MEDICAL AND
ECONOMIC MALACOLOGY

MEDICAL AND ECONOMIC MALACOLOGY

Emile A. Malek
DEPARTMENT OF TROPICAL MEDICINE AND PARASITOLOGY
TULANE UNIVERSITY
SCHOOL OF PUBLIC HEALTH AND TROPICAL MEDICINE
NEW ORLEANS, LOUISIANA

Thomas C. Cheng
INSTITUTE FOR PATHOBIOLOGY
CENTER FOR HEALTH SCIENCES
LEHIGH UNIVERSITY
BETHLEHEM, PENNSYLVANIA

ACADEMIC PRESS   New York and London   1974
A Subsidiary of Harcourt Brace Jovanovich, Publishers

ACADEMIC PRESS, INC.
111 Fifth Avenue, New York, New York 10003

United Kingdom Edition published by
ACADEMIC PRESS, INC. (LONDON) LTD.
24/28 Oval Road, London NW1

Library of Congress Cataloging in Publication Data

Malek, Emile Abdel, Date
  Medical and economic malacology.

  Includes bibliographies.
  1.   Mollusks as carriers of disease.   2.   Shellfish
culture.   3.   Parasites–Mollusks.   4.   Mollusks.
I.   Cheng, Thomas Clement, joint author.   II.   Title.
[DNLM: 1.   Disease vectors.   2.   Mollusca.   3.   Shell-
fish.   QL403 M245m 1973]
RA641.M6M34   594'.06'5   73-9435
ISBN 0–12–466150–5

Contents

5. Snail Hosts of Human-Infecting Trematodes

6. Mollusks as Hosts of Human-Infecting Nematodes

7. Pathogens of Medically and Economically Important Mollusks

8. Hematology

9. Internal Defense Mechanisms

15.   Field Work: Equipment and Methods

Preface

This volume is intended as an introduction to applied malacology as it pertains to public health and shellfisheries. Although both medical malacology and shellfisheries biology have been recognized for decades as important aspects of the study of mollusks, with the exception of a few laboratories there has been essentially no communication between individuals working or teaching in the two areas. Yet, as this book hopefully points out, there are many aspects of these subdisciplines that are of mutual interest. For example, an understanding of the internal defense mechanisms of mollusks and the basic features of molluscan pathology should comprise the training of both types of malacologists. Furthermore, in order to understand molluscan pathology and internal defense mechanisms there should be some basic knowledge of molluscan blood cells, and individuals intending to conduct laboratory studies on a variety of problems at the cellular level should be aware of the "state of the art" relative to molluscan cell and tissue culture. Such information is included in this volume.

Despite the common denominators, there are certain areas of these two subdisciplines that do not overlap. Consequently, in order to satisfy the needs of both medical malacology and shellfisheries biology, chapters devoted to topics of particular interest to one or the other of the two groups are also included. For example, the role of certain species of mollusks as hosts of parasites and their relationship to these parasites are discussed as are methods for the control of these mollusks. These chapters obviously are meant for students of medical malacology as are the laboratory exercises and techniques presented in Chapters 14 and 15. On the other hand, a chapter dealing with aquaculture is included for students of shellfisheries biology. Although the material in these chapters may appear to be of interest only to one or the other group, we are of the opinion that it will prove to be of interest to all malacologists.

The initial plan was also to include a chapter on the basic physiology of mollusks, for such information is essential in the training of any malacologist. However, in view of the fact that three excellent publications have appeared in recent years dealing with various aspects of molluscan physiology, it was thought that the duplication was unnecessary. Therefore, the reader is referred to the following three treatises for basic physiological information:

Wilbur, K. M., and Yonge, C. M. (eds.) (1964, Vol. I; 1966, Vol. II). "Physiology of Mollusca." Academic Press, New York.

Fretter, V. (ed.) (1968). "Studies in the Structure, Physiology and Ecology of Molluscs." Academic Press, New York.

Florkin, M., and Scheer, B. T. (eds.) (1972). "Chemical Zoology," Volume VII. "Mollusca." Academic Press, New York.

Malacology, at least certain aspects of the discipline, is rapidly being recognized as an important area of applied biology. Not only do species of mollusks serve as vectors of human and animal pathogens but certain marine species are also important foods for humans. As entomology and nematology have been recognized as being of sufficient importance to warrant the establishment of distinct departments in our universities and governmental agencies, malacology is rapidly receiving increased attention. It may be some time yet before universities decide to establish departments devoted exclusively to the subject, but it is a fact that several institutions have already developed formal courses in malacology. It is hoped that this volume will serve as an aid in the teaching of such courses.

Mollusks are often thought of by invertebrate zoologists as interesting schizocoelous protostomates, by comparative physiologists as animals with fascinating muscles and nervous systems, and by ecologists as extremely well-adapted organisms with interesting distribution patterns. Although all of these are legitimate and important viewpoints, it is our intent that this volume will also serve to point out that these animals are extremely important as carriers of disease-causing organisms and as food for the ever-increasing world population. Hence, hopefully, this introductory volume will also serve to enhance an appreciation of the role of mollusks in the world of public health and natural resources.

The senior author wishes to acknowledge support from the U.S. Public Health Service in the form of a Research Career Award (K6-AI-18,424) and the junior author wishes to acknowledge the support by a grant from the U.S. Public Health Service (FD-00416-01-02) during the preparation of sections of this volume.

EMILE A. MALEK
THOMAS C. CHENG

MEDICAL AND ECONOMIC MALACOLOGY

1 The Phylum Mollusca

The phylum Mollusca includes those animals commonly referred to as snails, slugs, clams, oysters, chitons, squids, octopods, and nautili. These animals all possess a structure called the "mantle," which envelops the internal organs, and most species secrete a shell of calcium carbonate. A foot is used by snails for creeping over surfaces, by clams for plowing through mud and sand, and by squids for seizing their prey.

According to fossil records and modern carbon-dating methods, the mollusks had their origin during the Cambrian period, about 600 million years ago, and all the major groups were established by the end of the Cambrian. The exact number of species of mollusks living today is not known; however, it has been estimated that there are about 80,000 to 150,000 extant species. In addition, at least 35,000 fossil species have been reported. It can be concluded from these figures that the mollusks are among the most successful animals. They occur in all types of ecological niches, ranging from the abyssal depths of the oceans to highly arid terrestrial regions.

With the advent of the interest of biologists in the role of mollusks as hosts of helminth parasites, beginning with Swammerdam (1737), the importance of mollusks as carriers of pathogenic parasites has been gradually recognized, and this aspect of malacology has rapidly gained impetus. On the other hand, mollusks have always been economically important. The shells of certain species have served as money, can be fashioned into jewelry and buttons, and were important components of kitchen middens of prehistoric man. Furthermore, such species as scallops, clams, oysters, squids, and octopuses are important as food even today, and considerable research has been carried out to learn how to conserve and propagate these species. It is primarily the medical and economic aspects of malacology that are emphasized in this volume.

Classes of the Mollusca

There are six classes of mollusks.

CLASS MONOPLACOPHORA

The members of this class are saucer-shaped and possess a shell covering a bilaterally symmetrical body (Fig. 1-1). Five pairs of gills (or ctenidia) surround the foot on the ventral suface. The mantle is completely covered by the single-piece, oval shell. The mantle cavity is shallow and contains the gills. The class is represented by the living *Neopilina*, which is found in deep oceans.

CLASS AMPHINEURA

The members of this class, known as chitons, are bilaterally symmetrical (Fig. 1-1). They have a dorsally situated, flat shell of eight calcareous plates, and they have many pairs of gill lamellae. The mantle is extensive and covers the dorsal and lateral surfaces.

CLASS GASTROPODA (*GASTRO* 'STOMACH'; *PODA* 'FOOT')

This class includes the snails, which are superficially asymmetrical and possess a spirally coiled shell; the limpets, which possess a low, conical unspiraled shell; and the slugs, which possess a concealed shell or no shell at all (Fig. 1-1).

CLASS SCAPHOPODA (*SCAPHO* 'SPADE', i.e., DIGGING)

This class includes the elephants' tusk shells (Fig. 1-1). These mollusks are marine, have tubular shells that are open at both ends, and are bilaterally symmetrical. The foot is cylindrical and pointed. The sexes are separate and there are no special genital ducts.

CLASS CEPHALOPODA (*CEPHALO* 'HEAD')

This class includes the squids, octopods, and nautili (Fig. 1-1). These mollusks are all marine, portray bilateral symmetry, possess a foot divided into arms with suckers around the "head" and mouth, and have either an internal shell or no shell at all. They move by jet propulsion. There are many extinct forms.

Fig. 1-1. Classes of the Mollusca. (A) *Neopilina*, a representative of the class Monoplacophora. (B) Chiton, a representative of the class Amphineura. (C) Elephant's tusk, a representative of the class Scaphopoda. (D) Snail, a representative of the class Gastropoda. (E) Squid, a representative of the class Cephalopoda. (F) Clam, a representative of the class Bivalvia.

CLASS BIVALVIA (ALSO KNOWN AS PELECYPODA OR LAMELLIBRANCHIATA) (*PELECY* 'AX')

This class comprises the clams, mussels, oysters, and scallops. (Fig. 1-1). These mollusks are bilaterally symmetrical, possess a shell of two valves with corresponding lobes of the mantle, and have no tentacles, no eyes, no "head," and no radula. There is a dorsal ligament that, together with teeth formed from the valves, constitute the hinge. These mollusks are primarily marine although a number of species are also found in brackish and freshwater. All the species have a hatchetlike foot and gills in the form of lamellae.

2 Classification and Structure of the Gastropoda

Classification

There are three divisions of the gastropods regarded by various authors as subclasses (Table 2-1).

SUBCLASS PROSOBRANCHIATA (COMMONLY REFERRED TO AS THE PROSOBRANCHS OR OPERCULATES)

The designation "prosobranch" indicates that the gills (branchia), located in the body cavity, are anterior to the heart. This subclass contains the majority of the gastropods—marine, freshwater, and land snails. The shell aperture is usually with a calcareous or horny operculum. Their respiration is through gills (except in the few terrestrial species), and the sexes are separate. The subclass is divided into three orders.

Order Archaeogastropoda

These are the more primitive prosobranchs. Each snail has two auricles, two internal gills, and two kidneys. The gonads discharge through the right kidney directly into water.

Order Mesogastropoda

This order includes the majority of the prosobranchs that possess one auricle, one gill, and one kidney. The gonads open independently through a separate genital tract. The shell is sometimes provided with a siphonal canal.

TABLE 2-1

Classification of the Molluscan Class Gastropoda

Gastropoda

Subclass	Prosobranchiata			Opisthobranchiata	Pulmonata				
					Order Basommatophora			Stylommatophora	Systellommatophora
	Freshwater	Brackish water and marine	Terrestrial		Freshwater	Brackish water and marine	Amphibious or terrestrial	Terrestrial snails	Slugs
Family[a]	Hydrobiidae* Thiaridae*§ Pleuroceridae*§ Viviparidae§ Pilidae*§	Potamidae* Littorinidae* Nassariidae* Muricidae Conidae* Neritidae	Helicinidae Pomatiasidae Truncatellidae	Akeridae*	Planorbidae*§ Lymnaeidae*§ Physidae*§ Ancylidae*§	Siphonaridae Gadiniidae	Ellobiidae Carychiidae	Helicidae* Limacidae† Polygyridae*± Philomycidae§± Endodontidae§± Arionidae§†± Succineidae§± Bulimulidae Cionellidae* Zonitidae± Enidae*	Veronicellidae*±

[a]Symbols indicate the following points: *medical importance; §intermediate hosts for trematodes other than those parasitic in humans; †intermediate hosts for some cestodes; ±intermediate hosts for some nematodes.

Order Neogastropoda

Snails belonging to this order are identical to the mesogastropods except that a more or less elongated siphonal canal of the shell and the radula are different from those of the Mesogastropoda.

Families in freshwater include the following: Hydrobiidae (representatives: *Amnicola*, *Oncomelania*, and *Pomatiopsis*); Synceridae or Assimineidae (representative: *Syncera*); Thiaridae (representatives: *Thiara*, *Brotia*, and *Cleopatra*); Pleuroceridae (representatives: *Goniobasis*, *Pleurocera*, and *Semisulcospira*); Viviparidae (representatives: *Campeloma* and *Viviparus*); and Pilidae or Ampullaridae (representatives; *Pila* and *Pomacea*).

Families in fresh, brackish, and seawater include the following: Neritidae (representative: *Neritina*); Potamidae or Cerithiidae (representatives: *Pirenella* and *Cerithidea*); Littorinidae (representative: *Littorina*); Nassariidae (representative: *Nassarius*); Muricidae (representative: *Urosalpinx*); and Conidae (representative: *Conus*).

Families on land include the following: Helicinidae (representatives: *Helicina*, *Hendersonia*, and *Lucidella*); Truncatellidae (representative: *Truncatella*); and Pomatiasidae (representatives: *Chondropoma* and *Opisthosiphon*).

SUBCLASS OPISTHOBRANCHIATA

The subclass Opisthobranchiata includes marine forms exclusively. The gill, when present, is posterior to the heart. The shell is reduced or absent, and calcareous spicules are present in naked forms. The opisthobranchs are hermaphroditic and live among seaweeds and under rocks.

SUBCLASS PULMONATA

The members of Pulmonata are mainly freshwater and terrestrial snails. A few, however, occur in marine and brackish waters. They have no gills, and a part of the mantle cavity serves as a lung, hence the designation Pulmonata. The shell, when present, is usually in the form of a simple, regular spire, which may be only rudimentary. In many terrestrial species an "epiphragm" of hardened mucus temporarily closes the aperture of the shell. The pulmonates are hermaphrodites, usually oviparous, but sometimes ovoviviparous. They are inoperculates except for the members of the marine genus *Amphibola*. There are three subdivisions of the pulmonates that are regarded as orders.

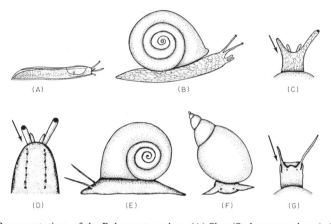

Fig. 2-1. Representatives of the Pulmonate orders. (A) Slug (Stylommatophora). (B) Terrestrial snail (Stylommatophora). Notice occurrence of scales and eyes at the tip of the posterior (or dorsal) tentacles. (C) Anterior portion of a stylommatophoran with a portion of the left posterior tentacle inverted (indicated by arrow), and, hence, the eye is not visible. (D) Slug, *Veronicella* sp. (Systellommatophora), with contracted left posterior tentacle (indicated by arrow). (E) Planorbid snail (Basommatophora). (F) Lymnaeid snail (Basommatophora). (G) Anterior portion of a basommatophoran showing a contracted tentacle (indicated by arrow) and eyes situated at the base of the tentacles.

Order Basommatophora (Fig. 2-1)

The members of this order are mostly freshwater snails, but there are a few terrestrial or marine ones. They possess one pair of contractile tentacles with eyes at the bases. The shell is conical, discoidal, or patelliform. Male and female genital tracts open separately to the exterior, but the two apertures are closely situated.

The freshwater families include Planorbidae (representatives: *Helisoma* and *Biomphalaria*); Lymnaeidae (representative: *Lymnaea*); Physidae (representative: *Physa*); and Ancylidae (representative: *Ferrissia*). The members of the family Carychiidae (representative: *Carychium*) are terrestrial, and the members of the family Ellobiidae (representatives: *Melampus, Detracia*, and *Phytia*) are terrestrial or semiamphibious, living in damp places or near the margin of the sea but not in the water. Aquatic families living in salt or brackish water along the seashore include the Siphonaridae (representative: *Siphonaria*) and the Gadiniidae (representative: *Gadinia*).

Order Stylommatophora (Fig. 2-1)

The members of this order are land snails and slugs. Each specimen possesses two pairs of tentacles, with eyes at the tips of the posterior (dorsal) tentacles. These tentacles can be everted and inverted. The land snails possess well-developed and conspicuous shells while the slugs possess rudimentary and concealed shells or have no shells. The head–foot region of the land snails is covered with scales.

Among the families of land snails are Helicidae (representative: *Helix*); Helicellidae (representatives: *Hygromia, Helicella,* and *Cochlicella*); Bradybaenidae (representative: *Bradybaena*); Polygyridae (representative: *Polygyra*); Endodontidae (representatives: *Anguispira* and *Helicodiscus*); Succineidae (representative: *Succinea*); Bulimulidae (representative: *Bulimulus*); Cionellidae (representative: *Cionella*); Zonitidae (representative: *Zonitoides*); and Helminthoglyptidae (representatives: *Cepolis, Monadenia,* and *Helminthoglypta*).

Among the families of slugs are Limacidae (representatives: *Deroceras* and *Limax*); Philomycidae (representatives: *Philomycus* and *Pallifera*); and Arionidae (representative: *Arion*).

Order Systellommatophora (Fig. 2-1)

This order includes those species of slugs that are mostly tropical. The family Veronicellidae (representative: *Veronicella*) is a member of this order. The members of the Veronicellidae possess two pairs of contractile tentacles, with eyes at the tip of the posterior (dorsal) pair. These slugs have neither an external nor an internal shell. Representatives of the Systellommatophora have been introduced into the southern United States.

Structure

SHELL

The gastropod shell is comprised of conchiolin infiltrated with calcium carbonate (aragonite). To protect the shell from erosion by the carbonic acid in the water, it is covered by a horny substance called the "epidermis," or "periostracum." Much of the surface marking of the shell is found in the periostracum layer and is lost when this layer is removed. The periostracum is secreted by the mantle edge, whereas the inner calcareous layers are secreted by the entire dorsal surface of the mantle. The latter continues to add to the shell throughout the life of the snail.

BODY REGIONS

Gastropods have a head, foot, mantle region (pallial region), and a visceral mass. The head and foot are united to form a head–foot region, which bears the tentacles and eyes. Gastropods also possess a mantle that covers the pallial region and that is continuous with a tunica propria covering the visceral mass.

DEVELOPMENT OF TORSION AND OTHER EVOLUTIONARY TRENDS

The development of body torsion is of considerable importance during the evolutionary history of gastropods. As the result of this process, the mantle cavity has shifted forward, and the visceral and pallial regions have become twisted through a 180° angle in relation to the head–foot region. This process is independent of the spiral coiling of the shell and the visceral mass that many of the gastropods exhibit. Some gastropods are not coiled, but all of them have undergone torsion at some time during their evolutionary development. The head and foot still retain the pretorsion bilateral symmetry.

Among the prosobranchs, the diotocardia* and the monotocardia† have been altered considerably due to torsion. Their gills, which in their untwisted ancestors occurred behind the heart and projected into the posteriorly directed mantle cavity, now face forward and lie anterior to the heart, hence the name "prosobranchs." The members of the second subclass of gastropods, the opisthobranchs, are shell-less, sluglike animals that are superficially symmetrical, and, according to Fretter and Graham (1962), have evolved from a monotocardian ancestor of the prosobranchs through a process of detorsion that has restored the original relationships of gill and heart, hence the name "opisthobranchs."

Fretter and Graham (1962) are of the opinion that the pulmonates are also derived from a monotocardian ancestor since the mantle cavity still lies above the animal's head and faces forward. The shell has been retained by the majority of the pulmonates for protection and to help them withstand desiccation. Another evolutionary trend among the pulmonates has led to the land slugs. Among these gastropods there is a tendency toward a naked body and freer movement. Furthermore, the visceral hump is not coiled but is present in a hollowed foot.

Among the pulmonates another evolutionary trend has occurred. Specifically, the gill has disappeared, and vascularization of a part of the mantle cavity has occurred to form the lung. The presence of this organ permits these animals, including the aquatic species, to breathe air.

---

*With two auricles comprising the heart as among the Archaeogastropoda.
†With a single auricle comprising the heart as among the Mesogastropoda and Neogastropoda.

DIGESTIVE SYSTEM

The digestive tract of gastropods opens anteriorly through the mouth. The mouth leads into the buccal cavity, which contains a radula, and the buccal cavity leads into a tubular esophagus. The latter leads into the stomach, which, in turn, is connected to the intestine. The intestinal tract communicates with the exterior through the anus, which is situated anteriorly on the mantle collar.

The mouth is provided with two jawlike horny plates opposed to which is a chitinous rasping ribbon, the radula, resting on a tongue, or odontophore. The great diversity in the arrangement and sizes of the teeth comprising the radula in different groups of gastropods has been used in the classification of these animals.

Secretory glands associated with the digestive tract are (1) the salivary glands, which open into the buccal cavity; (2) the esophageal glands, sometimes in the form of pouches, situated around the esophagus; and (3) the midgut gland (or digestive gland), which is connected with the stomach.

The stomach consists of a globular, anterior region and, in some species, a posterior, or distal, tubular region known as the style sac. The digestive gland consists of a large number of blind-ending tubules, each with a duct that is connected with the stomach. Each duct may be branched, and the branches are connected with the stomach. The digestive gland is not only an organ for secretion of enzymes but also an organ of absorption, phagocytosis, nutrient storage, and excretion.

NERVOUS SYSTEM

The nervous system consists of two cerebral ganglia, paired pedal and visceral ganglia, and two or three additional pairs of ganglia. All the ganglia are united by commissures. Nerve fibers, emanating from the ganglia and commissures, innervate the various organs.

RESPIRATORY SYSTEM

The majority of gastropods breathe through gills or lungs. The gills are filamentous or tuftlike. In some species they are branched or appear as "feathered" lobes of the integument. The gills occur in the mantle cavity, and, rarely, they project freely on the back or at the sides. Some groups, like the Ampullaridae and Siphonaridae, possess both lungs and gills. The lung opens to the outside through a respiratory pore, the pneumostome.

REPRODUCTIVE SYSTEM

Considerable differentiation of the reproductive organs occurs among the gastropods. The prosobranchs are dioecious, whereas the pulmonates are usually monoecious. The male and female genital tracts open through a common opening in the land snails and slugs (Stylommatophora), while among the Basommatophora the genital tracts open separately. Differences in the reproductive organs will be dealt with in subsequent sections of this chapter. The embryonic stages of gastropods are completed in the egg, there being no postembryonic metamorphoses as in many of the Bivalvia.

The two main subclasses of the gastropods, the Prosobranchiata and the Pulmonata, will be considered separately.

PROSOBRANCHIATA

The prosobranchs exhibit great variation in structure, in shell shape, and in mode of life. The Archaeogastropoda are the oldest and, with the exception of the Neritacea, are all marine, as are the Neogastropoda. The Mesogastropoda are marine, freshwater, or terrestrial. Some prosobranchs are pelagic. Others, such as the members of the family Ianthidae, are planktonic; for example, the fragile, violet snail, *Ianthina fragilis*. This snail drifts in schools on the ocean surface. Its head is prolonged into a large snout, its radula is large, and its small foot is attached to a gelatinous float filled with air bubbles to which the egg capsules are attached.

A few prosobranchs possess reduced shells in addition to modified structures employed for swimming. An example of the latter is portrayed by members of the family Atlantidae, for example, *Atlanta turriculata*. This mollusk swims with its shell pointed downward and with sudden jerks. Its ability to swim is enhanced by its finlike foot. It rests by attaching to floating objects.

With a few exceptions, the shell of prosobranchs is provided with an operculum (Fig. 14-2). The operculum is usually thin and consists of a hornlike substance that is not chitin but is similar to the conchiolin of the shell. However, the operculum also may be thick and calcareous.

The shell of prosobranchs is generally conical, turreted, fusiform, or spindle in shape. It may also be flattened or may be of the limpet type, that is, with complete loss of spiral coiling. Those families with a long, turreted spire include the Cerithiidae (representatives: *Cerithidea cingulata* and *C. scalariformis*), Turritellidae (representative: *Turritella turebra*), Scallidae (representatives: *Scala communis* and *S. angulata*), Pleuroceridae (representatives: *Pleurocera acuta*, *Semisulcospira libertina*, and *Goniobasis livescens*, as in Fig. 4-15), and Thiaridae (representative: *Thiara tuberculata*, as in Fig. 4-15). Among those with a fusiform or spindle-shaped shell with an anterior canal are the members of the families Fasciolariidae (representatives: *Fusus longissimus* and *Fasciolaria tulipa*), Buccinidae (representative: *Siphonalia kellettii*), Muricidae (representatives: *Urosalpinx cinerea*, *Murex brassica*, and *Purpura patula*). Among the limpets are the members of the families Calyptraeidae (representatives: *Calyptraea mammilaris*, *Crepidula fornicata*, and *Crucibulum striatum*), Fissurellidae (representatives: *Fissurella volcano*, *Lucapina crenulata*, and *Diodora alternata*), and Patellidae (representative: *Patella vulgata*). Among those that possess conical-topped shells are the periwinkles, which are members of the family Littorinidae (representatives: *Littorina irrorata*, as in Fig. 4-15, and *L. littorea*).

The mantle embraces the neck of the snail and is continuous posteriorly with the wall of the visceral mass. In some prosobranchs an elongation from the mantle, known as the siphon, fits into the siphonal, or anterior, canal of fusiform or spindle-shaped shells. The siphon varies in length depending on the species. If the siphonal canal is absent, the siphon is curved back over the animal as in members of the families Conidae and Olividae. In members of the freshwater family Ampullaridae, the siphon is well developed and can extend to more than the body length. Although generally regarded to be respiratory in function, Morton (1958) is of the opinion that the siphon has an additional function. With the chemosensitive osphradium at its base, this

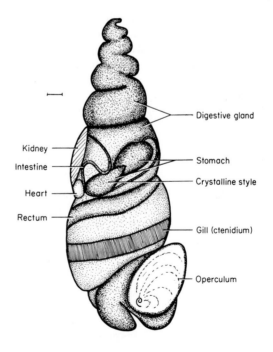

Fig. 2-2. *Thiara granifera*. Specimen with shell removed showing positions of certain internal organs. Bar = 1 mm.

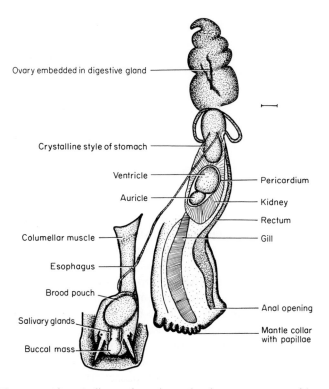

Ovary embedded in digestive gland

Crystalline style of stomach

Ventricle

Auricle

Columellar muscle

Esophagus

Brood pouch

Salivary glands

Buccal mass

Pericardium

Kidney

Rectum

Gill

Anal opening

Mantle collar with papillae

Fig. 2-3. *Thiara granifera.* A dissected specimen showing arrangement of internal organs. Bar = 1 mm.

structure may be employed as a movable nostril and a forward-seeking exploratory organ. The osphradium is a chemoreceptor and is believed to function in testing the quality of the water entering the mantle cavity. In carnivorous mollusks the osphradium assumes a large size, for example, among the whelks and cones. In these prosobranchs the large siphon can detect living and dead animal food from some distance. In the Archaeogastropoda and lower Mesogastropoda, the simplest osphradia occur. These are in the form of either a patch or as a line of sensory cells. In the more advanced species, the osphradium is pectinate, resembling a small accessory gill, as it is in the case of *Buccinum.*

In addition to one or two osphradia, the pallial complex also includes one or two gills, one or more glandular areas, each known as a hypobranchial gland, and the terminal parts of the excretory, digestive, and reproductive systems. The gill (Figs. 2-2 and 2-3) is attached to the mantle and consists of a varying number of filaments that are connected to a longitudinal bar in which the blood sinuses are located. In some small prosobranchs reared in the laboratory, such as certain members of the family Hydrobiidae, the gill can be seen clearly through the thin, transparent shell. Although the presence of one or two gills characterizes most of the proso-branchs, they are absent in members of such terrestrial families as the Pomatiasidae, Cyclophoridae, Acmidae, and Helicinidae. In these, respiration is carried out by a highly vascularized area of the mantle. The large, amphibious members of the family Ampullaridae, which occur in South America, Asia, and Africa, portray a vascularized area of the mantle in addition to the gill.

In the more primitive prosobranchs, for example, the Archaeogastro-poda, the heart consists of one ventricle and two auricles and hence the designation Diotocardia. In the more advanced prosobranchs, for example, the Mesogastropoda and Neogastropoda, there is only one ventricle and one auricle, and hence the designation Monotocardia.

In addition to the heart, the circulatory system consists of a number of vessels, but is composed mainly of sinuses, or lacunae, with connective tissue walls (Fig. 2-4). Actually, the hemolymph bathes the tissues, and, in this manner, the exchange of gases and nutrients occurs. The venous hemolymph is collected from the proboscis and head by the proboscidal sinus and from the foot by the pedal sinus. These two sinuses unite in the large cephalopedal sinus, which, in turn, joins the subrenal sinus. The hemolymph from the visceral mass is collected by the perivisceral sinus, which also opens into the subrenal sinus. Most of the hemolymph passes through the kidney and is conducted from there in numerous channels into the branchial vessels in the gill. After oxygenation, the hemolymph is collected in the efferent branchial vessel, which leads directly into the auricle. A main aorta arises from the ventricle, and it soon becomes divided into an anterior and a posterior aorta, each further subdividing to give rise to branches that supply oxygenated hemolymph to the various parts of the body.

The kidney is the excretory organ. It is situated near the pericardial sac at the beginning of the visceral mass (Fig. 2-3). At its anterior end, the kidney empties to the exterior at a point on the mantle roof close to the anus. At the posterior end, the cavity of the kidney is connected with the pericardial cavity by renopericardial canals. Among diotocardians, where there are two gills, there are also two kidneys. However, among the monotocardians there is only one kidney.

Relative to feeding habits, the archaeogastropods are herbivores or deposit scrapers, the neogastropods are carnivores, and the mesogastropods are either deposit scrapers, carnivores, or collect their food by employing the ciliary current of their gills. In some mesogastropods the gill filaments become well developed and, in addition to their respiratory function, have become adapted to serve in the collection of food particles by means of their

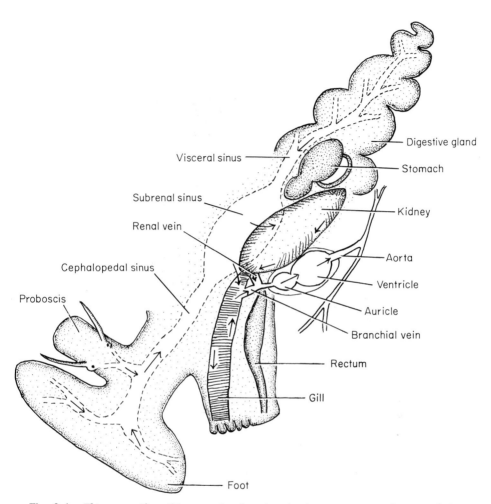

Visceral sinus

Subrenal sinus

Renal vein

Cephalopedal sinus

Proboscis

Digestive gland

Stomach

Kidney

Aorta

Ventricle

Auricle

Branchial vein

Rectum

Gill

Foot

Fig. 2-4. *Thiara granifera.* Diagram showing the circulatory system and some of the internal organs. Arrows indicate the direction of flow of the hemolymph. Broken lines indicate position of the spongy connective tissue walls of the hemolymph sinuses. Adapted from Malek, in Alicata (1962).

cilia. Such ciliary feeding is exhibited not only by some marine species but also by members of the freshwater family Viviparidae. Certain glandular and ciliated tracts on the gill filaments, in addition to the hypobranchial gland, contribute mucus employed for food collection.

The members of the family Eulimidae (= Mellanellidae) are ectoparasites on echinoderms. These small mollusks are parasitic on sea urchins and sea cucumbers. The foot of eulimids is poorly to moderately developed, but a

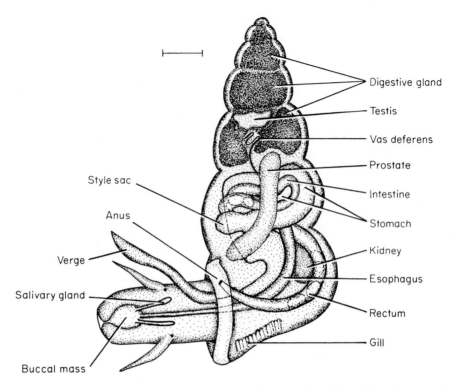

Fig. 2-5. *Oncomelania hupensis nosophora.* Drawing of male adult with shell removed showing positions of various internal systems. Bar = 1 mm.

proboscis is present and can be employed to reach around the host for feeding. Jaws, radula, and salivary glands are absent in these mollusks, which occur from the Arctic to the tropic seas. *Eulima micans* and *E. intermedia* are examples of the Eulimidae.

   The organizational plan of the digestive system of prosobranchs is similar to that described for the gastropods in general; however, the proximal globular region of the stomach is characterized by the occurrence of a ciliated region of grooves and ridges. In addition, there is a raised cuticular area known as the gastric shield. In many prosobranchs the stomach is evaginated anteriorly to form the style sac (Figs. 2-2, 2-3, and 2-5). This sac contains an acellular, semitransparent rod known as the crystalline style. The sac lies alongside the anterior portion of the intestine with which it may communicate; however, it is usually not connected with the intestinal tract. The crystalline style is a hyaline rod. As it rotates and is thrust into the stomach, the style releases amylolytic enzymes gradually and continuously. The style sac and style are confined to herbivorous prosobranchs that feed by ciliary currents or on vegetation. The feeding process is aided by radular action, and the continuous stream of minute food particles are passed into the stomach. In carnivorous prosobranchs, however, the style sac, the style, and the sorting area of the stomach are absent, and the stomach is reduced in size.

The digestive gland (Figs. 2-2, 2-3, and 2-5) is a multipurpose organ, and the tubules comprising it consist of at least two types of cells. One of these types of cells is pyramidal in shape and includes darkly staining cytoplasm. The function of this type of cell is believed to be secretory and excretory, in addition to serving as a storage site of calcium. The second type of cell is more numerous and is primarily digestive in function, although these cells may also carry on secretion, absorption, phagocytosis, and nutrient storage. Furthermore, these cells might pass through a cycle of several phases. For an analysis of the activities of the digestive gland in various prosobranchs, and gastropods in general, see Owen (1966) and Hyman (1967).

With very few exceptions, the sexes in the prosobranchs are separate. The gonad is always single and is embedded in the digestive gland in the top whorls of the spire of the shell (Figs. 2-3 and 2-5). In order to accomodate fertilization and egg production, the female reproductive system is more complicated than the reproductive organs in the male. After arising from the ovary, a part of the oviduct, the visceral oviduct, is situated along the visceral mass. It then enters the mantle cavity where it is confined to the roof alongside the rectum and communicates with the exterior near the anus. The pallial portion of the oviduct is an enlarged tube (Fig. 2-6), which is highly glandular. In viviparous species the pallial portion of the oviduct, or brood

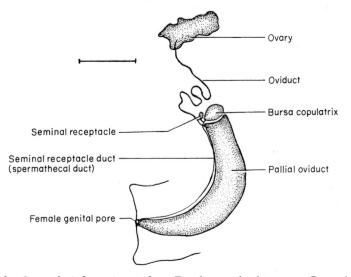

Fig. 2-6. *Oncomelania hupensis nosophora.* Female reproductive organs. Bar = 1 mm.

pouch, is even more enlarged (Fig. 2-3). It accomodates the embryos developing in it. In the small, hydrobiid, viviparous species, the brood pouch and the embryos can be seen through the thin, transparent shell (Malek and Little, 1971). One to several small sacs, the seminal receptacle or spermathecae, are connected to the oviduct at the junction of the visceral and pallial portions of the oviduct.

The testis occupies the same topographic relationship with the digestive gland as does the ovary. The male duct, after leaving the testis, bears a number of tuberclelike thickenings, the seminal vesicles. A part of the male duct either functions as a prostate gland or it receives the duct of a distinct prostate gland. Distal to this, the sperm duct lies along the floor of the mantle cavity to the point where it is connected with the base of the penis (verge) (Fig. 2-5) or to the male genital pore, if the penis is absent. In members of the Viviparidae the right tentacle is short and includes the penis. Variations occur in the structure and shape of the penis, and such variations are utilized as taxonomic characteristics (p. 335). The penis may be bifid and bears papillae (Fig. 14-10) and/or cup-shaped glandular invaginations, or it might be simple and devoid of such structures.

PULMONATA

The pulmonates possess a typical spiral shell that varies in shape and that may be reduced or absent. Among the slugs, the shell is absent, as in members of the family Veronicellidae, or reduced to a small piece carried on the posterior end of the animal, as in *Testacella*. In some cases the small piece may be concealed completely by the mantle.

Pulmonates vary from minute snails measuring a few millimeters in length, as in the terrestrial family Pupillidae, to large snails reaching 2 to 3 inches in length, as in the terrestrial families Achatinidae and Strophocheilidae.

Among the members of the Basommatophora the shell varies from discoidal or globose as among the Planorbidae, for example, *Biomphalaria glabrata* (Fig. 4-6) and *Bulinus* (*Bulinus*) *truncatus* (Fig. 4-8); to patelliform or limpet-shaped as among the Ancylidae, for example, *Ferrissia dalli*; to conical or fusiform as among the Lymnaeidae, for example, *Lymnaea stagnalis* (Fig. 4-12) and *Acella haldemani*, and the Physidae, for example, *Physa anatina*. Among the Stylommatophora the shell may be pupilliform, for example, *Cerion incanum* of the family Cerionidae and *Pupoides albilabris* of the family Pupillidae; succiniform, for example, *Succinea saleana* (Fig. 4-17) of the family Succineidae; spindle-shaped, for example, *Cionella lubrica* (Fig. 4-17) of the family Cionellidae; bulimoid, for example, *Liguus fasicatus* and *Bulimulus alternatus* of the family Bulimidae; fusiform or conical, for example, *Euglandina rosea* (Fig. 4-17) of the family Oleacinidae and *Achatina fulica*, *Subulina octona*, and *Lamellaxis gracilis* of the family Achatinidae; globose, for example, *Helix pomatia* and *Otala lactea* of the family Helicidae, *Zachrysia provisoria* of the family Camaenidae, and *Stenotrema depilatum* of the family Polygyridae; or depressed, for example, *Mesomphyx inornatus* of the family Zonitidae.

In the pulmonate shell there is never an anterior canal as in the shells of many prosobranchs, and an operculum is also absent except in members of the marine genus *Amphibola*. Instead, however, there are teeth and ridges present at the aperture as found among some members of the families Pupillidae, Streptaxidae, Polygyridae, and Planorbidae. Among the Stylommatophora a hardened mucous covering of the aperture, known as the epiphragm, is developed during aestivation.

The body surface is smooth among freshwater basommatophorans. However, among the terrestrial stylommatophorans the surface is provided with protuberances known as scales (Fig. 2-1). Among these scales is found a network of grooves that are mucous ducts. The head of basommatophorans bears a single pair of tentacles, while there are two pairs of tentacles on stylommatophorans (Fig. 2-1). An eye is located at the base of each tentacle on basommatophorans. On the stylommatophorans, the eye is situated at the club-shaped end of each of the posterior tentacles.

Among pulmonates a gill and a hypobranchial gland are usually absent in the mantle cavity, but instead most of the cavity is vascularized to form a lung (Figs. 2-8 and 2-9), which opens to the exterior by the pneumostome. The latter is drawn out into a short siphon in members of the basommatophoran families Planorbidae, Lymnaeidae, and Physidae. In some genera of the fourth basommatophoran family, the Ancylidae, however, there is no lung or pneumostome, but there is an accessory respiratory structure, the pseudobranch, situated externally. Also, in the Planorbidae there is a pseudobranch situated externally near the pneumostome (Fig. 2-8). There is no osphradium in the terrestrial stylommatophorans, but it is usually present in the aquatic basommatophorans. It functions, as in prosobranchs, as a chemoreceptor. The medically important planorbid, *Biomphalaria glabrata*, can locate food such as lettuce a few minutes after their introduction in the aquarium.

The kidney is situated along the roof of the pulmonary cavity (Figs. 2-8 and 2-9) and extends anteriorly from the pericardium and heart. The rectum and the genital tracts lie beneath the floor of the pulmonary cavity. On the ventral surface of the kidney of the neotropical species *Biomphalaria glabrata* and the African subgenus *Physopsis* of the genus *Bulinus* is found a ridge, the renal ridge (Fig. 14-8), which is important as a taxonomic characteristic of the group. The kidney is connected posteriorly to the pericardial cavity by

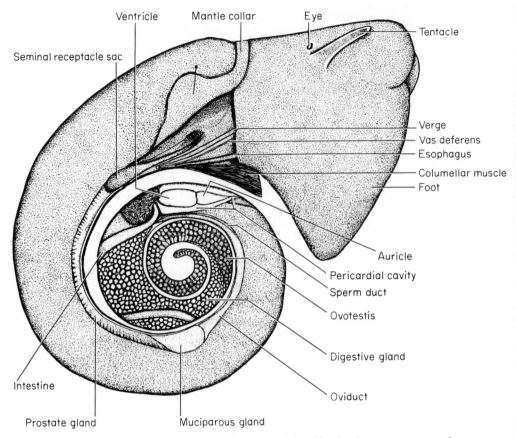

Fig. 2-7. *Biomphalaria alexandrina.* View from right side showing arrangement of some internal organs. After Malek (1955).

one or more renopericardial canals that open anteriorly at or near the pneumostome. The kidney varies in length and width among the various pulmonates, and a ureter is generally present as a straight, flexed, or curved duct (Fig. 2-9). Folded excretory epithelium occupies the interior of the kidney (Malek, 1952). In addition to the kidney, excretion is also carried out by cells of the digestive gland and by the pericardial wall.

Based on studies of both terrestrial and aquatic species, in general, the circulatory system of pulmonates is less open than that of other gastropods. There are networks of capillaries and vessels occurring on the surface or in the interior of all organs (Malek, 1955; Basch, 1969; Pan, 1971). The circulation in the gill is replaced by that in the lung. Otherwise, the general organizational plan of the circulatory system is similar to that of the prosobranchs (p. 14).

The heart of pulmonates consists of an auricle and a ventricle, and

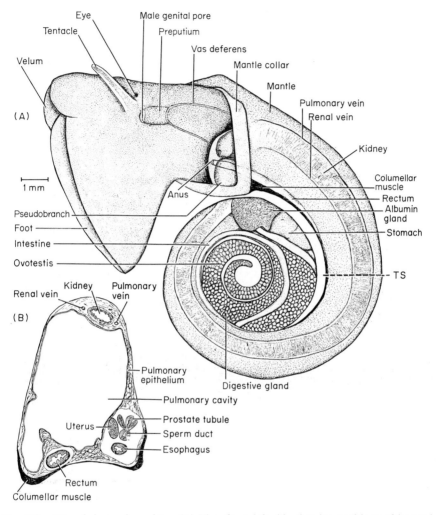

Fig. 2-8. *Biomphalaria alexandrina.* (A) View from left side showing positions of internal organs. (B) Transverse section in pulmonary region as indicated by TS in part A. After Malek (1955).

the pericardial sac is located posterior to the lung and kidney and is embraced by posteriormost portion of the kidney (Figs. 2-7 and 2-9). Numerous branches of the afferent pulmonary arteries infiltrate into the capillary network in the roof of the pulmonary sac. It is at this site that hemolymph is aerated. From this capillary network numerous efferent pulmonary veins discharge into a main pulmonary vein that, in turn, is connected with the adjacent auricle. The pulmonary vein is situated lateral and parallel to the kidney (Figs. 2-8 and 2-9). Hemolymph is collected from

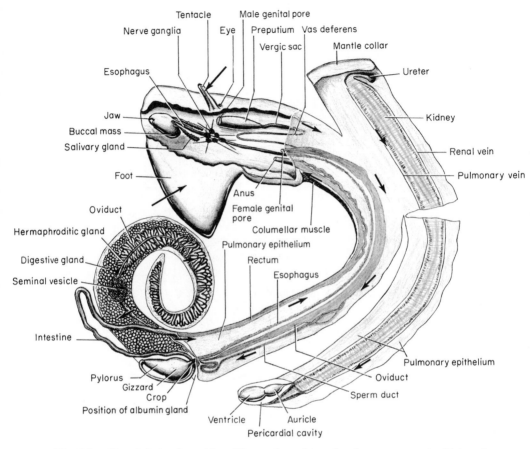

Fig. 2-9. *Biomphalaria alexandrina.* Dissected specimen showing arrangement of internal organs. Arrows indicate sites of penetration of the miracidia of *Schistosoma mansoni*, the migration route of daughter sporocysts to the posterior organs, and the migration route of cercariae anteriorly to the exterior from the region of the mantle collar, pseudobranch, and neighboring tissues. After Malek (1955).

the renal sinuses by capillaries, which discharge into the renal vein that joins the pulmonary vein prior to its entering the auricle.

The pulmonates are mainly herbivores, feeding on decayed leaves, other vegetation, and microorganisms constituting the periphyton in aquatic environments. In all pulmonates the radula is a broad, lingual ribbon consisting of many teeth (Fig. 14-7) that are employed to scrape vegetation or other nutrient materials deposited on the vegetation. Some stylommatophorans are carnivores, living mainly on other land snails and slugs. *Euglandina rosea*, a species occurring in the southern United States and Central America, is an example of a voracious carnivore.

Along the digestive tract a foregut gland (salivary gland) occurs as a pair of elongate glands (Fig. 2-9) lying on the esophagus and is connected with the roof of the pharynx. These glands anastomose posteriorly. The general opinion of recent investigators is that there is but one morphological type of cell comprising the salivary glands, although many different functional phases occur. The salivary glands are composed of large gland cells that are bound together by an external envelope of connective tissue and are grouped around the ramifications of the salivary ducts. In *Biomphalaria glabrata*, Pan (1958) has reported a single type of cell that is tall and includes a basophilic net holding droplets of secretion. Carriker and Bilstad (1946) have recognized the following structural phases in the salivary gland cells of *Lymnaea stagnalis*: finely reticular, granular, finely alveolar, and grossly alveolar. These authors have stated that in *L. stagnalis* the secretion of the salivary glands contains amylase.

The esophagus, especially in land snails, is widened posteriorly to form the crop, in which food is stored and digested. In freshwater pulmonates the stomach is partly or wholly muscularized to form a gizzard, which is absent among stylommatophoran pulmonates. The gizzard (Fig. 2-9) is posteriorly connected to the pyloric end of the stomach, into which empty the ducts of the digestive gland and from which a small cecum protrudes. The stomach is followed by the intestine. Working with *Lymnaea stagnalis*, Carriker (1947) has differentiated histologically and functionally a prointestine, a mid-intestine, and a postintestine. In general, the intestine is short in carnivorous pulmonates and is longer and often looped in herbivorous pulmonates.

A typical sac with style, as found in prosobranchs and bivalves, is absent in pulmonates. Carriker (1947), however, has reported the occurrence of a typhlosole in the beginning of the intestine in *Lymnaea stagnalis*. The typhlosole arises as an infolding of the ventral muscular wall of the anterior portion of the intestine, and it is projected at a right angle into the intestinal lumen. Baker (1945) considers the fingerlike process or the blind cecum on the underside of the pylorus near the duct of the digestive gland in all planorbid snails as the style sac. It would appear that such structures in members of the Lymnaeidae and Planorbidae may not function as a style and style sac but may represent them.

The digestive gland of pulmonates contains two histological types of cells (Fig. 2-10): (1) the digestive cells (the designation being synonymous with liver, ferment, palisade, hepatic, resorption, secretion, excretory, and vacuolar cells of some investigators) and (2) the lime cells (also known as calcium, or chalk cells). Carriker and Bilstad (1946) have stated that in *Lymnaea stagnalis* the digestive cells constitute the bulk of the digestive gland tubules and are polyphasic. Considerable variations in cell size and appearance occur as related to physiological function or condition. These cells are all capable of secretion, excretion, absorption, digestion, and stor-

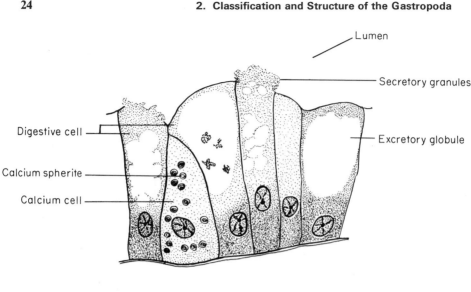

Fig. 2-10. Histology of digestive gland tubule. Section of a portion of the digestive gland of *Biomphalaria glabrata* showing types of cells and inclusions present.

age of fat and glycogen. In *Lymnaea, Helisoma,* and *Biomphalaria* the lime cells are found scattered throughout the digestive gland tubules in small groups. These cells contain large bodies that are calcareous (Malek, 1952).

All pulmonates are hermaphroditic. There is a common genital aperture in the stylommatophoran land snails, but separate male and female apertures occur in the basommatophorans. The plan of organization of the reproductive system is basically the same throughout the Basommatophora. A description of a planorbid reproductive system serves as an example Fig. 2-11).

The gonad is called the "ovotestis" if both sperm and ova are produced. A part of the ovotestis is free within the top, or distalmost, whorl of the shell while the remaining portion is embedded in the digestive gland. The ovotestis consists of many follicles known as acini. A main duct, a hermaphroditic duct, arises from the ovotestis, and along its course there are a number of outgrowths known as seminal vesicles. This duct bifurcates to form the male and female tracts, which are situated parallel to each other. In the male tract, a sperm duct receives the secretions of a prostate gland and then differentiates into a tubular vas deferens that leads to the penial complex. This complex consists of a vergic sac that houses the verge or penis, a preputium that opens to the exterior through the male genital pore, and a

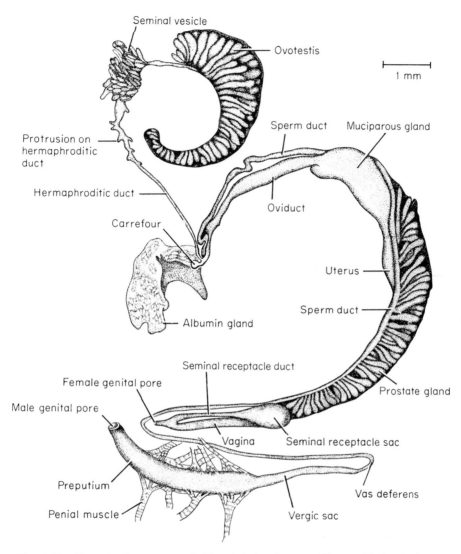

Seminal vesicle

Ovotestis

1 mm

Protrusion on hermaphroditic duct

Sperm duct

Muciparous gland

Hermaphroditic duct

Oviduct

Carrefour

Uterus

Sperm duct

Albumin gland

Seminal receptacle duct

Female genital pore

Male genital pore

Prostate gland

Vagina

Seminal receptacle sac

Preputium

Vas deferens

Penial muscle

Vergic sac

Fig. 2-11. Reproductive system of *Biomphalaria obstructa*. The positions of the reproductive organs in this species is quite characteristic of all the members of the Planorbidae. After Malek (1969).

number of penial muscles. Along the female tract, the oviduct receives the secretion from a large muciparous gland before becoming differentiated into a uterus, which receives secretions from an oöthecal gland. The uterus leads into the vagina, which opens to the exterior through the female genital pore. A seminal receptacle duct and sac are connected to the vagina.

References

Alicata, J. E. (1962). Life cycle and developmental stages of *Philophthalmus gralli* in the intermediate and final hosts. *J. Parasitol.* **48**, 47–54.

Baker, F. C. (1945). "The Molluscan Family Planorbidae." Univ. of Illinois Press, Urbana.

Basch, P. F. (1969). The arterial system of *Biomphalaria glabrata* (Say). *Malacologia* 7, 169–181.

Carriker, M. R. (1947). Morphology of the alimentary system of the snail *Lymnaea stagnalis appressa* Say. *Wis. Acad. Sci. Arts. Lett.* **38**, 1–88.

Carriker, M. R., and Bilstad, N. M. (1946). Histology of the alimentary system of the snail *Lymnaea stagnalis appressa* Say. *Trans. Amer. Microsc. Soc.* **65**, 250–275.

Fretter, V., and Graham, A. (1962). "British Prosobranch Molluscs." Ray Society, London.

Hyman, L. H. (1967). "The Invertebrates," Vol. VI. McGraw-Hill, New York.

Malek, E. A. (1952). Morphology, bionomics and host-parasite relations of Planorbidae (Mollusca: Pulmonata). Ph.D. thesis, University of Michigan, Ann Arbor, Michigan.

Malek, E. A. (1955). Anatomy of *Biomphalaria boissyi* as related to its infection with *Schistosoma mansoni*. *Amer. Midl. Natur.* **54**, 394–404.

Malek, E. A. (1969). Studies on "tropicorbid" snails (*Biomphalaria*: Planorbidae) from the Caribbean and Gulf of Mexico areas, including the southern United States. *Malacologia* 7, 183–209.

Malek, E. A. and Little, M. D. (1971). *Aroapyrgus colombiensis* n. sp. (Gastropoda: Hydrobiidae), snail intermediate host of *Paragonimus caliensis* in Colombia. *Nautilus* 85, 20–26.

Morton, J. E. (1958). "Molluscs." Hutchinson University Library, London.

Owen, G. (1966). Digestion. *In* "Physiology of Mollusca" (K. M. Wilbur and C. M. Yonge, eds.), Vol. 2, pp. 53–96. Academic Press, New York.

Pan, C. T. (1958). The general histology and topographic microanatomy of *Australorbis glabratus*. *Bull. Mus. Comp. Zool., Harvard Univ.* **119**, 237–299.

Pan, C. T. (1971). The arterial system of the planorbid snail *Biomphalaria* glabrata. *Trans. Amer. Microsc. Soc.* **90**, 434–440.

3 Classification and Structure of the Bivalvia

The members of the class Bivalvia, commonly known as clams, oysters, and mussels, are of worldwide distribution. All the species are aquatic, with the majority being marine, but there are some that are freshwater. They vary in length from a few millimeters to more than 70 cm. The giant marine clam *Tridacna* is an example of the latter size. The bivalves live half-buried in, and move slowly on, muddy or sandy bottoms, but many species are sedentary, as in the case of *Spondylus, Ostrea*, and others. Some bivalves live in cavities, which they excavate either in wood like *Teredo* or in stone, as in the case of *Lithophaga* and *Pholas*. Some are commensals or parasites that live in or on echinoderms such as *Montacuta*. Boss (1965) has reviewed the literature relative to the relationships of bivalves of the superfamily Erycinacea and other invertebrates. He has concluded that the relationship is predominantly commensalistic but may also be mutualistic or even ectoparasitic. Among the hosts cited are some species of Porifera, Coelenterata, Bryozoa, Annelida, other Mollusca, Echinodermata, and Arthropoda. By comparison to other mollusks the Bivalvia are greatly modified; however, they constitute a more uniform class than the gastropods.

Classification

There are three divisions of the Bivalvia regarded as subclasses. The following classification is after Morton and Yonge (1964).

27

SUBCLASS PROTOBRANCHIA

Gills with flat, nonreflected filaments, hypobranchial glands retained. Foot opening out to expose flattened ventral surface with numerous retractors. Feeding primarily by means of extensile proboscides from enlarged labial palps. With primitive but also very specialized characters.

SUBCLASS LAMELLIBRANCHIA

Gills much larger relative to labial palps and forming feeding organs; filaments greatly elongated and reflected, forming two-sided lamellae the arms of which are usually united by lamellar junctions. Adjacent filaments attached by ciliary junctions (filibranch) or united by tissue (eulamellibranch). Six orders are recognized under this subclass, and these are differentiated mainly on gill structure and arrangement. These orders are Taxodonta, Anisomyaria, Heterodonta, Schizodonta, Adapedonta, and Anomalodesmata.

SUBCLASS SEPTIBRANCHIA

Adductors equal and mantle edges not extensively fused. Gills transformed into a muscular septum pumping water through the mantle cavity. Macrophagous feeding upon animal remains, often at considerable depth.

Structure

The bivalves have no head, tentacles, buccal mass, jaws, or radula. Their ancestors were probably limpetlike, and later underwent lateral compression. In modern species the shell is divided into two calcified valves, which are connected dorsally by a noncalcified ligament consisting of conchiolin. The two valves are secreted by two corresponding mantle flaps. The shell is secreted by the entire surface of the mantle, and the external layer is secreted by the thickened mantle edge only. Although primarily symmetrical, the valves are asymmetrical in certain species such as *Arca, Pecten*, and *Ostrea*. The valves articulate along the dorsal border by the hinge consisting of a system of teeth and sockets and can be firmly held closed by the adductor muscles. On their inner surface each valve exhibits the insertions of a number of pairs of muscles (Fig. 3-1A).

The foot is an ax-shaped structure (hence the designation Pelecypoda often employed for this class of mollusks). It usually extends from the anterior portion of the shell and by lodgment to the substrate, drags the animal slowly forward.

The animal has two openings posteriorly: the lower, or branchial, siphon through which water enters, passes anteriorly aerating the gills, and carries

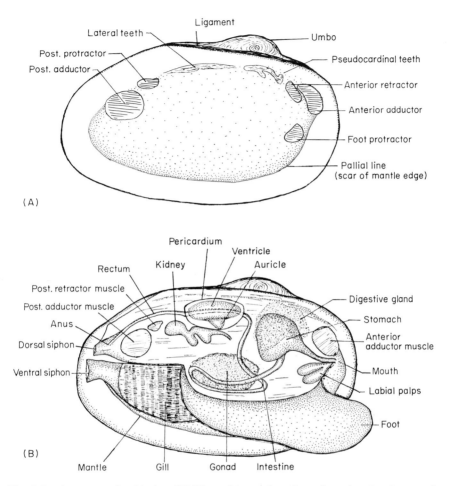

Fig. 3-1. Anatomy of a bivalve. (A) View of internal surface of a valve showing muscle scars. (B) Internal organs of a bivalve.

food to the mouth; and the dorsal, or anal, siphon, which accomodates the current of water leaving the mantle cavity. Sometimes the siphons are referred to as the inhalent and exhalent siphons. The gills are paired and each consists of two demibranchs suspended in the mantle cavity, at each side of the foot. In most bivalves each demibranch is V-shaped so the pair is W-shaped (Fig. 3-2). The gills are divided into a series of water tubes by septa or partitions through which water is circulated by means of ciliary action. However, the shape and structure of the gills do vary, and the differences are employed as taxonomic characteristics among the major groups of bivalves.

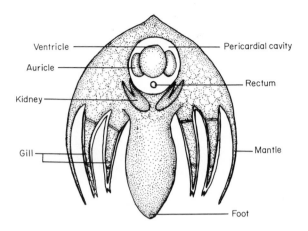

Fig. 3-2. Lamellibranch morphology. Schematic drawing of a transverse section through the pericardial region of a bivalve showing characteristic structure of the gills. In many species of bivalves the ventricle is traversed by the rectum.

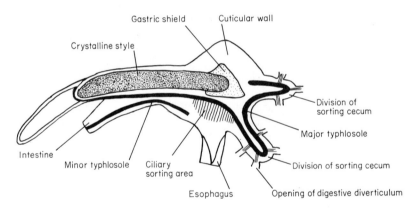

Fig. 3-3. Schematic drawing of the stomach of a eulamellibranch. Redrawn after Morton (1958).

Most Bivalvia are ciliary feeders, and their food consists mainly of fine deposits of microscopic diatoms and other microflora. However, a few, such as members of the subclass Septibranchia and other abyssal species, are carnivorous, feeding on animal remains.

The mouth opens at the anterior end of the body, and on each side of it is located a flap, or palpus (the labial palps), which, together with the gills, guide the food to the mouth. The mouth leads directly into a short esophagus, which opens into the stomach (Fig. 3-1B). The saccular stomach is large and generally laterally compressed. Bivalves also possess a style sac and style similar to those found in prosobranch gastropods (Fig. 3-3). As in the proso-branchs, the style consists primarily of mucoproteins secreted by the edge of a number of typhlosoles that isolate the style sac from the intestine. The style always contains amylase and glycogenase, which are set free in the stomach as its anterior terminal dissolves. According to Morton (1958), the stomach of bivalves functions in sorting a mixture of particles, carrying undigested materials to the intestine, conveying fine fragments after preliminary extra-cellular digestion to the digestive gland diverticula, and ensuring that waste matter returning from the digestive gland diverticula reaches the intestine without remixing with the food. In some forms the style sac is fused with the anterior end of the intestine and communicates with it by a narrow, longi-tudinal slit. Pelseneer (1906) has reported that such a condition occurs in *Arca, Mytilus, Ostrea, Pecten, Cardium, Mya*, members of the Unionidae, and other species.

The digestive diverticula (digestive gland) consists of a pair of large, more or less symmetrical, acinar structures that occupy the entire space surround-ing the stomach. As is the case in gastropods, cells of the digestive gland tubules are capable of phagocytizing particles from the lumen and carrying on intracellular digestion. Fragmentation of the luminal edges of the cells (Fig. 3-4) and their return to the stomach helps in eliminating the residual waste material after intracellular digestion.

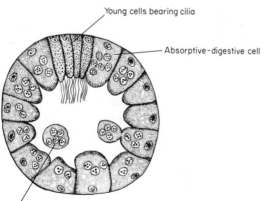

Young cells bearing cilia

Absorptive-digestive cell

Bud given off by digestive cell

Fig. 3-4. Morphology of bivalve digestive gland. Drawing of a section of a terminal lobule showing cell types present. Redrawn after Morton (1958).

The intestine coils a few times prior to leading to the rectum (Fig. 3-1B), which passes ventral to, dorsal to, or traverses the ventricle of the heart. The anus is situated on the midline behind the posterior adductor muscle.

As in gastropods, the circulatory system of bivalves is the open system type. It is composed of a number of vessels and sinuses with connective tissue walls. The heart consists of a median ventricle and two auricles that are usually symmetrical (Fig. 3-1B and 3-2). An aortic trunk arises from the ventricle, and it usually divides into an anterior and a posterior aorta, which supply the various parts of the body with oxygenated hemolymph. The hemolymph actually seeps into the sinuses and bathes the various tissues. The most prominent sinuses are the pallial sinuses, the pedal sinus, and the median ventral sinus (subrenal sinus). The latter extends between the pericardium and the foot. Hemolymph passes from this sinus to the kidneys and from there flows to the gills. The directional flow of hemolymph in this part of the circulatory system is similar to that in the prosobranch gastropods (Fig. 2-4). In addition to its function in the exchange of gases, the hemolymph serves as a hemoskeleton providing turgidity to such structures as the mantle, the siphons, and the foot. The hemolymph constitutes an important tissue of the body and often amounts to half of the shell-less animal's weight. Nucleated cells similar to those of gastropods are present in the plasma (Chapter 8). In the case of some neotropical, marine species, nonamoeboid corpuscles containing hemoglobin also occur. The hemoglobin need not be within hemolymph cells; it may occur within the gill cells (Read, 1965).

The kidneys are symmetrical organs situated below the pericardium in the postero-dorsal region of the body (Fig. 3-2). They generally extend back to the posterior adductor muscle. The kidneys open into the pallial cavity through orifices situated at their anterior ends, while at the posterior end they open into the pericardium through two renopericardial or internal renal orifices. Each kidney appears as a sac folded on itself and thus is U-shaped. The two kidneys are either connected with one another or are separate. They portray ramifications and extend over the whole surface of the visceral mass in the oyster *Ostrea*. In addition to the kidneys, excretion is also carried out by the pericardial glands. These glands are specialized areas of the epithelial wall of the pericardium. As they do in gastropods, hemolymph cells in bivalves carry out excretory activities by carrying particles into the lumen of the gut, into the pericardium and renal organ, and through the outer body wall. These cells may migrate from the blood spaces in the gills onto the surfaces, where they phagocytize food particles and then either retreat into the epithelium or are ingested through the mouth.

The reproductive system of bivalves is simple when compared with that of gastropods. The gonads (Fig. 3-1B) are paired or fused along the midline. Their ducts are short and include no glands. According to Morton (1958), in primitive bivalves, such as *Nucula*, these ducts open into the kidneys and through them into the mantle cavity. In the more advanced species, however, they become separate and open on a papilla shared with the nephridiopore, or the gonoducts communicate with the exterior at a site spatially separate from the nephridiopore. Internal fertilization never occurs; however, in many species the sperm and eggs make contact within the mantle cavity. In some bivalves there is a brood chamber, or marsupium, which is the inter-lamellar space of the inner or outer gills, and in this space the eggs are maintained for a period prior to their escape as larvae. In the larviparous oysters the mantle cavity serves as a temporary brood chamber (p. 268). In the viviparous species the newly hatched glochidium remains within the parent for a period that varies from species to species, ranging from about 4 weeks to about 6 months. Members of the freshwater family Sphaeriidae (fingernail clams) liberate small replicas of the adult from between the gills, but in the freshwater unionid mussels the young are liberated at a much earlier stage. The larvae, known as glochidia, attach themselves by spines and/or a byssus to fish. After a period of growth as a parasite of fish, they drop off and become independent. The glochidial valve is retained as a nucleus around which the growing valve of the adult is deposited.

Species belonging to the oyster family are either larviparous, for example, *Ostrea edulis* and *O. lurida*, or oviparous, for example, *Crassostrea virginica, C. angulata, C. gigas*, and *C. cucullata*. The larviparous species produce late, short-swimming larvae from the mantle cavity, while the oviparous species shed eggs that are fertilized externally and give rise to long-swimming veligers (Chapter 12).

Bivalvia are in general dioecious, but hermaphrodites occur among some groups. The gonad is comprised of acini and is ramified, as in *Ostrea* and other forms. Many of the species of oysters are dioecious, for example, *Crassostrea virginica*, but other species are hermaphrodites. In some herma-phroditic species the entire gonad is hermaphroditic while in other species parts of the gonad are hermaphroditic while other parts produce either sperm or ova. In still other species, the gonad is differentiated into regions, with the anterior region being male and the posterior being female. This is the case in *Pecten* spp. Changing of sex is known to occur among dioecious bivalves. The best known examples of this are the oysters. Intensive work with the freshwater naiad group of the United States (van der Schalie, 1970) has shown that most of the species are dioecious, with only four being usually hermaphroditic while several are occasional hermaphrodites. *Anodonta imbecillus, Lasmigona compressa, Lasmigona subviridis*, and *Carun-culina parva* have been shown to be hermaphroditic.

Sexual dimorphism is only exhibited in a few species of bivalves. The females of certain species of *Unio* and *Lampsilis* are broader than the males, and in *Astarte* the border of the shell is smooth in the male and crenelated in the female.

References

Boss, K. J. (1965). Symbiotic erycinacean bivalves. *Malacologia* **3**, 183–195.

Morton, J. E. (1958). "Molluscs." Hutchinson University Library, London.

Morton, J. E., and Yonge, C. M. (1964). Classification and structure of the Mollusca. *In* "Physiology of Mollusca" (K. M. Wilbur and C. M. Yonge, eds.), Vol. 1, pp. 1–58. Academic Press, New York.

Pelseneer, P. (1906). *In* "A Treatise on Zoology" (E. R. Lankester, ed.), Part V, Mollusca, Adam & Black, London.

Read, K. R. H. (1965). The characterization of the hemoglobins of the bivalve mollusc *Phacoides pectinatus* (Gmelin). *Comp. Biochem. Physiol.* **15**, 137–158.

van der Schalie, H. (1970). Hermaphroditism among North American freshwater mussels. *Malacologia* **10**, 93–112.

4 Systematic Account of the Gastropoda

Since the gastropods are by far the most important group of mollusks from the standpoint of medical malacology, this, and especially the following two chapters, are devoted to a systematic account of the Gastropoda and their roles as hosts for parasites of public health importance.

The first section of this chapter deals with the freshwater snails. The families are considered: first those subordinate to the Pulmonata, then those belonging to the Prosobranchiata. For each family there is information regarding (1) the recognition characters of the shell and animal; (2) the subfamilies, if considered to be of importance; and (3) the genera, their diagnostic features, important species, geographical distribution, and some of the trematodes for which they serve as intermediate hosts. In the second section the families of brackish and marine snails are considered. In the third section the land snails are only dealt with in the form of a key to the important genera, including their characteristics, some representative species, and some of the trematodes that they harbor. Throughout the chapter the list of trematodes after each molluscan species is by no means complete. Only a few examples are cited to acquaint the reader with the types of trematodes one might expect to find in different categories of snails.

FRESHWATER SNAILS

Key to Families

1. Snail with an operculum .... Prosobranchiata   2
   Snail without an operculum .... Pulmonata   6
2. Operculum concentric   3
   Operculum spiral   4
3. Shell very large; with eyes on short peduncles at base of tentacles;
   anterior part of proboscis protruding as two processes resembling
   tentacles .... Pilidae (=Ampullaridae)   (p. 69)
   Shell large, but smaller than Ampullaridae; tentacles long and slender;
   in male right tentacle shorter than left, forming a sheath for the
   penis .... Viviparidae   (p. 68)
4. Operculum multispiral, circular; shell generally less than 7 mm in width,
   wider than high, often with carinae (Fig. 4-2) .... Valvatidae

   Operculum paucispiral   5
5. Shell thick and heavy, shell whorls generally very flat sided, spire narrowly pointed; adult shell more than 15 mm in height; aperture sometimes angulate .... Pleuroceridae   (p. 67)
   Shell small, not thick or heavy, aperture never angulate ..... Hydrobiidae   (p. 58)
6. Shell patelliform .... Ancylidae   **(p. 56)**
   Shell spiral   7
7. Shell discoidal, orblike .... Planorbidae   **(p. 37)**
   Shell with elongated spire   8
8. Shell dextral .... Lymnaeidae   **(p. 53)**
   Shell sinistral .... Physidae   **(p. 57)**

The medically important family Thiaridae is widely distributed outside of the continental United States. It can be fitted in the key given above. Like the Pleuroceridae, the thiarids have high, **turreted, and** thick shells and a spiral, corneous operculum (multispiral or **paucispiral**). To group 3 is added the hydrobiid genus *Bulimus* (= *Bithynia*), with a concentric operculum. Its shell is small, however, being 2–11 mm in height, and its aperture is elongated.

In the Mediterranean area and in some African countries the distribution of the Physidae and the subfamily Bulininae of the family Planorbidae over-laps. Members of the Bulininae possess shells that are sinistral and physoid or globose in shape. The above key can, in this case, be extended as follows:

8. Shell dextral .... Lymnaeidae
   Shell sinistral   9
9. Pseudobranch present, hemolymph red .... Bulininae
   Pseudobranch absent, hemolymph colorless .... Physidae

Subclass Pulmonata
(The Pulmonates)

FAMILY PLANORBIDAE

The family Planorbidae is one of the most important families from the standpoint of public health. The shell is discoidal, sinistral (ultradextral), and may be globose or physoid. The animal is sinistral with its pulmonary and genital apertures situated on the left side. The tentacles are long, filiform, and cylindrical, with eyes situated at their inner bases. The structure of the penial complex is variable, but always consists of a preputium and a vergic sac. The radula includes a bicuspid central tooth, large bi- or tricuspid lateral teeth, and the marginal teeth are long, narrow, and multicuspid. A highly vascular pseudobranch is present on the left side. Members of this family include hemoglobin in their hemolymph and hence are reddish in color. For more details about this family see Baker (1945).

Key to Subfamilies

1. Shell globose or turreted .... Bulininae   (p. 43)
   Shell discoidal   2
2. Well-developed, cup-shaped preputial gland present, usually with a duct
      (Fig. 14-11C), gland may be reduced in size   3
   Preputium without a gland, only pilasters, or with an appendage attached
      to pilasters. (Fig. 14-11A)   4
3. Prostate with multiple diverticula, fan-shaped in cross section, ovotestis
      of several diverticula arranged like a fan (Fig. 14-12C)
      .... Helisomatinae   (p. 49)
   Prostate forming a finger-shaped pattern with a few diverticula, preputial
      gland duct inside preputium, ovotestis with paired diverticula
      .... Planorbulinae   (p. 52)
4. Appendage may be present inside preputium, vergic sac with external
      flagella (short or long) near its junction with vas deferens (Fig.
      14-11D) .... Segmentininae   (p. 48)
   No preputial gland, vergic sac without flagella (Fig. 14-11A)
      .... Planorbinae   (p. 37)

Subfamily Planorbinae

Key to Genera of Planorbinae

1. Verge with stylet, pear-shaped at base .... *Gyraulus*
   Verge without stylet   2
2. Vergic sac less than one-fourth length of preputium, prostate gland with
      a number of unbranched tubules arising from prostate duct ....
                                                              Planorbis

Vergic sac as long as preputium or longer, prostate tubules branched, no
prostate duct .... *Biomphalaria*

Genus *Gyraulus* Charpentier.   Members of the genus *Gyraulus* possess
small shells that are greatly depressed with carinate or subcarinate peri-
pheries and include three or four rapidly increasing whorls. The aperture
is oblique, the verge has a horny stylet, and a separate prostate duct is
present. The radula has bi- or tricuspid lateral teeth and six-cuspid marginal
teeth. *Gyraulus* is worldwide in its distribution, being present in North
America, northern South America, Europe, Asia, Africa, Australia, Malaysia, and the Philippines.

Gyraulus parvus (Say) (Fig. 4-1c) is the intermediate host of both the avian
schistosome *Gigantobilharzia gyrauli* and the plagiorchid *Haematoloechus
parviplexus*, which as an adult is parasitic in frogs. *Gyraulus similaris* is the

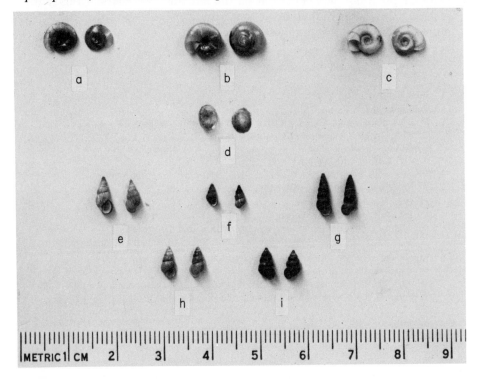

Fig. 4-1.   Shells of some snails. (a) *Hippeutis umbilicalis* (Benson) from Taiwan. (b) *Segmentina
hemisphaerula* (Benson) from Taiwan. (c) *Gyraulus parvus* (Say) from Michigan. (d) *Ferrissia
dalli* Walker from Louisiana. (e) *Oncomelania hupensis hupensis* (Gredler) from China. (f) *Oncomelania hupensis quadrasi* (Moellendorff) from the Philippines. (g) *Oncomelania hupensis nosophora* (Robson) from Japan. (h) *Oncomelania hupensis formosana* (Pilsbry and Hirase) from
Taiwan. (i) *Pomatiopsis lapidaria* (Say) from Louisiana.

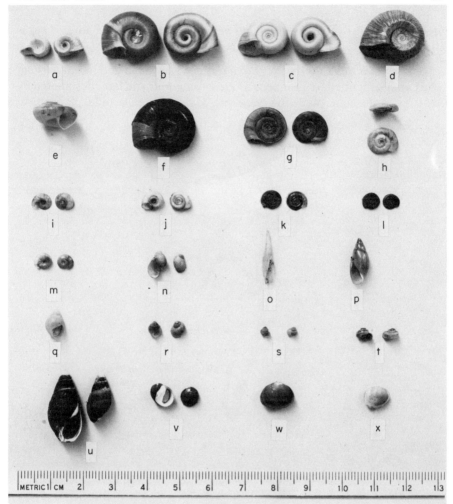

Fig. 4-2. Some molluscan shells. (a) *Helisoma anceps* (Menke) from Michigan. (b) *Helisoma trivolvis* (Say) from Michigan. (c) *Helisoma campanulatum* (Say) from Michigan. (d) *Helisoma corpulentum* (Say) from Minnesota. (e) *Carinifex newberryi* (Lea) from California. (f) *Planorbarius corneus* (Linn.) from Holland. (g) *Planorbis planorbis* (Linn.) from Holland. (h) *Planorbis philippi* (Monterosato from Egypt. (i) *Promenetus exacuous* (Say) from Michigan. (j) *Planorbula armigera* (Say) from Michigan. (k) *Drepanotrema cultratum* (D'Orbigny) from Texas. (l) *Drepanotrema cimex* (Moricand) from Brazil. (m) *Segmentorbis angustus* (Jickelli) from Sudan. (n) *Plesiophysa* sp. from Brazil. (o) *Acella haldemani* (Binney) from Michigan. (p) *Apleza hypnorum* (Linn.) from Michigan. (q) *Bulimus* (= *Bithynia*) *tentaculata* (Linn.) from Michigan. (r) *Somatogyrus subglobosus* (Say) from Michigan. (s) *Amnicola limosa* (Say) from Michigan. (t) *Valvata tricarinata* (Say) from Michigan. (u) *Melanopsis praemrosa* (Linn.) from Lebanon. (v) *Neritina jordani* Sowerby from Lebanon. (w) *Sphaerium striatinum* (Lamarck) from Michigan. (x) *Musculium partumeium* (Say) from Michigan.

intermediate host of *Haematoloechus breviplexus*, which as an adult is parasitic in frogs.

Genus *Planorbis* Geoffrey.   *Planorbis* is a European and North African genus, first described by Linnaeus as *Helix planorbis* and later designated by Geoffrey as the generotype for *Planorbis*. Many of the discoidal planorbids,

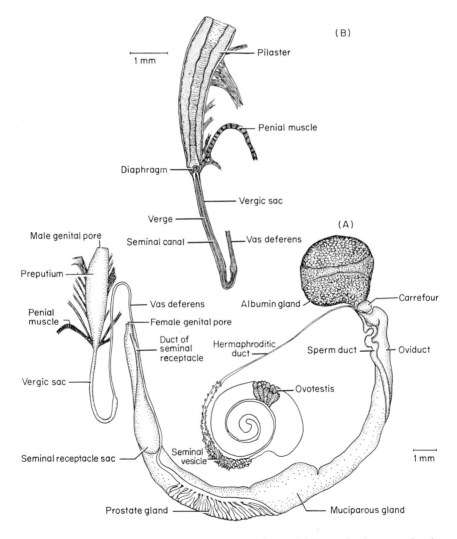

Fig. 4-3. Reproductive system of *Biomphalaria glabrata*. (A) Reproductive tract showing constituent parts. (B) Sagittal view of penial complex. After Malek (1952a).

including those serving as intermediate hosts for schistosomes, were included in this genus, for example, *Planorbis boissyi* Potiez and Michaud, *Planorbis pfeifferi* Krauss (now considered species of *Biomphalaria*), and others, which are not intermediate hosts of schistosomes and which are now assigned to the genera *Helisoma, Drepanotrema*, and others.

Planorbis planorbis (Linn.) is an intermediate host for the cyclocoelid trematode *Tracheophilus sisowi*, parasitic in ducks, and for *Paramphistomum cervi*, parasitic in sheep and cattle. Its shell includes a few whorls that increase regularly in diameter. The left and right sides are flattened and keeled. The

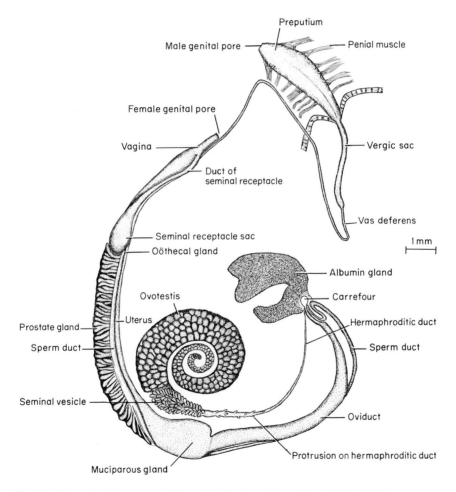

Fig.4-4. Reproductive system of *Biomphalaria alexandrina*. After Malek (1954b).

pseudobranch is small, leaf-shaped, and flattened. No conspicuous ridges are present on the rectum or the kidney. *Planorbis philippii* Monterosato from Alexandria, Egypt, is depicted in Fig. 4-2h.

Genus *Biomphalaria* Preston. The generotype for this genus is *Biomphalaria smithi* Preston (1910) originally collected in Lake Edward in Uganda. The shell is subdiscoidal planulate, with a concave spire, and the last whorl is very large. The umbilicus is in the form of a shallow depression. The shell has a gaping aperture, and the labrum is greatly receded below. There is a deviation towards the left of the last half whorl. Viewed dextrally, the last part of the whorl drops below the periphery.

Several species of *Biomphalaria* occur in Africa, South America, the Caribbean, and southwestern Asia (Saudi Arabia and Yemen). Many of the species serve as intermediate hosts for *Schistosoma mansoni*. Cercariae of other trematodes have also been reported from these species. The genitalia of *Biomphalaria glabrata* (Say) are depicted in Fig. 4-3 while those of *B. alexandrina* (Ehrenberg) are illustrated in Fig. 4-4 and in Fig. 4-5d.

Members of the genera *Australorbis* Pilsbry, *Tropicorbis* Pilsbry and Brown, and *Taphius* Adams and Adams are neotropical, and several planorbid species that are actual and potential intermediate hosts for *Schistosoma mansoni* have been placed in these genera. Their diagnostic features and those of *Biomphalaria* do not justify their being recognized as distinct genera, and efforts have been made to decide upon name applicable to all of them. A ruling by the International Commission on Zoological Nomenclature (1965) has given preference to *Biomphalaria* over the earlier generic designations such as *Planorbina, Taphius*, and *Armigerus*, and this decision is followed in this book (also see Barbosa *et al.*, 1961).

In Fig. 4-6 are depicted the shells of some species of *Biomphalaria* from Africa and the Western Hemisphere. *Biomphalaria glabrata* is an important intermediate host for *Schistosoma mansoni* on some Caribbean islands and in South America. *Biomphalaria straminea* (Dunker) and *B. tenagophila* (D'Orbigny) are known intermediate hosts in Brazil. *B. philippiana* (Dunker), *B. chilensis* (Anton), *B. albicans* (Pfeiffer), and *B. riisei* (Clessin) are potential intermediate hosts since they have been demonstrated to be experimentally susceptible to *S. mansoni*.

Distribution and systematics of the neotropical potential hosts of *S. mansoni* were reported by Malek (1969). These used to be included in the genus *Tropicorbis* but are now considered under *Biomphalaria*.

The African species of *Biomphalaria*, on the other hand, are almost all natural hosts of *S. mansoni*. Their systematics and distribution in the Central African and Ethiopian plateaus and in the Nile basin were worked out by Malek (1958), and in Africa in general by Mandahl-Barth (1958).

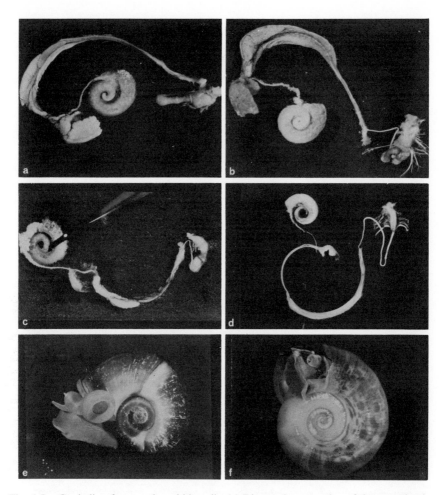

Fig. 4-5. Genitalia of some planorbid snails. (a) Dissected preparation of the reproductive system of *Helisoma trivolvis*. (b) Dissected preparation of the reproductive system of *Helisoma corpulentum*. (c) Dissected preparation of the reproductive system of *Helisoma campanulatum*. (d) Dissected preparation of the reproductive system of *Biomphalaria alexandrina*. (e) Everted penial complex of *Helisoma trivolvis*. (f) Everted penial complex of *Biomphalaria alexandrina*. After Malek (1952a).

Subfamily Bulininae

The genus *Bulinus* Müller is African, Middle Eastern, and southern European in distribution. Another genus included in this subfamily is *Indoplanorbis* Annandale and Prashad, which occurs in India, Thailand, the

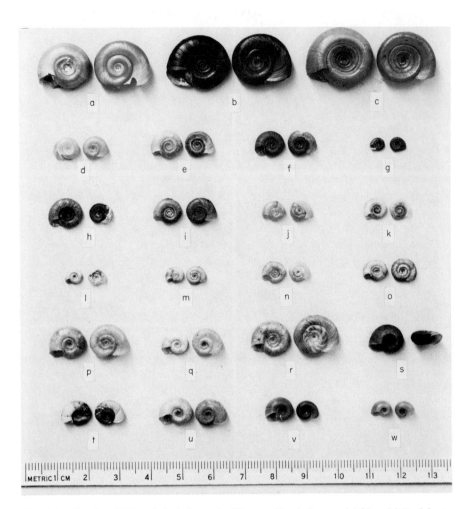

Fig. 4-6. Species of *Biomphalaria* from the Western Hemisphere and Africa. (a) *B. glabrata* (Say) from Puerto Rico. (b) *B. glabrata* from Brazil. (c) *B. tenagophila* (D'Orbigny) from Brazil. (d) *B. straminea* (Dunker) from Brazil. (e) *B. riisei* (Dunker) from Puerto Rico. (f) *B. straminea* (Dunker) from Brazil. (g) *B. schrammi* (Crosse) from Brazil. (h) B. peregrina (D'Orbigny) from Brazil. (i) *B. peregrina* from Argentina. (j) *B. philippiana* (Dunker) from Ecuador. (k) *B. fieldii* (Tryon) from El Salvador. (l) *B. liebmani* (Dunker) from Mexico. (m) *B. obstructa* (Morelet) from Baton Rouge, Louisiana. (n) *B. obstructa* from New Orleans, Louisiana. (o) *B. obstructa* from Louisiana. (p) *B. alexandrina* (Ehrenberg) from Egypt. (q) *B. ruppellii* (Dunker) Sudan. (r) *B. sudanica* Martens from Sudan. (s) *B. smithi* (Preston) from Lake Edward, Uganda. (t) *B. pfeifferi* (Krauss) from Ghana. (u) *B. pfeifferi gaudi* (Ranson) from Sudan. (v) *B. pfeifferi gaudi* from Gambia. (w) *B. choanomphala* (Martens) from Lake Albert, Uganda.

Malay Penninsula, and Sumatra. The genus *Camptoceras* Benson, which occurs in Japan, can also be placed in this subfamily.

Indoplanorbis exustus Larambergue is the intermediate host for several species of trematodes among which are the mammalian schistosomes *Schistosoma spindale*, *S. indicum*, and *S. nasale* and the amphistome *Gastrodiscus secundus*, parasitic as an adult in equines.

Genus *Bulinus* Müller. The shell of members of the genus *Bulinus* is sinistral, ovate or higher to almost cylindrical, and turreted. The height ranges from 4 to 23 mm. The whorls are usually evenly rounded. The aperture is high and wide in snails with a low spire and relatively narrow in specimens with a high spire. The columellar margin is either straight, more or less twisted, or truncate. The sculpture consists of spirally arranged rows of small transverse impressions, or the shell may possess ribs (costate). The general arrangement of the radular teeth is similar to that of members of the Planorbinae. In most species, marginal teeth four to seven are cuspid; the lateral and marginal teeth, however, show great individual variation. The pseudobranch is deeply folded (hence different from that of the Planorbinae). The genitalia are also different from those of the Planorbinae (Fig. 4-7). Specifically, the ovotestis includes a smaller number of acini, the prostate gland is compact and fan-shaped, the verge is introverted and coiled inside the vergic sac when not in use (designated as an "ultrapenis"), and, when everted, it is long and club-shaped. The preputium is more or less similar to that of the Planorbinae. The vagina and the seminal receptacle duct are short (also see Mandahl-Barth, 1958).

The genus *Bulinus* is divided into the following two subgenera.

SUBGENUS *Physopsis*. The characteristics of *Physopsis* are (1) columella is truncate, (2) the shell sculpture consists of spirally arranged rows of small, transverse impressions or nodules, and (3) the ventral surface of the kidney has a distinct renal ridge.

Most species transmit the human blood fluke *Schistosoma haematobium* and some schistosomes of animals in Africa south of the Sahara Desert.

SUBGENUS *Bulinus sensu stricto.* Among the members of *Bulinus* the columella is usually straight, although it is sometimes slightly twisted and/or reflexed, but it is never truncate. Furthermore, it leaves a narrow umbilicus in some subspecies. The shell is usually costate, and there is no renal ridge in the animal. This subgenus is comprised of the following: *Bulinus (Bulinus) truncatus* (Audouin) and its varieties. Among members of this species the spire is low, and the height of the shell is medium, usually 10 mm. However, the Egyptian representatives of *Bulinus truncatus* may in exceptional cases attain a height of 20 mm, and the Sudanese representatives about 14 mm. The

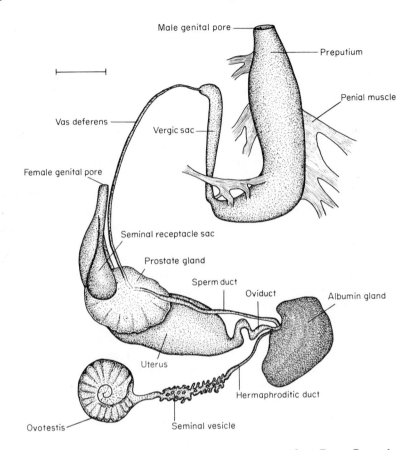

Fig. 4-7. Reproductive system of *Bulinus (Bulinus) truncatus* from Egypt. Bar = 1 mm.

aperture is high and wide, and aphalic specimens are common. *Bulinus (B.) truncatus* (Fig. 4-8a) is distributed over the Mediterranean area including some islands, the Middle East, as far east as Iran, and in Africa as far as the Great Lakes (also see Malek, 1958).

Bulinus (B.) truncatus is the recognized intermediate host of *S. haematobium* in Iran, Iraq, Syria, Egypt, the Sudan, and along the North African coast. The role that some varieties play in the transmission of urinary schistosomiasis in some African countries is not known. *Bulinus (B.) truncatus* also serves as the intermediate host for *Schistosoma bovis* and the amphistome trematode *Paramphistomum microbothrium*, parasitic in cattle, sheep, and goats.

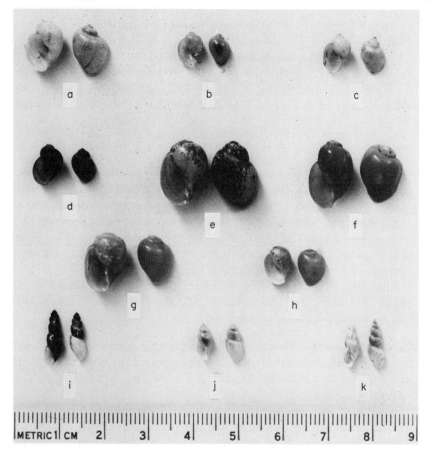

Fig. 4-8. Shells of some bulinid snails. (a) *Bulinus* (*Bulinus*) *truncatus* (Audouin) from Egypt. (b) *B.* (*B.*) *truncatus rohlfsi* (Clessin) from Senegal. (c) *B.* (*B.*) *coulboisi* (Bourguignat) from the Congo. (d) *B.* (*B.*) *tropicus* (Krauss) from Rhodesia. (e) *B.* (*Physopsis*) *africanus* (Krauss) from Uganda. (f) *B.* (*Ph.*) *globosus* (Morelet) from Angola. (g) *B.* (*Ph.*) *ugandae* Mandahl-Barth from Sudan. (h) *B.* (*Ph.*) *jousseaumei* from Gambia. (i) *B.* (*B.*) *forskalii* (Ehrenberg) from Tanzania. (j) *B.* (*B.*) *senegalensis* (Müller) from Gambia. (k) *B.* (*B.*) *forskalii* (Ehrenberg) from Sudan. After Malek (1962).

Bulinus (*B.*) *forskalii* (Ehrenberg) and its varieties, for example, *B.* (*B.*) *senegalensis*, possess a shell with a long, slender spire. The shell is costate, but sometimes the costae are not distinct. The columella is usually twisted.

Bulinus (*B.*) *forskalii* is a known host in nature for certain schistosomes of animals in some African countries and for the human intestinal schistosome, *Schistosoma intercalatum*, in Gabon. It is a potential intermediate host for *S. haematobium*, although some of the varieties are known to be actual transmitters of this parasite. *Bulinus (B.) forskalii* is one of the hosts for the amphistomes *Gastrodiscus aegyptiacus* of equines and *Paramphistomum microbothrium* of cattle, sheep, and goats.

Bulinus (B.) forskalii, formerly referred to as *Pyrgophysa forskalii*, is widely distributed in Africa, south of the Sahara. It also occurs in the Nile Valley, and some of its varieties are on the islands of Mauritius and Madagascar.

Subfamily Segmentininae

The members of Segmentininae are small planorbids with low, bright, smooth, and very glossy discoidal shells. The last whorl embraces the shell, and the aperture is nearly heart-shaped. The prostate tubules are in the form of simple sacs arranged in a single row along the prostate duct. There are one or two flagella at the end of the vergic sac, and in some genera there is a preputial appendage attached to the pilasters. The kidney of members of this subfamily is without a ridge.

The important genera of the Segmentininae are *Segmentina* Fleming, *Hippeutis* Charpentier, and *Drepanotrema* Crosse and Fischer. These are the intermediate hosts for several trematodes.

Genus *Segmentina* Fleming. The shells in *Segmentina* have four or more small, calcareous barriers, or lamellae, inside the whorls. There is a glandular appendage in the preputium, and there are two short flagella at the end of the vergic sac.

Segmentina hemisphaerula (Benson) has a glossy, reddish brown to light brown shell about 3 mm in height and 9 mm in diameter. The umbilicus is very deep (Fig. 4-1b). It is the intermediate host of the intestinal fluke *Fasciolopsis buski* of pigs and man. The snail is widely distributed throughout Japan, Taiwan, and China.

Segmentina angustus (Jickeli) occurs in the Sudan and Uganda. Mandahl-Barth (1954) has assigned the African species in a new genus, *Segmentorbis*. These African planorbids are sympatric with the biomphalarid hosts of *Schistosoma mansoni*, and the two groups can only be distinguished by an experienced investigator.

Genus *Hippeutis* Charpentier. The shell of *Hippeutis* is similar to that of *Segmentina*, although it is flattened and without internal lamellae. The animal possesses a preputial appendage and two short flagella on the vergic sac.

Hippeutis umbilicalis (Benson) (Fig. 4-1a) occurs in Taiwan, southern China, Vietnam, Laos, Cambodia, and India.

Hippeutis cantori (Benson) is present throughout China and is the snail host of *Fasciolopsis buski*.

Genus *Drepanotrema* Crosse and Fischer. The shell of *Drepanotrema* is small, and the body whorl is large and expanded to embrace the previous whorl; the whorls are rounded or carinated and usually overlapping. There is a pronounced depression on the umbilical side, and there are no barriers or lamellae in the shell. The animal is long, its preputium is without appendage, and there are both long and short flagella on the vergic sac. The sperm duct is long, and there are a few unbranched prostate tubules of different sizes associated with it.

Drepanotrema is an American genus with species occurring in southern Texas, Mexico, Central and South America, and on many of the Caribbean islands.

The species of *Drepanotrema* are of significance because they are found with biomphalarid planorbids, which are actual and potential hosts of *Schistosoma mansoni* in the Western Hemisphere. *Drepanotrema cultratum* (D'Orbigny) from Texas (Fig. 4-2k) and *Drepanotrema cimex* (Moricand) from Brazil (Fig. 4-2l) are examples.

Subfamily Helisomatinae

In this subfamily the prostate is fan-shaped in cross section; the prostate tubules are compound, branching several times; and the prostate duct is short. The preputial gland is well developed, cup-shaped, and with the duct situated externally between the preputium and the vergic sac. This duct is absent in a few species. *Planorbarius* Froriep is the only representative genus in Europe and North Africa. The other genera belonging to this subfamily are American.

Genus *Planorbarius*. *Helix cornea* Linn. was selected by Froriep as the generotype for this genus, hence *Planorbarius corneus*. The shell is large, discoidal, solid, and portrays gradually enlarging whorls. The preputium is large and pyriform while the vergic sac and verge are very small. The vergic sac is situated at the summit of the preputium and lies on it. The preputial gland is located at the base of the preputium and, while still within the preputium, tapers into an appendage that terminates in two lateral swellings. There is no gland duct present (Fig. 14-11B).

Planorbarius metidgensis (Forbes) (= *P. dufourii*), which occurs in Algarve, Portugal, is the reported intermediate host of *Schistosoma haematobium* within a small focus in that country. It is, however, believed to be under control. It has also been reported that *P. metidgensis* could be experimentally infected with *S. mansoni*.

Planorbarius corneus is an intermediate host of the cyclocoelid trematode *Tracheophilus sisowi*, the adult of which parasitizes ducks. It is also a suitable intermediate host for *Bilharziella polonica*, the blood fluke of ducks, and certain other species of trematodes.

Genus *Helisoma* (Swainson) (See Malek, 1952a, 1952b, 1954a). *Planorbis bicarinatus* Say (= *P. anceps* Menke) was selected by Sowerby as the generotype for this genus, hence *Helisoma bicarinatus*. No member of *Helisoma* has been incriminated as an intermediate host for a parasite of humans; however, a large number of other species of trematodes are harbored by the many species and varieties of this genus in the United States and Canada.

Among the members of *Helisoma* the preputial gland is well developed and cup-shaped. Besides its secretory functions, it is a holdfast organ that serves to attach one mate to the neck of its partner during copulation. The reproductive system of *Helisoma trivolvis* is shown in Fig. 4-9.

Key to Common Species of North American *Helisoma*

1. Basal whorls regularly wound, not funicular, adult shell more than 13 mm in
   diameter 2
   Base funicular whorls sharply carinated above, below, or both, adult shell
   13 mm or less in diameter ....*H. anceps*   (Fig. 4-2a)
2. Aperture greatly expanded, bell-shaped (campanulate) ..*H. campanulatum* (Fig. 4-2c)
   Aperture not expanded, shell large 3
3. Whorls carinate, high, with raised growth lines ....*H. corpulentum* (Fig. 4-2d)
   Whorls rounded, low, growth lines not raised ....*H. trivolvis* (Fig. 4-2b)

Helisoma trivolvis (Say) is the molluscan intermediate host for several species of trematodes among which are the following: the amphistomes *Allassostoma parvum*, a parasite of frogs and turtles, and *Megalodiscus temperatus*, a parasite of frogs; the echinostomes *Petasiger nitidus*, a parasite of grebes, and *Echinostoma revolutum*, a parasite of birds and mammals; the psilostome *Psilostomum ondatrae*, a parasite of gulls and muskrats; the clinostomes *Clinostomum complanatum*, a parasite of herons, and *C. attenuatum*, a parasite of bitterns; the strigeid *Crassifiala ambloplitis*, a parasite of the kingfisher; the spirorchids *Spirorchis artericola*, *S. elephantis*, and *S. parvus*, all parasites of turtles; the cyclocoelid *Tracheophilus cymbius*, a parasite of grebes; the allocreadiid *Macroderoides typicus*, a parasite of fishes; the plagiorchid *Alloglosidium corti*, also a parasite of fishes; and the lissorchiid *Lissorchis fairporti*, another parasite of fishes.

Helisoma anceps (Menke) [= *H. antrosum* (Conrad)] is the molluscan host for the amphistomes *Zygocotyle lunatum*, a parasite of ducks and rats, and *Wardius zibethicus*, a parasite of muskrats; the clinostomes *Clinostomum complanatum*, a parasite of herons, and *C. attenuatum*, a parasite of bitterns; the echinostomes *Petasiger nitidus*, a parasite of grebes, and *Echinostoma revolutum*, a parasite of birds and mammals; the psilostome *Psilostomum ondatrae*, a parasite of gulls and muskrats; and the cephalogonimid *Cephalogonimus americanus* under experimental conditions.

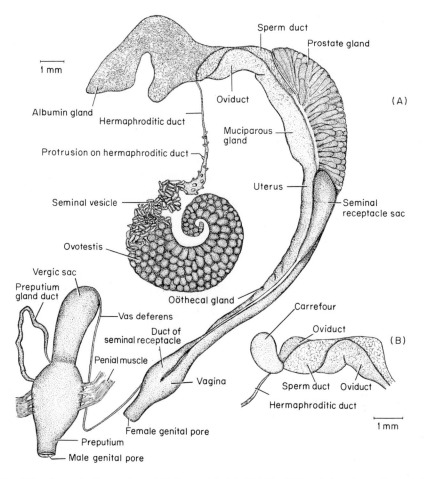

Fig. 4-9. Reproductive system of *Helisoma trivolvis*. (A) Genital tract showing various parts. (B) Sperm duct and oviduct near point of bifurcation of hermaphroditic duct. After Malek (1954a).

Larvae of the following trematodes have been reported in *Helisoma campanulatum* (Say): *Spirorchis elephantis*, *S. parvus*, *Alloglosidium corti*, *Petasiger nitidus*, *Allassostoma parvum*, and *Alaria marcianae*; the last under experimental conditions.

Helisoma corpulentum (Say) is the molluscan host for *Crassifiala ambloplitis* and *Petasiger chandleri*, both being parasites of grebes, and several other trematodes (Malek, 1953).

Subfamily Planorbulinae

To this subfamily belong the North American genera *Planorbula* Halde-man and *Promenetus* Baker. These are small planorbids that serve as interme-diate hosts for several species of trematodes. *Planorbula armigera* (Say) is the first intermediate host of the strigeid *Alaria mustelae* of dogs and cats and the plagiorchid *Haematoloechus medioplexus* of frogs and toads.

Promenetus exacuous (Say) and *Planorbula armigera* (Say) occur in Michi-gan. Members of the genus *Gyraulus* Charpentier of the subfamily Planor-binae are of similar size to those of *Promenetus* and *Planorbula*, for example, less than 6 mm in shell diameter. In certain areas they occur together, and, besides anatomical differences, they can be distinguished by use of the following key based on shell differences:

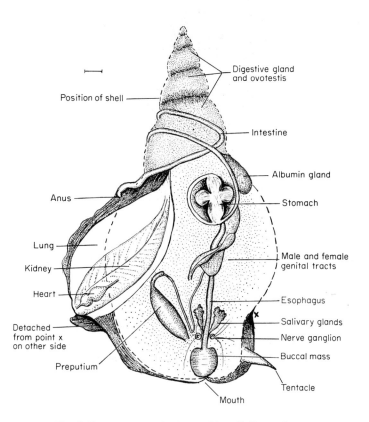

Fig. 4-10.   Anatomy of a lymnaeid snail. Bar = 1 mm.

1. Aperture of shell with lamellae or ridges; whorls regularly and slowly increasing in diameter; last whorl abruptly deflected near aperture
....*Planorbula*   (Fig. 4-2j)
   Aperture of shell without lamellae   2
2. Outer whorl partly enveloping others; periphery noticeably keeled
....*Promenetus*   (Fig. 4-2i)
   Whorls with rounded or subangulated periphery, all whorls visible from
   above and below ....*Gyraulus*   (Fig. 4-1c)

FAMILY LYMNAEIDAE

Among members of the family Lymnaeidae the shell is dextral and ovately oblong. Furthermore, the spire is more or less attenuated, and it varies considerably in height. The columellar axis is typically gyrate (spiraled) or twisted. The shell varies in thickness and in the size of the body whorl.

The soft parts of the animal are dextrally coiled, and the tentacles are flattened and triangular rather than filiform. The central tooth of the radula is unicuspid, while the lateral teeth are bi- or tricuspid. There are a number of intermediate teeth, and the marginal teeth are multicuspid or serrated (Fig. 14-7). The kidney is large and pear-shaped (Fig. 4-10), while the ureter proceeds directly forward without flexure. A pseudobranch is wanting. The genital apertures and the anus are situated on the right side.

The large preputium of lymnaeids (Fig. 4-11) may have a sarcobellum, for example, in *Pseudosuccinea* Baker, or may lack a sarcobellum, for example, in *Fossaria* Westerlund. The vergic sac varies in length. It is two-thirds the length of the preputium in *Fossaria*, half the length of the preputium in *Pseudosuccinea*, one and a quarter times the length of preputium in *Bulimnea* Haldeman, and one-fourth the length of the preputium in *Lymnaea* Lamarck. The prostate is either bulblike, as in *Lymnaea*, or cylindrical, as in *Bulimnea* and *Pseudosuccinea*. The seminal receptacle is round with a thin duct.

Malacologists disagree on the taxonomic status of members of this family. Some consider all lymnaeids to belong to one genus, *Lymnaea*; others recognize additional genera, for example, *Pseudosuccinea, Bulimnea, Acella* Haldeman, *Fossaria*, and *Stagnicola* Jeffreys; and still others regard the latter genera as subgenera of *Lymnaea* (see Baker, 1911, 1928; Hubendick, 1951).

Key to North American Lymnaeids Based on Shell Characters
(Adapted from F. C. Baker, 1928)

1. Spire elongated, as long as or longer than aperture ....
   Spire acute, much shorter than the elongated aperture, shell thin
   ....*Pseudosuccinea* (Fig. 4-12b)

2. Shell large, body whorl wide, much inflated 3
   Shell small or of medium size, body whorl slightly inflated, spire as long
      as or a little longer than aperture 4
3. Shell horn color, thin, spire acute ....*Lymnaea* (Fig. 4-12g)
   Shell greenish or reddish, rather solid, aperture purplish, spire wide
      ....*Bulimnea*
4. Shell very slender, thin, and fragile; spire much longer than aperture
      ....*Acella* (Fig. 4-2o)
   Shell more or less inflated, usually rather solid; spire as long as or a
      little longer than aperture 5
5. Surface with distinct spiral sculpture. Spire usually acute, columella twisted
      or plaited, body whorl compressed or slightly inflated, size variable
      ....*Stagnicola* (Fig. 4-12c)
   Surface usually without distinct spiral sculpture, columella smooth, shell
      usually small, 10 mm or less in height ....*Fossaria* (Fig. 4-12a)

The lymnaeid snails are intermediate hosts for several species of trematodes. Some of the most important species are listed below with their molluscan hosts.

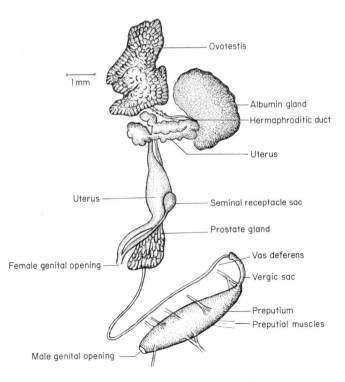

Fig. 4-11. Reproductive system of a lymnaeid snail. Bar = 1 mm.

Fig. 4-12. Shells of some lymnaeid and physid snails. (a) *Fossaria cubensis* (Pfeiffer) from Louisiana. (b) *Pseudosuccinea columella* (Say) from Louisiana. (c) *Stagnicola palustris* (Müller) from Michigan. (d) *Stagnicola emarginata angulata* (Sowerby) from Michigan. (e) *Fossaria* (*Lymnaea*) *truncatula* (Müller) from Holland. (f) *Lymnaea natalensis* (Krauss) from Sudan. (g) *Lymnaea stagnalis appressa* (Say) from Michigan. (h) *Lymnaea swinhoei* (Adams) from Taiwan. (i) *Physa gyrina* Say from Michigan. (j) *Physa parkeri* "Currier" DeCamp from Michigan. After Malek (1962).

Lymnaea natalensis (Krauss) (= *L. caillaudi* Bourguignant) (Fig. 4-12f): *Fasciola gigantica* in Africa (Malek, 1959).

    Fossaria truncatula (Müller) (Fig. 4-12e): *Fasciola hepatica* in Europe and North Africa.

    Lymnaea swinhoei (Adams) (Fig. 4-12h): First and sometimes second intermediate host for *Echinostoma revolutum* in Formosa.

    Lymnaea rubiginosa (Michelin): First and second intermediate hosts for *Echinostoma audyi* in Malaysia. The same species in Thailand is the molluscan host for the schistosomes *Trichobilharzia maegraithi* and *Orientobilharzia harinasutai*.

Pseudosuccinea columella (Say) (Fig. 4-12b) and *Fossaria cubensis* (Pfeiffer) (Fig. 4-12a): *Heterobilharzia americana* of raccoons, dogs, nutrias, and rabbits in Louisiana (Malek, 1967). *Fossaria cubensis* is also the intermediate host for *Paramphistomum microbothrium* (= *Cotylophoron cotylophorum*) of cattle and sheep and for *Fasciola hepatica* in Louisiana.

For geographical distribution of *Pseudosuccinea*, see Malek and Chrosciechowski (1964).

Stagnicola palustris (Müller): Intermediate host for the schistosomes *Schistosomatium douthitti* of rodents and *Trichobilharzia ocellata* of ducks and teals and a first intermediate host for the echinostomes *Echinoparyphium flexum* of ducks and *Protechinostoma mucronisertulatum* of rails in Michigan.

Stagnicola emarginata angulata (Sowerby) (Fig. 4-12d): Intermediate host for the avian schistosome *Trichobilharzia stagnicolae,* the diplostomid *Diplostomum flexicaudum* of gulls, the strigeid *Cotylurus communis* of gulls, the notocotylid *Notocotylus urbanensis* of birds, the echinostome *Euparyphium beaveri* of mink and otters, the plagiorchids *Plagiorchis micracanthus* of bats and mice, and *Eustomus chelydrae* of turtles. *Stagnicola emarginata angulata* is also a first and second intermediate host of the plagiorchids *Plagiorchis muris* of rats, pigeons, and man; *P. proximus* of muskrats and mice; and the strigeid *Cotylurus flabelliformis* of ducks.

Stagnicola bulimoides (Lea): First and second intermediate hosts for the plagiorchid *Opisthioglyphe locellus* of frogs and toads.

Stagnicola reflexa (Say): Second intermediate host of the strigeid *Cotylurus flabelliformis* and the molluscan host of the fasciolid *Fascioloides magna* of deer.

Stagnicola caperata (Say): Also molluscan host for *Fascioloides magna*.

Lymnaea stagnalis appressa (Say): (Fig. 4-12g): Molluscan host for the plagiorchids *Opisthioglyphe ranae*, *O. rastellus*, and *Glypthelmins hyloreus* and the diplostomids *Diplostomum spathecum* and *D. flexicaudum*. This snail is both the first and second intermediate host for the strigeid *Cotylurus flabelliformis* and the intermediate host of the avian schistosome *Trichobilharzia ocellata* and the mammalian schistosome *Schistosomatium douthitti*. The cercariae of *T. ocellata* and *S. douthitti* are species that cause cercarial dermatitis in man.

FAMILY ANCYLIDAE

The shell of members of the Ancylidae is usually patelliform (caplike or limpet-shaped) and is rarely modified. The modified shells may be dextrally spiraled or neritiform. The animal itself is either sinistrally or dextrally coiled and has a large oval foot. Furthermore, its tentacles are short, blunt, and cylindrical with eyes situated on their inner bases. A pseudobranch is present and is very important in respiration as these mollusks rarely come to the surface. The radula is comprised of a uni- or bicuspid central tooth, bicuspid or comblike lateral teeth, and comblike marginal teeth. The genitalia are variable in shape, but the vas deferens is always enlarged near the vergic sac to form a structure that is homologous to the epiphalus of land snails, and there is a flagellum opening into the vergic sac. The verge in some species resembles the ultrapenis of *Bulinus*, a member of the family Planorbidae (see Basch, 1963).

The family Ancylidae is worldwide in distribution, and the common genera are *Ferrissia* Walker and *Gundlachia* Pfeiffer.

Ferrissia tenuis (Bourguignant) has been reported as a suitable intermediate host for *Schistosoma haematobium* near Bombay, India. This report, however, has been received with some reservation by many.

Ferrissia novangliae (Walker) is a snail host of the amphistome *Megalodiscus temperatus* of frogs in Michigan. The same species has also been found shedding brevifurcate, pharyngeate, strigeid cercariae; brevifurcate, apharyngeate, spirorchid cercariae; and an echinostome cercaria.

Ferrissia parallela (Haldeman) is infected with the plagiorchid *Haematoloechus* sp., a lung fluke of frogs, in Michigan.

FAMILY PHYSIDAE

In members of the family Physidae the shell is spiral, sinistrally coiled, thin, and smooth or with microscopic transverse striae, shining or dull, and the spire may be elongated or very short.

The animal is sinistrally coiled, its tentacles are long, slender, and cylindrical, and its foot is narrow and pointed posteriorly. There is no pseudobranch, and the inner margin of the mantle is plain or digitate and extends over the shell. The radula is arranged in V-shaped rows; the central tooth is multicuspid. The lateral and marginal teeth are obliquely bent, comblike, multicuspid, and have a process at their external angle. The vergic sac is usually twice as long as the preputium, but it varies in length. The preputium has a large gland associated with its upper surface, the vergic sac is curved over the preputium, and the prostate is wide and flattened. There are representatives of this family in North America, Europe, Asia, Southeast Asia, some parts of Africa, and Australia.

Where there is an overlap in distribution of physids and species of *Bulinus*, for example, in the Mediterranean area, the Middle East, North Africa, and some other African countries, the snails can be distinguished by the following main characteristics.

1. In *Physa* the foot tapers considerably towards its posterior end, while in the species and subspecies of *Bulinus* (not *Physopsis*), the foot is broader than in *Physa*.

2. When a *Bulinus*, being a planorbid, is crushed, the seeping hemolymph

is red due to the presence of hemoglobin. The hemolymph of *Physa* is color-less.

3. There is no pseudobranch in *Physa*, whereas there is one in *Bulinus*.

4. *Physa* has characteristic V-shaped rows of teeth on its radular ribbon while in *Bulinus* the rows are straight. Furthermore, as indicated, the structures of the teeth are different.

Key to Genera of American Physidae

Shell elongate, slender, smooth, polished, inner edge of mantle simple, not digitate ....
Aplexa Fleming
Shell less elongate, spire short, body whorl usually inflated, smooth or with macroscopic or microscopic revolving striae; edge of mantle usually digitate, extending over the columellar portion of shell ....*Physa* Draparnaud

Some representative species of *Physa*, known to serve as intermediate hosts for digenetic trematodes, are listed below.

Physa parkeri DeCamp (Fig. 4-12j): Intermediate host for *Trichobilharzia physellae*, a parasite of water birds. The cercaria of this trematode (*Cercaria physellae*) causes cercarial dermatitis in man in Michigan and elsewhere. It is also the intermediate host of the hemiurid *Halipegus occidentalis* of frogs and the monostome *Notocotylus urbanensis* of ducks and muskrats.

Physa gyrina Say [=*Physella gyrina* (Say)] (Fig. 4-12i): Molluscan host of the diplostomids *Posthodiplostomum minimum* of herons and *Fibricola cratera* of opossums and raccoons; the heronimid *Heronimus chelydrae* of turtles; the plagiorchids *Lechriorchis tygarti*, *L. primus*, *Zeugorchis syntomentera*, and *Z. eurinus* of snakes; and the avian schistosome *Gigantobilharzia huronensis* in Michigan and elsewhere. This snail is also a second intermediate host of *Cotylurus flabelliformis*.

Physa integra Haldeman: Molluscan host of the plagiorchid *Pneumatophilus variabilis* of snakes, the telorchid *Telorchis medius* of turtles and snakes, the echinostome *Echinoparyphium flexum* of ducks, the spirorchid *Vasotrema robustum* of turtles, and the monostome *Notocotylus urbanensis* of birds.

Physa heterostropha (Say): Snail host for the diplostomid *Posthodiplostomum minimum* and the plagiorchid *Lechriorchis tygarti*.

Physa occidentalis Tryon: First and second intermediate hosts for *Echinostoma revolutum*, a parasite of birds and mammals.

Subclass Prosobranchiata (The Operculates)
(See Abbott, 1948; Malek, 1966)

FAMILY HYDROBIIDAE

In members of the Hydrobiidae the shell is small, dextrally coiled, and is conical or subconical. It has four to eight whorls and is imperforate or umbilicate. The operculum is concentric or paucispiral and corneous or calcarious. The periostracum usually is without color markings.

The animal itself has a long snout, long tentacles, which are thin and round, a long foot, a smooth mantle edge, and platelike gills consisting of twenty to fifty lamellae. The sexes are separate. The male has an exserted verge situated on the dorsal surface of the neck. This verge is simple, bifid or trifid. It lies near the margin of the mantle, median or slightly to the right. The central tooth of the radula is multicuspid and includes basal denticles. The lateral radular teeth are hatchet-shaped and multicuspid, while the marginal teeth are slender and multicuspid.

Subfamily Hydrobiinae (= Amnicolinae)

In members of the Hydrobiinae the operculum is thin and paucispiral. There are about seventy-five rows of teeth, each with seven teeth. The verge is simple, curved, and fleshy and may be bifid or trifid. The eggs are laid singly.

In the Orient, several species of *Oncomelania* Gredler serve as the intermediate host for *Schistosoma japonicum*. In the United States, two species of *Pomatiopsis* Tryon are potential intermediate hosts for *S. japonicum* and an actual intermediate host for *Paragonimus kellicotti* and a few other species of trematodes. Also representatives of this subfamily in the United States are *Amnicola* Gould and Haldeman, *Paludestrina* D'Orbigny, *Pyrgulopsis* Call and Pilsbry, *Littoridina* Souleyet, and *Littoridinops* Pilsbry.

Genus *Oncomelania* Gredler.   In members of this genus the outer lip of the shell aperture is slightly thickened, and the operculum is thin and paucispiral. The snout of the animal is blunt, the tentacles are slender and long, and an important characteristic is the pigmentation at the inner base of the tentacles, which is usually yellow around the eyes, thus forming "eyebrows" (Fig. 4-13). The verge is simple, exserted, and may be covered by the mantle. The gill is comprised of fourteen to sixty lamellae. The formula for the central radular tooth indicates the arrangement of the cusps on the anterior edge and the basal denticles; it is usually 2–1–2/3–3, but may be 1–1–1/3–3 (Fig. 14-7).

Oncomelanids are amphibious snails that are found along the moist, weedy, earth banks of canals, at the water's edge or up to a few inches above the surface of the water. The eggs are small, laid singly, and are usually covered with sand. All the species of *Oncomelania* (Fig. 4-1) are transmitters of *Schistosoma japonicum*. According to Davis (1971), all oncomelanid snails are subspecies of *Oncomelania hupensis*.

Oncomelania hupensis hupensis (Gredler) (Fig. 4-1e) is usually higher than the other species, being 7 to 10 mm. There are six to nine shell whorls. The shell has strong axial striae, or ribs, which vary in number

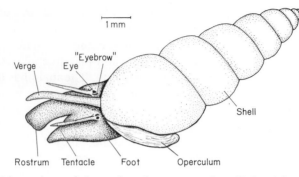

Fig. 4-13. Male specimen of *Oncomelania hupensis nosophora* (Robson) from Japan. Notice that the verge, or penis, is depicted in the erected condition; when not in this state, it is usually in the form of a stumpy knob situated above the "neck" of the snail. The presence of this knob is used to determine the sex of the specimen.

from ten to thirty on each whorl. This snail is found in the Yangtze River drainage system in China.

Oncomelania hupensis nosophora (Robson) (Fig. 4-1g) measures from 5 to 9 mm in height. Its shell is smooth except for very fine axial growth lines. It occurs in Japan and occasionally in some parts of southern China.

Oncomelania hupensis quadrasi (Moellendorff) (Fig. 4-1f) measures from 3 to 5 mm in height, and its shell includes six to seven whorls. It is smooth except for fine axial growth lines. It occurs in the Philippines.

Oncomelania hupensis formosana (Pilsbry and Hirase) (Fig. 4-1h) measures from 4 to 6 mm in height, and its smooth shell includes six to seven whorls, resembling that of *O. hupensis nosophora*. It occurs on Taiwan (Formosa) where it transmits an animal or zoophilic strain of *Schistosoma japonicum*, but it can be infected experimentally with certain human strains of this schistosome.

Oncomelania hupensis lindoensis is the snail host of *S. japonicum* in the Lake Lindu area of Celebes, Indonesia. Its anatomy has been described by Davis and Carney (1973).

Genus *Pomatiopsis* Tryon.   *Pomatiopsis lapidaria* (Say) (Fig. 4-1i), a member of this genus, is found in the United States in the Mississippi River drainage and in most of the eastern part of the country. It always occurs close to freshwater, being found along banks and flood plains of rivers and streams and near marshy areas. Anatomically it is very similar to *Oncomelania*, but certain minor differences exist. The gill, verge, radula, shell, and operculum are similar to those of *Oncomelania*.

Pomatiopsis cincinnatiensis (Lea) occurs in Michigan and elsewhere in the midwestern United States. The two species of *Pomatiopsis* mentioned, that is, *P. lapidaria* and *P. cincinnatiensis*, can be distinguished in that *P. cincinnatiensis* is considerably more pigmented than *P. lapidaria*, and its verge has a long filament at its tip, which is not present in *P lapidaria* (Dundee, 1957).

The shells of the two species can be distinguished by use of the following key:

Elongated shell, six to seven whorls, adult 7 mm long .... *P. lapidaria*
Broadly conical shell, five whorls, adult 5 mm long .... *P. cincinnatiensis*

Although members of the genus *Pomatiopsis* share many features in common with those of the Hydrobiidae, some malacologists have recommended, on the basis of anatomical details, that *Pomatiopsis* should be placed in a separate family, the Pomatiopsidae. *Oncomelania* may belong not only to this family but also to the genus *Pomatiopsis*.

In addition to *Paragonimus kellicotti*, the North American lung fluke, *P. lapidaria* serves as the molluscan host for *Nudacotyle novicia*, a parasite of the meadow mouse; *Euryhelmis monorchis*, a parasite of mink; and *Cercaria pomatiopsidis* and *C. geddesi*.

Genus *Amnicola* Gould and Haldeman.   The shell of members of this genus is small, oval–conical, umbilicate, and rather short. The spire is subacute, and the body whorl is convex. The shell aperture is oval and less than half the height of the shell. The columella is not thickened nor reflected. The operculum is thin, corneous, and paucispiral. The verge is bifid. There is a tongue-shaped process in the middle of the anterior surface of the central radular tooth.

Amnicola limosa (Say) (Fig. 4-2s) is the molluscan host of the azygid trematode, *Azygia longa*, of fishes; the opisthorchids *Opisthorchis tonkae* of muskrats and *Metorchis canadensis* of dogs, cats, and mink; the heterophyid *Apophallus brevis* of birds; the echinostome *Echinochasmus donaldsoni* of grebes; and the prosthogonimid *Prosthogonimus macrorchis* of birds.

Amnicola pilsbryi Walker is the snail host of the microphallids *Maritrema obstipum* and *Levinseniella amnicolae*, both being parasites of ducks.

Amnicola peracuta Pilsbry and Walker is the snail host of the allocreadid *Homalometron armatum* of fish.

Genus *Paludestrina* (D'Orbigny).   In members of this genus the shell is more slender and elongate than that of members of *Amnicola*. Furthermore, the shell is imperforate, the whorls are inflated, and the sutures are deep. The central tooth of the radula is without the tongue-shaped process, and the verge is bifid.

Genus *Pyrgulopsis* Call and Pilsbry.   The shell of members of this genus is ovate–conical, imperforate, and the whorls are flattened or slightly carinate.

Genus *Littoridina* Souleyet.   The shell of members of this genus is narrowly umbilicate, the aperture is pyriform, and the body whorl is subangulate. The radula is the same as that in *Amnicola*. The verge is large and includes five or six small digitate processes.

Genus *Littoridinops* Pilsbry (See Thompson, 1968).   *Littoridinops tenuipes* (Couper), a member of this genus, is the molluscan host for the heterophyid *Ascocotyle pachycystis*.

Genus *Aroapyrgus* Baker.   Representatives of this hydrobiid genus occur in small streams in Central and South America. *Aroapyrgus colombiensis* is the intermediate snail host of *Paragonimus caliensis* in Colombia (Malek and Little, 1971). *Paragonimus mexicanus* has been discovered in Costa Rica (Brenes and Zeledon, personal communication); *Aroapyrgus costaricensis* is its snail host.

Subfamily Buliminae (= Bithyninae)

In members of this subfamily the shell is ovate, comparatively large (10 mm), and the peristome is generally thickened. The operculum is thick, calcareous, and usually concentric, with a small subcentral spiral nucleus. The verge is exserted, curved, fleshy, and bifid. The central radular tooth includes numerous basal denticles.

This subfamily is represented in the Orient by the genera *Parafossarulus* and *Bulimus*, which are of public health importance. *Parafossarulus* has a shell characterized by raised spiral ridges or keels, and the lip of its aperture is thickened. *Bulimus* Scopoli* is thinner than *Parafossarulus* Annandale and Prashad. It is smooth except for the presence of axial growth lines, and its shell lip is slightly thickened.

Parafossarulus manchouricus (Bourguignant) (Fig. 4-14g): The shells of *P. manchouricus* vary from 7 to 10 mm in height, and they are usually yellowish brown in color. This species occurs in China, Taiwan, and Japan. It is synonymous with *P. striatulus* (Benson) and is the principal first intermediate host for *Clonorchis sinensis*, the Chinese liver fluke, in Japan, and one of the important intermediate hosts in China. It is also a host for *Echinochasmus perfoliatus*, an echinostome occasionally found in man.

---

*Bulimus is also referred to in the literature as *Bithynia* Leach, *Bithinia* Gray, or *Bythinia* (a misspelling for *Bithynia*).

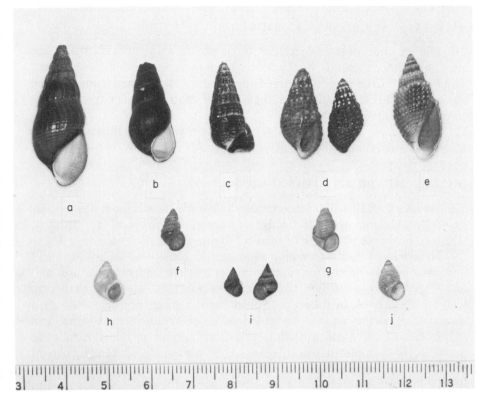

Fig. 4-14. Shells of some gastropods from the Orient. (a) *Semisulcospira libertina* (Gould) from Japan. (b) *Semisulcospira libertina* from Taiwan. (c) *Cerithidea cingulata* (Gmelin) from Japan. (d) *Thiara granifera* (Lamarck) from Taiwan. (e) *Thiara granifera* (Lamarck) from the Philippines. (f) *Parafossarulus sinensis* (Neumary) from China. (g) *Parafossarulus manchouricus* (Bourguignat) from Japan. (h) *Bulimus fuschsianus* (Moellendorff) from China. (i) *Syncera* (=*Assiminea*) *lutea* Adams from China. (j) *Parafossarulus manchouricus* from Taiwan. After Malek (1962).

Bulimus fuchsianus (Moellendorff) (Fig. 4-14h): The shells of adults of this species are about 10 mm in height. It is an important first intermediate host of *Clonorchis sinensis* in China.

Bulimus tentaculata (Linn.) (Fig. 4-2q): This species was introduced into the United States from Europe and is found in the area of the Great Lakes. The shiny shell, which varies from being transparent to opaque, ranges in color from yellowish to greenish. The operculum is calcareous, thick, concentric, and rounded ovate.

B. tentaculata is the intermediate host for several species of tremotodes, for example, the psilostome *Psilotrema spiculigerum* of ducks and the strigeid *Apatemon gracilis*, also of ducks.

FAMILY SYNCERIDAE (=ASSIMINEIDAE)

The members of the Synceridae are amphibious and are about the same size as the oncomelanids, but the outer lip of the aperture of syncerids is not thickened. Furthermore, *Syncera* Gray can be distinguished from *Oncomelania* by the presence of only a single pair of short eye stalks instead of the prominent tentacles.

Syncera lutea Adams (Fig. 4-14i) is the intermediate host for *Paragonimus iloktsuenensis* in southern China.

FAMILY THIARIDAE (=MELANIIDAE)

Members of Thiaridae are worldwide in their distribution. They occur in fresh and brackish waters and in temperate, subtropical, and tropical regions. Some members are of medical importance.

The shells of thiarids are high and turreted, sometimes measuring 1 to 2 inches. The whorls are rounded with moderate or impressed sutures and usually include conspicuous sculpture, spiral, and axial intersections to form ridges, ribs, knobs, or tubercles. Spines are sometimes present, although a few species portray smooth sculpturing. The operculum is dark brown and corneous with a spiral growth (multispiral) and a central or subcentral nucleus, for example, in *Brotia* Adams, or it is paucispiral with an eccentrical nucleus, for example, in *Thiara* Roding. The mantle edge is smooth or with digitiform processes. The snout is as long as the foot, and the tentacles are round and slightly tapered. There are seven teeth in each row of the radula. The central tooth is small with five to seven denticles on the anterior edge, but there are no basal denticles. The lateral tooth (1) and the marginal teeth (2) have few cusps in some species and numerous cusps in others (Fig. 14-7).

A few members of the Thiaridae are oviparous. Many others are ovoviviparous with "brood pouches" situated on the dorsal side of the mother snail where the eggs hatch, for example, in *Thiara*. Apparently few males occur, and many females are parthenogenetic. Thus, one individual can initiate a new colony if transported to a new suitable habitat. This may explain the very wide geographic distribution of members of this family.

Genus *Thiara* Roding.   The shell of *Thiara* measures from 1 to 2 inches in height, and the sutures are deep or moderately so. The sculpture is usually beeded, and a few species portray shell spines. The shell is imperforate, the aperture is more or less vertical, and the operculum is pear-shaped with an eccentric nucleus at the narrow, basal end. The mantle edge bears ten to fourteen papillae. The members of this genus are ovoviviparous. They occur in tropical and subtropical Africa and Asia, but some species occur in Japan and northern Australia. They are also abundant in the Malay Archipelago, the Philippines, and on various Pacific Islands.

Thiara granifera (Lamarck) (=*Melanoides granifera*, = *Tarebia granifera*) (Fig. 4-14d,e) occurs on Taiwan, the Philippines, and the islands of Southeast Asia. Its body whorl is wide, and there are distinct spiral rows of beeds. The mantle edge bears finger-shaped fringes.

T. granifera is the first intermediate host for the mammalian lung fluke *Paragonimus westermani* and the mammal-infecting heterophyids *Haplorchis taichui, Stellantchasmus* (=*Diorchitrema*) *formosanum*, and *Metagonimus yokogawai*. This species has been introduced into the continental United States, and a colony has been reported in the Lithia Springs of Hillsborough County, Florida. It is also found in Hawaii and in Puerto Rico. In Hawaii it is the intermediate host of the eye fluke of birds, *Philophthalmus gralli*, and certain species of heterophyid trematodes. A dissected specimen is depicted in Fig. 2-3. It is also found in southwest Texas.

Thiara tuberculata (Müller) [=*Melanoides tuberculata* (Müller)]: The shell in *T. tuberculata* is uniformly turreted and bears eight to eleven whorls separated by deep sutures. Compared with *T. granifera*, the shell is slender and somewhat higher. The sculpture is reticulate or nodular, varying from heavy to light. The body whorl is not as wide as that of *T. granifera* (Fig. 4-15f). The mantle edge bears finger-shaped fringes.

This species, and several of its varieties, are distributed all over Africa and Asia. It is one of the molluscan hosts for *Paragonimus westermani* and the heterophyid *Stellantchasmus formosanum*. In certain geographic foci of schistosomiasis in the Middle East, this species has been erroneously incriminated on epidemiological evidence. It is, however, an intermediate host for many other species of trematodes; for example, in Egypt it is the molluscan host for the lecithodendrid *Prosthodendrium pyramidum*, an intestinal parasite of bats.

Genus *Brotia* Adams. In members of this genus the shell is large, measuring up to 2 or 3 inches. The axial ribs are heavy and clear, and the operculum is round, multispiral, and has a central or nearly central nucleus.

Brotia asperata (Lamarck) occurs in the Philippines.

Brotia variabilis (Benson) occurs in India, Burma, the Malay Peninsula, and Sumatra and Java, both in Indonesia.

Some members of the family Thiaridae that are of medical importance have been misidentified in the past as *Brotia* by some investigators, and as the result, certain species of *Brotia* are sometimes incriminated as intermediate hosts for some species of trematodes of medical importance.

Genus *Cleopatra* Troschel. This genus includes a number of small melanid snails, occurring in Africa and Madagascar, that are intermediate

Fig. 4-15. Shells of some gastropods. (a) *Goniobasis livescens* Menke from Michigan. (b) *Goniobasis floridensis* (Reeve) from Florida. (c) *Pleurocera acuta* Rafinesque from Michigan. (d) *Cleopatra cyclostomoides* (Küster) from Sudan. (e) *Cleopatra bulimoides* (Olivier) from Sudan. (f) *Thiara tuberculata* (Müller) from Egypt. (g) *Campeloma decisum* (Say) from Michigan. (h) *Campeloma floridense* Call from Louisiana. (i) *Viviparus georgianus* (Lea) from Florida. () *Viviparus georgianus* from Louisiana. (k) *Marisa cornuarietis* (Linn.) from Puerto Rico. (1) *Lanistes bolteniana* (Chemnitz) from the Sudan. (m) *Pila ovata* (Olivier) from the Sudan. (n) *Pomacea paludosa* (Say) from Louisiana. (o) *Pomacea paludosa* from Florida. (p) *Neritina reclivata* Say from Louisiana. (q) *Littorina irrorata* (Say) from Louisiana. After Malek (1962).

hosts of many species of trematodes. *Cleopatra bulimoides* (Olivier) (Fig. 4-15e) is common in Egypt, and its range extends eastward into Syria and southward into the Sudan. It is the intermediate host of *Prohemistomum vivax*, a parasite of dogs, cats, kites, and occasionally of man. *C. cyclostomoides* (Küster) also occurs in Egypt and the Nile Valley in the Sudan, and *C. guillemei* Bourguignant and *C. nyanzae* Mandahl-Barth have been reported from Uganda.

FAMILY PLEUROCERIDAE

The members of the family Pleuroceridae have a thick and solid shell with whorls that are generally flat sided and a spire that typically tapers into a point. The shell aperture is entire or more or less canaliculate at the base. The operculum is paucispiral, and the animal is either oviparous or ovoviviparous. The pleurocerids do not occur west of the Mississippi Valley drainage, except for a few isolated species that occur in the northern Pacific states. The genus *Semisulcospira* Boettger, which was included in the family Thiaridae, has been transferred to the Pleuroceridae.

Genus *Pleurocera* Rafinesque. In *Pleurocera acuta* Rafinesque (Fig. 4-15c) from Michigan the aperture of the shell is angulate and prolonged into a short canal at the bottom. The columella is twisted and not callously thickened. The species belonging to *Pleurocera* occur in rivers in Kentucky, Tennessee, and Alabama, in the Great Lakes, and extend west to the Mississippi. *Pleurocera acuta* is the snail host of the allocreadid trematode *Lepidauchen ictulari*, a parasite of fish.

Genus *Goniobasis* Lea. In *Goniobasis livescens* Menke (Fig. 4-15a) from Michigan the shell aperture is less angulate than that of *Pleurocera*, and there is a tendency to form a canal below. The columella is simple in this species, and the shell is smooth, striate, or tuberculate (Dazo, 1965).

Goniobasis livescens is the molluscan host for the pronocephalid trematode *Macravestibulum obtusicaulum*, a parasite of turtles, and the heterophyid *Apophallus venustus*, a parasite of birds. It is also of interest to note that the azygid trematode *Proterometra dickermani* completes its life cycle in *G. livescens*, the only host in its life cycle.

Goniobasis plicifera silicula (Gould) is the snail host for the allocreadid *Plagioporus siliculus*, a parasite of fishes; the heterophyid *Metagonimoides oregonensis*, a parasite of raccoon; and the troglotrematid *Troglotrema salmincola*, the so-called salmon-poisoning fluke, a parasite of dogs, cats, and foxes.

Goniobasis proxima (Say) is an intermediate host for the heterophyid *Metagonimoides oregonensis*, a parasite of raccoons, and *Goniobasis*, sp. is the molluscan host for the azygid *Proterometra sagittaria*, a parasite of fishes.

Genus *Io* Lea. Shells of *Io fluvialis* (Say) from Tennessee possess very pronounced spines, especially on the body whorl.

Genus *Semisulcospira* Boettger. The members of this genus have a smooth shell with slightly flattened whorls. There may, however, be very low, short ribs forming the axial sculpture. The operculum is ovate paucispiral with the nucleus nearer to the center than that of *Thiara*. The mantle edge is smooth.

Semisulcospira libertina (Gould) (= *Melania libertina* Gould) (Fig. 4-14a,b) is an ovoviviparous species that occurs in Japan, Korea, and Taiwan. Davis (1969) has contributed a comprehensive taxonomic study of some species of *Semisulcospira* in Japan. He later (1972) dealt with the geographic variation of *S. libertina*.

According to Ito *et al.* (1959) in Shizuoka Prefecture, Japan, the following species of cercariae were shed by a large number of *S. libertina* examined: *Paragonimus westermani, Pseudoxorchis major, Centrocestus armatus, Metagonimus* spp., *Notocotylus magniovatus, Pseudobilharziella corvi, Cercaria nipponensis, C. incerta, C. monostyloides, C. yoshidae, C. innominatum, C. pseudodivaricata, C. introverta, C. manei, C. longicerca,* and several echinostomes.

FAMILY VIVIPARIDAE

In members of the family Viviparidae the shell is moderately large, imperforate, or subumbilicate. The operculum is concentric with a subcentral nucleus. The tentacles are long and slender, and, in the male, the right one is shorter than the left, forming a sheath for the verge. The viviparids are ovoviviparous.

Genus *Viviparus* Montfort. The shell of members of this genus is subconic, the whorls convex, and the color is olivaceous, dark brown, or banded. Several species may be found in the Mississippi Valley and from Ohio and Indiana south to the Gulf of Mexico. Representative species also occur in Europe, Asia, and Africa. The viviparids serve as intermediate hosts for relatively few species of trematodes and almost all the species that have been found have been echinostomes. Representatives of this family are *Viviparus angularis* Müller in China and *V. georgianus* (Lea) in Florida, Georgia, Alabama, and Louisiana (Fig. 4-15i,j). The so-called mystery snail of aquarium keepers is a species of *Viviparus*, specifically, *V. malleatus*. This species has become established in many freshwater lakes and ponds along the east coast of the United States. It is known to occur in Massachusetts, New York, Connecticut, New Jersey, Pennsylvania, and Maryland. It is the molluscan host for *Echinochasmus elongatus* and *E. rugosus* in Japan.

Species belonging to the genus *Viviparus* but occurring in Africa and southern and eastern Asia have been placed in another genus, *Bellamya* Jousseaume, for example *Bellamya unicolor* (Olivier), which occurs in the Nile Valley.

Genus *Campeloma* Rafinesque. In members of this genus the shell is solid and thick, and the aperture is oval. Furthermore, the body whorl is narrower, and the spire is more elongated than that of *Viviparus*. These snails have an olivaceous green shell and only occur in North America, ranging from the Mississippi Valley east to the Atlantic and from the St. Lawrence Valley south to the Gulf of Mexico.

Campeloma decisum (Say) (Fig. 4-15g) is the common species in the northern states, while *C. floridense* Call (Fig. 4-15h) is the common species in the southern states. *Campeloma decisum* is the first and second intermediate host for the brachylaimid trematode *Leucochloridiomorpha constantiae*, a parasite of birds. The metacercariae of *L. constantiae* occur within the uterus of this snail. *Campeloma decisum* is also the intermediate host for certain species of trematodes belonging to the family Aporocotylidae.

Campeloma rufum (Haldeman) is an intermediate host for *Troglotrema mustelae*, a parasite of dogs, cats, and mink.

FAMILY PILIDAE (= AMPULLARIDAE)

Members of the family Pilidae are commonly known as the "apple snails." The shell is very large, smooth, and green or brown in color. The spire is short, and the body whorl is inflated. The shell is umbilicate, and the lip of the aperture is simple. The operculum is large, calcareous or corneous, and it is concentric with a subcentral nucleus. The tentacles are long and filiform. The pilids are oviparous. Although they are freshwater snails, many members can lead an amphibious life on mud when the water recedes. Representative species occur in Africa, Asia, Central and South America, and southern United States.

Included in the Pilidae are the following genera: *Pila* Roding, *Pomacea* Perry, *Lanistes* Montfort, *Afropomus* Pilsbry and Bequaert, *Saulea* Gray, *Asolene* D'Orbigny, and *Marisa* Gray.

Pomacea paludosa (Say) (Fig. 4-15n,o) occurs in Georgia and Florida, *Pila ovata* (Olivier) (Fig. 4-15m) occurs in the Nile Valley, *Pila globosa* (Swainson) is a native of Southeast Asia, *Marisa cornuarietis* (Linn.) (Fig. 4-15k) occurs in Puerto Rico, and *Lanistes bolteniana* (Chemnitz) (Fig. 4-15l) is found in the Nile Valley.

Pila luzonica, which occurs on Luzon Island in the Philippines, is the second intermediate host for *Echinostoma ilocanum*, an echinostome that has been reported to parasitize man.

TABLE 4-1

Diagnostic Characteristics of the Major Genera of the Family Pilidae[a]

Genus	Shape of shell	Operculum	Respiratory siphon	Oviposition site	Behavior	Geographical distribution
Pila	Dextral, subovate to globose	Calcareous	Brevisiphonate	On banks or mud-flats near water	Amphibious	Africa and Asia
Lanistes	Sinistral, subovate	Corneous	Brevisiphonate	On submerged vegetation	Aquatic or slightly amphibious	Africa
Pomacea	Dextral, subovate ovate or globose	Corneous	Longisiphonate	On emergent parts of aquatic vegetation	Moderately amphibious	S. America, Central America, West Indies, southern United States
Marisa	Dextral, secondarily planorboid	Corneous	Longisiphonate	On submerged vegetation	Aquatic	S. America, West Indies

[a]After Michelson (1961).

Marisa cornuarietis is a voraceous species that has been advocated for the biological control of the planorbid snails that serve as intermediate hosts for the human-infecting schistosomes (for anatomy see Demian, 1964).

Table 4-1 shows the diagnostic characteristics of the major genera of the family Pilidae.

MARINE AND BRACKISH WATER SNAILS
(See Abbott, 1954)

Subclass Prosobranchiata

FAMILY NERITIDAE

The family Neritidae includes primarily marine and brackish water snails. A few representatives occur in freshwater near the sea in the tropics and subtropics. This family is, therefore, appropriately placed at the beginning of this section.

The shell of members of the Neritidae is dextrally coiled. It is imperforate, globose, and has a short spire. The shell aperture is semiovate, and the columellar region is expanded, flattened, and usually thickened. The tentacles are long and slender, and the eyes are situated on peduncles located at the external base of the tentacles. The gill is large and triangular. The sexes are separate, and the female is oviparous. The radula consists of a quadrate or broadly triangular central tooth with a broad cusp, five lateral, and numerous marginal teeth. Specifically, there are sixty or more marginal teeth with long, narrow stalks and small blades.

Genus *Neritina* Lamarck.   The members of this genus possess semicircular opercula, which are calcareous and paucispiral. The opercular edge bears two projecting processes, which articulate with the columella. A number of species occur in brackish and freshwater in Florida and the Gulf of Mexico. Two representatives are *Neritina reclivata* Say (Fig. 4-15p) from the delta of the Mississippi River in Louisiana and *Neritina jordani* Sowerby (Fig. 4-2v) from Lebanon.

FAMILY POTAMIDAE (=CERITHIIDAE)

In members of the family Potamidae the columella is tightly coiled, and the whorls include heavy spiral striations. The shell aperture usually ends in a canal situated at the base. The animal bears tentacles that are thick at the base, but the distal end narrows abruptly.

Members of this family occur in subtropical and tropical regions of all continents, living in tidal zones, brackish estuaries, and brackish fish ponds and lakes.

Pirenella conica (Blainville): This species occurs along the coast of the Mediterranean and Red Sea and in lakes in those regions. It is the first intermediate host for *Heterophyes heterophyes*, an intestinal fluke of man, dogs, cats, and other fish-eating mammals.

Cerithidea cingulata (Gmelin) (Fig. 4-14c): The species has been implicated in the life cycle of *Heterophyes heterophyes* and other flukes in Japan. It also occurs in India, Ceylon, Malaysia, southern China, the Philippines, and New Guinea. The shell is high conical with many whorls. The shell sculpture is in the form of ridges or beads, and the shell aperture is small, ending in a siphonal canal at the base. The operculum is circular and horny with many concentrical whorls situated around a central nucleus.

Cerithidea scalariformis (Say): In members of this species the shell has a high turreted spire, and there are about nine whorls with deep sutures and longitudinal ribs. The outer lip is partly reflected. *Cerithidea scalariformis* is commonly known as the "ribbed horn shell," and it is found from Georgia to Texas, being very abundant in the Florida Keys. In Florida it is intermediate host of the avian schistosome, *Austrobilharzia penneri*, and the philophthalmid *Parorchis acanthus*, an intestinal trematode of gulls. *Austrobilharzia penneri* is known to cause "clam diggers' itch" or cercarial dermatitis in man.

Cerithidea californica Haldeman: This species is found from Baulinas Bay to San Diego in California. It is the intermediate host of the monostome *Catatropis johnstoni*, a parasite of birds; the heterophyids *Phocitremoides ovale*, a parasite of cats and chicks (experimental) and *Euhaplorchis californiensis*, a parasite of gulls; the echinostome *Himasthla* sp., a parasite of birds; and the philophthalmid *Cloacitrema michiganensis*, also a parasite of birds.

Batillaria minima (Gmelin): The members of this species possess a black or deep brown shell and are commonly known as the "black horn shells." The shell sculpture is in the form of low, longitudinal ribs and nodular spiral ridges. It is a common gastropod on the muddy coasts of Florida. It is the intermediate host of the avian schistosome *Ornithobilharzia canaliculata*, which can cause cercarial dermatitis in man.

FAMILY LITTORINIDAE

The members of the family Littorinidae are commonly known as the "periwinkles." They live in salt and brackish waters clinging to rocks and other substrates occurring in the littoral zone. They are also abundant on vegetation found in brackish waters. The shells are thick, imperforate, conical with a pointed low spire, and include shallow sutures and a horny operculum.

Littorina planaxis (Philippi): This is the common "flat periwinkle" or "eroded periwinkle." Its shell includes three to four whorls and is grayish brown with bluish white spots and flecks. This species is found on the West Coast of the United States, from Puget Sound to lower California, and is the intermediate host of the avian schistosome *Austrobilharzia variglandis*, which is a causative agent of cercarial dermatitis in man.

Littorina pintado (Wood): This subtropical species is characterized by a shell that includes about five whorls. Furthermore, the spire is pointed, and the sutures are indistinct. It is yellowish to bluish white with minute brown dots. The inside of the aperture is reddish brown. It is the most common periwinkle on the rocks and embankments along the Hawaiian coasts. On some of the offshore islands in Hawaii it serves as the intermediate host for the dermatitis-producing avian schistosome *Austrobilharzia variglandis.*

Littorina irrorata (Say): *Littorina irrorata* (Fig. 4-15g) is the "gulf periwinkle" or the "marsh periwinkle." This snail is found among the edges of brackish water marshes or on marine vegetation. It is abundant in the Gulf of Mexico and extends north to New Jersey and New York. It is off-white in color with spiral lines of chestnut brown dots, which are usually obscured because of the accumulation of algae on its surface.

Littorina saxatilis (Olivi): This species and another species, *L. obtusata*, are the first intermediate hosts of the echinostome *Himasthla littorinae*, a parasite of gulls along the coasts of Massachusetts and Rhode Island. *Littorina saxatilis* possesses an obvious but variable spire, and its shell, measuring up to 13 mm long, is rough with irregular, raised lines. The color of adult specimens varies but is commonly greenish yellow. The females are viviparous.

Littorina obtusata possesses a flattened spire, and its shell is very smooth and shiny. The coloration is variable but is commonly clear yellow orange. Bands may be present. This species occurs in the lower littoral zone, associated with fucoid seaweeds. *Littorina saxatilis*, on the other hand, occurs higher up in the littoral zone.

Littorina littorea (Linn.): This is the most common species along the Atlantic Coast of North America and in northern Europe. Commonly known as the "common periwinkle," it occurs at midlevel in the littoral zone. It is characterized by a moderate spire that expands more rapidly after the first tiny whorls. The young of this species are usually black, but the older specimens are variable in color, although always dull. It serves as the intermediate host for a large number of marine trematodes. Along the Atlantic Coast of North America, ranging from the maritime provinces of Canada to

South Carolina, the most common trematode in *L. littorea* is *Himasthla quissetensis*, an echinostome parasite of gulls.

FAMILY NASSARIIDAE

The members of this family are small carnivorous snails that are world-wide in distribution. The shell is thick, and its aperture is drawn into a short canal.

Nassarius obsoletus (Say): This is one of the most common snails along the Atlantic Coast of the United States, where it is usually found on mud flats. It is dark reddish or purplish black in color. The shell consists of about six whorls, its spire is elevated, and there is a large number of beads on its surface.

Nassarius obsoletus is the intermediate host of the human dermatitis-causing avian schistosome *Austrobilharzia variglandis*; the lepocreadid *Lepocreadium setiferoides*, a parasite of fish; the acanthocolpid *Stephanostomum tenuis*, another parasite of fish; and the echinostome *Himasthla quissetensis*, a parasite of birds.

FAMILY MURICIDAE

The snails belonging to the family Muricidae possess thick, solid shells, and many members bear spines. They are carnivorous and live on rocky bottoms. They are worldwide in distribution but are especially prevalent in the tropics.

Urosalpinx cinerea (Say): This is the common "oyster drill." Its shell is gray, and it measures a little more than an inch in height. It is the intermediate host of the philophthalmid trematode *Parorchis acanthus*, a parasite of marine birds. This snail is of considerable economic importance since it is an active predator of oysters.

FAMILY CONIDAE

Among the medically important mollusks are the stinging or venomous gastropods that belong to the family Conidae. These mollusks are commonly known as the "poison cone shells."

Members of this family of tropical mollusks are sluggish animals that live among rocks and corals and crawl on sand. A few species inhabit the coasts of the United States. The shells are so colorful and attractive that they are favorites of shell collectors. The shell is large and solid and has several whorls, a very low spire, and a high body whorl and aperture.

The species found in American waters are fortunately not dangerous, but all the cones in the Indo-Pacific area should be considered potentially dangerous. Their effect should not be overlooked by swimmers, divers, and shell collectors in the tropics. Most of these species possess a venom apparatus and are capable of causing serious and sometimes fatal wounds. The bite paralyzes the prey, usually other shellfish, and in man it causes local pain, swelling, numbness, and paralysis.

The mechanism of the actual delivery of the poison is still not very clear in all species. Clench and Kondo (1943), Abbott (1948), and Halstead (1959) have studied the process. When the animal adheres to its prey or when held in the human hand, its long proboscis protrudes very quickly. Harpoon-shaped radular teeth are released into the pharynx and from thence to the proboscis, which thrusts the teeth into the flesh of the prey. Venom is ejected from a special gland and is transported to the coiled tooth by a venom duct.

Kohn *et al.* (1960) have reported that injections of small quantities of extracts of the venom duct (tubular venom gland) of several species of *Conus* Linn. proved lethal to other mollusks, fishes, and mice. Sarramegna (1965) made an extensive study of the cones of New Caledonia and the Indo-Pacific region. He has elaborated on the poison apparatus of various species of *Conus*, the chemical composition of the poison, and conducted toxicity experiments on animals.

Cruider (1961) has noted the great care with which fishermen in certain areas of Thailand handle the cone shells, but, at the same time, they roast and eat some of the poisonous ones.

The species that have been recorded as dangerous in the Indo-Pacific region are *Conus geographus* Linn., *C. aulicus* Linn., *C. tulipa* Linn., *C. textile* Linn., and *C. marmoreus* Linn. Some of these are illustrated in Fig. 4-16. Along the coasts of the United States the following nondangerous species are found: *Conus spurius atlanticus* Clench, *C. regius* Gmelin, *C. floridanus*, *C. citrimus* Gmelin, *C. jaspireus* Gmelin, and *C. verrucosus* Hwass.

LAND SNAILS
(See Pilsbry, 1940–1948; Burch, 1962)
Key to Some Common Land Snails and Slugs

Land Snails
1. With an operculum* 2
   Without an operculum 4
2. Shell elongate; sutures deep; with five to seven whorls; amphibious
   .... *Pomatiopsis* Tryon†
   Shell strongly depressed to conic, with few whorls 3

*Included in this key are a few operculates (Prosobranchiata), otherwise the key is mainly for the terrestrial pulmonates belonging to the orders Stylommatophora and Systellommatophora.

†*Pomatiopsis* occurs in flood plains. See also page 60, under "hydrobiids."

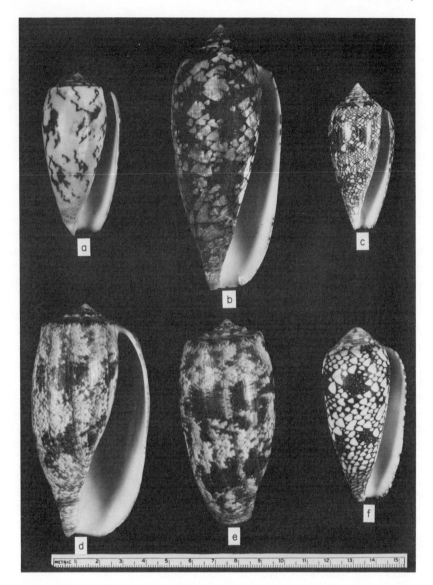

Fig. 4-16. Cone shells from the Indo-Pacific area. (a) *Conus striatus* Linn. (b) *Conus aulicus* Linn. (c) *Conus textile* Linn. (d) *Conus geographus* Linn. (e) *Conus geographus*. (f) *Conus textile*. After Malek (1962).

3. Shell with distinct axial striations, shell small (about 2.5 mm), yellowish, depressed, with rounded perifery .... *Lucidella tantilla* (Pilsbry)
  In southern Florida and tropical America shell larger, about 7 mm, depressed but with a conic spire (subglobose), aperture small, semicircular, peristome thickened .... *Hendersonia occulta* (Say) (Fig. 4-17y)
  Shell with smooth surface, or with indistinct corrugation, spire highly conic, or of medium height .... *Helicina* Lamarck
  .... *H. orbiculata* (Say) (Fig. 4-17z)
  .... *H. clappi* Pilsbry
  Species of this genus are found in tropical and subtropical America. In the United States they occur in Florida, Louisiana, Texas, Arkansas, Oklahoma, and Missouri

4. Spire high, shell ovate–conic or subconic 5
  Spire low, shell heliciform, broader than high 10

5. Aperture more than one-half the shell height 6
  Aperture one-third shell height ...... *Cionella* Jeffreys (= *Cochlicopa* Risso) e.g., *C. lubrica* (Müller), (Fig. 4-17wt), shell shining brown, lip not reflected. In this section also belong the genera *Gastrocopta, Vertigo, Carychium,* and *Pupoides.*

6. Aperture usually one-half shell height 7
  Aperture more than one-half shell height; shell, thin, and yellowish .... *Succinea* Draparnaud 8

7. Shell solid, rounded whorls, distinct umbilicus, chalky white with ashy streaks and spots .... *Bulimulus* Leach
  .... *B. exilis* (Gmelin) (Fig. 4-17x)
  Tapering spire, blunt apex, spire and interior pink, surface glossy, first three whorls more or less smooth, the rest irregularly sculptured with longitudinal striae, whorls moderately convex
  .... *Euglandina* Crosse and Fischer
  .... *E. rosea* (Férussac) (Fig. 4-17v)

8. Aperture more or less round, spire obvious, one-fifth of shell height, a small species .... *Succinea avara* Say
  Aperture ovate three-fourths to four-fifths shell height, spire rudimentary 9

9. Aperture regularly ovate, greenish or yellowish .... *Succinea ovalis* Say (Fig. 4-17s)
  Aperture three-fourths shell height, little expanded at lower part
  .... *S. retusa* (Lea)
  Aperture three-fourths shell height, little expanded at lower part . . . . .
  S. salleana Pfeiffer (= *Oxyloma saleana* (Pfeiffer) (Fig. 4-17t)

10. Aperture with broadly reflected peristome 16
  Peristome not reflected, lip of aperture sharp 11

11. Shell large, 10 mm or more in diameter 12
  Shell less than 10 mm in diameter 14

12. Shell dull, with about six closely ribbed whorls, shell flattened on top and rounded on base, wide umbilicus .... *Anguispira* Morse
  Shell more or less polished, usually smooth, may be minutely ribbed 15

13. Body whorl keeled, especially in young snails; all whorls with interrupted oblique, irregular spots or red brown, $d = 21, h = 10*$ ....
  Anguispira alternata (Say) (Fig. 4-17p)

*d = diameter, h = height; both in millimeters.

Whorls rounded, brown or red with two dark, well-marked, usually wide
and revolving bands, $d = 23$, h $= 14$* ...... *Anguispira solitaria* (Say)

14. Shell disclike, flattened, with four whorls and several parallel revolving
ridges; aperture small round with a number of small white teeth, $d = 4$,
$h = 1.5$* .... *Helicodiscus parallelus* (Say)

Shell with a low spire or dome-shaped (pyramidal) $d = 4$, $h = 3$ ....
Euconulus Reinhardt, *E. flavus* (Müller)

$d = 1.5$, $h = 1$ .... *Punctum* Morse, *P. pygmaeum* (Draparnaud)

$d = 5$, $h = 3$ .... *Zonitoides* Lehmann, *Z. arboreus* (Say)   (Fig. 17-r)

pyramidal, $d = 15$, $h = 9.5$ .... *Gastrodonta* Albers, *G. ligera* (Say)   (Fig. 4-17u)

15. Shell flattened on top, aperture small and oblique, shining but not vitreous,
five whorls, umbilicus wide and deep, $d = 16.5$, $h = 8$ ....
Haplotrema Ancey ($= Circinaria$ Beck)

Spire slightly elevated, aperture large, shining dark brown, with five well-
rounded, finely striated whorls, $d = 23$, $h = 14$–15 ....
Mesomphix Beck ($= Omphalina$ Rafinesque)
M. cupreus (Rafinesque)   (Fig. 4-17n)

16. Shell large and dull, much more than 5 mm in diameter .... Polygyridae   18

Shell small, less than 3 mm in diameter   17

17. Shell pyramidal and ribbed, $d = 2.5$, $h = 2$ ....
Strobilops Pilsbry, *S. labyrinthica* (Say)

Shell with low spire, chalky white, $d = 2.5$, $h = 1.2$ ....
Vallonia Risso, *V. pulchella* Müller)

18. Shell umbilicate   19

Shell imperforate   20

19. Shell dentate ....
Mesodon thyroidus (Say)
Light to dark brown, thin, with five and one-half whorls, umbilicus
partly closed, small white tooth on parietal wall, $d = 25$, $h = 17$.

Triodopsis monodon (Rackett)
Reddish brown, with small apex, bluntly convex, six whorls, white
elongate short tooth on parietal wall, $d = 8$, $h = 6$.

Triodopsis fraudulenta (Pilsbry) Fig. 14-17c)
Yellow brown to nearly black. Nearly twice as wide as it is high, with
six whorls, rounded. One stout tooth on parietal wall, two smaller teeth
on thickened outer lip (peristomal teeth), $d = 13$, $h = 7.5$

Shell edentate
Allogona profunda (Say)
Twice as wide as high; yellow or brown with darker revolving lines and
bands, with five whorls, growth lines oblique and distinct. Aperture
round, basal part of lip slightly elevated at one point, $d = 30$, $h = 15$.

20. Shell dentate
Mesodon elevatus (Say) (Fig. 4-17e)
Yellow brown, spire elevated, thus height subequal to diameter.
One stout white tooth on parietal wall, $d = 21$, $h = 17$.

Mesodon zaletus (Binney)
Yellow to brown, rather large, globose, with five to six rounded whorls,
body whorl very large, aperture nearly round. One tooth on parietal wall
often not appearing except in adults. In large specimens, $d = 28$, $h = 23$.

Mesodon inflectus (Say)

Whitish yellow to nearly black; very much depressed; with five to six convex whorls; one curved tooth on parietal wall, two sharply pointed teeth on inner part of reflected lip, $d = 10$–12, $h = 6$.

Triodopsis obstricta (Say)

Whorls sharply angled; stout tooth on parietal wall.

Stenotrema hirsutum (Say) (Fig. 4-17j)

Dark red or brown, small, bluntly conic; aperture narrow and elongate; long ridgelike tooth on parietal wall; basal reflected lip with a notch in the middle; surface covered with minute stiff bristles, $d = 8$, $h = 5$.

Shell edentate

Triodopsis multilineata (Say) (Fig. 4-17d)

Rather thin, yellow or reddish with a number of revolving lines or bands; with six convex whorls; aperture rounded, $d = 21$, $h = 14$.

Triodopsis albolabris (Say)

Yellow to dark brown; with six convex whorls; fine regularly spaced growth lines; aperture nearly round; outer lip broadly reflected and small callosity on basal lip, $d = 32$, $h = 15$.

Slugs

1. Mantle covering only small portion of animal .... Limacidae   2
   Mantle covering all or most of animal   5
2. Large, adults usually more than 5 cm; body with bands or spots   3
   Medium or small, less than 4 cm; without bands or spots, may be mottled
   .... *Deroceras* Rafinesque (= *Agriolimax* Mörch) spp. In Europe and nearby parts of Africa and Asia, introduced into United States.
3. Light brown; mantle and back with dark longitudinal bands, mucus colorless ...... *Limax marginatus* Müller. European, introduced into several areas of United States.
   Yellowish to gray; mantle and back usually spotted or mottled ....
4. Mantle and back black-spotted, mucus colorless .. *Limax maximus* (Linn.) In Europe, Asia Minor, Algeria; introduced into North and South America.
   Mantle and body gray with yellow spots, mucus yellow ....
   Limax flavus Linn.
   Introduced from Europe into many parts of United States.
5. Eyes on contractile (not inversible) tentacles; mantle covering the entire back of the animal .... Veronicellidae
   Primitive slugs found in the tropics. *Veronicella floridana* (Leidy) is the only species native to the United States, being found in Florida and probably states bordering the Gulf of Mexico.
   Eyes on inversible tentacles; mantle covering most of animal   6
6. Large, adults 8–10 cm, back yellow or white with or without brown and black spots on mantle ....
   Philomycus Férussac, *P. carolinianus* (Bosc)
   Small, adult about 2.5 cm   7
7. Mantle unspotted; ashy or dark gray .... *Pallifera dorsalis* (Binney)
   Mantle white or flesh colored, with a few black spots ....
   Pallifera fosteri Baker

Fig. 4-17. Some representative terrestrial snails. (a) *Triodopsis palliata* (Say) from Michigan. (b) Triodopsis tridentata (Say) from Michigan. (c) *Triodopsis fraudulenta* (Pilsbry) from Michigan. (d) *Triodopsis multilineata* (Say) from Michigan. (e) *Mesodon elevatus* (Say) from Michigan. (f) *Mesodon thyroidus* (Say) from Louisiana. (g) *Mesodon sayanus* (Pilsbry) from Michigan. (h) *Mesodon clausus* (Say) from Michigan. (i) *Polygyra septemvolva* Say from Louisiana. (j) *Stenotrema hirsutum* (Say) from Michigan. (k) *Stenotrema fraternum* (Say) from Michigan. (l) *Oxychilus cellarius* (Müller) from Michigan. (m) *Haplotrema concavum* (Say) from Michigan. (n) *Mesomphix cupreus* (Rafinesque) from Louisiana. (o) *Bradybaena similaris* (Férussac) from Louisiana. (p) *Anguispira alternata* (Say) from Louisiana. (q) *Goniodiscus perspectivus* (Say) from Michigan. (r) *Zonitoides arboreus* (Say) from Michigan. (s) *Succinea ovalis* Pfeiffer from Louisiana. (t) *Succinea saleana* Pfeiffer from Louisiana. (u) *Ventridens* (=*Gastrodonta*) *ligera* (Say) from Michigan. (v) *Euglandina rosea* (Férussac) from Louisiana. (w) *Cionella lubrica* (Müller) from New York. (x) Bulimulus exilis (Gmelin) from Puerto Rico. (y) *Hendersonia occulta* (Say) from Iowa. (z) *Helicina orbiculata* (Say) from Louisiana. After Malek (1962).

The following is a list of some digenetic trematodes that utilize many of the above mentioned land snails and slugs and others, as first or second intermediate hosts, or both.

In general members of the trematode families Brachylaemidae, Leucochloridiidae, Dicrocoeliidae, and Brachycoeliidae develop in these mollusks. The following is by no means a complete list, only a few examples are given:

Postharmostomum helicis (rodents).* First intermediate host, *Anguispira alternata* (Say); second intermediate host, *A. alternata, Ventridens* (= *Gastrodonta*) *ligera* (Say), *Triodopsis fraudulenta* (Pilsbry), *Stenotrema hirsutum* (Say), *Triodopsis multilineata* (Say), *Allogona profunda* (Say), *Mesodon thyroidus* (Say), *Zonitoides arboreous* (Say), *Deroceras laeve* (Müller).

Postharmostomum gallinum (chicken).* First intermediate host, *Bradybaena* (= *Eulota*) *similaris* (Férussac) and *Subulina octona* (Bruguiere).

Brachylaema virginiana (opossum).* *Mesodon thyroidus* (Say) serves as first and second intermediate hosts and *Mesomphix cupreus* as second intermediate host.

Brachylaema nicolli (birds).* In *Helicella* sp., *Helix aspersa* Müller, *Oxychilus cellarius* (Müller), *Deroceras reticulatum* (Müller) (= *Agriolimax agrestis* Linn.).

Ectosiphonus rhomboideus (short-tailed shrew).* In *Ventridens ligera* (Say), as first and second intermediate hosts.

Entosiphonus thompsoni (short-tailed shrew).* In *Retinella indentata* (Say) as first intermediate host and in *Succinea ovalis* (Say), *Ventridens ligera* (Say), *Deroceras laeve* (Müller), *Zonitoides nitidus* (Müller), and *Retinella indentata* (Say) as second intermediate hosts.

Hasstilesia tricolor (rabbits).* In *Vertigo ovata* Say and *Vertigo ventricosa elatior* Sterki as first and second intermediate hosts.

Panopistus pricei (short-tailed shrew).* In *Ventridens ligera* (Say), *Zonitoides arboreous* (Say), and *Deroceras laeve* (Müller) as first intermediate hosts and *Zonitoides arboreous* (Say), *Z. nitidus* (Say), *Ventridens ligera* (Say), *Deroceras laeve* (Müller), and *Stenotrema monodon* (Rackett) as second intermediate hosts.

Leucochloridium spp. (birds).* In several species of *Succinea* Draparnaud, *Quickella* Boettger, and *Oxyloma* Westerlund.

Dicrocoelium dendriticum (sheep, cattle, deer, rabbit, and man).* In *Cionella lubrica* (Müller), in New York, and in *Zebrina detrita* (Müller), *Helicella* sp., and *Helicella ericetorum* (Müller) in Europe.

Platynosomum fastosum (cats and opossum).* In *Subulina octona* (Bruguiere).

*Indicates the definitive host.

Eurytrema procyonis (raccoon).* In *Mesodon thyroidus* Say.
Eurytrema pancreaticum (cattle).* In *Bradybaena similaris* (Férussac) in Malaysia.
Brachylecithum sp. (ruffed grouse).* Experimentally in *Zonitoides arboreous, Cionella lubrica* (Müller), and *Deroceras laeve* (Müller) in the United States.
Conspicuum icteridorum (grackles).* In *Zonitoides arboreous* (Say).
Brachycoelium obesum (amphibians).* In *Ventridens ligera* (Say) and *Deroceras reticulatum* (Müller).
Brachycoelium louisianae (amphibians).* In *Polygyra septemvolva* Say.

References

Abbott, R. T. (1948). Handbook of medically important mollusks of the Orient and the Western Pacific. *Bull. Mus. Comp. Zool., Harvard Univ.* **100**, 245–328.

Abbott, R. T. (1954). "American Sea Shells. A Guide to the Shells of the Atlantic, Pacific and Gulf Shores of the United States, Canada, Central America and the Islands of the Caribbean." D. von Nostrand Co., Princeton, New Jersey.

Baker, F. C. (1911). "The Lymnaeidae of North and Middle America." Spec. Publ. No. 3, Chicago Acad. Sci., Chicago, Illinois.

Baker, F. C. (1928). "The Freshwater Mollusca of Wisconsin, Part I. Gastropoda." Wis. Acad. Arts Lett. Madison, Wisconsin.

Baker, F. C. (1945). "The Molluscan Family Planorbidae." Univ. of Illinois Press, Urbana, Illinois.

Barbosa, F. S., Hubendick, B., Malek, E. T. A., and Wright, C. A. (1961). The generic names *Australorbis, Biomphalaria, Platytaphius, Taphius* and *Tropicorbis* (Mollusca, Pulmonata). *Ann. Mag. Natur. Hist., Ser. 13,* **4**, 371–375.

Basch, P. F. (1963). A review of recent freshwater limpet snails of North America (Mollusca: Pulmonata). *Bull. Mus. Comp. Zool., Harvard Univ.* **129**, 399–461.

Burch, J. B. (1962). "How to Know the Eastern Land Snails." W. C. Brown, Dubuque, Iowa.

Clench, W. J., and Kondo, Y. (1943). The poison cone shells. *Amer. J. Trop. Med.* **23**, 105–120.

Cruider, F. N. (1961). Medical and public health importance of marine mollusks. M. P. H. thesis, Tulane University Medical School.

Davis, G. M. (1969). A taxonomic study of some species of *Semisulcospira* in Japan (Mesogastropoda: Pleuroceridae). *Malacologia* **7**, 211–294.

Davis, G. M. (1971). Mass cultivation of *Oncomelania* (Prosobranchia: Hydrobiidae) for studies of *Schistosoma japonicum. In* "Culturing *Biomphalaria* and *Oncomelania* (Gastropoda) for large-scale studies of schistosomiasis." *Bio-Medical Reports, 406 Med. Lab.* No. 19, 85–161.

Davis, G. M. (1972). Geographic variation in *Semisulcospira libertina* (Mesogastropoda: Pleuroceridae). Proc. Malac. Soc. London **40**, 5–32.

Davis, G. M., and Carney, W. P. (1973). Description of *Oncomelania hupensis lindoensis*, first intermediate host of *Schistosoma japonicum* in Sulawesi (Celebes). *Proc. Acad. Natur. Sci. Philadelphia* **125**, 1–34.

Dazo, B. C. (1965). The morphology and natural history of *Pleurocera acuta* and *Goniobasis livescens* (Gastropoda: Cerithiacea: Pleuroceridae). *Malacologia* **3**, 1–80.

Demian, E. S. (1964). The anatomy of the alimentary system of *Marisa cornuarietis* (L.). *Medd. Goteb. Mus. Zool. Avdel. Ser. B.*, **138**, 1–75.

Dundee, D. S. (1957). Aspects of the biology of *Pomatiopsis lapidaria* (Say) (Mollusca: Gastropoda; Prosobranchia). *Misc. Publ. Mus. Zool. Univ. Mich.* No. 100.

Halstead, B. W. (1959). "Dangerous Marine Animals." Cornell Maritime Press, Cambridge, Massachusetts.

Hubendick, B. (1951). Recent Lymnaeidae. Their variation, morphology, taxonomy, nomenclature and distribution. *Kungl. Svenska Vet-Akade-miens Handlinger* Stockholm, Band 3, No. 1.

International Commission on Zoological Nomenclature. (1965). Opinion 735. *Biomphalaria* Preston, 1910 (Gastropoda): Granted under the plenary powers of precedence over *Planorbina* Haldeman, 1842, *Taphius* J. & A. Adams, 1855, and *Armigerus* Classin, 1884. *Bull. Zool. Nomenclature* **22**, 94–99.

Ito, J., Mochizuki, H., and Noguchi, M. (1959). Studies on the cercariae parasitic in *Semisulcospira libertina* in Shizuoka Prefecture. *Jap. J. Parasitol.* **8**, 913–922 (in Japanese).

Kohn, A. J., Saunders, P. R., and Wiener, S. (1960). Preliminary studies on the venom of the marine snail *Conus. Ann. N.Y. Acad. Sci.* **90**, 706–725.

Malek, E. A. (1952a). Morphology, bionomics and host-parasite relations of Planorbidae (Mollusca: Pulmonata). Ph. D. thesis, University of Michigan, Ann Arbor.

Malek, E. A. (1952b). The preputial organ of snails in the genus *Helisoma* (Gastropoda: Pulmonata). *Amer. Midl. Natur.* **48**, 94–102.

Malek, E. A. (1953). Life history of *Petasiger chandleri* (Trematoda: Echinostomatidae) from the pied-billed grebe, *Podilymbus podiceps podiceps*, with some comments on other species of *Petasiger. J. Parasitol.* **39**, 152–158.

Malek, E. A. (1954a). Morphological studies on the family Planorbidae (Mollusca: Pulmonata). I. Genital organs of *Helisoma trivolvis* (Say) (Subfamily Helisomatinae F. C. Baker, 1945). *Trans. Amer. Micros. Soc.* **73**, 103–124.

Malek, E. A. (1954b). Morphological studies on the family Planorbidae (Mollusca: Pulmonata). II. The genital organs of *Biomphalaria boissyi* (Subfamily Planorbinae, H. A. Pilsbry, 1934). *Trans. Amer. Micros. Soc.* **73**, 285–296.

Malek, E. A. (1958). Distribution of the intermediate hosts of bilharziasis in relation to hydrography, with special reference to the Nile basin and the Sudan. *Bull. W.H.O.* **18**, 691–734.

Malek, E. A. (1959). Trematode infections in some domesticated animals in the Sudan. *J. Parasitol.* **45**, (Suppl.), 21.

Malek, E. A. (1962). "Laboratory Guide and Notes for Medical Malacology." Burgess Co., Minneapolis, Minnesota.

Malek, E. A. (1966). Medically important mollusks. *In* "A Manual of Tropical Medicine" (Hunter, Frye, and Swartzwelder, eds.), pp. 667–684. Saunders, Philadelphia, Pennsylvania.

Malek, E. A. (1967). Experimental infection of several lymnaeid snails with *Heterobilharzia americana. J. Parasitol.* **53**, 700–702.

Malek, E. A. (1969). Studies on "tropicorbid" snails (*Biomphalaria*: Planorbidae) from the Caribbean and Gulf of Mexico areas, including the Southern United States. *Malacologia* **7**, 183–209.

Malek, E. A., and Chrosciechowski, P. (1964). *Lymnaea* (*Pseudosuccinea*) *columella* from Venezuela, and notes on distribution of *Pseudosuccinea. Nautilus* **78**, 54–56.

Malek, E. A., and Little, M. D. (1971). *Aroapyrgus colombiensis* n. sp. (Gastropoda: Hydrobiidae), snail intermediate host of *Paragonimus caliensis* in Colombia. *Nautilus* **85**, 20–26.

Mandahl-Barth, G. (1954). The freshwater mollusks of Uganda and adjacent territories. *Ann. Mus. Roy. Congo Belge* **32**, 1–206.

Mandahl-Barth, G. (1958). Intermediate hosts of *Schistosoma*. African *Biomphalaria* and *Bulinus*. W.H.O. Monograph. Series, No. 37.

Michelson, E. H. (1961). On the generic limits in the family Pilidae (Prosobranchiata: Mollusca). No. 133, 1–10. Breviora, Cambridge, Massachusetts.

Pilsbry, H. A. (1940–1948). Land mollusca of North America (North of Mexico) Monog. No. 3, vols. 1 and 2. Acad. Natur. Sci. Philadelphia.

Preston, H. B. (1910). Additions to the non-marine molluscan fauna of British and German East Africa and Lake Albert and Edward. *Ann. Mag. Natur. Hist.* **6**, 526–536.

Sarramegna, R. (1965). Poisonous gastropods of the Conidae family found in New Caledonia and the Indo Pacific. South Pacific Commission, Technical Paper No. 144, Noumea, New Caledonia.

Thompson, F. G. (1968). "The Aquatic Snails of the Family Hydrobiidae of Peninsular Florida." University Florida Press, Gainsville.

5 Snail Hosts of Human-Infecting Trematodes

With very few exceptions, mollusks serve as the only or as one of the intermediate hosts of the digenetic trematodes. Among this group of endo-parasites, a number of species are of public health and veterinary importance since they are known to cause debilitating diseases, with some being more severe than others (Cheng, 1973; Malek, 1961a, 1970 for schistosomiasis and paragonimiasis). A number of species that are of importance are listed in Table 5-1.

In analyzing the compatibility (and incompatibility) of larval trematodes and their molluscan hosts, it has become apparent that there is a high degree of specificity among trematodes in general for their snail inter-mediate hosts, for example, they have become adapted to a single or a few species of snails. Furthermore, in the latter case these mollusks belong to the same genus or the same family. It is noted that a miracidium of a given trematode species may penetrate several species of snails, but its subsequent fate within the tissues of the snails is apparently determined by a series of yet uncertain physiological and biochemical phenomena associated with strain differences. The parasites may develop and produce cercariae in some species of mollusks or are encapsulated in others as a result of cellular reactions (Newton, 1952; McQuay, 1952; Brooks, 1953; Sudds, 1960; Malek, 1967b). Although such reactions are not produced in susceptible snails, Pan (1965) has shown that cellular reactions do occur in a susceptible strain of *Biomphalaria glabrata* parasitized by *Schistosoma mansoni* if the parasites become moribund. Specifically, a marked, generalized proliferative tissue reaction is elicited by cercariae trapped or dying in the loose, vascular con-

TABLE 5-1

Medically Important Trematodes and Their Molluscan Intermediate Hosts [a]

Trematode	Definitive host	Species	Family	Geographical distribution
Schistosomes				
Mammalian				
schistosomes				
Schistosoma mansoni	Human	*Biomphalaria glabrata*	Planorbidae	Puerto Rico, Dominican Republic, St. Kitts, Guadeloupe, Martinique, St. Lucia, Dutch Guiana, Venezuela
Schistosoma mansoni	Human, opossum, several species of rodents	*B. glabrata*	Planorbidae	Brazil
		B. tenagophila	Planorbidae	Brazil
		B. straminea	Planorbidae	Brazil
		B. philippiana	Planorbidae	Ecuador[b]
		B. chilensis	Planorbidae	Chile[b]
		B. albicans	Planorbidae	Puerto Rico[b]
		B. riisei	Planorbidae	Puerto Rico[b]
	Human	*B. pfeifferi gaudi*	Planorbidae	Gambia, Portuguese Guinea, Sierra Leone, Liberia, Guinea, Mauritania, Senegal, Le Soudan, Ivory Coast, Ghana, Nigeria
		B. sudanica	Planorbidae	Cameroons, Congo, Kenya, Uganda, Tanzania, Malawi, Sudan
Schistosoma mansoni	Human	*B. ruppellii*	Planorbidae	Congo, Sudan, Eritrea, Ethiopia, Kenya, Uganda, Tanzania
Schistosoma mansoni	Human	*B. pfeifferi*	Planorbidae	Uganda, Tanzania, Rhodesia, South Africa, Mozambique, Madagascar

Parasite	Host	Snail	Family	Location
		B. choanomphala, B. smithi, B. stanleyi	Planorbidae	Uganda
	Human, gerbils, shrews	B. alexandrina	Planorbidae	Egypt
	Human	B. alexandrina	Planorbidae	Saudi Arabia, Yemen
	Human, rodents, shrews	B. ruppellii	Planorbidae	Congo
		B. sudanica	Planorbidae	Congo
		B. bridouxiana	Planorbidae	Congo
	Human, dogface baboon	B. ruppellii	Planorbidae	Kenya
Schistosoma rodhaini	Rodents, dog, felines, human	B. bridouxiana	Planorbidae	Congo
		B. sudanica		
Schistosoma haematobium	Human	*Bulinus (Bulinus) truncatus*	Planorbidae	Morocco, Algeria, Tunisia, Libya, Egypt, Sudan, Turkey, Syria, Israel, Saudi Arabia, Yemen, Iraq, Iran
	Human	*B. (B.) truncatus rohlfsi*, *B. (B.) guernei*	**Planorbidae**	Cameroons, Ghana, Gambia, Mauritania
		B. (B.) senegalensis	**Planorbidae**	Gambia, Senegal
	Human	*B. (Physopsis) jousseaumei*	Planorbidae	Gambia, Portuguese Guinea, Le Soudan
		B. (Ph.) globosus	Planorbidae	Gambia, Portuguese Guinea, Sierra Leone, Liberia, Cameroons, Ghana, Nigeria, Angola, Sudan, Uganda, Tanzania
		B. (Ph.) globosus, *B. (Ph.) africanus*	Planorbidae	Rhodesia, South Africa, Mozambique
	Human, dogface baboon, monkeys	*B. (Ph.) globosus*, *B. (Ph.) nasutus*, *B. (B.) coulboisi*	Planorbidae	Kenya
	Human	*Ferrissia tenuis*	Ancylidae	India
	Human	*Planorbarius metidjensis* (= *P. dufourii*)	Planorbidae	Portugal

87

TABLE 5-1 (continued)

Trematode	Definitive host	Species	Family	Geographical distribution
			Molluscan intermediate host	
Schistosoma intercalatum	Human	*B. (Ph.) globosus*, *B. (Ph.) africanus*	Planorbidae	Congo
S. mattheei	Human	*B. (B.) forskalii*	Planorbidae	Gabon
	Cattle, sheep, goat, impala, zebra, human	*B. (Ph.) africanus*, *B. (Ph.) globosus*	Planorbidae	South Africa, Transvaal, Rhodesia
Schistosoma, bovis	Sheep, goat, cattle,	*Bulinus (B.) truncatus*	Planorbidae	Southern Europe, southwestern Asia
S. bovis	Sheep, goat, cattle, equines	*B. (B.) truncatus*, *B. (Ph.) nasutus*, *B. (B.) forskalii*, *B. (B.) senegalensis*	Planorbidae	Africa
S. bovis	Sheep, goat, **cattle,** human, pig, **equines,** camel	*B. (B.) truncatus*, *B. (Ph.) ugandae*	Planorbidae	Sudan
S. spindale	Cattle, buffalo	*Indoplanorbis exustus*	Planorbidae	India, Malaysia, Sumatra
S. leiperi	Cattle, sheep, goat, antelopes, buffalo	*B. (Ph.) africanus*, *B. (Ph.) globosus*	Planorbidae	Zambia
S. indicum	Horse, goat, sheep, dog, camel	*Indoplanorbis exustus*	Planorbidae	India
Schistosoma incognitum	Pig, dog	*Lymnaea luteola*	Lymnaeidae	India
S. nasale	Cattle	***Indoplanorbis exustus*** *Lymnaea luteola* *L. acuminata*	Planorbidae Lymnaeidae Lymnaeidae	India

Parasite	Host	Snail	Family	Location
Schistosoma japonicum	Human, dog, cat, rat, mice, cattle, water buffalo, pig, horse, sheep goat, badger Dog, water buffalo goat, pig	*Oncomelania nosphora,* *O. hupensis,* *O. quadrasi* *O. formosana*	Hydrobiidae	Japan China Philippines Formosa
*S. japonicum*like species	Human, dog	*Lithoglyphopsis aperta*	Hydrobiidae	Laos, Cambodia
Bivitellobilharzia loxodontae	Elephant	*Lymnaea* sp.	Lymnaeidae	Congo
Schistosomatium douthitti	Muskrat, deer, meadow mice, and other small rodents	*Stagnicola palustris,* *Lymnaea stagnalis*	Lymnaeidae	Northern United States, Canada, and Alaska
Heterobilharzia americana	Raccoon, bobcat, dog, nutria, rabbit	*Fossaria cubensis,* *Pseudosuccinea columella*	Lymnaeidae	Louisiana, Florida, Texas, North Carolina
Orientobilharzia turkestanicum	Sheep, goat, water buffalo, cattle, equines, camel	*Lymnaea tenera euphratica*	Lymnaeidae	Iraq, Iran
O. dattae	Water buffalo, cattle	*Lymnaea luteola*	Lymnaeidae	India
Avian schistosomes				
Ornithobilharzia canaliculata	Royal tern	*Batillaria minima*	Potamidae (=Cerithiidae)	Florida
Austrobilharzia variglandis	Ruddy tern stone	*Littorina pintado*	Littorinidae	Hawaii
A. variglandis	Lesser scaup duck	*Nassarius obsoletus*	Nassariidae	Rhode Island, New Jersey
A. variglandis	Red-breasted merganser	*Nassarius obsoletus*	Nassariidae	Connecticut
A. variglandis		*Littorina planaxis*	Littorinidae	California
Austrobilharzia penneri	Chick, pigeon (exp.)	*Cerithidea scalariformis*	Cerithiidae	Florida
Gigantobilharzia huttoni	White pelican	*Haminoae antillarum guadeloupensis*	Akeridae	Florida

TABLE 5-1 (continued)

Trematode	Definitive host	Molluscan intermediate host		
		Species	Family	Geographical distribution
G. sturniae	Large starling, sparrow, wagtail	*Segmentina hemisphaerula*	Planorbidae	Japan
G. gyrauli	Blackbird	*Gyraulus parvus*	Planorbidae	Wisconsin
G. huronensis	Goldfinch, cardinal	*Physa gyrina*	Physidae	Michigan
Trichobilharzia ocellata	Duck, teal	*Lymnaea stagnalis, Stagnicola palustris*	Lymnaeidae	Europe, Canada, Michigan, Wisconsin
T. physellae	Duck	*Physa anatina*	Physidae	Louisiana
T. physellae	Duck	*Physa parkeri*	Physidae	Canada, Michigan, Wisconsin
T. stagnicolae	Canary (experimental)	*Stagnicola emarginata*	Lymnaeidae	Canada, Michigan, Wisconsin
T. yokogawai	Duck	*Lymnaea swinhoei*	Lymnaeidae	Formosa
Trichobilharzia sp.	Duck, cormorant	*Lymnaea natalensis*	Lymnaeidae	Congo
Liver flukes				
Fasciola hepatica	Sheep, cattle and other herbivores, human	*Fossaria truncatula*	Lymnaeidae	Europe, North Africa, Egypt, Eastern and Central Asia, Asia Minor
		Stagnicola bulimoides, Pseudosuccinea columella, Fossaria modicella	Lymnaeidae	South, Southwest, West, North Central United States
		F. cubensis	Lymnaeidae	Puerto Rico, Louisiana
		L. bogotensis	Lymnaeidae	Columbia
		L. viatrix		Argentina
		L. rubiginosa		Malaya
		L. philippensis	Lymnaeidae	Philippines
		L. swinhoei		

Parasite	Host	Snail	Family	Distribution
Fasciola gigantica	Sheep, cattle, other herbivores, human	*L. pervia, L. japonicum*	Lymnaeidae	Japan
		L. tenuistriatus	Lymnaeidae	Australia
		Lymnaea natalensis	Lymnaeidae	Africa
		L. auricularia rufescens	Lymnaeidae	Pakistan, India
		L. acuminata	**Lymnaeidae**	India
		Fossaria ollula, Pseudosuccinea columella (experimental)	Lymnaeidae	Hawaii
		L. auricularia rubiginosa	Lymnaeidae	Malaya
Fascioloides magna	Cattle, horse, **sheep**, deer	*Fossaria parva, F. modicella*	Lymnaeidae	North America
Clonorchis sinensis	Human, dog, **cat**	*Parafossarulus manchouricus*	Hydrobiidae	China, Japan, Formosa, Korea
		Bithynia (= Bulimus) fuchsianus	Hydrobiidae	China
Opisthorchis felineus	Cat, dog, human	*Bithynia (= Bulimus) leachi*	Hydrobiidae	Central and Eastern Europe and Siberia
Dicrocoelium dendriticum	Sheep, cattle, deer, rabbit, human	*Helicella candidula, Zebrina detrita*	Helicellidae	Europe
			Enidae	
Dicrocoelium dendriticum	Sheep, cattle	*Cionella lubrica*	Cionellidae	United States
Intestinal flukes				
Fasciolopsis buski	Human, pig	*Segmentina hemisphaerula, Hippeutis cantori,*	**Planoribidae**	China, Indochina, Formosa
				India (Assam)

TABLE 5-1 (continued)

Trematode	Definitive host	Molluscan intermediate host		
		Species	Family	Geographical distribution
Echinostoma ilocanum	Rats, human	*Segmentina trochoideus*		India (Assam)
		1st intermediate host:		
		Gyraulus convexiusculus	Planorbidae	Philippines
		Hippeutis umbilicalis	Planorbidae	Philippines
		Gyraulus prashadi	Planorbidae	India
		G. convexiusculus	Planorbidae	Java
		2nd intermediate host:		
		Pila conica	Pilidae	Philippines
		Viviparus javanicus	Viviparidae	Java
Echinochasmus perfoliatus	Dog, cat, human	*Parafossarulus manchouricus*	Hydrobiidae	Orient
Gastrodiscoides hominis	Pig, human	*Helicorbis coenosus*	Planorbidae	India (Assam)
Heterophyes heterophyes	Cat, dog, fox, human	*Cerithidea cingulata*	Potamidae (= Cerithiidae)	Japan
Heterophyes heterophyes	Cat, dog, fox, human	*Pirenella conica*	Potamidae (= Cerithiidae)	Egypt

Parasite	Definitive hosts	Snail host	Snail family	Geographical distribution
Metagonimus yokogawai	Cat, dog, human	*Semisulcospira libertina*	Pleuroceridae	Orient
Haplorchis taichui and *H. pumilio*	Birds, mammals (experimental)	*Thiara granifera* *Thiara granifera, Semisulcospira libertina*	Thiaridae Thiaridae Pleuroceridae	Orient Orient
Stellantchasmus formosanum	Birds	*Thiara granifera* *Thiara tuberculata, Semisulcospira libertina*	Thiaridae Thiaridae Pleuroceridae	Orient Orient Orient
Prohemistomum vivax	Cat, dog, kite	*Cleopatra bulimoides*	Thiaridae	Egypt
Paragonimus vestermani Lung fluke	Human, tiger, lion, cat, dog, badger	*Semisulcospira libertina* *Thiara granifera, T. toucheana T. tuberculata*	Pleuroceridae Thiaridae	Japan, China, Korea, Formosa China, Formosa

[a]For detailed information on the geographical distribution of the snail hosts of the human schistosomes see Malek (1961a) and Wright (1973).
[b]Experimental infection.

93

nective tissue. In addition, daughter sporocysts maturing in the digestive gland may provoke a reaction intermediate between the focal and generalized types of tissue response.

The specificity of trematodes relative to their molluscan hosts is demonstrated by the human-infective schistosomes and other species. The following examples support the host-specificity concept.

Members of the *Schistosoma haematobium* complex in Africa and in the Middle East develop only in certain species of gastropods of the genus *Bulinus*. On the other hand, *Schistosoma mansoni* and related species in Africa and in the Western Hemisphere develop in species of *Biomphalaria*. *Schistosoma japonicum* matures in several species of the operculate *Oncomelania* in various countries in the Orient. These species of snails are closely related and are known to hybridize among themselves (Malek, 1961a).

Similarly, the Chinese liver fluke, *Clonorchis sinensis* (=*Opisthorchis sinensis*), develops in species of the operculates *Parafossarulus* and *Bulimus* belonging to the same subfamily, the Buliminae of the family Hydrobiidae. The oriental intestinal fluke *Fasciolopsis buski* develops in planorbid snails of the genera *Segmentina* and *Hippeutis*.

The intermediate hosts of *Fasciola* spp. are lymnaeid snails. Specifically, *Fossaria truncatula* (= *Lymnaea truncatula*), *Fossaria cubensis*, and related amphibious species living on the wet banks of shallow water bodies serve as intermediate hosts for *Fasciola hepatica* and *Lymnaea natalensis* in Africa, and several varieties of *Lymnaea auricularia* in Asia serve as intermediate hosts for *Fasciola gigantica*.

It is known that there are special adaptations by African schistosomes to local strains of mollusks. For example, *Bulinus* (*Bulinus*) *truncatus* is the intermediate host for *S. haematobium* in North Africa and the Middle East; however, south of the Sahara and at corresponding latitudes in East Africa, most of the *Bulinus* (*Physopsis*) spp. serve as the transmitters of *S. haematobium*, *S. mattheei*, *S. bovis*, and *S. intercalatum*. In West Africa only a few species of the subgenus *Bulinus* serve as hosts, for example, *Bulinus* (*Bulinus*) *truncatus rohlfsi* and *B.* (*B.*) *senegalensis*. In addition, *B.* (*B.*) *truncatus rohlfsi* and *B.* (*Ph.*) *globosus* have been found to be only susceptible each to its respective local strain of this schistosome in two nearby villages in West Africa. It is evident, therefore, that the presence of a compatible snail host is of primary importance for the establishment of endemicity or enzooticity of the trematode infection. Since these snails have special habitat requirements and geographical distributions, it follows that the trematodes also have a spotty and characteristic distribution, even within the same general area. It is noted that the absence of the infection with a certain species of trematode in some areas where the susceptible species of snail is present is sometimes difficult to explain. Such situations are undoubtedly due to other factors, be these ecological, for example, topographic and other types of barriers; behavioral, for example, feeding and other types of ethological phenomena; or physiological, for example genetic differences that are reflected as incompatible phenotypes. Other factors are undoubtedly also involved. In order to present a clearer picture of the complexity of trematode—mollusk relationships, a brief review of what is known follows. Those unfamiliar with the developmental biology of digenetic trematodes as related to mollusks are referred to Cheng (1973).

It has long been known that compatibility and incompatibility need not be "all or none" phenomena, since, as suggested earlier, both interspecific and intraspecific (or strain) differences do occur. These can be indirectly measured by the rate of parasite development, infectivity of the cercariae or metacercariae, the number of progeny produced by delayed polyembryony, and so on. In fact, an understanding of the factors governing compatibility and incompatibility, in turn, most probably will provide answers for why these manifestations occur.

After the initial host—parasite contact, the invasion process, the establishment of the parasite within the host, and the escape process are distinct aspects of a successful parasitic relationship. One would expect factors correlated with all these phases to contribute to some degree in regulating compatibility and/or incompatibility, and, indeed, available evidence indicates that this is so.

Initial Host—Parasite Contact

Periodically the question of the importance of host attraction in governing host specificity in mollusk—trematode relationships is raised. This topic, which has been critically reviewed by Cheng (1967), among others, is becoming less controversial as evidence increases. The former controversy is not whether host attraction does occur since the studies by Faust and Meleney (1924), Faust (1934), Faust and Hoffman (1934), Barlow (1925), Tubangui and Pasco (1933), Mathias (1925), Kloetzel (1958, 1960), Kawashima *et al.* (1961a), Campbell (1961), Davenport *et al.* (1962), Etges and Decker (1963), and MacInnis (1965) have all demonstrated rather conclusively that attraction between miracidia and mollusks does occur. This is a subtle phenomenon, however, which is operative only within very restricted distances and can be observed only with the application of quantitative techniques. The moot point is whether chemotaxis is in any way related to host specificity and hence influences compatibility. Although the studies of Faust and Meleney (1924), Barlow (1925), Neuhaus (1953), and Etges and Decker (1963) suggest that miracidial attraction is host specific, the results of Malek

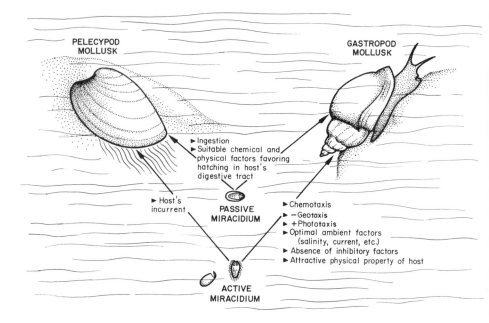

Fig. 5-1. Diagrammatic drawing illustrating factors that may govern or influence miracidium–mollusk contact during the preinvasion phase. After Cheng (1968).

(1950, 1958, 1967a, 1967b), Sudds (1960), Kawashima *et al.* (1961a), Barbosa (1965), Cheng (1968), and Chernin (1970, 1972) suggest that attraction of miracidia to a specific mollusk or to water conditioned by the mollusk need not be correlated with subsequent compatibility.

It is noted that the effectiveness of the "host factor"*—a term introduced by Davenport (1955) to designate the stimulatory material of host origin—in guiding miracidia to their molluscan host is doubtful under certain circumstances. For example, Etges and Decker (1963) have pointed out that the naturally occurring negative geotaxis and positive phototaxis of *Schistosoma mansoni* miracidia most probably eclipse the chemotactic effect of the "host factor." Even between these taxes, Chernin and Dunavan (1962) have demonstrated that the negative geotaxis is a more powerful determinant of miracidial behavior than is positive phototaxis. Thus, it is only under those conditions where naturally occurring taxes guide the miracidia to the immediate proximity of the mollusk that the influence of the "host factor," which is operative only within short distances, is effective (Fig. 5-1).

*The term "miraxone" has been coined by Chernin (1970) as a more specific one for this factor.

In addition to the influence of the "host factor," a number of physico-chemical factors present in the environment are known to influence miracidia–mollusk contact (Upatham, 1972; Sturrock and Upatham, 1973). These include the volume of water, pH, salinity, and turbidity. It is noted that in the case of the miracidia of *Schistosoma haematobium*, Shiff (1969) has demonstrated that, unlike the miracidia of *S. mansoni*, they appear to be positively geotactic and negatively phototactic since experiments have indicated that caged snails confined to the bottom in the shade are more frequently infected.

It should also be mentioned that it is highly doubtful if chemotactic forces are influential during the preinvasion relationship between miracidia and pelecypod mollusks, since the ability of this group of mollusks to effect incurrents, through either their siphons or shell edges, undoubtedly results in the passive intake of miracidia via the currents (Fig. 5-1).

Besides innate taxes, the nature of the environment is known to determine whether attraction between mollusk and miracidium can be effective (Fig. 5-1). An excellent example of this has been contributed by Kawashima *et al.* (1961b). Earlier, these investigators (1961a) had demonstrated that, although the miracidium of *Paragonimus ohirai*, a mammalian lung fluke, is attracted to three species of brackish-water snails of the genus *Assiminea* (*A. parasitologica*, *A. japonica*, and *A. latericea miyazakii*), only one of the three, *A. parasitologica*, is a compatible host. *A. latericea miyazakii* is an incompatible host, while *A. japonica* can be infected experimentally, but the level of infection is consistently low. Thus, it would appear that in nature some other factor or factors must be operative to bring about the selection of *A. parasitologica* by miracidia. It was subsequently shown, in a study of the locomotive speed and survival of *P. ohirai* miracidia in various concentrations of NaCl, that the lower the salt concentration is the more active the miracidia become, with the optimum salinity being 0.25% NaCl or less. Concurrent studies on the ecology of the three species of snails revealed that the optimum salinity for *A. parasitologica* is 0.25%, that for *A. latericea miyazakii* is 0.4%, and that for *A. japonica* is 0.6%. These findings demonstrate that an environmental factor, salinity in this case, can serve as a mechanism determining host selection. Thus, these investigators have demonstrated that the influence of the mollusks' attractants can be masked by an ambient factor and have also revealed further evidence that attraction of miracidia to mollusk need not mean successful subsequent development.

Relative to the nature of the "host factor," Wright (1959) has suggested that it may be in the form of species-specific substances incorporated in the body-surface mucus of mollusks; Kawashima *et al.* (1961a) have demonstrated that *Paragonimus ohirai* miracidia are attracted to amino acid mixtures placed in cellophane bags; and MacInnis (1965) has found that butyric acid, galactose, L-cysteine, HCl, and even 1.0 mM HCl will stimulate "contact with return" of over 80% of *S. mansoni* miracidia in an artificial test system. Moreover, it should be pointed out that, although organic molecules, possibly amino acids, fatty acids, and sugars are the attractants, there is also some evidence indicating that the pH or some other physical property of the host may be responsible, at least in part, for the attraction (Kawashima *et al.*, 1961a). This most probably explains the attraction of *S. mansoni* miracidia for dilute HCl, as demonstrated by MacInnis. In addition, R. B. Short (personal communication) has found that the presence of calcium in water does affect contact between *S. mansoni* miracidia and *Biomphalaria glabrata*. Thus, ionic calcium appears to be an important factor relative to miracidia–mollusk contact although its role remains to be elucidated.

More recently, Chernin (1970) has demonstrated that the miracidial stimulant emitted by *Biomphalaria glabrata* is thermostable, will retain its activity during prolonged storage, has a molecular weight of < 500, and is thus probably a structurally simple molecule. Furthermore, Chernin (1972) has shown that the factor is water soluble and emanates from specimens of strains susceptible and nonsusceptible to *Schistosoma mansoni.*

In the case of the miracidia of *Schistosoma haematobium*, Shiff (1968, 1969) has demonstrated that they are unable to infect *Bulinus* (*Physopsis*) *globosus* in moderately fast-flowing water unless turbulence occurs near the snails. Furthermore, these miracidia apparently dive to the bottom of bodies of water and subsequently locate the snail hosts by chemotaxis. This chemotactic factor, like that of *Biomphalaria glabrata*, is also water soluble (Shiff and Kriel , 1970).

In the case of those species of trematodes that do not include a free-swimming miracidial stage, successful host–parasite contact is dependent upon the ingestion of the egg by the mollusk, followed by hatching within the latter's alimentary tract (Fig. 5-1). Although some information is available pertaining to the hatching process of eggs in water (Standen, 1951; Rowan, 1956, 1957; Wilson, 1968), surprisingly little information is available on the factor or factors that influence hatching of trematode eggs in mollusks. It is generally believed that the mollusk's digestive juices in some manner stimulate hatching (Krull and Mapes, 1952; Timon-David, 1965; and others), although the exact mechanisms have not been studied. Nevertheless, it is apparent that the biochemistry and physical properties of the mollusk's digestive tract could serve as determinants of compatibility, as manifested by hatching, or of incompatibility, as manifested by non-hatching.

There are certain digenetic trematodes whose miracidia normally hatch and infect the snail by penetration, but they can also be transmitted if their eggs are ingested by the snail. Beaver *et al.* (1964) demonstrated that fully embryonated eggs of *Paragonimus kellicotti*, in leached-out feces, were ingested by the amphibious snail *Pomatiopsis lapidaria* and caused its infection as evidenced later by the emergence of the cercariae. The study of the mechanism of hatching of such eggs, in the water or in the snail's digestive tract, would be of value.

The Invasion Process

Because of obvious immediate medical implications, considerable information is available about factors governing the penetration of cercariae into mammals and other vertebrate hosts. On the other hand, little is known about miracidial penetration into mollusks, either from the exterior or through the gut wall. Nevertheless, this barrier could be a factor determining compatibility or incompatibility.

Certain aspects of the processes involved during the successful penetration of *Lymnaea truncatula* and *L. auricularia* by *Fasciola hepatica* and *F. gigantica*, respectively, have been studied by Dawes (1959, 1960a,b,c). According to him, the miracidium first becomes attached to the molluscan host's integument by suctorial action resulting from application of the "cup" formed by the inversion of the anterior papilla assisted by mucus. This is followed by the secretion of cytolytic enzymes from ". . . the gut and the unicellular pharyngeal 'glands' into the 'cup'." The subsequent enzymatic activity results in the lysis of the host's epithelial and subepithelial tissues. Only after the host's integument has been perforated does the parasite enter, but not before it has sloughed its ciliated epidermis. For this reason, Dawes considers the penetrating form to be a sporocyst and not a miracidium. Recently, Wilson *et al.* (1971) have investigated the penetration of *L. truncatula* by *F. hepatica* miracidia by employing electron microscopy. They have reported that, although miracidial attachment can be stimulated in the absence of the snail by chemicals, the surface to which the miracidium attaches must have the correct physical configuration for the parasite to form a stable attachment. The cytolytic enzymes secreted by the miracidium originate from the apical gland as well as accessory glands, the latter being comprised by pairs of uninucleate cells situated on each side of the apical gland (Wilson, 1971).

The hypothesis that the attachment surface of the miracidium must fit the molluscan surface to be penetrated may also hold true in the case of *Schistosoma mattheei* miracidia and *Bulinus africanus* since Kinoti (1971) has demonstrated, by employing electron microscopy, that the surface of the apical epidermis of the miracidium of *S. mattheei* consists of branching and anastomosing microvilli. Kinoti has suggested that this arboreal arrangement serves to attach the miracidium to the body surface of the snail host during penetration.

As the miracidium of *Fasciola* penetrates, its ciliated cells are shed in sequence from anterior to posterior. According to Wilson *et al.* (1971), the sporocyst newly transformed from the miracidium is covered by a new body surface consisting of material extruded from a group of vesiculated cells that lie beneath the musculature of the body wall.

Inasmuch as cytolytic enzymes are involved in the penetration process of miracidia, the question may be asked as to whether the miracidial cytolytic enzymes must be chemically specific for the integument of specific species of mollusks. If this is the case, the compatibility of enzymes to substrate could serve as a factor governing successful penetration, hence host compatibility (Fig. 5-2). Indeed, Lie (1963) has expressed the opinion that the prevention of penetration of certain echinostome miracidia by unnatural snails is responsible for incompatibility. Similarly, Kinoti (1970) has demonstrated that the incompatibility of *Schistosoma mattheei* with *Bulinus truncatus* is mostly due to the failure of the schistosome miracidia to penetrate. This is in contradiction with Malek's (1958) results, with regard to the susceptibility of *Bulinus* (*Physopsis*) *ugandae* to *S. haematobium* miracidia. *Bulinus* (*Ph.*) *ugandae* in the Sudan and Uganda is either non-susceptible or shows very poor susceptibility to *S. haematobium*. In spite of this, the miracidia have no difficulty penetrating the snails but later fail to develop in all or most of them. The ability of the miracidia of *S. haematobium* to penetrate *B.* (*Ph.*) *ugandae* is similar to that of the miracidia of *S. bovis*, for which *B.* (*Ph.*) *ugandae* is an effective natural host (Malek, 1969).

In addition to the miracidium's cytolytic enzymes, Dawes (1960c) has

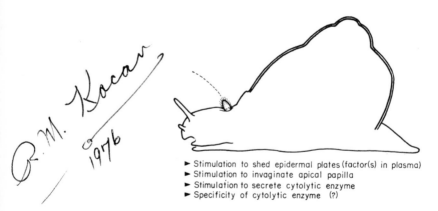

► Stimulation to shed epidermal plates (factor(s) in plasma)
► Stimulation to invaginate apical papilla
► Stimulation to secrete cytolytic enzyme
► Specificity of cytolytic enzyme (?)

Fig. 5-2. Diagrammatic drawing illustrating factors that may govern or influence successful penetration of the molluscan host by a miracidium. After Cheng (1968).

expressed the view that the shedding of the ciliated epidermis by the miracidium, thus transforming it to a sporocyst, is a prerequisite for successful infection of the snail. This hypothesis has been challenged by Lengy (1962), who has demonstrated that *Schistosoma bovis* miracidia do not shed their ciliated epidermis prior to penetrating. Similarly, Maldonado and Acosta-Matienzo (1947) demonstrated earlier that *S. mansoni* miracidia do not shed their plates until after successful penetration; Heyneman (1966) has successfully initiated the infection of *Lymnaea rubiginosa* with *Echinostoma audyi* miracidia and of *Indoplanorbis exustus* with *Echinostoma malayanum* miracidia by inoculating these miracidia through the mantle via a minute hole drilled in the mollusks' shells, thus suggesting that the shedding of the miracidial epidermal plates is not a prerequisite to successful infection, at least in these species. It remains true, nevertheless, that certain species of fasciolid miracidia may shed their plates prior to penetration. Campbell and Todd (1955), for example, have reported that *Fascioloides magna* miracidia shed their ciliated plates (more appropriately referred to as ciliated cells) on the exterior after a brief contact with the molluscan host's tissues, and Barlow (1925) has found the transformation of *Fasciolopsis buski* miracidia into sporocysts when bathed in "snail tissue juices." Cheng (1968) has observed that *Fasciola gigantica* miracidia shed their plates when placed in concentrated and 1 : 10 dilutions of the plasma of *Galba ollula*, the natural host, and in similar concentrations of the plasma of *Helisoma duryi normale*, an incompatible host, but not in the plasma of *Thiara granifera* and *Littorina pintado*, both of which are also incompatible hosts. Similar phenomena were not observed when miracidia were placed in tissue extracts of all four species of snails, nor were they observed in greater dilutions of *G. ollula* and *H. duryi normale* plasma. Thus, this phenomenon is apparently not related to host compatibility. Rather, it suggests that miracidia that possess the innate ability to shed their epidermal cells prior to penetration can be stimulated to do so by some factor(s). Nevertheless, it would appear that the occurrence of the stimulatory factor(s) in the natural hosts could influence compatibility during this phase of host–parasite relationship, especially if Dawes' contention is true among fasciolid trematodes.

No information is yet available relative to the nature of the stimulatory factor(s); however, the fact that *F. gigantica* miracidia did not shed their plates when placed in extracts of desanguinated and aqueously perfused snails indicates the factor is present in plasma rather than in tissue fluids.

It is also significant that *F. gigantica* miracidia were stimulated to shed their plates only in concentrated plasma and in a 1 : 10 dilutions of plasma. This may be interpreted to mean that in nature the stimulatory effect would occur only when miracidia become intimately associated with or are in actual contact with the snail, since plasma, seeping from the wound resulting

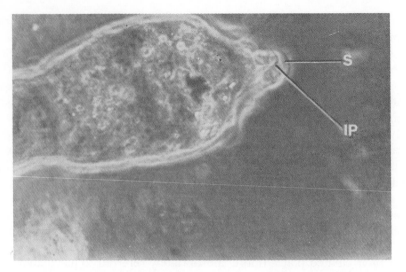

Fig. 5-3. Photomicrograph showing invagination of the apical papilla of the miracidium of *Fasciola gigantica* and secreted lytic enzyme after exposure to concentrated *Galba ollula* plasma. IP, Invaginated papilla; S, secreted material (× 120). After Cheng (1968).

from the parasite's lytic enzymes, would be rapidly diluted as it diffuses through the aqueous medium.

In addition to the shedding of epidermal plates, invagination of the apical papilla as well as the secretion of some substance, perhaps the lytic enzyme, were also noticed in *F. gigantica* miracidia exposed to plasma from *G. ollula* and *H. normale*. Thus, it would appear that the formation of the apical "cup," as well as secretion, are stimulated not by physical contact but by some factor(s) present in the mollusk's plasma (Fig. 5-3).

It is noted that in the case of the penetrative activity of *Schistosoma mansoni* miracidia Chernin (1972) has shown that it is nonspecific, for example, the miracidia will attack susceptible as well as nonsusceptible snails and even agar. Earlier, Malek (1950) has shown that the initial reaction of the miracidia of *S. mansoni* during their random movement, toward a living susceptible or nonsusceptible snail, is similar to their reaction toward an empty snail shell. They later penetrated both susceptible and nonsusceptible snails.

Establishment of the Parasite

Successful establishment of germinal sacs (sporocysts, rediae, or both) within the mollusk implies that the form that has invaded the host will reach a suitable site, overcome the host's internal defense mechanisms, be the target

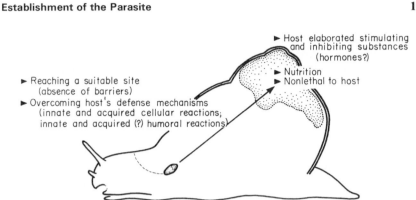

Fig. 5-4. Diagrammatic drawing illustrating factors that may govern or influence the successful establishment of trematode larvae in a mollusk. The arrow indicates path of the larva to digestive gland (shaded). After Cheng (1968).

of host-elaborated growth and development-stimulating factors, be able to obtain its required nutrients, and at the same time not kill its host (Fig. 5-4). These requirements are considered separately.

REACHING A SUITABLE SITE

Although tissue specificity still remains one of the unsolved problems in parasitology, it is a well-documented phenomenon. For example, for a large number of species among the Digenea the molluscan host's digestive gland or gonad appear to be the preferred sites of normal larval development. This does not mean that aberrant parasites cannot develop in ectopic sites. Indeed, such exceptions to the rule are known. Investigations into the nature and development of larvae that grow at ectopic sites not only can provide insights into the physicochemical requirements of these parasites but also can reveal some of the factors that inhibit or prevent the parasite from reaching its normal developmental site. A series of such studies is summarized to illustrate this point.

Among members of the trematode order Plagiorchioidea, the mother sporocysts of certain species are known to be attached to the external surface of their molluscan hosts' alimentary tracts (Cort *et al.*, 1954; Rankin, 1944; Leigh, 1946; Schell, 1961, 1962a; Cheng, 1961a,b; and others). Surrounding each of the daughter sporocysts arising from these mother sporocysts is a so-called paletot. The question is, What is the origin of this paletot? According to Cort and Olivier (1943), Cort and Ameel (1944), and Cort *et al.* (1954), the paletot is formed from the multiplication of the cells of the mother sporocyst wall, which invaginates and surrounds each daughter sporocyst. More recently Schell (1961, 1962a), who studied the sporocysts of *Hap-*

lometrana intestinalis and *Glypthelmins quieta*, both intestinal parasites of amphibians, has expressed the opinion that the paletot is not of parasite origin but represents an enveloping membrane that has resulted from the proliferation of the basement membrane surrounding the snail's gut, thus preventing further invasion by the mother sporocyst beyond that space delimited by the intestinal epithelium on one side and the basement membrane on the other. If Schell's observations are correct, the reason why mother sporocysts of *H. intestinalis* and *G. quieta* are found abutting upon their molluscan hosts' alimentary tracts rather than between the digestive gland lobules—as is the case with certain other plagiorchid trematodes—is that the migration of these sporocysts becomes restricted by their hosts' basement membranes. Although the mother sporocysts of both *H. intestinalis* and *G. quieta* become successfully established at this site and produce daughter sporocysts, the migration of the mother sporocysts does become restricted. Schell (1962a) has stated: "In following the development of *G. quieta* it became evident that the thin basement membrane beneath the intestinal epithelium of the host snail plays an important role in protecting the snail from invasion by the parasite." Is it possible, then, that certain species of trematodes, which could not undergo normal development at the site restricted by the basement membrane, would in this way be prevented from becoming established? Although examples of this, as far as we have been able to determine, have not yet been described among mollusk–larval trematode relationships, the condition known as schistosome dermatitis caused by avian schistosome cercariae in human skin is an example of the inability of these cercariae to successfully penetrate the depth of the abnormal host's skin. Unable to survive in the surfacial areas of the skin, they die. In this connection, Lewert and Lee (1954), Lewert (1958), and Lewert and Mandlowitz (1963) have demonstrated that the physical and chemical natures of the basement membrane and ground substance do determine whether the entrance of invasive forms of helminths will be successful.

The evidence presented indicates that barriers, especially in the form of basement membrane and perhaps ground substances, situated in the path of invading trematode larvae could prevent them from reaching a satisfactory site for further development and thus serve as determinants of host incompatibility.

HOST'S INTERNAL DEFENSE MECHANISMS

What is known about the nature of internal defense mechanisms in mollusks, both cellular and humoral, is considered in Chapter 9. The role of certain molluscan leukocytes and fibrous elements in innate immunity, caused by the encapsulation of trematode larvae, is well established. As mentioned earlier, the results of Newton (1952, 1954), Brooks (1953), Sudds (1960), Malek (1967b) and others strongly indicate that encapsulation generally occurs around larvae in incompatible hosts. However, slight and restricted encapsulation may also occur around larvae in their natural hosts (Cheng and Cooperman, 1964; Probert and Erasmus, 1965; Schell, 1961, 1962a,b; Pan, 1965), but these extremely light capsules usually inflict little or no damage upon the parasites. On the other hand, the extensive capsules that surround parasites in totally or partially incompatible hosts usually result in destruction of the parasites. The chemical basis for this destruction remains undetermined; nevertheless, it may be generalized that encapsulation by leukocytes and/or fibers resulting in death is by far the most effective form of innate defense mechanism in mollusks against incompatible trematode larvae.

In connection with the internal defense mechanism in compatible snail hosts the following observations are relevant. Malek (1961b,c), based on field and laboratory work on schistosomiasis in Egypt and the Sudan, used the term "spontaneous cure," or arrest in the development and discharge of the cercariae, in dealing with the schistosome–snail relationship. It was observed that some naturally and laboratory infected snails, which were not subjected to any environmental stress, ceased to produce cercariae into the water. In Egypt and the Sudan, *Biomphalaria alexandrina* and *B. sudanica* were "cured" of their infections with *Schistosoma mansoni*, and *Bulinus truncatus* of its infection with *S. haematobium*, after the cercariae had been emerging from the snails for several months. Later Malek (1969) reported that some Sudanese *Bulinus* (*Physopsis*) *ugandae* were also cured of their infections with *Schistosoma bovis*. When cured snails were dissected, the sporocysts were found to contain a few living cercariae, but the majority were motionless, and autolysis was evident. Moreover, during 15 years of dealing with *Biomphalaria glabrata* infected with *S. mansoni* (Puerto Rican strain), one of us (E. A. M.) has also observed the same phenomenon to occur among a few of the snails, which had not been subjected to any changes in the environment, especially temperature. When one of these snails was sectioned, only a slight host reaction around the sporocysts was evident, and the majority of the cercariae had undergone autolysis. Thus, it seems that in a compatible snail–schistosome relationship of long duration the snail's internal defense mechanism (whether cellular and/or humoral) becomes operative and terminates the infection in the case of a few individuals.

Although supposedly innate humoral factors in mollusks have been reported by various workers (see review by Cheng, 1967), their effectiveness as defense mechanisms against invading trematode larvae is unknown or uncertain. Recently, however, Heyneman (1966) has successfully demonstrated in transplantation studies that the inability of *Echinostoma malayanum* to become established in *Lymnaea rubiginosa* and of *E. audyi* in *Indoplanorbis exustus* is due to "physiological rejection within snail tissues distinct from the factors responsible for failure of miracidia to attach to or penetrate the body wall of the nonadapted host." Although it would be tempting to interpret Heyneman's findings to indicate the occurrence of an innate humoral factor, the destruction of *E. malayanum* and *E. audyi* larvae could very well have resulted from encapsulation. Unfortunately, follow-up histological studies that would confirm this conclusion are not available.

Two other examples of possible occurrence of innate humoral immunity that prevents the establishment of larval trematodes have been reported. Benex and Lamy (1959) have shown that tissue extracts from the planorbid snail *Planorbis corneus* will immobilize *S. mansoni* miracidia, and these French workers suggest that species of snails that are refractory to *S. mansoni* infection may possess "immunelike" immobilizing substances. Sudds (1960) has shown that when *Trichobilharzia elvae* miracidia penetrate two abnormal hosts, *Bulimnaea megasoma* and *Fossaria abrussa*, the parasites die and begin to degenerate within 1.5–6 days, without any indication of a host-tissue reaction. Again, it would be tempting to interpret these findings as indications of the presence of innate humoral immunity, but, under the conditions of the experiments, other possible explanations cannot be completely ruled out.

Occasionally suggestions have appeared in the literature that snails at different ages present different degrees of susceptibility to infection by trematode larvae. Most, if not all, of these reports have resulted from either field studies (where the ages of snails have been estimated by their sizes) or qualitative assays of infectivity. Whether such age-correlated resistance is due to some innate humoral factor or even to a cellular factor remains unknown. At least in the case of the Egyptian snail *Biomphalaria alexandrina* Malek (1950) has shown that age has little or no influence on their susceptibility to infection with an Egyptian strain of *Schistosoma mansoni*. A few strains of Brazilian *Biomphalaria glabrata*, however, show different degrees of susceptibility with regard to age. Moreover, 2–4 week old *Bulinus truncatus* from the Sudan was the most susceptible to Sudanese *Schistosoma haematobium* (Malek, 1958).

The only evidence of acquired cellular immunity available at this time is that presented by Barbosa and Coelho (1956). These investigators have demonstrated that, although *Biomphalaria glabrata* previously "cured" of *Schistosoma mansoni* infection can be reinfected, some tissue reaction involving leukocytes and fibrous elements is evoked in reinfected snails, a phenomenon not found in initial infections. This finding could mean that some type of incomplete acquired immunity exists in *B. glabrata* after the initial infection and is manifested during reinfection as cellular response.

The belief held by some workers that acquired humoral immunity can occur in mollusks stems primarily from the reports of Winfield (1932) and Nolf and Cort (1933). These investigators reported that the presence of *Cotylurus flabelliformis* sporocysts in varieties of *Lymnaea stagnalis* prevents almost all the cercariae of this trematode from successfully penetrating and encysting as metacercariae. Later, Cort *et al.* (1945) repeated these studies and reported that the same phenomenon occurs in *Stagnicola emarginata angulata* parasitized by *C. flabelliformis* sporocysts. They noted that the few cercariae that did succeed in penetrating were inhibited from developing into metacercariae unless they entered sporocysts and were thus presumably protected from the host's antibodies. On the basis of these reports, Culbertson (1941) concluded that "... it is clear that snails acquire an immunity after infection by trematodes. ..." Several later authors, especially Michelson (1963) and Cheng (1967), have cautioned that this generalization is unwarranted since, as of this date, the ability of mollusks to produce antibodies has not been conclusively demonstrated.

The results of two other studies suggest the occurrence of acquired humoral immunity. Chowaniec (1961) has reported that only a small proportion of snails already harboring *Fasciola hepatica* could be infected with the same parasite, while most of the control snails could be readily infected. In the second study, Lie *et al.* (1966) have demonstrated that only 5% of *Lymnaea rubiginosa* infected with one species of echinostome could be superinfected with a second, while 89% of uninfected control snails could be infected. In neither of these studies, however, were antibodies demonstrated. It is of interest that, in the case of *L. rubiginosa*, Lie *et al.* have stated another possible explanation: young invading sporocysts of the second species are killed and ingested by the rediae of the first species.

It should be remembered, however, that several reports emanating from parasitologists at the Michigan and Minnesota Biological Stations, from Canada, and from other areas have indicated the common occurrence of natural double and sometimes triple larval trematode infections among snails. In schistosomiasis areas, Malek (1959) reported on *Bulinus* (*Physopsis*) *ugandae* in the Sudan naturally infected with both *Schistosoma bovis* and an amphistome, proven to be *Paramphistomum microbothrium*. These reports seem to indicate the lack of any acquired internal defense mechanism or of competition among at least certain species of larval trematodes. Of course, in some cases, the possibility cannot be excluded that the miracidia of two or three trematodes have penetrated the same snail at about the same time and thus were able to develop simultaneously.

Another example of the lack of an acquired internal defense mechanism in some cases of trematode–snail relationships is the following: a nonpatent infection of the Egyptian *Biomphalaria alexandrina* with a noncompatible strain of *S. mansoni* (a Puerto Rican strain) apparently did not confer any acquired resistance on the snails. The snails later became infected and produced cercariae when they were reexposed to an Egyptian strain of *S. mansoni* (Malek, 1950).

The most convincing indirect evidence of acquired humoral immunity in mollusks is that contributed by Michelson (1963, 1964), who demonstrated that *Schistosoma mansoni* miracidia-immobilizing substances occur in the tissue extracts of *Biomphalaria glabrata* infected with this trematode. Although Michelson found that his controls (extracts of other species of uninfected snails, extracts of snails infected with an acid-fast bacillus, an echinostome metacercaria, the nematode *Daubaylia potomaca*, snails inoculated with bovine albumin, *S. mansoni* eggs and polystyrene spheres, uninfected *B. glabrata*, and water) all gave positive results, in no instance did the percentage of immobilization reach the level observed in extracts of *S. mansoni*-infected snails. Michelson cautiously states, "Although the suggestion that the immobilizing phenomenon might be associated with an antigen–antibody interaction is an appealing one, data are lacking to substantiate this hypothesis. The possibility that the immobilizing substance(s) might be related either to parasite-produced toxins or to products resulting from alternations in the snail's metabolism cannot be excluded."

It may be concluded, then, that innate cellular immunity appears to be the most efficient mechanism by which trematodes are prevented from developing in incompatible mollusks, although acquired cellular immunity may occur. The role of humoral factors, either innate or acquired, remains in doubt. In fact, the concensus of opinion at this time is that mollusks do not produce antibodies.

INFLUENCE OF HOST-ELABORATED GROWTH AND DEVELOPMENT-STIMULATING OR INHIBITING SUBSTANCES

This vast area of host–parasite relationships has hardly been investigated. From what is known about the metabolic interaction between larval trematodes and mollusks, it is inconceivable that compatible hosts do not influence in some manner the growth and differentiation processes of their parasites and thus enhance their normal sequence of development or, conversely, that incompatible hosts do not in some manner inhibit the normal developmental sequences of their parasites.

Meade and Pratt (1966) have reported that when rediae of *Metagonimoides oregonensis* are experimentally transplanted from naturally infected *Oxytrema silicula*, in which the gonads had been destroyed, to young uninfected snails with healthy gonads, a certain number will survive but that differences are apparent between the transplanted rediae, their progeny, and those in naturally infected snails. They noted that the transplanted rediae more than doubled their natural size, "mucus and debris" were included in their ceca, and the enclosed metacercariae were no longer distinguishable. Burns and Pratt (1953) had shown earlier that the rediae of *M. oregonensis* give rise to both cercariae and metacercariae within their brood chambers and that no daughter rediae occur. Furthermore, although some metacercariae, released from transplanted rediae into the body cavities of acceptor snails, survived for up to 6 weeks, none of these were infective when fed to a known compatible experimental definitive host, the golden hamster. These uninfective metacercariae also exhibited some behavioral and morphological peculiarities. They displayed greater activity, their eyespots disappeared, and the prominent Y-shaped excretory vesicle, which normally appears black, was often enlarged and possessed fewer granules. Meade and Pratt are of the opinion that these differences in the transplanted rediae and metacercariae had resulted from the influence of their new host's gonadal hormone(s). The same hormone(s) presumably was present at a very much lower level or not present at all in the original castrated hosts. Whether this conclusion is justified must await more direct evidence.

From the study cited above, it would appear that some host factor(s), perhaps hormones, in *O. silicula* with healthy gonads does disrupt the normal development of *M. oregonensis* rediae and metacercariae during the later phase of the relationship. The significance of this finding to our discussion is that it is an example of a host-elaborated substance that "inhibits" normal development and thus promotes incompatibility. The phenomenon reported by Meade and Pratt, however, does not appear to hold true in all transplanted mollusk–larval trematode associations. Chernin (1966), for example, has reported that successful transplants of *S. mansoni* mother and daughter sporocysts from *B. glabrata* to acceptor snails of the same species was followed by normal cercarial formation. Perhaps this difference can be explained by the fact that *M. oregonensis* includes a redial stage while *S. mansoni* includes sporocyst stages. It is well known that rediae inflict significantly more damage upon mollusks than do sporocysts. Thus, perhaps the donor *B. glabrata* is never completely castrated, and *S. mansoni*, as the result of a long relationship with *B. glabrata* and exposure to its hormones, is not adversely affected by hormones during the later phases of its development, as is *M. oregonensis*.

Another example of possible host-stimulated developmental alterations among larval trematodes has been reported by James (1964) and discussed by Cable (1965). James has reported that the intramolluscan life cycle stages of the gymnophallid trematode *Parvatrema homoeotecnum* include a "primary germinal sac" with adult features, including an oral sucker, ventral sucker, pharynx, and bifid ceca, and a "daughter germinal sac," which is unique in that, in addition to the adult features found on the "primary germinal sac," it also possesses a bifurcate tail. The "daughter germinal sacs" increase in size and lose their tails while still within the "primary germinal sac." Further development does not occur until they rupture out of primary sacs. Daughter sacs then continue to develop in one of three possible ways. (1) Most produce cercariae and metacercariae; (2) a few produce a second generation of "daughter germinal sacs"; and (3) very occasionally, cercariae, metacercariae, and second-generation "daughter germinal sacs" are produced in the same "daughter germinal sac." These larval stages are found in the hemocoelic spaces of the digestive gland and gonad of the littoral prosobranch *Littorina saxatilis tenebrosa.* According to James, the "primary germinal sac" could be interpreted to be a metacercaria; while, according to Cable, the "daughter germinal sac" could be considered a cercaria. Thus, the usual sequence of larval stages is reversed in *P. homoeotecnum.* Since the usual life history pattern among related gymnophallids includes two molluscan intermediate hosts, both being marine pelecypods, Cable (1965) has given the following as one possible explanation for this variation. "It may be significant that metacercariae of other gymnophalline species live in loose, even superficial association with their hosts whereas the species that James (1964) described invades the snail to the extent commonly seen in mollusks serving as the first intermediate host of trematodes in general. As a result, that species probably gets a double exposure of the most intimate sort to the tissues and body fluid of mollusks." This, of course, implies that the tissues and body fluids of mollusks may have influenced that unusual developmental sequence. Although in this instance the presumably host-stimulated developmental alterations do not affect the parasite deleteriously, it is conceivable that such changes could in certain instances deter or inhibit delayed polyembryony and thus render the host incompatible.

NUTRIENT REQUIREMENTS

Available evidence indicates that trematode parasites utilize carbohydrates as their primary energy source. They acquire their carbohydrates in the form of glucose resulting from the degradation of the host's stored glycogen (Malek, 1952), or, if there is not stored glycogen in the vicinity of their natural habitat, they utilize the mollusk's blood sugars (Cheng, 1963a; Cheng and Lee, 1971). In addition to sugars these larvae apparently utilize free amino acids from the mollusk's hemolymph and perhaps even from the surrounding host cells that are lysed or ruptured mechanically. In the case of *Schistosoma mansoni,* Lee and Cheng (1972) have provided evidence that the parasite may hydrolyze the hemoglobin from the hemolymph of *Biomphalaria glabrata,* and the iron-containing moiety, possibly heme, is taken up.

Lipids, in the form of short-chain fatty acids, are also taken up by germinal sacs but are primarily stored, rather than utilized, in cercariae and in certain species in the walls of germinal sacs. The current belief that these stored fatty acids are not utilized in energy production while they are within the mollusk's digestive gland stems from von Brand's (1952) belief that this environment is essentially anaerobic and hence is not conducive to lipid metabolism.

Cheng and Snyder (1962a,b, 1963), by employing histochemistry, arrived at the conclusion that glucose and fatty acids are taken up by sporocysts through their body walls. Recent electron microscope studies tend to corroborate this with the finding of conspicuous microvilli along the outer surfaces of sporocysts. In the case of rediae, Cheng (1962, 1963b) found that the ingestion of the host's cells is the primary method of nutrient acquisition, although some absorption may occur through the body wall also. This, again, appears to be corroborated by the finding of microvilli on redial walls. For a review of the fine structure and nutrient uptake by larval trematodes, see Erasmus (1972).

Relative to the relationship between nutrition and compatibility and incompatibility, it may be asked whether the introduction of germinal sacs into a foreign host or to some site within the trematode's natural molluscan host, where the physicochemical nature of the host–parasite interphase prevents the uptake of nutrients, could cause the parasite to fail to become established. For example, could the destruction of heavily encapsulated germinal sacs in incompatible hosts actually represent, at least in part, death due to starvation?

It is known that the rate of cercarial development is dependent upon the amount of food assimilated by the snail host and upon the number of larvae competing for the available nutrients in the snail, among other factors (Kendall, 1949). It would follow that, if the host–parasite interphase is favorable for nutritional uptake but nutrients are not sufficiently available as the result of a poorly nourished host or because of competition between a large number of germinal sacs, normal development could not occur—and this would constitute incompatibility.

LETHALITY TO HOST

Surprisingly little information is available pertaining to the lethality of trematode larvae to mollusks. Some investigators (Rees, 1931; Kendall, 1964; James, 1965) have suggested that during certain mollusk–trematode associations death of the host does not occur. Yet Schreiber and Schubert (1949) and Pan (1965), both working with *Biomphalaria glabrata* parasitized with *Schistosoma mansoni*, have shown that a high incidence of mortality does occur. These known mortalities, however, cannot be considered to reflect incompatibility, since the parasites do develop normally, and death, as Faust and Hoffman (1934), Schreiber and Schubert (1949), and Pan (1965) have pointed out, has resulted from the rapid multiplication of larvae and mass emergence of cercariae. From the available information, it would appear that the death of mollusks resulting from invasion by "pathogenic" trematodes is extremely rare. No indisputable examples have yet been reported, although Kendall (1950) has shown that *Fasciola hepatica* does inflict conspicuous deleterious effects on *Lymnaea stagnalis*, *L. palustris*, and *L. glabra* but not on *L. auricularia*. The fact that mass mortality seldom occurs could be interpreted to mean that the defense mechanisms of mollusks are highly efficient.

It appears appropriate at this point to interject the following comment. Death of mollusks due to a pathogenic trematode infers extremely severe pathogenicity, a topic that has been reviewed recently (Cheng, 1967). Yet, despite known instances of drastic histopathological alterations in parasitized mollusks caused by trematode larvae, few proven cases of rapid and virulent deaths are known.

Escape Process

Our present knowledge concerning the passive and/or active mechanisms employed by cercariae while escaping from their molluscan hosts is based primarily on studies carried out on the human-infecting species of schistosomes (see reviews by Probert and Erasmus, 1965; Cheng, 1967), although some information is also available on *Fasciola hepatica* (Kendall and McCullough, 1951). All these studies have been concerned with the processes that make possible successful escape and, hence, in a manner of speaking, govern compatibility. On the other hand, if some factor or factors within the mollusk interfere with cercarial escape and thus prevent the parasites from continuing their normal course of development, this factor or factors may contribute to host incompatibility. In seeking evidence for this hypothetical possibility, one should be cautious in distinguishing between consistent barriers, either structural or physiological, which prevent escape and in so doing endanger the perpetuation of the parasite species, and an occasional accidental arrest of the escape of a few cercariae. An example of the latter is the report by Pan (1965) that some escaping *Schistosoma mansoni* cercariae do become trapped in the loose vascular connective tissue of *Biomphalaria glabrata* and die. Yet, in the latter case the frequency of this event suggests that it is a normal occurrence. If all the cercariae were thus trapped, one could cite this as an example of incompatibility due to prevention of escape. It is of interest to note that if a similar phenomenon is not found in other mollusk–trematode associations, one might consider *B. glabrata* as being partially incompatible with *S. mansoni* as far as escape is concerned. Indeed, available information indicating the incompatibility of different strains of *B. glabrata* with strains of *S. mansoni* does suggest that this relationship is not completely free of factors favoring incompatibility, but we believe that structural barriers are not included among these factors. Faust and Hoffman (1934) asserted that a definite septum completely splits the planorbid visceral mass into a proximal and a distal portion and thus is a barrier for schistosome and other larval trematodes. In a study devoted to the anatomy of *Biomphalaria alexandrina* in relation to its infection with *Schistosoma mansoni*, Malek (1955) found that (1) no structural barriers exist in this or other planorbid snails to hinder the migration of daughter sporocysts and cercariae; (2) the circulatory system is an efficient vehicle in transporting the daughter sporocysts and cercariae during the normal route of movement of the snail's hemolymph; (3) some daughter sporocysts fail to reach the posterior (distal) organs, that is, the digestive gland and ovotestis, and settle in various organs among which are the kidney, the lung, around the rectum, on the prostate, uterus, and sperm duct. Our observations on escape of cercariae of *S. mansoni* from *B. glabrata* confirm those of Pan (1965) in that some of the cercariae become trapped, and we consider this a normal occurrence. The escape of the cercariae of *Schistosoma bovis* from its snail host *Bulinus* (*Physopsis*) *ugandae* was also investigated (Malek, 1969).

References

Barbosa, F. S. (1965). Ecology of the larval parasitic stages of *Schistosoma mansoni*. *Rev. Inst. Med. Trop. Sao Paulo* **7**, 112–120.

Barbosa, F. S., and Coelho, M. V. (1956). Pesquisa de immunodade adquirida homologa em *Australorbis glabratus*, nas infestacoes por *Schistosoma mansoni*. *Rev. Brasil. Malariol. Doencas Trop.* **8**, 49–56.

Barlow, C. H. (1925). The life cycle of the human intestinal fluke *Fasciolopsis buski* (Lankester). *Amer. J. Hyg., Monogr. Ser.* **4**, 1–98.

Beaver, P. C., Malek, E. A., and Little, M. D. (1964). Development of *Spirometra* and *Paragonimus* eggs in Harada-Mori cultures. *J. Parasitol.* **50**, 664–666.

Benex, J., and Lamy, L. (1959). Immobilisation des miracidiums de *Schistosoma mansoni* par extraits de planorbes. *Bull. Soc. Pathol. Exot.* **52**, 188–193.

Brooks, C. P. (1953). A comparative study of *Schistosoma mansoni* in *Tropcorbis havenensis* and *Australorbis glabratus*. *J. Parasitol.* **39**, 159–163.

Burns, W. C., and Pratt, I. (1953). The life cycle of *Metagonimoides oregonensis* Price (Trematoda: Heterophyidae). *J. Parasitol.* **39**, 60–67.

Cable, R. M. (1965). "Thereby hangs a tail." *J. Parasitol.* **51**, 3–12.

Campbell, W. C. (1961). Notes on the egg and miracidium of *Fascioloides magna* (Trematoda). *Trans. Amer. Microsc. Soc.* **80**, 308–319.

Campbell, W. C., and Todd, A. C. 1955. *In vitro* metamorphosis of the miracidium of *Fascioloides magna* (Bassi, 1875) Ward, 1917. *Trans. Amer. Microsc. Soc.* **74**, 225–228.

Cheng, T. C. (1961a). Description, life history, and developmental pattern of *Glypthelmins pennsylvaniensis* n. sp. (Trematoda: Brachycoeliidae), new parasite of frogs. *J. Parasitol.* **47**, 469–477.

Cheng, T. C. (1961b). Studies on the morphogenesis, development and germ cell cycle on the sporocysts and cercariae of *Glypthelmins pennsylvaniensis* Cheng, 1961 (Trematoda: Brachycoeliidae). *Proc. Pa. Acad. Sci.* **35**, 10–22.

Cheng, T. C. (1962). The effects of parasitism by the larvae of *Echinoparyphium* Dietz (Trematoda: Echinostomatidae) on the structure and glycogen deposition in the hepatopancreas of *Helisoma trivolvis* (Say). *Amer. Zool.* **2**, 513.

Cheng, T. C. (1963a). Histological and histochemical studies on the effects of parasitism of *Musculium partumeum* (Say) by the larvae of *Gorgodera amplicava* Looss. *Proc. Helminthol. Soc. Wash.* **30**, 101–107.

Cheng. T. C. (1963b). The effects of *Echinoparyphium* larvae on the structure of and glycogen deposition in the hepatopancreas of *Helisoma trivolvis* and glycogenesis in the parasite larvae. *Malacologia* **1**, 291–303.

Cheng. T. C. (1967). Marine molluscs as hosts for symbioses: With a review of known parasites of commercially important species. *Advan. Mar. Biol.* **5**, 1–424.

Cheng. T. C. (1968). The compatibility and incompatibility concept as related to trematodes and molluscs. *Pac. Sci.* **22**, 141–160.

Cheng, T. C. (1973). "General Parasitology." Academic Press, New York.

Cheng, T. C., and Cooperman, J. S. (1964). Studies on host-parasite relationships between larval trematodes and their hosts. V. The invasion of the reproductive system of *Helisoma trivolvis* by the sporocysts and cercariae of *Glypthelmins pennsylvaniensis*. *Trans. Amer. Microsc. Soc.* **83**, 12–23.

Cheng, T. C., and Lee, F. O. (1971). Glycose levels in the mollusc *Biomphalaria glabrata* infected with *Schistosoma mansoni*. *J. Invertebr. Pathol.* **18**, 395–399.

Cheng, T. C., and Snyder, R. W., Jr. (1962a). Studies on host-parasite relationships between larval trematodes and their hosts. I. A review. II. The utilization of the host's glycogen by the intramolluscan larvae of *Glypthelmins pennsylvaniensis* Cheng, and associated phenomena. *Trans. Amer. Microsc. Soc.* **81**, 209–228.

Cheng, T. C., and Snyder, R. W., Jr. (1962b). Studies on host-parasite relationships between larval trematodes and their hosts. III. Certain aspects of lipid metabolism in *Helisoma trivolvis* (Say) infected with the larvae of *Glypthelmins pennsylvaniensis* Cheng and related phenomena. *Trans. Amer. Microsc. Soc.* **81**, 327–331.

Cheng, T. C., and Snyder, R. W., Jr. (1963). Studies on host-parasite relationships between larval trematodes and their hosts. IV. A histochemical determination of glucose and its role in the metabolism of molluscan host and parasite. *Trans. Amer. Microsc. Soc.* **82**, 343–346.

Chernin, E. (1966). Transplantation of larval *Schistosoma mansoni* from infected to uninfected snails. *J. Parasitol.* **52**, 473–482.

Chernin, E. (1970). Behavioral responses of miracidia of *Schistosoma mansoni* and other trematodes to substances emitted by snails. *J. Parasitol.* **56**, 287–296.

Chernin, E. (1972). Penetrative activity of *Schistosoma mansoni* miracidia stimulated by exposure to snail-conditioned water. *J. Parasitol.* **58**, 209–212.

Chernin, E., and Dunavan, C. A. (1962). The influence of host-parasite dispersion upon the capacity of *Schistosoma mansoni* miracidia to infect *Australorbis glabratus*. *Amer. J. Trop. Med. Hyg.* **11**, 455–470.

Chowaniec, W. (1961). Influence of environment on the development of liver fluke, and the problem of superinvasion and reinvasion in the intermediate host. *Acta Parasitol. Pol.* **9**, 463–479.

Cort, W. W., and Ameel, D. J. (1944). Further studies on the development of the sporocyst stages of plagiorchiid trematodes. *J. Parasitol.* **30**, 37–50.

Cort, W. W., and Olivier, L. (1943). The development of the larval stages of *Plagiorchis muris* Tanabe, 1922, in the first intermediate host. *J. Parasitol.* **29**, 81–99.

Cort, W. W., Brackett, S., Olivier, L., and Nolf, L. O. (1945). Influence of larval trematode infections in snails on their intermediate host relations to the strigeid trematode, *Cotylurus flabelliformis* (Faust, 1917). *J. Parasitol.* **31**, 61–78.

Cort, W. W., Ameel, D. J., and Van der Woude, A. (1954). Germinal development in the sporocysts and rediae of the digenetic trematodes. *Exp. Parasitol.* **3**, 185–225.

Culbertson, J. T. (1941). "Immunity Against Animal Parasites". Columbia Univ. Press, New York.

Davenport, D. (1955). Specificity and behavior in symbioses. *Quart. Rev. Biol.* **30**, 29–46.

Davenport, D., Wright, C. A., and Causley, D. (1962). Technique for the study of the behavior of motile microorganisms. *Science* **135**, 1059–1060.

Dawes, B. (1959). Penetration of the liver-fluke, *Fasciola hepatica*, into the snail *Limnaea truncatula. Nature* (*London*) **184**, 1334–1335.

Dawes, B. (1960a). Penetration of *Fasciola gigantica* Cobbold, 1856 into snail hosts. *Nature* (*London*) **185**, 51–53.

Dawes, B. (1960b). The penetration of *Fasciola hepatica* into *Limnaea truncatula*, and of *F. gigantica* into *L. auricularia. Trans. Roy. Soc. Trop. Med. Hyg.* **54**, 9–10.

Dawes, B. (1960c). A study of the miracidium of *Fasciola hepatica* and an account of the mode of penetration of the sporocyst into *Lymnaea truncatula. In* "Libro Homenaje al Dr. Eduardo Caballero y Caballero," pp. 95–111. Inst. Politecnico Nacional, Escuela Nac. Cien. Biol., Mexico.

Erasmus, D. A. (1972). "The Biology of Trematodes." Arnold, London.

Etges, F. J., and Decker, C. L. (1963). Chemosensitivity of the miracidium of *Schistosoma mansoni* to *Australorbis glabratus* and other snails. *J. Parasitol.* **49**, 114–116.

Faust, E. C. (1934). The reactions of the miracidia of *Schistosoma japonicum* and *S. haematobium* in the presence of their intermediate hosts. *J. Parasitol.* **49**, 114–204.

Faust, E. C., and Hoffman, W. A. (1934). Studies on schistosomiasis mansoni in Puerto Rico. III. Biological studies. I. The extramammalian phases of the life cycle. *P. R. J. Pub. Health Trop. Med.* **10**, 1–97.

Faust, E. C., and Meleney, H. E. (1924). Studies on schistosomiasis japonica. *Amer. J. Hyg., Monogr. Ser.* **3**, 1–339.

Heyneman, D. (1966). Successful infection with larval echinostomes surgically implanted into the body cavity of the normal snail host. *Exp. Parasitol.* **18**, 220–223.

James, B. L. (1964). The life cycle of *Parvatrema homoeotecnum* sp. nov. (Trematoda: Digenea) and a review of the family Gymnophallidae Morozov, 1955. *Parasitology* **54**, 1–41.

James, B. L. (1965). The effects of parasitism by larval Digenea on the digestive gland of the intertidal prosobranch *Littorina saxatilis* (Olivi) subsp. *tenebrosa* (Montagu). *Parasitology* **55**, 93–115.

Kawashima, K., Tada, I., and Miyazaki, I. (1961a). Host preference of miracidia of *Paragonimus ohirai* Miyazaki, 1939 among three species of snails of the genus *Assiminea. Kyushu J. Med. Sci.* **12**, 99–106.

Kawashima, K., Tada, I., and Miyazaki, I. (1961b). Ecological analysis on the mechanism of the host preference of miracidia of *Paragonimus ohirai* Miyazaki, 1939 in natural condition. *Kyushu J. Med. Sci.* **12**, 143–151.

Kendall, S. B. (1949). Nutritional factors affecting the rate of development of *Fasciola hepatica* in *Limnaea truncatula*. *J. Helminthol.* **23**, 179–190.

Kendall, S. B. (1950). Snail hosts of *Fasciola hepatica* in Britain. *J. Helminthol.* **24**, 63–74.

Kendall, S. B. (1964). Some factors influencing the development and behavior of trematodes in their molluscan hosts. *In* "Host-Parasite Relationships in Invertebrate Hosts" (A. E. R. Taylor, ed.), pp. 51–73. Blackwell, Oxford.

Kendall, S. B., and McCullough, F. S. (1951). The emergence of the cercariae of *Fasciola hepatica* from the snail *Limnaea truncatula*. *J. Helminthol.* **25**, 77–92.

Kinoti, G. K. (1970). Observations on the infection of bulinid snails with *Schistosoma mattheei*. II. The mechanism of resistance to infection. *Parasitology* **62**, 161–170.

Kinoti, G. K. (1971). The attachment and penetration apparatus of the miracidium of *Schistosoma*. *J. Helminthol.* **45**, 229–235.

Kloetzel, K. (1958). Observacoes sobre o tropismo de miracidio do *Schistosoma mansoni* pelo molusco *Australorbis glabratus*. *Rev. Brazil. Biol.* **18**, 223–232.

Kloetzel, K. (1960). Novas observacoes sobre o tropismo de *Schistosoma mansoni* pelo molusco *Australorbis glabratus*. *Rev. Inst. Med. Trop. Sao Paulo* **2**, 341–346.

Krull, W. H., and Mapes, C. R. (1952). Studies on the biology of *Dicrocoelium dendriticum* (Rudolphi, 1819) Looss, 1899 (Trematoda: Dicrocoeliidae), including its relation to the intermediate host, *Cionella lubrica* (Miller). V. Notes on infections of *Dicrocoelium dendriticum* in *Cionella lubrica*. *Cornell Vet.* **42**, 339–351.

Lee, F. O., and Cheng, T. C. (1972). Incorporation of ^{59}Fe in the snail *Biomphalaria glabrata* parasitized by *Schistosoma mansoni*. *J. Parasitol.* **58**, 481–488.

Leigh, W. H. (1946). Experimental studies on the life cycle of *Glypthelmins quieta* (Stafford, 1900), a trematode of frogs. *Amer. Midl. Natur.* **35**, 460–483.

Lengy, J. (1962). Studies on *Schistosoma bovis* (Sonsino, 1876) in Israel. I. Larval stages from egg to cercaria. *Bull. Res. Counc. Isr., Sect. E* **10**, 1–36.

Lewert, R. M. (1958). Invasiveness of helminth larvae. *Rice Inst. Pam.* **45**, 97–113.

Lewert, R. M., and Lee, C. L. (1954). Studies on the passage of helminth larvae through host tissues. I. Histochemical studies of extracellular changes caused by penetrating larvae. II. Enzymatic activity of larvae *in vitro* and *in vivo*. *J. Infec. Dis.* **95**, 13–51.

Lewert, R. M., and Mandlowitz, S. (1963). Innate immunity to *Schistosoma mansoni* relative to the state of connective tissue. *Ann. N. Y. Acad. Sci.* **113**, 54–62.

Lie, K. J. (1963). The life history of *Echinostoma malayanum* Leiper, 1911. *Trop. Geogr. Med.* **15**, 17–24.

Lie, K. J., Basch, P. F., and Umathevy, T. (1966). Studies on Echinostomatidae (Trematoda) in Malaya. XII. Antagonism between two species of echinostome trematodes in the same lymnaeid snail. *J. Parasitol.* **52**, 454–457.

MacInnis, A. J. (1965). Responses of *Schistosoma mansoni* miracidia to chemical attractants. *J. Parasitol.* **51**, 731–746.

McQuay, R. M. (1952). Susceptibility of a Louisiana species of *Tropicorbis* to infection with *Schistosoma mansoni*. *Exp. Parasitol.* **1**, 184–188.

Maldonado, J. F., and Acosta-Matienzo, J. (1947). The development of *Schistosoma mansoni* in the snail intermediate host, *Australorbis glabratus*. *P. R. J. Pub. Health Trop. Med.* **22**, 331–373.

Malek, E. A. (1950). Susceptibility of the snail *Biomphalaria boissyi* to infection with certain strains of *Schistosoma mansoni*. *Amer. J. Trop. Med.* **30**, 887–894.

Malek, E. A. (1952). Morphology, bionomics and host-parasite relations of Planorbidae (Mollusca: Pulmonata). Ph. D. thesis, University of Michigan, Ann Arbor.

Malek, E. A. (1955). Anatomy of *Biomphalaria boissyi* as related to its infection with *Schistosoma mansoni*. *Amer. Midl. Natur.* **54**, 394–404.

Malek, E. A. (1958). Natural and experimental infection of some bulinid snails in the Sudan with *Schistosoma haematobium*. *Proc. 6th Int. Congr. Trop. Med. Malaria* **2**, 5–13.

Malek, E. A. (1959). Trematode infections in some domesticated animals in the Sudan. *J. Parasitol.* (Suppl.) **45**, 21.

Malek, E. A. (1961a). The ecology of schistosomiasis. *In* "Studies in Disease Ecology" (J. M. May ed.), pp. 261–327. Hafner Co., New York.

Malek, E. A. (1961b). The biology of mammalian and bird schistosomes. *Bull. Tulane Univ. Med. Faculty* **20**, 181–207.

Malek, E. A. (1961c). Some epidemiological and public health aspects of schistosomiasis. *Bull. Tulane Univ. Med. Faculty* **21**, 31–42.

Malek, E. A. (1967a). Experimental infection of several lymnaeid snails with *Heterobilharzia americana. J. Parasitol.* **53**, 700–702.

Malek, E. A. (1967b). Susceptibility of tropicorbid snails from Louisiana to infection with *Schistosoma mansoni. Amer. J. Trop. Med. Hyg.* **16**, 715–717.

Malek, E. A. (1969). Studies on bovine schistosomiasis in the Sudan. *Ann. Trop. Med. Parasitol.* **63**, 501–513.

Malek, E. A. (1970). Diseases of the respiratory system: Paragonimiasis (Endemic Haemoptysis). *In* "Diseases of Children in the Subtropics and Tropics". (D. B. Jelliffe, ed.), pp. 242–248. Edward Arnold Ltd., London.

Mathias, P. (1925). Recherches experimentales sur le cycle évolutif de quelques trématodes. *Bull. Biol. Fr. Belg.* **59**, 1–123.

Meade, T. G., and Pratt, I. (1966). Changes in the redia and metacercaria of *Metagonimoides oregonensis* Price, 1931, transplanted from infected to uninfected snails. *Proc. Helminthol. Soc. Wash.* **33**, 35–37.

Michelson, E. H. (1963). Development and specificity of miracidial immobilizing substances in extracts of the snail *Australorbis glabratus* exposed to various agents. *Ann. N. Y. Acad. Sci.* **113**, 486–491.

Michelson, E. H. (1964). Miracidia-immobilizing substances in extracts prepared from snails infected with *Schistosoma mansoni. Amer. J. Trop. Med. Hyg.* **13**, 36–42.

Neuhaus, W. (1953). Uber den chemischen Sinn der Miracidien von *Fasciola hepatica. Z. Parasitenk.* **15**, 476–490.

Newton, W. L. (1952). The comparative tissue reaction of two strains of *Australorbis glabratus* to infection with *Schistosoma mansoni. J. Parasitol.* **38**, 362–366.

Newton, W. L. (1954). Tissue response to *Schistosoma mansoni* in second generation snails from a cross between two strains of *Australorbis glabratus. J. Parasitol.* **40**, 1–4.

Nolf, L. O., and Cort, W. W. (1933). On immunity reactions of snails to the penetration of the cercariae of the strigeid trematode, *Cotylurus flabelliformis* (Faust). *J. Parasitol.* **20**, 38–48.

Pan, C. T. (1965). Studies on the host-parasite relationship between *Schistosoma mansoni* and the snail *Australorbis glabratus. Amer. J. Trop. Med. Hyg.* **14**, 931–976.

Probert, A. J., and Erasmus, D. A. (1965). The migration of *Cercaria X* Baylis (Strigeida) within the molluscan intermediate host *Lymnaea stagnalis. Parasitology* **55**, 77–92.

Rankin, J. S. (1944). A review of the trematode genus *Glypthelmins* Stafford, 1905, with an account of the life cycle of *G. quieta* (Stafford, 1900) Stafford, 1905. *Trans. Amer. Miscrosc. Soc.* **63**, 30–43.

Rees, F. G. (1931). Some observations and experiments on the biology of larval trematodes. *Parasitology* **23**, 428–440.

Rowan, W. B. (1956). The mode of hatching of the egg of *Fasciola hepatica. Exp. Parasitol.* **5**, 118–137.

Rowan, W. B. (1957). The mode of hatching of the eggs of *Fasciola hepatica*. II. Colloidal nature of the viscous cushion. *Exp. Parasitol.* **6**, 131–142.

Schell, S. C. (1961). Development of the mother and daughter sporocysts of *Haplometrana intestinalis* Lucker, a plagiorchioid trematode of frogs. *J. Parasitol.* **47**, 493–500.

Schell, S. C. (1962a). Development of the sporocyst generations of *Glypthelmins quieta*

Stafford, 1900) (Trematoda: Plagiorchioidea), a parasite of frogs, *J. Parasitol.* **48**, 387–394.

Schell, S. C. (1962b). The life history of *Telorchis bonnerensis* Waitz (Trematoda: Reniferidae), a parasite of the long-toed salamander, *Ambystoma macrodactylum* Baird. *Trans. Amer. Microsc. Soc.* **81**, 137–146.

Schreiber, F. G., and Schubert, M. (1949). Experimental infection of the snail *Australorbis glabratus* with the trematode *Schistosoma mansoni* and the production of cercariae. *J. Parasitol.* **35**, 364–366.

Shiff, C. J. (1968). Location of *Bulinus* (*Physopsis*) *globosus* by miracidia of *Schistosoma haematobium. J. Parasitol.* **54**, 1133–1140.

Shiff, C. J. (1969). Influence of light and depth on location of *Bulinus* (*Physopsis*) *globosus* by miracidia of *Schistosoma haematobium. J. Parasitol.* **55**, 108–110.

Shiff, C. J. and Kriel, R. L. (1970). A water-soluble product of *Bulinus* (*Physopsis*) *globosus* attractive to *Schistosoma haematobium* miracidia. J. Parasitol. **56**, 281–286.

Standen, O. D. (1951). The effects of temperature, light and salinity upon the hatching of the ova of *Schistosoma mansoni. Trans. Roy. Soc. Trop. Med. Hyg.* **45**, 225–241.

Sturrock, R. F. and Upatham, E. S. (1973). An investigation of the interactions of some factors influencing the infectivity of *Schistosoma mansoni* miracidia to *Biomphalaria glabrata. Int. J. Parasitol.* **3**, 35–41.

Sudds, R. H., Jr. (1960). Observations of schistosome miracidial behavior in the presence of normal and abnormal snail hosts and subsequent tissue studies of these hosts. *J. Elisha Mitchell Sci. Soc.* **76**, 121–133.

Timon-David, J. (1965). Infestation expérimentale d'une hélicelle par huit espèces de trématodes digénétiques appartenant à quatre familles différentes. *Ann. Parasitol. Hum. Comp.* **40**, 149–154.

Tubangui, M. A., and Pasco, A. M. (1933). The life history of the human intestinal fluke, *Euparyphium ilocanum* (Garrison, 1908). *Philipp. J. Sci.* **51**, 581–603.

Upatham, E. S. (1972). Effects of some physico-chemical factors on the infection of *Biomphalaria glabrata* (Say) by miracidia of *Schistosoma mansoni* Sambon in St. Lucia, West Indies. *J. Helminthol.* **46**, 307–315.

von Brand, T. (1952). "Chemical Physiology of Endoparasitic Animals." Academic Press, New York.

Wilson, R. A. (1968). The hatching mechanism of the egg of *Fasciola hepatica* L. *Parasitology* **58**, 79–89.

Wilson, R. A. (1971). Gland cells and secretions in the miracidium of *Fasciola hepatica. Parasitology* **63**, 225–231.

Wilson, R. A., Pullin, R., and Denison, J. (1971). An investigation of the mechanism of infection by digenetic trematodes: The penetration of the miracidium of *Fasciola hepatica* into its snail host *Lymnaea truncatula. Parasitology* **63**, 491–506.

Winfield, G. F. (1932). On immunity of snails infested with the sporocysts of the strigeid, *Cotylurus flabelliformis*, in the penetration of its cercariae. *J. Parasitol.* **19**, 130–133.

Wright, C. A. (1959). The application of paper chromatography to a taxonomic study in the molluscan genus *Lymnaea. J. Linn. Soc. London*, Zool. **44**, 222–237.

Wright, W. H. (1973). Geographical distribution of schistosomes and their intermediate hosts. *In* "Epidemiology and Control of Schistosomiasis (Bilharziasis)". (N. Ansari, ed.), pp. 32–249. S. Karger, Basel and University Park Press, Baltimore.

6 Mollusks as Hosts of Human-Infecting Nematodes

Terrestrial Snails and Slugs

The importance of terrestrial snails and slugs as intermediate and paratenic hosts for certain species of nematodes, although long recognized, has been overshadowed by the role of snails in the life cycles of medically and economically important trematodes. In recent years, however, land snails and slugs have received increased attention because of the roles of certain species in perpetuating important zoonoses in some parts of the world.

Chitwood and Chitwood (1937) distinguished the nematodes occurring in snails as belonging to six groups based on differences in life cycle patterns. Their scheme appears to be an appropriate way of classifying the nematodes found in snails. It is noted, however, that a few species cannot be fitted into any of the categories at this time because of lack of information pertaining to their life cycles. The six groups proposed by Chitwood and Chitwood are as follows.

1. Normally free-living (living upon decaying plant or animal matter) and plant parasitic nematodes that may pass through an animal's digestive tract uninjured. The association of these nematodes with snails is apparently facultative and purely accidental. Examples: *Leptodera foecunda* (= *Pelodytes hermaphroditius*) in slime of the slug *Arion empiricorum*; *Aphelencus parietinus*, *Rhabditis dolichura*, and *Tylenchus lameliformis* in feces of *Helix pomatia* and in the intestines of other species of terrestrial snails.

2. Obligatorily parasitic nematodes living in the host's digestive tract. Examples: members of the families Angiostomidae and Cosmocercidae.

Specifically, *Leptodera angiostoma* (= *Angiostoma limacis*) in the intestines of *Limax rufus* and *Arion ater*; *Cosmocercoides* spp. in the intestines of *Opeas goodalli* and *Deroceras agreste* and with larvae in eggs of the latter slug.

3. Nematodes with parasitic larvae occurring in the foot muscles of the host and with a free-living adult stage. Example: *Alloionema appendiculata* in *Arion ater*.

4. Adult nematodes living in the genital organs of the host. Example: *Leptodera flexilis* in *Limax* sp.

5. Agamic nematodes and nematomorphs that live in the lung and body spaces of the host and that leave the host upon reaching maturity to lead a free-living existence. Examples: *Mermis nigrescens* in *Limax agrestis*; *Mermis albicans* in *Succinea putris*.

6. Parasitic nematodes of vertebrates, the larvae of which occur in snails. Examples: *Mullerius capillaris*, a parasite of sheep with larvae reported from *Limax cinereus*, *L. flavus*, *Deroceras agreste*, *Arion circumscriptus*, *A. hortensis*, *Helix pomatia*, *Hygromia bispida*, *Monacha umbrosa*, and *Cepaea hortensis* (Hobmaier and Hobmaier, 1935); *Aeleurostrongylus abstrusus* and *Anafilaroides rostratus*, which are both lung parasites of cats and utilize the snails *Bradybaena similaris* and *Subulina octona* as intermediate hosts (Alicata, 1947; Ash, 1962).

A recently discovered parasitic disease of man, meningoencephalitic angiostrongylosis, or parasitic meningoencephalitis,* caused by the rat lung-worm *Angiostrongylus cantonensis*, is known to be transmitted by a number of gastropods (Table 6-1). Among these, the giant African snail, *Achatina fulica*, is believed to be the most important carrier. In addition, *Bradybaena similaris* and *Subulina octona* are commonly infected in the Pacific Basin. In addition to the disease in man caused by *A. cantonensis*, another type of angiostrongylosis, designated as abdominal angiostrongylosis, has been found in Costa Rica (Morera and Céspedes, 1971a,b; Céspedes *et al.*, 1967; Morera, 1967). This disease is caused by *A. costaricensis*.

Human meningoencephalitic angiostrongylosis has been reported from a number of islands in the Pacific, including Hawaii, Tahiti, the New Hebrides Islands, the Loyalty Islands, and New Caledonia. Cases have also been reported in Vietnam, Thailand, Sumatra, the Philippines and Taiwan. For a detailed review of the life cycle of *Angiostrongylus cantonensis* and a discussion of how humans become infected, see Alicata and Jindrak (1970). In

---

*The designation of "parasitic meningoencephalitis" is not the preferred one since other parasites, such as *Paragonimus westermani*, can also cause eosinophilic meningoencephalitis in man.

TABLE 6-1

Molluscan Intermediate Hosts for *Angiostrongylus cantonensis*

Molluscan host[a]	Geographic distribution
Terrestrial snails	
Achatina fulica (N,	Pacific Islands, Malaysia, Thailand
Allopeas kyotoensis (E)	
Bradybaena similaris (N)	Pacific Islands
Euglandina rosea (E)	
Euhadra peliomphala (E)	
Euhadra quaesita (E)	
Fruticicola despecta sieboldiana (E)	
Helicina orbiculata (E)	
Macrochlamys resplendens (N)	Malaysia
Mesodon thyroidus (E)	
Opeas javanicum (N)	Pacific Islands
Pupina complanata (N)	Pacific Islands
Subulina octona (N)	Pacific Islands
Zonitoides arboreus (E)	
Aquatic snails	
Bellamya ingallsiana (N)	Malaysia
Biomphalaria glabrata (E)	
Biomphalaria heliophila (E)	
Biomphalaria obstructa (E)	
Biomphalaria pallida (E)	
Biomphalaria pfeifferi (E)	
Biomphalaria straminea (E)	
Biomphalaria tenagophila (E)	
Bulinus forskalii (E)	
Bulinus globosus (E)	
Bulinus senegalensis (E)	
Bulinus tropicus (E)	
Bulinus truncatus (E)	
Cipangopaludina chinensis (N)	Taiwan
Drepanotrema simmonsi (E)	
Ferrissia tenuis (E)	
Balba viridis (E)	
Helisoma sp. (E)	
Indoplanorbis exustus (N)	Malaysia
Lymnaea swinhoe (E)	
Lymnaea volutata (E)	
Marisa cornuarietis (E)	
Physa sp. (E)	
Physa acuta (E)	
Pila ampullacea (N)	Thailand
Pila angelica (E)	
Pila gracilis (N)	Thailand
Pila polita (N)	Thailand

TABLE 6-1 (continued)

Molluscan host[a]	Geographic distribution
Aquatic snails (continued)	
Pila scutata (N)	Malaysia
Pila turbinis (N)	Thailand
Plesiophysa hubendicki (E)	
Segmentina hemisphaerula (E)	
Sinotaia quadrata (E)	
Sinotiana martensiana (N)	Thailand
Terrestrial slugs	
Deroceras laeve (N)	Pacific Islands
Deroceras reticulatum (E)	
Girasia peguensis (N)	Malaysia
Microparmarion malayanus (N)	Malaysia
Limax flavus (E)	
Limas maximus (E)	
Vaginulus plebeius (N)	Pacific Islands
Veronicella alte (N)	Pacific Islands, Malaysia

[a]N = natural infections; E = experimental infections.

brief, the most common method by which humans become infected is via the intentional or accidental ingestion of mollusks harboring the infective third-stage larvae of this parasite.

In Louisiana, a wide range of local land snails and slugs can be infected with *A. cantonensis*. Infective stage larvae have been recovered from the following terrestrial snails: *Bradybaena similaris, Mesodon thyroidus, Helicina orbiculata*, and *Euglandina rosea*. In addition, the slugs *Limax flavus* and *Deroceras laeve* can also serve as intermediate hosts. Inside the snail or slug the larvae of *A. cantonensis* are found encapsulated by the mollusk's connective tissue fibers (see Chapter 9).

Two common methods for detecting and isolating nematode larvae, including those of *A. cantonensis*, in mollusks are (1) by pressing the molluscan host between two glass plates and examining the preparation with a dissection microscope, and (2) by artificial digestion of the macerated molluscan tissue in 100 ml of 1% HCl containing 0.5 g of pepsin followed by filtering and sedimenting the digest. Four layers of cotton surgical gauze provide adequate filteration. The first method is most convenient in the case of small snails and slugs, while the second method can be employed for both small (*Subulina octona, Bradybaena similaris*) and large (*Achatina fulica*, veronicellid slugs) mollusks.

Human abdominal angiostrongylosis, characterized by eosinophilia, prolonged fever, anorexia, abdominal pain, vomiting, intestinal granulomas, and occasionally bowl obstruction and death, is contracted when individuals accidentally ingest the molluscan intermediate host, the slug *Vaginulus plebeius. A. costaricensis* is normally a parasite of wild rodents, especially the cotton rat, *Sigmodon hispidus*, and the common rat, *Rattus rattus*. In addition, it has been found in *Liomys adsperus*, *Oryzomys fulvescens*, and *Zygodontomys microtimus* in Panama (Tesh *et al.*, 1973). When humans ingest slugs harboring the infective third-stage larvae, this nematode localizes in the mesenteric arteries. The occurrence of larvae in slugs can be detected by employing the same methods as for *A. cantonensis* larvae. For a discussion of the molluscan host of *A. costaricensis*, see Morera and Ash (1970).

In addition of *A. cantonensis* and *A. costaricensis*, a third species, *A. vasorum*, is of potential importance to human health. This nematode is a parasite of carnivores in nature and utilizes slugs, *Arion rufus*, as the intermediate host. However, according to Eckert and Lammler (1972), a number of other species of mollusks are suitable as intermediate hosts under experimental conditions. These include the slugs *Deroceras agreste* and *D. laeve*, the terrestrial snail *Vitrea diaphana*, and the freshwater snails *Anisus leucostomus* and *Lymnaea tomentosa*.

Angiostrongylus vasorum does not include a cerebral migration phase in its development in its normal definitive hosts, and hence it is unlikely that it would produce a disease in the central nervous system of humans if third-stage larvae are ingested accidentally. This parasite has been reported from dogs and foxes in Europe and Asia, from dogs in Uganda, Australia, and South America, and from *Tayra barbara senex* in Mexico.

Freshwater Snails

Chitwood and Chitwood (1937) have listed several species of nematodes that parasitize freshwater snails and have placed them in Group 5; that is, they live as agamic forms in the lungs and body spaces of mollusks and probably leave them upon reaching sexual maturity. An example of this category of nematodes includes *Daubaylia potomaca*, a parasite of *Helisoma trivolvis*, first reported by Chitwood and Chitwood (1934) in snails collected along the Potomac River in Washington, D.C., and later found by Chernin *et al.* (1960) in *Helisoma trivolvis* as well as in *H. campanulatum* in Michigan. Chernin *et al.* have been able to infect *Biomphalaria glabrata*, the most common intermediate host for *Schistosoma mansoni*, with this nematode (p. 138). Although the complete life cycle of *D. potomaca* is not known, eggs, larvae, and adult male and female worms have been found in the deep tissues of *Helisoma*.

It is of interest to note that *Biomphalaria glabrata* is a suitable experimental intermediate host for *Angiostrongylus cantonensis* (Richards and Merritt, 1967).

In addition to larval nematodes, several species of larval nematomorphs have been reported from freshwater snails. For example, *Gordius aquaticus* have been reported from *Lymnaea* sp., *L. vulgaris*, and *L. ovata*; *Gordius villoti* has been reported from *Lymnaea ovata*; *Paragordius tricuspidatus* has been found in *Lymnaea ovata*; and *Parachordodes tolosanus* has been found in *Lymnaea* sp. Although these nematomorphs are of no great medical or economic importance, they are being briefly mentioned here since they may be encountered by those examining freshwater snails for larval nematodes. For a review of the biology of nematomorphs, see Cheng (1973a).

Marine Mollusks

The role of marine mollusks as transmitters of nematodes of public health importance is essentially unexplored. However, as the result of the work of Cobb (1930), the larva of a species of *Porrocaecum** (Fig. 6-1) is

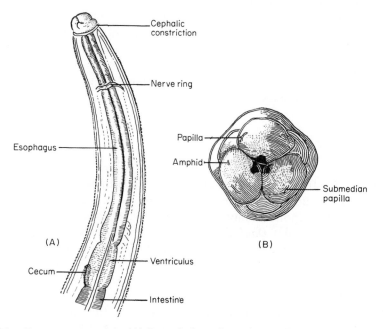

Fig. 6-1. *Porrocaecum pectinis.* (A) Lateral view of anterior portion of larva. (B) Face on view of anterior terminal of larva. Redrawn after Cobb (1930).

*Cobb (1930) described this nematode as *Paranisakis pectinis.* It is now known as *Porrocaeum pectinis.*

known to occur in the scallop *Aequipecten*. This parasite, originally found at Beaufort, North Carolina, has since been also reported from *Aequipecten maximus* by Gutsell (1930), from *A. gibbus* by Hutton (1964), and from *A. irradians* by Cheng (1973b) off the coasts of North Carolina, South Carolina, and Florida. Larval *Porrocaecum* (along with the larvae of *Anisakis, Phocanema*, and *Contracaecum*) are known to cause gastric granuloma formation in humans if accidentally ingested in inadequately cooked food.

Host—Parasite Relationships

Considerably more is known about the relationship between mollusks and trematodes than between mollusks and nematodes. It is generally assumed that the larval nematodes that utilize gastropods as intermediate hosts enter these hosts via the oral route. This, however, need not always be the case. For example, Cheng and Alicata (1965) have studied the modes of infection of *Achatina fulica* with *Angiostrongylus cantonensis*. One group of snails was infected orally while the second group was infected by placing the larvae on the extended foot of each snail. By comparing the percentages of third-stage larvae of the nematode recovered from the foot musculature it was ascertained that both methods of infection were possible and equally as efficient. Under natural conditions both methods of infection are believed to occur. In addition, the cannibalistic habits of *A. fulica* are believed to be responsible for the transmission of nematode larvae from one snail to another.

In the case of pelecypods, very often the location of the larval nematode within the molluscan host gives some idea of the route of entry. In the case of *Porrocaecum* in scallops, for example, the parasite is usually found embedded in the adductor muscle, and it is generally assumed that the infective larva burrows into the muscle after having been swept into the mantle cavity by the incurrent resulting from the bivalve's pumping action. On the other hand, larval nematodes occurring in the lumen of the mollusk's digestive tract or embedded in the connective tissue that envelopes the digestive tract are believed to have arrived at these sites after being ingested. In the case of those in the connective tissue mentioned, they have arrived therein by burrowing through the wall of the alimentary tract.

As a rule, larval nematodes occurring in the tissues of mollusks are encapsulated (p. 192), and the capsule is usually comprised of host cells, usually leukocytes. Furthermore, there is some evidence that the chemotactic agent that attracts the host's reaction cells is the nematode's molting fluid, at least in part (Cheng, 1966). In the case of the third-stage larva of *Angiostrongylus cantonensis* encapsulated in the musculature of *Achatina fulica*, the capsule is comprised of host myofibers that have become fused and infiltrating leukocytes (Fig. 6-2) (Cheng and Rifkin, 1970).

Since encapsulated nematode larvae are essentially arrested, their entrance into the definitive or paratenic host is dependent upon the ingestion of the molluscan host in which they occur by the subsequent host. This situation is exemplified by *A. cantonensis*.

Nothing is known at this time about a variety of physiological and biochemical interactions that must occur within mollusks harboring nematode parasites. For example, although understood to some degree in the case of nematodes in mammals (Rogers, 1966), the host-provided stimulus for molting on the part of parasite in mollusks has not yet been explored. Similarly, the nutritional requirements of intramolluscan nematode larvae have not been investigated.

It is of interest to note that recently Brockelman and Jackson (1972) have reported that an inhibitor occurring in *Helix aspersa* prevents the maturation of the third-stage larva of *Rhabditis manpasi*. Under natural conditions this nematode, which inhabits the mantle cavity of its snail host, only attains the third larval stage. However, it can develop to maturity if cultured on sterile rabbit kidney slices supported by dextrose agar slants. *R. maupasi* will also develop to maturity in a liquid medium containing raw rabbit extract. If raw

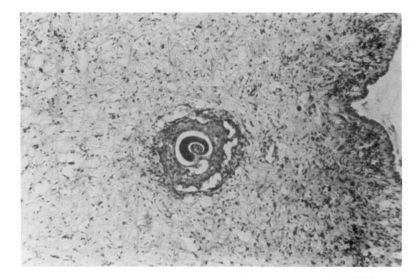

Fig. 6-2. *Angiostrongylus cantonensis.* Photomicrograph of third-stage larva in the foot of *Achatina fulica* encapsulated by a cyst comprised of fused myofibers infiltrated by leukocytes (× 45).

H. aspersa extract is added to either culture medium, development of the nematode beyond the third stage is suppressed. The inhibitory substance, which has not yet been identified, is apparently proteinaceous since its activity is destroyed after digestion by bacteria or with trypsin or chymotrypsin. If the substance is inactivated, the nematode will reach maturity and reproduce in snail extracts. This interesting discovery serves as an example of a development-inhibiting substance of host origin.

References

Alicata, J. E. (1947). Parasites and parasitic diseases of domestic animals in the Hawaiian Islands. *Paci. Sci.* 1, 69–84.

Alicata, J. E., and Jindrak, K. (1970). "Angiostrongylosis in the Pacific and Southeast Asia." Thomas, Springfield, Illinois.

Ash, L. R. (1962). Helminth parasites of dogs and cats in Hawaii. *J. Parasitol.* **48**, 63–65.

Brockelman, C. R., and Jackson, G. J. (1972). Axenic cultivation of the nematode, *Rhabditis maupasi*, and its inhibition with a factor from the snail host, *Helix aspersa. Program. Abstr., 47th Annu. Meet, Amer. Soc. Parasitol.* p. 73.

Céspedes, R., Salas, J., Mekbel, S., Troper, L., Mullner, F., and Morera, P. (1967). Granulomas entéricos y linfaticos con intensa eosinophilia tisular producidos por un estrongilideo (Strongylata) 1. Patalogia. *Acta Médica Cost.* **10**, 235–255.

Cheng, T. C. (1966). Perivascular leucocytosis and other types of cellular reactions in the oyster Crassostrea virginica experimentally infected with the nematode *Angiostrongylus cantonensis. J. Invertebr. Pathol.*, **8**, 52–58.

Cheng, T. C. (1973a). "General Parasitology." Academic Press, New York.

Cheng, T. C. (1973b). Human parasites transmissible by seafood and related problems. *In* "Microbiological Quality of Seafoods" (C. O. Chichester and H. Graham, eds.), pp. 163–189. Academic Press, New York.

Cheng, T. C., and Alicata, J. E. (1965). On the modes of infection of *Achatina fulica* by the larvae of *Angiostrongylus cantonensis. Malacologia* **2**, 267–274.

Cheng, T. C., and Rifkin, E. (1970). Cellular reactions in marine molluscs in response to helminth parasitism. *In* "A Symposium on Diseases of Fishes and Shellfishes" (S. F. Snieszko, ed), Spec. Publ. No. 5, *Amer. Fisher. Soc.*, pp. 443–496. Washington, D.C.

Chernin, E., Michelson, E. H., and Augustine, D. L. (1960). *Daubaylia potomaca*, a nematode parasite of *Helisoma trivolvis*, transmissible to *Australorbis glabratus. J. Parasitol.* **46**, 599–607.

Chitwood, B. G., and Chitwood, M. B. (1934). *Daubaylia potomaca* n. sp., a nematode parasite of snails, with a note on other nemas associated with molluscs. *Proc. Helminthol. Soc. Wash.* **1**, 8–9.

Chitwood, B. G. and Chitwood, M. B. (1937). Snails as hosts and carriers of nematodes and nematomorpha. *Nautilus* **50**, 130–135.

Cobb, N. A. (1930). A nemic parasite of *Pecten. J. Parasitol.* **17**, 104–105.

Eckert, J., and Lammler, G. (1972). Angiostrongylose bei Mensch und Tier. *Z. Parasitenk.* **39**, 303–322.

Gutsell, J. S. (1930). Natural history of the bay scallop. *Bull. U.S. Fish. Bur.* **46**, 569–631.

Hobmaier, A., and Hobmaier, M. (1935). Intermediate hosts of *Aeleurostrongylus abstrusus* of cat. *Proc. Soc. Exp. Biol. Med.* **32**, 1641–1647.

Hutton, R. F. (1964). A second list of parasites from marine and coastal animals of Florida. *Trans. Amer. Microsc. Soc.* **83**, 439–447.

Morera, P. (1967). Granulomas entéricos y limfáticos con intensa eosinofilia tisular producidos por un estrongilideo. 2. Aspecto parasitologico. *Acta Médica Cost.* **10**, 257–265.

Morera, P., and Ash, L. R. (1970). Investigación del hesped intermediario de *Angiostrongylus costaricensis* (Morera y Céspedes, 1971). *Bol. Chileno Parasitol.* **25**, 135.

Morera, P., and Céspedes, R. (1971a). *Angiostrongylus costaricensis* n. sp. (Nematoda: Metastrongyloidea), a new lungworm occurring in man in Costa Rica. *Rev. Biol. Trop.* **18**, 173–185.

Morera, P. and Céspedes, R. (1971b). Angiostrongylosis abdominal. *Acta Médica Cost.* **14**, 159–173.

Richards, C. S., and Merritt, J. W. (1967). Studies on *Angiostrongylus cantonensis* in molluscan intermediate hosts. *J. Parasitol.* **53**, 382–388.

Rogers, W. P. (1966). Exsheathment and hatching mechanisms in helminths. *In* "The Biology of Parasites" (E. J. L. Soulsby, ed.), pp. 33–39. Academic Press, New York.

Tesh, R. B., Ackerman, L. J., Dietz, W. H., and Williams, J. A. (1973). *Angiostrongylus costaricensis* in Panama: Prevalence and pathologic findings in wild rodents infected with the parasite. *Amer. J. Trop. Med. Hyg.* **22**, 348–356.

7 Pathogens of Medically and Economically Important Mollusks

Chapters 5 and 6 have been concerned with the role of mollusks as intermediate hosts for helminth parasites, which eventually develop to sexual maturity within a vertebrate definitive host. Because of the nature of this book, the emphasis has been placed on those species of helminths that, as adults, are parasites of humans. Despite this emphasis, one should keep in mind that the larval stages of helminths are true parasites of mollusks, and some of them are equally as pathogenic to the mollusk as they are to the human host. Pathologic alterations in mollusks associated with parasitic infections are discussed in Chapter 10 and to some extent in Chapter 11. Furthermore, as pointed out on page 220, the pathogenicity of certain larval helminths, such as *Schistosoma mansoni*, can have severe implications as far as the health of the molluscan host is concerned, including drastic reductions in its fecundity and longevity. Thus, the parasites considered in the two previous chapters should also be considered as pathogens of their molluscan hosts, although the degree of pathogenicity varies and in most instances remains undetermined.

If the larval helminths mentioned in the previous chapters are pathogens of their molluscan hosts, then why is the material comprising this chapter treated separately? There are two reasons: (1) the emphasis in Chapters 5 and 6 is on the role of mollusks as intermediate hosts of parasites, and (2) interest in organisms pathogenic to medically and economically important mollusks stems from their potential role as biological control agents and as killers of shellfish, respectively. Therefore, those parasites that cause sublethal and/or chronic diseases in their molluscan hosts commonly have not been considered "pathogens" in invertebrate pathology. This, of course, is an artificial separation of "pathogen" from "parasite," although not all parasites, especially metazoan parasites, cause recognizable disease, especially if present in small numbers (Cheng, 1973).

In view of the distinct practical rationales for studying pathogens of medically and economically important mollusks, it appears more appropriate to discuss the known pathogens of these two categories of mollusks separately.

Pathogens of Medically Important Mollusks

The literature pertaining to potential pathogens, parasites, and predators as possible biological control agents for medically important mollusks has been reviewed by Michelson (1957) and Malek (1958) and very little has been added to date.

VIRUSES

Although some undoubtedly exist, no virus has yet been identified or isolated from any species of medically important mollusk. The major reason for this rests with the fact that the successful establishment of cell lines from these mollusks, or all mollusks for that matter, has not yet been achieved (Chapter 11). Since viruses are intracellular, obligatory parasites of their hosts' cells, molluscan virology has yet to become a reality.

BACTERIA

A few species of bacteria have been reported from freshwater gastropods of medical importance. Berry (1949) has reported a gram-negative bacterium that caused an epizootic with high mortality in laboratory colonies of *Biomphalaria glabrata*, *B. pfeifferi*, and *Physopsis africana*. The disease was characterized by swelling of the tentacular tips, followed by necrosis, hemorrhage, and neuromuscular involvements. This bacterium, unfortunately, has not been maintained in culture.

Dias (1953, 1954, 1955) has reported a gram-variable bacterium from the ovotestis of *Biomphalaria glabrata*. This bacterium was originally designated BET (*bacilo de esporo terminal*) and later (Cruz and Dias, 1953) named it *Bacillus pinottii*. Dias has described it as being saprophytic and as developing a high degree of virulence after repeated serial passage in *B. glabrata*. Although Texera and Scorza (1954) in Venezuela and Dias and Dawood (1955) in Egypt have reported killing *B. glabrata* in the field and in the laboratory with *B. pinottii*, Tripp (1961), as the result of carefully controlled laboratory experiments involving *B. pinottii* from Dias's laboratory, has reported that this bacterium is apparently nonpathogenic to *B. glabrata*.

Another bacterium that may be of value from the standpoint of biological control is the species of *Mycobacterium* reported by Michelson (1961) from *Helisoma anceps*. This acid-fast bacillus is pathogenic and has been successfully maintained in pure culture. The isolation and cultivation methods employed by Michelson are presented in detail since they could be applied by those interested in isolating potential bacterial pathogens of mollusks.

The entire snail (minus the alimentary tract), or selected tissues, is homogenized in a sterile mortar containing 2 ml of sterile distilled water, and the homogenate is transferred to a sterile test tube to which is added 2 ml of 3% HCl plus a drop of bromocresol purple indicator. The contents of the tube are mixed thoroughly and permitted to stand at room temperature (25°C) for 2 hours, after which 3% NaOH is added until the mixture becomes slightly alkaline. It is then centrifuged at 1500 rpm for 15 minutes, and the sediment is used to inoculate tubes of Petragnani and Dorset's egg media. The culture tubes are maintained at 25°C and 37°C for 30 days, and those showing bacterial growth may be stored at 5°C for 30 days or are routinely transferred.

TABLE 7-1

Transmission of the Snail Acid-Fast Bacillus to Various Species of Gastropods[a]

Molluscan species	Method of exposure	Infection rate	Day infection first noted
Helisoma anceps	Environmental	11/20	15
Helisoma trivolvis	Stab wound[b]	4/10	6
Helisoma trivolvis fallax	Environmental	7/20	17
Helisoma trivolvis fallax	Environmental	4/10	28
Helisoma trivolvis fallax	Stab wound[b]	3/5	10
Biomphalaria glabrata	Infected snails	7/30	31
Biomphalaria glabrata	Environmental	5/20	20
Biomphalaria glabrata	Stab wound[b]	2/5	4
Biomphalaria glabrata	Inoculation[b]	12/20	6
Bulinus truncatus	Environmental	2/20	25
Biomphalaria pfeifferi	Environmental	1/10	43
Biomphalaria pfeifferi	Stab wound[b]	3/5	12
Biomphalaria pfeifferi	Inoculation[b]	4/10	5

[a]After Michelson (1961).

[b]In stab wound and inoculation infections the formation of a lesion in a tissue other than the site of infection was required for the snail to be considered as being infected.

Michelson was successful in infecting a percentage of several species of snails of the family Planorbidae, including *Biomphalaria glabrata* and *B. pfeifferi*, which are suitable intermediate hosts of *Schistosoma mansoni* and *Bulinus truncatus*, which is a host of *S. haematobium* (Table 5-1). Although some of the successful infections were transmitted by stab wounds and inoculation, which are obviously impractical from the standpoint of biological control, it is of interest to note that Michelson was successful in transmitting this pathogenic mycobacterium by dispersing it in the aquatic environment (Table 7-1). Infected snails portray prominent clubbing of the tentacular tips (Fig. 7-1), generally accompanied by a localized increase in pigmentation. Histologically, the bacteria can be observed intracellularly within amoebocytes (Fig. 7-2), which eventually accumulate in small aggregates and are subsequently walled off by fibroblasts to form tubercles (Fig. 7-3). Mortality data for infected snails are not available.

FUNGI

Although no pathogenic fungus has yet been cultured from a medically important species of mollusk, it is of interest to note that Malek (1952) has reported that a species belonging to the Fungi Imperfecti will kill both *Biomphalaria boissyi* and *Bulinus truncatus* in laboratory aquaria. In addition to this report of a pathogenic fungus, Cowper (1946) has observed a species of *Catenaria* invading and destroying the egg masses of *Biomphalaria glab-*

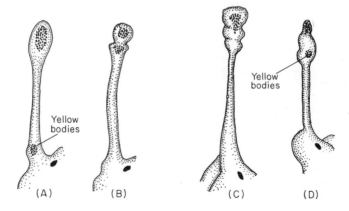

Fig. 7-1. Drawings of tentacles of snails infected with *Mycobacterium*. (A) and (B) Tentacles of *Biomphalaria glabrata*. (C) and (D) Tentacles of *Helisoma anceps*. Note the enlargement of the tips of the tentacles and the accumulation of pigment. Yellow bodies are present in A and D. Redrawn after Michelson (1961).

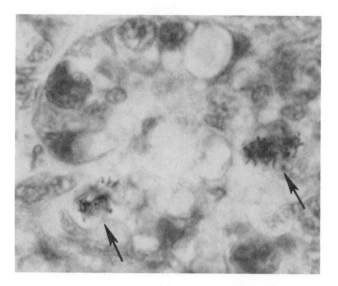

Fig. 7-2. Photomicrograph of section through the digestive gland of *Helisoma anceps* showing phagocytic leukocytes enclosing acid-fast bacilli. The snail had been exposed to the bacteria 7 days prior to sectioning (carbol fuchsin and Janus green) (× 1600). After Michelson (1961).

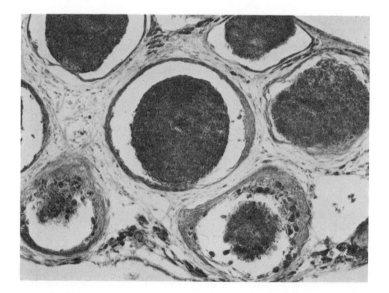

Fig. 7-3. Photomicrograph of a section through the mantle collar of *Helisoma anceps* showing well-defined tubercules filled with masses of acid-fast bacilli. The snail was infected 4 months prior to sectioning (carbol fuchsin and acid hemalum) (× 260). After Michelson (1961).

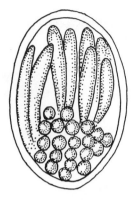

Fig. 7-4. *Pfeifferinella ellipsoides.* Oocyst from the digestive gland of *Planorbis corneus.* It measures 13–15 μm long. **Redrawn** after Wasielewski (1904).

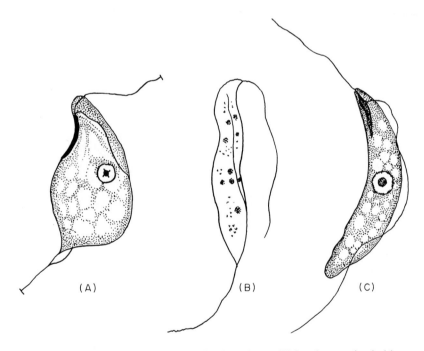

Fig. 7-5. *Cryptobia helicis.* (A) Fixed and stained specimen. (B) Specimen stained with neutral red. (C) Stained specimen. Parts A and B redrawn after Kozloff (1948); C redrawn after Bělař (1920).

rata (*Planorbis guadeloupensis*), and Michelson (1957) has reported that a personal communication from De Meillon informed him that an unidentified fungus has been observed to invade the tissues of unhatched, embryonic *Physopsis* in the laboratory. De Meillon is of the opinion that this fungus originated from the hay and grass infusions used to feed the snails.

PROTOZOA

Although a number of ciliates have been reported associated with freshwater gastropods (Leidy, 1877, De Leon, 1919; van den Berghe, 1934; Jarocki, 1935; Kay, 1946), none of these appear to be parasites, or at least pathogens, and hence hold little promise as biological control agents. Kudo (1954), however, has reported the occurrence of a coccidian, *Pfeifferinella ellipsoides* (Fig. 7-4), which appears to be a true parasite, in the digestive gland of the pulmonate *Planorbarius corneus*. It does not appear to be pathogenic, although this remains to be tested.

Hollande and Chabelard (1953) have reported heavy mortalities among laboratory colonies of *Lymnaea*, *Bithynia*, *Biomphalaria*, and *Bulinus* due to a flagellate, *Dimoeriopsis destructor*, and have suggested that this protozoan may hold promise as a biological control agent. Another flagellate, *Cryptobia* (= *Trypanoplasma*) *isidorae*, has been reported from the freshwater pulmonate *Isidora tropica* by Fantham (1923), but its pathogenicity is unknown. Another species of *Cryptobia*, *C. helicis* (Fig. 7-5), is known, to occur in the reproductive organ of various species of pulmonate snails including *Triodopsis albolabris*, *T. tridentata*, *Anguispira alternata*, *Helix aspersa*, and *Monadenia fidelis*. This flagellate is apparently nonpathogenic.

Among amoebae, Richards (1968) has reported the occurrence of two species, *Hartmannella biparia* (Fig. 7-6) and *H. quadriparia* (Fig. 7-7), in *Bulinus globosus* and *Biomphalaria pallida*, respectively. Because of the general structure of these amoebae, the occurrence of contractile vacuoles (which as a rule are not present in parasitic amoebae), and their sporadic occurrence in aquaria, Richards has concluded that these are free-living amoebae that have invaded the gastropods as facultative parasites.

Both *H. biparia* and *H. quadriparia* cause pathologic reactions within their hosts. Specifically, *H. biparia* occur as intracellular parasites with the host's amoebocytes, which, in turn, are surrounded by fibroblasts to form nodules. These nodules, each enclosing several infected ameobocytes, occur throughout the digestive tract, digestive gland, heart, kidney, reproductive system, and mantle. Parasitized snails may become moribund, and the presence of *H. biparia* is believed to affect the growth and reproduction of *Bulinus globosus*.

H. quadriparia also occurs within amoebocytes within nodules, and

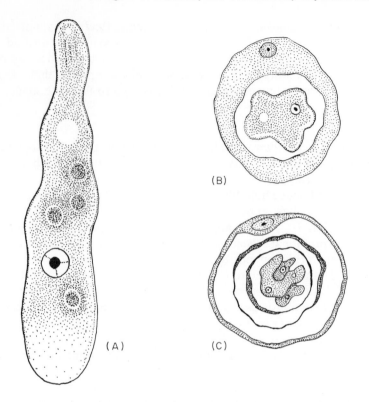

Fig. 7-6. *Hartmannella biparia.* (A) Drawing of motile trophozoite recently emerged from mollusk showing four refractile granules. (B) Single active amoeba in host cell. (C) Two active amoebae enclosed by two membranes within host cell. All parts redrawn after Richards (1968).

these nodules occur in the foot, tentacles, along the edge of the mantle collar, and in tissues lining the mantle cavity. Infected *Biomphalaria pallida* have been reported to be commonly sluggish and pale and may become moribund. Again, the growth and reproduction of infected snails are believed to be interfered with.

Richards has attempted to infect a number of other species of gastropods through exposure to amoebae. His results are summarized in Table 7-2. Furthermore, both species of amoebae could be cultured for several months in medium NCTC 109 diluted tenfold with autoclaved tap water.

Whether these two species of *Hartmannella* are of any use as biological control agents remains to be tested.

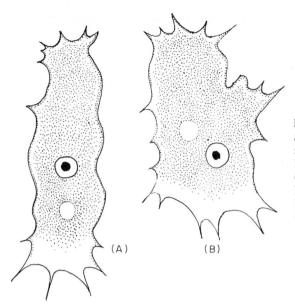

Fig. 7-7. *Hartmannella quadriparia.* (A) Trophozoite recently escaped from host that had been dissected in water. (B) Another trophozoite that had escaped from a dissected host. Parts A and B redrawn after Richards (1968).

(A)   (B)

TABLE 7-2

Occurrence of *Hartmannella biparia* **and** *H. quadriparia* **in Various Species of Gastropods**[a]

Molluscan species	*H. biparia*[b]	*H. quadriparia*[b]
Bulinus globosus	L	—
Bulinus forskalii	E	—
Bulinus guernei	L	O
Bulinus jousseaumi	L	O
Bulinus tropicus	L	O
Bulinus truncatus	L	—
Biomphalaria glabrata	L,F	—
Biomphalaria tenagophila	O	—
Biomphalaria pfeifferi	L	—
Biomphalaria helophila	E	E
Biomphalaria obstructa	L	E
Biomphalaria pallida	L	L
Biomphalaria riisei	F	O
Biomphalaria straminea	L	E
Drepanotrema simmonsi	—	E
Helisoma sp.	L	—
Indoplanorbis exustus	L	—
Bithynia sp.	E	E
Physa sp.	E	E

[a] After Richards (1968).

[b] L, Found infected in laboratory aquaria; E, found infected after experimental exposure; —, experimental infection unsuccessful; O, experimental infection not attempted.

METAZOAN PARASITES

It is well known that mollusks usually are the intermediate hosts of digenetic trematodes and occasionally serve in the same capacity for cestodes and nematodes. It is not the intent in this chapter to discuss the numerous species of larval trematodes harbored by mollusks of medical importance since these are the indirect targets of biological control rather than the tools. Nevertheless, those species of adult trematodes of medical importance are listed in Table 5-1.

No cestodes that hold promise as biological control agents are known at this time.

Among nematodes, Chernin *et al.* (1960) have reported the occurrence of *Daubaylia potomaca* adults in the hearts of *Helisoma trivolvis* and *H. campanulatum* collected in Michigan. This nematode was originally described by Chitwood and Chitwood (1934) in the "pulmonary cavity" of *H. trivolvis* in the Potomac River. As the result of placing *Biomphalaria glabrata* in containers with *H. trivolvis* naturally infected with this nematode and in water in which naturally infected *H. trivolvis* had died and decomposed, Chernin *et al.* were able to demonstrate that *B. glabrata* can be infected.

Although histological sections have revealed not only adult males and females of this nematode but also all the larval stages and eggs in nearly all the tissues and hemolymph sinuses in infected snails, there is little apparent pathology except the local destruction of muscle and connective tissue fibers. In some areas varying degrees of amoebocytic infiltration occurs. The pathogenicity of *D. potomaca* relative to killing *B. glabrata* remains undetermined, and, hence, the value of this nematode as a biological control agent cannot be assessed.

Pathogens of Economically Important Mollusks

As stated, interest in pathogens of economically important mollusks stems from the objective of preventing epizootics. Consequently, although a number of parasites are known to occur in shellfish (Cheng, 1967), only those species that are known to cause epizootics are being considered. Furthermore, because oysters have been the center of attention from the standpoint of pathobiological studies, most of the available information pertains to the several species of oysters. An excellent historical account of disease of oysters has been contributed by Sprague (1971), a synoptic review has been presented by Rosenfield (1969), and Sindermann (1970) has contributed an extensive review.

VIRUSES

It has only been since 1971 that the occurrence of viruses in economically important mollusks has been demonstrated, although a virus has been suspected for many years as the etiologic agent in one epizootic disease in *Crassostrea virginica*. Specifically, what is designated the "Malpeque Bay disease" is believed by some to be caused by a virus (Rosenfield, 1969). This

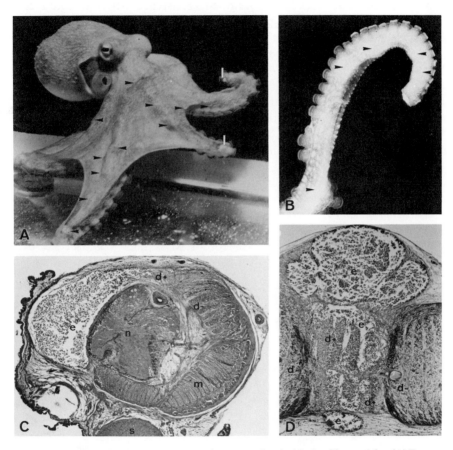

Fig. 7-8. Tumorous growths in *Octopus vulgaris* associated with viruslike particles. (A) Tumorous *Octopus* showing huge knobs (arrows) on the tentacles the terminals of which have been autophagized (white bars) (× 16). (B) Tentacular tip with tumors (arrows) visible through the skin. (C) Transverse section through a tentacle and developing tumor (× 10). (D) Section through a mantle tumor (× 16). e, Edematous region; d, area of decay; d −, initial stage of tumor development; d +, advanced stage of tumor development; m, muscle; n, nerve; s, sucker muscle. After Rungger *et al.* (1971).

disease virtually destroyed the oyster industry in Malpeque Bay, Prince Edward Island, Canada, in 1915, and over the years has spread to other areas of the Canadian Maritime Provinces (Orton, 1924; Logie, 1956; Mackin, 1960). Although the oyster industry in effected areas has recovered, the possible viral etiologic agent apparently is still present since oysters transplanted into endemic areas die within the first or second year after introduction. Based on this evidence, it has been postulated that the native oysters growing in endemic areas have developed a resistance to the etiologic agent.

The first virus or viruslike particle reported from a mollusk to date is that found by Rungger *et al.* (1971) in *Octopus vulgaris* from the Gulf of Naples. This viruslike pathogen causes edematous nodular tumors, mainly on the tentacles of octopuses (Fig. 7-8) and in more advanced stages the tumors also appear on the ventral side of the mantle and on the siphon. The disease leads to apathy of the animal and self-mutilation and is always fatal. The viruslike particles, as revealed by electron microscopy, are hexagonal and 120–140 nm long by about 100 nm wide (Fig. 7-9). They often appear in aggregates, sometimes surrounded by a multilayered, membranous envelope (Fig. 7-10).

The second virus or viruslike particle to be reported from a mollusk is what has been postulated to be a herpes-type virus by Farley *et al.* (1972) in *Crassostrea virginica*. The oysters from which this virus was reported had been transplanted from a site in the Piscataqua River near Eliot, Maine, to Marsh River, a tributary of the Sheepscot River near Wiscasset, also in

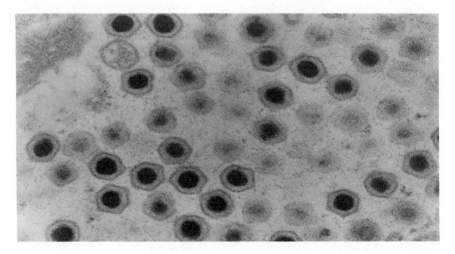

Fig. 7-9. Electron micrograph showing viruslike particles in tumor of *Octopus*. The hexagonal structure of the presumed capsid is clearly recognizable. Most of the capsids are filled with electron dense material ($\times$ 59,138). After Rungger *et al.* (1971).

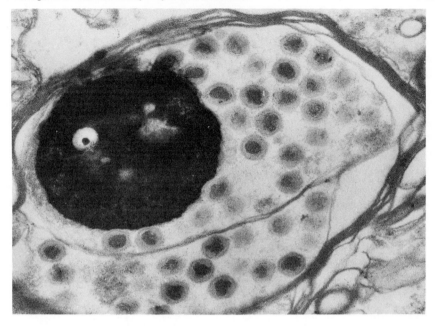

Fig. 7-10. Electron micrograph of small group of viruslike particles in tumor of *Octopus* surrounded by a multilayered, membranous envelope. Included within which is an electron dense mass (× 48,450). After Rungger *et al.* (1971).

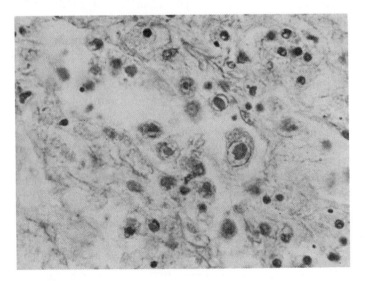

Fig. 7-11. Viruslike particles in *Crassostrea virginica*. Feulgen-stained section of an oyster infected with viruslike particles showing intranuclear inclusions (× 765). After Farley *et al.* (1972).

Maine. Farley *et al.* have reported that when infected oysters are maintained at 12°–18°C there is no mortality; however, if maintained at 28°–30°C, a lethal disease occurs. In histological sections of infected oysters, cells have been found frequently to contain intranuclear inclusion bodies comparable to those associated with herpesvirus infections in other animals (Fig. 7-11). When examined with the electron microscope, the viral particles within the nuclear inclusions were usually hexagonal, 70–90 nm in diameter, and with a single coat (Fig. 7-12). Some particles contained a dense nucleotide while others were empty. In addition, some were seen to have several fine filaments extending through the coat from a dense, eccentrically placed nucleoid, which give a flagellated appearance. The nuclear inclusions sometimes contained tubules each with a diameter measuring from 45 to 55 nm (Fig. 7-13). This virus is morphologically similar to the Lucké virus associated with kidney tumors in frogs.

Oysters infected with this herpes-type virus have dilated digestive diverticula, cellular infiltrates in the Leydig tissue surrounding the hemolymph sinuses, and, in advanced cases, massive cellular aggregates at these sites.

BACTERIA

It is well known that oyster larvae hatching in closed hatchery systems are often killed if heavy bacterial growth occurs; however, it remains unclear whether such bacteria are specific pathogens of the molluscan larvae or general fouling organisms that render the closed environment unsuitable for the survival of the delicate larvae, although the latter is suspected. It is noted, however, that Guillard (1959) and Tubiash *et al.* (1965) have isolated bacterial pathogens of bivalves larvae. These have been identified as members of the genera *Pseudomonas* and *Vibrio*, with the latter group including *Vibrio alginolyticus* and *V. anguillarum*. In addition, it is also now known that strains of *V. parahaemolyticus* are pathogenic to larval and young bivalves. All these bacteria will kill the larvae and juveniles of a number of species of commercially important mollusks including the American oyster, *Crassostrea virginica*, and the European oyster, *Ostrea edulis*.

Relative to adult oysters, several mass mortalities of the Pacific oyster, *Crassostrea gigas*, have been reported in Japan since the early 1950's, and Takeuchi *et al.* (1960) have implicated a gram-negative, motile bacillus, 1–3 μm long, probably a species of *Achromobacter*, in Hiroshima Bay. The fact that this organism has been isolated from healthy as well as moribund oysters is puzzling; however, there is no doubt that moribund oysters reveal diffuse cell infiltration, massive increase in the number of bacteria, and tissue necrosis.

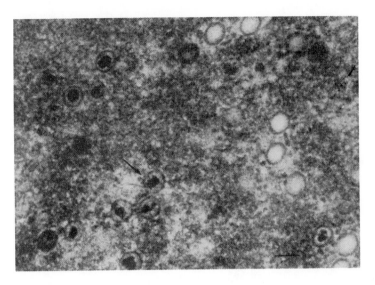

Fig. 7-12. Viruslike particles in *Crassostrea virginica*. Electron micrograph showing an intra-nuclear inclusion with various forms of viruslike particles, including empty particles and particles that appear flagellated (arrow) (× 68,000). After Farley *et al.* (1972).

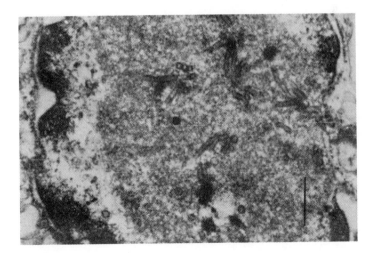

Fig. 7-13. Viruslike particles in *Crassostrea virginica*. Electron micrograph showing tubules within an intranuclear inclusion (× 23,000). After Farley *et al.* (1972).

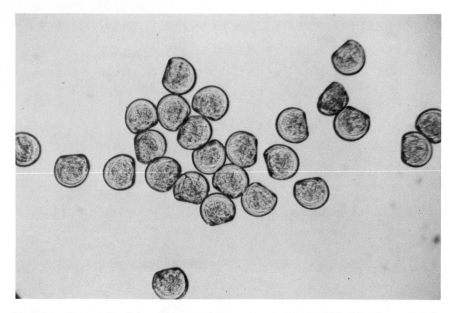

Fig. 7-14. Normal, live 2-day-old larvae of *Crassostrea virginica* (× 200). After Brown (1973).

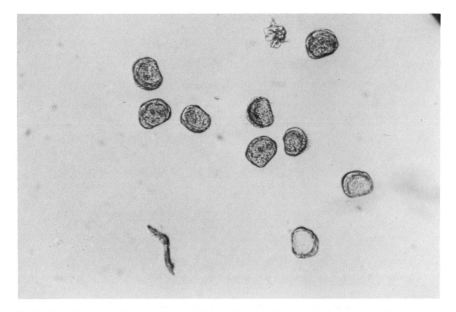

Fig. 7-15. Abnormal, live and dead 2-day-old larvae of *Crassostrea virginica*. These larvae had been challenged with a yet unidentified bacterium (OLM #12). Notice incomplete formation of shell and protruding velum (× 200). After Brown (1973).

Recently, Brown (1973) has conducted an experimental study of the pathogenicity of a number of strains of *Pseudomonas* and *Vibrio* on three developmental stages of *Crassostrea virginica* (at the first 48 hours of development, 2-day-old larvae, and presetting, 10-day-old larvae). She has found that twenty of the strains of bacteria tested will cause gross morphological abnormalities, decrease growth, and/or increase mortality for one or more of the three developmental stages (Figs. 7-14–7-17).

FUNGI

Several species of fungi have been reported as pathogens of marine pelecypods of economic importance. Some of these are known to have caused mortalities while others are suspected as causative agents.

Davis *et al.* (1954) isolated a fungus, which was identified as *Sirolpidium zoophthorum* from hatchery-raised oyster and clam larvae. Although infections are rare, this organism may cause epizootics that are fatal to the molluscan larvae in 2 to 4 days. Infected juveniles are reported to cease to grow and die soon after infection. Infected larvae contain large numbers of motile biflagellated zoospores of the fungus.

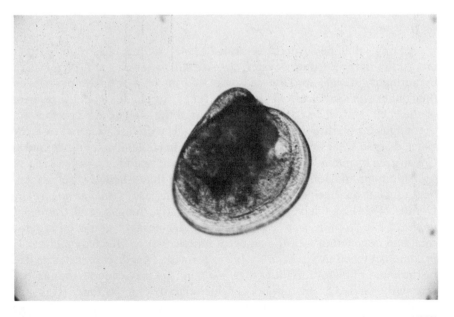

Fig. 7-16.   Normal, presetting larva of *Crassostrea virginica* (fixed) (× 200). After Brown (1973).

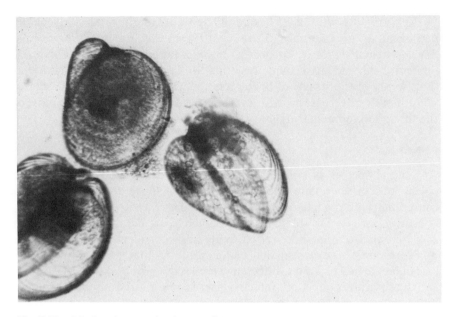

Fig. 7-17. Moribund, presetting larvae of *Crassostrea virginica*. These larvae had been challenged with an yet unidentified bacterium (ONML #2). Notice secondary invasion by ciliates and necrosis of tissues (× 200). After Brown (1973).

Among adult pelecypods, Korringa (1947, 1951a,b) has reported that mortalities of the European oyster, *Ostrea edulis*, beginning in 1930, is caused by a fungus, *Monilia* sp. Diseased oysters form green or brown pustules on their inner shell surfaces. Actually, the fungus originates from the exterior of the shell, and when the thinner portions of the shell become perforated, the fungus proliferates on the inner surfaces. The disease, referred to as the "shell disease," has been reported in *O. edulis* in Holland and France, and in *Crassostrea angulata*, the Portuguese oyster, in England.

Alderman and Jones (1967) have suggested that "shell disease" is identical to what has been designated as the "foot disease" (*maladie du pied*) by Dollfus (1921) and have identified the causative fungus as *Ostracoblabe implexa*. The "foot disease" aspect of the syndrome involves blistering of the shell and degeneration of the adjacent muscle tissue. Affected mucles may become detached as irregular cysts are formed. This disease is believed to be the cause of mass mortalities of *O. edulis* in 1877 at Arcachon, France. It is rare in the United States and not considered to be of importance (Galtsoff, 1964). It has also been reported from India in *Grassostrea gryphoides* (Durve and Bal, 1960).

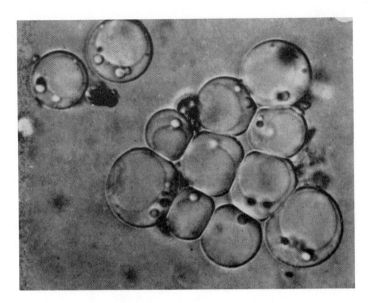

Fig. 7-18. *Labyrinthomyxa marina.* Photomicrograph of daughter cells resulting from the reproduction of cells from the pericardial fluid of an oyster that had been cultured in thioglycolate medium ($\times$ 1000). After Ray (1954).

The most important fungal pathogen of oysters in the United States is *Labyrinthomyxa marina* (Fig. 7-18). Originally described as *Dermocystidium marinum* by Mackin *et al.* (1950) in *Crassostrea virginica* from the Gulf Coast, it is now known to occur along the southern Atlantic Coast as well. The biology of this pathogen has been thoroughly reviewed by Ray (1954), Ray and Chandler (1955), Andrews and Hewalt (1957), and Mackin (1962).

Labyrinthomyxa marina is known to cause fatal epizootics, with infections and associated mortalities rising during the warm months and declining during the colder months. Infected oysters reveal inhibited gonadal development, retarded growth, and general emaciation. All tissues are invaded and multiple abscesses are formed. In addition to *C. virginica*, this fungus has been reported in the leafy oyster, *Ostrea frons*, and the horse oyster, *Ostrea equestris*, in Florida and Texas, respectively (Ray, 1954).

The infection is apparently direct since when the Olympia oyster, *Ostrea lurida*, is experimentally exposed to infected *C. virginica*, it becomes infected (Sindermann, 1970). In fact, Perkins and Menzel (1966) have described a motile biflagellated stage, which they believe is the infective form.

Laboratory studies on, as well as the diagnosis of *Labyrinthomyxa marina*

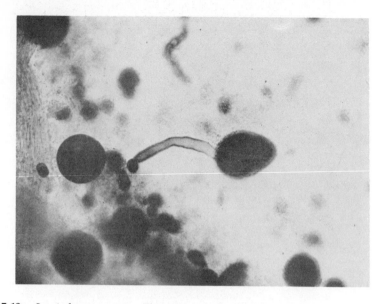

Fig. 7-19. *Layrinthomyxa marina.* Photomicrograph of iodine-stained specimen from oyster mantle tissue after incubation for 41 days in seawater containing yeast extract and dextrose (× 260). After Ray (1954).

have been greatly enhanced as the result of the development of a culture medium by Ray (1952). This medium consists of

```
Rehydrated thioglycolate medium  ..... 1000 ml
NaCl ................................ 20 g
Penicillin ........................... 250,000–500,000 units
Streptomycin ........................ 250,000–500,000 units
```

Small pieces of oyster tissue are placed in tubes containing this medium and incubated for 48 hours at 18°–30°C. Samples of the tissue are then stained with Lugol's iodine and examined under a microscope for the presence of the fungus (Fig. 7-19).

PROTOZOA

Although a number of protozoa have been reported as facultative or obligatory parasites of shellfish (Cheng, 1967), only a few are responsible for mass mortalities. These are reviewed briefly at this point.

The most important protozoan pathogen in the United States is *Minchinia nelsoni* (Fig. 7-20). Originally known as MSX (multinucleated sphere unknown), it was first discovered by L. A. Stauber and H. H. Haskin in sections

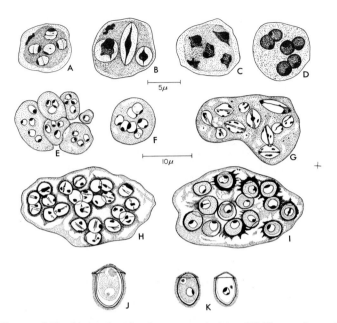

Fig. 7-20. Stages of *Minchinia nelsoni* in *Crassostrea virginica*. (A) Young plasmodium with small nuclei. (B) Older plasmodium with one large nucleus on each side of very large nucleus. (C) and (D) Forms of plasmodia commonly seen in parasitized Delaware Bay oysters. (E) Young plasmodia from oyster connective tissue. (F) Plasmodium with enlarged nuclei. (G) Nuclear division within enlarged plasmodium (early sporont). (H) Sporont containing sporoblasts. (I) Early sporocyst. (J) Fresh spore. (K) Fixed and stained spores. Upper scale refers to A–D, lower scale to E–K. Parts A–S redrawn after Haskin *et al.* (1966); E–K redrawn after Couch *et al.* (1966). Note: 1 μ = 1 μm.

of moribund oysters, *Crassostrea virginica*, taken from Delaware Bay. This parasite has caused extensive mortalities and a drastic decline of the oyster industry in Delaware Bay beginning in 1957 and in the lower Chesapeake Bay beginning in 1959. Mortalities in these areas have been as high as 95%. This pathogen is now known to occur from Connecticut to North Carolina.

Although the histopathology associated with *M. nelsoni* is usually not dramatic, leukocytosis (p. 191) is evident. The stage in the parasite's life cycle most commonly encountered in oyster tissues, especially in Leydig tissues surrounding the alimentary tract and in the gonad, is the multinucleated plasmodium (Fig. 7-20), although spores believed to be those of *M. nelsoni* have been observed. Death of infected oysters is generally attributed to the combined action of environmental and physiological stresses on oysters weakened by the effects of the disease.

It still remains unknown how oysters become infected, and the complete life cycle of *M. nelsoni* remains to be demonstrated experimentally, although Farley (1967) has offered a hypothetical pattern. For detailed reviews of the biology of this pathogen, see Cheng (1967) and Sindermann (1970).

A related haplosporidan parasite, *Minchinia costalis*, occurs in bays along the coasts of Maryland and Virginia, along the lower eastern shore of Virginia, and in Delaware Bay. First discovered in moribund and dead oysters from Hog Island Bay, Virginia, by Wood and Andrews (1962) and designated as SSO (seaside organism), this pathogen is believed to be responsible for sharp peaks of oyster mortality during the months of May and June.

HELMINTH AND ARTHROPOD PARASITES

Although a large number of helminths and arthropods, in addition to other groups of animals, have been reported as parasites of economically important marine mollusks all over the world, most of these do not appear to be lethal pathogens, nor do they cause mass mortalities, although histopathological changes are usually associated with each species (see Cheng, 1967, for review). The only species of metazoan parasite that has been reported to cause mass mortalities among shellfish, specifically the blue mussel, *Mytilus edulis*, is the copepod *Mytilicola intestinalis* (Figs. 7-21 and 7-22). It has been recorded as the causative agent of deaths among *M. edulis* in Europe (Korringa, 1950, in Chew *et al.*, 1963). Generally, however, parasitized mollusks, including *Mytilus galloprovincialis*, *M. edulis*, *Ostrea edulis*, *O. lurida*, *Cardium edule*, *Crassostrea gigas*, *Tapes semidecussata*, and several species of marine gastropods, only reveal poor conditions, being lean and watery.

OTHER DISEASES

Several other diseases of shellfish, especially of oysters, are known, but in each of these the etiologic agent has yet to be defined. Among the major diseases of this category are (1) the "gill disease" in France and other parts

Fig. 7-21. *Mytilicola intestinalis.* Ventral view of male adult. Redrawn after Steuer (1902).

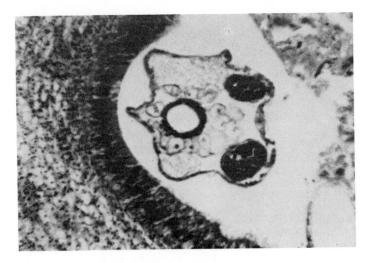

Fig. 7-22. Cross section of *Mytilicola intestinalis* in stomach of *Crassostrea gigas* from Washington. Courtesy of Dr. K. K. Chew.

of Europe (for reviews, see Franc and Arvy, 1970; Alderman and Gras, 1969); (2) the "Denman Island disease" of *Crassostrea gigas* in British Columbia (Quayle, 1961); (3) the "amber disease" of *Crassostrea virginica* in Louisiana (Mackin, 1962); and (4) the "mycelial disease" of *C. virginica* in certain local areas in Texas and Louisiana (Mackin, 1962).

References

Alderman, D. J., and Gras, P. (1969). Gill disease of Portuguese oysters. *Nature (London)* **224**, 616–617.

Alderman, D. J., and Jones, E. B. G. (1967). Shell diseases of *Ostrea edulis* L. *Nature (London)* **216**, 797–798.

Andrews, J. D., and Hewatt, W. G. (1957). Oyster mortality studies in Virginia. II. The fungus disease caused by *Dermocystidium marinum* in oysters of Chesapeake Bay. *Ecol. Mongr.* **27**, 1–26.

Belar, K. J. (1920). Die Kernteilung von Prowazekia. *Arch. Protistenk.* **41**, 308–320.

Berry, E. G. (1949). A recently observed snail disease. *Annu. Rep. Amer. Malacol. Union News Bull.* pp. 10–11.

Brown, C. (1973). The effects of some selected bacteria on embryos and larvae of the American oyster, *Crassostrea virginica*. *J. Invertebr. Pathol.* **21**, 215–223.

Cheng, T. C. (1967). Marine mollusks as hosts for symbioses: With a review of known parasites of commercially important species. *Advan. Mar. Biol.* **5**, 1–424.

Cheng, T. C. (1973). "General Parasitology." Academic Press, New York.

Chernin, E., Michelson, E. H., and Augustine, D. L. (1960). *Daubaylia potomaca*, a nematode parasite of *Helisoma trivolvis*, transmissible to *Australorbis glabratus*. *J. Parasitol.* **46**, 599–607.

Chew, K. K., Sparks, A. K. and Katkansky, S. C. (1963). First record of *Mytilicola orientalis* Mori in the California mussel *Mytilus californianus* Conrad. *J. Fish. Res. Bd. Can.* **21**, 205–207.

Chitwood, B. G., and Chitwood, M. B. (1934). *Daubaylia potomaca* n. sp., a nematode parasite of snails, with a note on other nemas associated with molluscs. *Proc. Helminthol. Soc. Wash.* **1**, 8–9.

Couch, J. A., Farley, C. A., and Rosenfield, A. (1966). Sporulation of *Minchina nelsoni* (Haplosporida, Haplosporidiidae) in *Crassostrea virginica* (Gmelin). *Science* **53**, 1529–1531.

Cowper, S. (1946). Some notes on the maintenance and breeding of schistosome vectors in Great Britain, with special reference to *Planorbis guadaloupensis* Sowerby. *Ann. Trop. Med. Parasitol.* **40**, 163–170.

Cruz, O., and Dias, E. (1953). *Bacillus pinotti* sp. n. *Trans. Roy. Soc. Trop. Med. Hyg.* **47**, 581–582.

Davis, H. C., Loosanoff, V. L., Weston, W. H., and Martin, C. (1954). A fungus disease in clam and oyster larvae. *Science* **120**, 36–38.

de Leon, W. (1919). *Balantidium haughworti*, new species parasitic in the intestinal tract of *Ampullaria* species; a morphological study. *Phillipp. J. Sci.* **15**, 389–409.

Dias, E. (1953). Novo possibilidade de combate aos moluscos transmissores des esquistos-somoses. *Minas Gerais, Bambui. Emprêssa Edit. Êco.* pp. 1–22.

Dias, E. (1954). Bacteriological Warfare on the intermediate hosts of human schistosomes. *Mem. Inst. Oswaldo Cruz* **42**, 315–327.

Dias, E. (1955). Isolamento e seleção de microorganismos de planorbideos utilizáveis em ensáios de luta biológica contra êstes invertebrados. *Hospital* (*Rio de Janeiro*) **47**, 111–116.

Dias, E., and Dawood, M. M. (1955). Preliminary trials on the biological snail control with *Bacillus pinottii* in Egypt. *Mem. Inst. Oswaldo Cruz* **53**, 13–29.

Dollfus, R. P. (1921). Sur les cellules a mucus de l'huître (*Ostrea edulis* L.) et la mycose de Pettit. *C. R. Soc. Biol.* **85**, 449–452.

Durve, V. S., and Bal, D. V. (1960). Shell disease in *Crassostrea gryphoides* (Schlotheim). *Curr. Sci.* **29**, 489–490.

Fantham, H. B. (1923). Some parasitic protozoa found in South Africa. VI. *S. Afr. J. Sci.* **20**, 493–500.

Farley, C. A. (1967). A proposed life cycle of *Minchinia nelsoni* (Haplosporida, Haplospori-diidae) in the American oyster *Crassostrea virginica*. *J. Protozool.* **14**, 616–625.

Farley, C. A., Banfield, W. G., Kasnic, G., Jr., and Foster, W. S. (1972). Oyster herpes-type virus. *Science* **178**, 759–760.

Franc, A., and Arvy, L. (1970). The development of gill disease in oysters and its causal agent *Thanatostrea polymorpha*. *Bull. Biol. Fr. Belg.* **104**, 3–19.

Galtsoff, P. S. (1964). The American oyster, *Crassostrea virginica* Gmelin, *U.S., Fish Wildl. Serv., Fish. Bull.* **64**, 1–480.

Guillard, R. R. L. (1959). Further evidence of the destruction of bivalve larvae by bacteria. *Biol. Bull.* **117**, 258–266.

Haskin, H. H., Stauber, L. A., and Mackin, J. G. (1966). *Minchinia nelsoni* n. sp. (Haplosporida, Haplosporidiidae): causative agent of the Delaware Bay oyster epizootic. *Science* **153**, 1414–1416.

Hollande, A., and Chabelard, R. (1953). Essai de lutte biologique par "*Dimoeriopsis destructor*" Hollande et Passen (protozoaire Flagellé) contra les bilharzioses et les distomatoses. *Minerva Urol.* **5**, 145.

Jarocki, J. (1935). Studies on ciliates from fresh-water molluscs. I. *Bull. Int. Acad. Cracovie, Ser. B. Sci. Natur. (II)* Nos. 6/7, pp. 201–230.

Kay, M. W. (1946). Observations on *Dogielella renalis* n. sp. (Astomata, Ciliophora) from the renal organ of *Physella* sp. *J. Parasitol.* **32**, 197–204.

Korringa, P. (1947). Les vicissitudes de l'ostréiculture hollandaise élucidées par la science ostréicole moderne. Ostréicult. *Cultivateur, Marseille* **16**, 3–9.

Korringa, P. (1951a). On the nature and function of "chalky" deposits in the shell of *Ostrea edulis* Linnaeus. *Proc. Calif. Acad. Sci.* **27**, 133–158.

Korringa, P. (1951b). Investigations on shell-disease in the oyster, *Ostrea edulis* L. *Rapp. Proces-Verb. Reunions, Cons. Perma. Int. Explor. Mer.* **128**, 50–54.

Kudo, R. R. (1954). "Protozoology," 4th ed. Thomas, Springfield, Illinois.

Leidy, J. (1877). Remarks on some parasitic infusoria. *Proc. Acad. Natur. Sci. Philadelphia* **29**, 259–260.

Logie, R. R. (1956). Oyster mortalities, old and new, in the Maritimes. *Fish. Res. Bd. Can., Progr. Rep. Atl. Coast Sta.* **65**, 3–11.

Mackin, J. G. (1960). Status of researches on oyster disease in North America. *Proc. Gulf Carib. Fish. Inst., 13th Annu. Sess.* pp. 98–113.

Mackin, J. G. (1962). Oyster disease caused by *Dermocystidium marinum* and other microorganisms in Louisiana. *Publ. Inst. Mar. Sci. Univ., Tex.* **7**, 132–229.

Mackin, J. G., Owen, H. M., and Collier, A. (1950). Preliminary note on the occurrence of a new protistan parasite, *Dermocystidium marinum* n. sp. in *Crassostrea virginica* (Gmelin). *Science* **111**, 328–329.

Malek, E. A. (1952). Morphology, Bionomics and Host-Parasite Relations of Planorbidae (Mollusca: Pulmonata). Ph.D. thesis, University of Michigan, Ann Arbor.

Malek, E. A. (1958). Factors conditioning the habitat of bilharziasis intermediate hosts of the family Planorbidae. *Bull. W.H.O.* **18**, 785–818.

Michelson, E. H. (1957). Studies on the biological control of schistosome-bearing snails. Predators and parasites of fresh-water Mollusca: A review of the literature. *Parasitology* **47**, 413–426.

Michelson, E. H. (1961). An acid-fast pathogen of fresh water snails. *Amer. J. Trop. Med. Hyg.* **10**, 423–427.

Orton, J. H. (1924). An account of investigations into the cause or causes of the unusual mortality among oysters in English oyster beds during 1920 and 1921. Part I. *Fish. Invest., London Ser. 2* **6**, 1–199.

Perkins, F. O., and Menzel, R. W. (1966). Morphological and cultural studies of a motile stage in the life cycle of *Dermocystidium marinum*. *Proc. Nat. Shellfish. Ass.* **56**, 23–30.

Quayle, D. B. (1961). Diseases of oysters. *Fish. Res. Bd. Can. Ms. Rep. Ser. (Biol.)* **713**, 1–9.

Ray, S. M. (1952). A culture technique for diagnosis of infections with *Dermocystidium marinum* Mackin, Owen, and Collier in oysters. *Science* **116**, 360–361.

Ray, S. M. (1954). Biological studies of *Dermocystidium marinum*, a fungus parasite of oysters. *Rice Inst. Pam.* Spec. Issue, pp. 1–114.

Ray, S. M., and Chandler, A. C. (1955). *Dermocystidium marinum*, a parasite of oysters. *Exp. Parasitol.* **4**, 172–200.

Richards, C. S. (1968). Two new species of *Hartmannella* amoebae infecting freshwater mollusks. *J. Protozool.* **15**, 651–656.

Rosenfield, A. (1969). Oyster diseases in North America and some methods for their control. *In* "Artificial Propagation of Commercially Valuable Shellfish." pp. 67–78. University of Delaware, Newark.

Rungger, D., Rastelli, M., Braendle, E., and Malsberger, R. G. (1971). A viruslike particle associated with lesions in the muscles of *Octopus vulgaris*. *J. Invertebr. Pathol.* **17**, 72–80.

Sindermann, C. J. (1970). "The Principal Diseases of Marine Fish and Shellfish." Academic Press, New York.

Sprague, V. (1971). Diseases of oysters. *Annu. Rev. Microbiol.* **25**, 211–230.

Steuer, A. (1902). *Mytilicola intestinalis* n. gen. n. sp. *Arb. Zool. Inst. Univ. Wien* **15**, 1–46.

Takeuchi, T., Takemoto, Y., and Matsubara, T. (1960). Haematological study of bacteria affecting oysters. *Rep. Hiroshima Pref. Fish. Exp. Sta.* **22**, 1–7.

Texera, D. A., and Scorza, J. V. (1954). Investigaciones sobre una forma bacteriana parecida al *Bacillus pinittii* hallada en Venezuela con acción patógena sobre el *Australorbis glabratus* Say. *Arch. Venez. Med. Trop. Parasitol. Med.* **2**, 235–242.

Tripp, M. R. (1961). Is *Bacillus pinottii* pathogenic in *Australorbis glabratus*? *J. Parasitol.* **47**, 464.

Tubiash, H. S., Chanley, P. E., and Leifson, E. (1965). Bacillary necrosis, a disease of larval and juvenile bivalve mollusks. I. Etiology and epidemiology. *J. Bacteriol.* **90**, 1036–1044.

van den Berghe, L. (1934). Sur un ciliate parasite des pontes de mollusques d'eau douce, *Glaucoma paedophthera* n. sp. *C.R. Soc. Biol.* **115**, 1423.

von Wasielewski, T. K. W. (1904). Studien und Mikrophotogramme zur Kenntnis der pathogenen Protozoen. 1 Heft, Leipzig.

Wood, J. L., and Andrews, J. D. (1962). *Haplosporidium costale* (Sporozoa) associated with a disease of Virginia oysters. *Science* **136**, 710–711.

8   Hematology

It has become increasingly more evident that a thorough understanding of the functional morphology, physiology, and biochemistry of the cellular constituents of the hemolymph of mollusks is of critical importance if we are to understand how this group of animals (1) reacts against foreign bodies, biotic and abiotic; (2) digests and transports nutrients; (3) accumulates various noxious substances such as heavy metals, pesticides, and so on; and (4) carries on respiration and gaseous transport. An understanding of these processes is equally as important in the investigation of many aspects of host–parasite relationships and in the rearing and utilization of mollusks as a food source. In this chapter some of the more salient aspects of structure and composition of the cellular elements and plasma of molluscan hemolymph are considered.

Morphology of Hemolymph Cells

In recent years, Andrew (1965), Hill and Welsh (1966), Cheng *et al.* (1969), Cheng and Rifkin (1970), Feng *et al.* (1971), Ruddell (1971a,b), and Foley and Cheng (1972) have all presented information on the several categories of hemolymph cells occurring in the various classes of mollusks. These contributions should be consulted for detailed information. Presented herein is a summary of what is known.

Molluscan hemolymph cells are typically eukaryotic. Each cell is delimited by a unit membrane and includes a compact nucleus enveloped by a

155

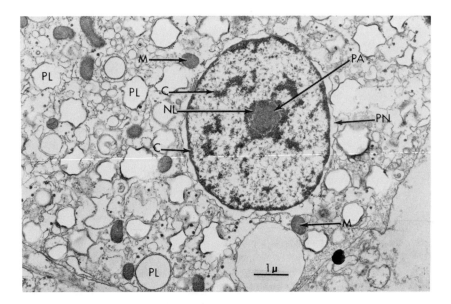

Fig. 8-1. Electron micrograph of a portion of a granular leukocyte of the American oyster, *Crassostrea virginica*, showing nucleus, phagosomelike bodies, and mitochondria (glutaraldehyde-osmium fixation, lead citrate stained) (× 9,750). C, Chromatin; M, mitochondria; NL, nucleolonema; PA, nucleolar pars amorpha; PL, phagosomelike body; PN, perinuclear cisterna. After Cheng and Rifkin (1970). Note: 1 μ = μm.

double-membraned nuclear envelope. A nucleolus may or may not be present. If present, it is usually situated near the center of the nucleus. When examined with the electron microscope, what appears to be a nucleolonema complex surrounds the nucleolus, at least in the large granular leukocytes (Fig. 8-1) (Cheng and Rifkin, 1970). The nucleolonema, consisting of an extremely fine-textured matrix in which dense granules are embedded, most probably represents the ribonucleoprotein component of the nucleolus.

When examined with the light microscope, the cytoplasm of molluscan hemolymph cells are either granular or agranular; however, when studied with the electron microscope, a variety of organelles and inclusions have been identified (Rifkin *et al.*, 1969; Ruddell, 1971a,b; Feng *et al.*, 1971; Cheng *et al.*, 1973). These include mitochondria with well-defined tubular cristae, smooth and/or rough endoplasmic reticulum. Golgi bodies, free and bound ribosomes, lipid droplets, glycogen granules, lysosomes, and phagosomelike bodies.

Behavior of Hemolymph Cells

All molluscan hemolymph cells are capable of pseudopodial movement, although critical studies on selected species have revealed that movements characteristic of specific types of cells can be recognized *in vitro*. Cells of the American oyster, *Crassostrea virginica*, when removed from the adductor muscle sinus and placed on glass slides at 21°–22°C, tend to form clumps consisting of 3 to 4 up to 100 to 200 cells. In time, the cells migrate away from the clump and spread against the substrate. The large granulocytes (see below) are positively thigmotactic and are capable of considerably more spreading than the smaller hyalinocytes. Furthermore, there are certain rearrangements of the cytoplasm and its inclusions, which are quite characteristic. Specifically, in granulocytes the ecto- and endoplasm become distinct, with the former becoming intimately adhered to the substrate. The cytoplasmic granules are exclusively limited to the endoplasm (Fig. 8-2). The pseudopods appearing along the periphery of the cell are filopodlike, although, unlike true filopods, they include semirigid "ribs" extending from

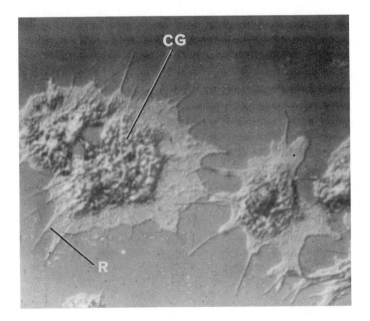

Fig. 8-2. Granulocytes of the American oyster, *Crassostrea virginica*. Nomarski reflected light interference photomicrograph showing riblike cytoplasmic rays (glutaraldehyde fixation, Giemsa stain. CG, Cytoplasmic granules; R, cytoplasmic ray. After Foley and Cheng (1972).

the endoplasm along the length of each pseudopod and terminating at the external point of the pseudopod (Fig. 8-2). The cytoplasm occurring in between the spokelike filopods forms thin webs (Fig. 8-2), which, according to Bang (1961), serve as "nets" for trapping bacteria (and possibly other foreign bodies) that become phagocytized.

The small hyalinocytes, although also capable of pseudopod formation, are more sluggish and produce small, blunt lobopods.

Types of Hemolymph Cells

With few exceptions, there is no total agreement yet as to how many types of cells occur in mollusks; only that all species possess leukocytes and some also possess hemoglobin-enclosing erythrocytes (Griesbach, 1891; Dawson, 1932; Sato, 1931; Hill and Welsh, 1966). It is noted, however, that in those species that have hemoglobin, this respiratory pigment need not be confined to within erythrocytes. For example, in the case of *Biomphalaria glabrata* the hemoglobin is suspended in the plasma.

Although some earlier investigators have reported that all molluscan leukocytes include cytoplasmic granules (Cuénot, 1891), while others have reported that all the cells are agranular (Kollmann, 1908), it is now evident as the result of studies by George and Ferguson (1950), de Bruyne (1895), Drew (1910), Takatsuki (1934a), Dundee (1953), Cheng and Rifkin (1970), Feng *et al.* (1971), and Foley and Cheng (1972) that both gastropods and pelecypods include both granular and agranular leukocytes. Several types of cells have also been reported in monoplacophorans (Lemche and Wingstrand, 1959), and cephalopods (Cuénot, 1891).

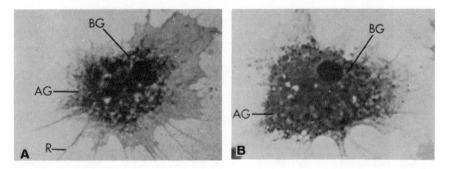

Fig. 8-3. Granulocytes of the American oyster, *Crassostrea virginica.* (A) Granulocyte containing acidophilic (AG) and some basophilic (BG) granules. Notice fine cytoplasmic rays (R). (B) Granulocyte containing acidophilic (AG) and basophilic (BG) granules (glutaraldehyde fixation, Giemsa stain). After Foley and Cheng (1972).

As the result of examining stained cells from eleven species of freshwater pelecypods, Dundee (1953) has concluded that the granular cells may be distinguished as either eosinophilic or basophilic granular cells; however, both Feng *et al.* (1971) and Foley and Cheng (1972) have found that this difference is unreliable since, at least in the oyster *Crassostrea virginica*, granulocytes commonly include both acidophilic and basophilic granules (Fig. 8-3). In addition, they have found that oyster granulocytes may include a third type of cytoplasmic granule designated as refractile granules. These are chromaphobic and are highly refractile (Fig. 8-4). Although some cells may include

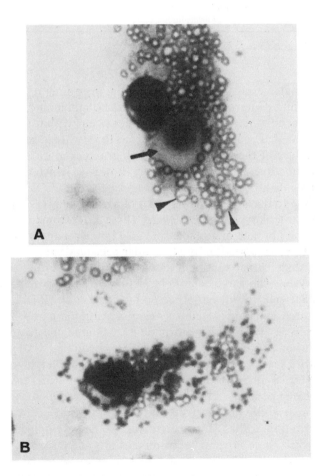

Fig. 8-4. Granulocytes of *Crassostrea virginica* containing refractile granules. (A) Granulocyte containing refractile granules and a phagocytized chicken erythrocyte (arrow). Note the presence of a few exceptionally large granules (arrow heads). (B) Granulocyte containing refractile granules as well as basophilic and acidophilic granules. Parts A and B after Feng *et al.* (1971).

TABLE 8-1

Classification of Hemolymph Cells of the American Oyster, *Crassostrea virginica*[a]

Large cells		
Granulocytes	With acidophilic granules	With combination of
	With basophilic granules	3 types of granules
	With refractile granules	
Fibrocytes	Primary fibrocytes	
	(with lobate nucleus)	
	Secondary fibrocytes	
	(with spherical or ovoid nucleus)	
Small cells		
Hyalinocytes	Agranular	
	Slightly granular	

[a]After Foley and Cheng (1972).

refractile granules exclusively, it is also common to find cells that include refractile granules intermingled with either acidophilic and/or basophilic granules. Since mixtures of types of granules occur within the same cells, it is suspected that, contrary to Dundee's (1953) classification, all these granulocytes are of the same type but with granules at different stages of physiologic function. It is still not known, however, which type of granule differentiates into which other type.

In addition to the large granulocytes, Foley and Cheng (1972) have found large agranular leukocytes in *C. virginica*. These differ from the granulocytes not only in the absence of granules, but also in their manner of pseudopod formation. The pseudopods of the agranular cells tend to be produced bipolarly, rather than formed randomly along the entire cell surface as in the case of granulocytes. The large, agranular leukocytes are designated "fibrocytes." Similar cells have been observed by Tripp *et al.* (1966).

As indicated in Table 8-1, fibrocytes of *C. virginica* can be further subdivided into two types, based on morphology of their nuclei. In one category, known as primary fibrocytes, the nucleus is lobed (Fig. 8-5), while in the other, known as secondary fibrocytes, the nucleus is spherical or ovoid but not lobate (Fig. 8-6). Since there are no other known differences between these two categories of fibrocytes, it may be questioned whether they actually represent two distinct types of terminal cells.

As indicated in Table 8-1, a second class of hemolymph cells occurs in some mollusks. These are smaller in dimensions and also in their nuclear–cytoplasmic ratios. Such cells, designated "hyalinocytes" (Fig. 8-7), have been recognized by George and Ferguson (1950) in the marine gastropods *Busycon carica*, *C. canaliculatum*, and *Fasciolaria tulipa*; and by Cheng and Rifkin (1970), Feng *et al.* (1971), and Foley and Cheng (1972) in *Crassostrea*

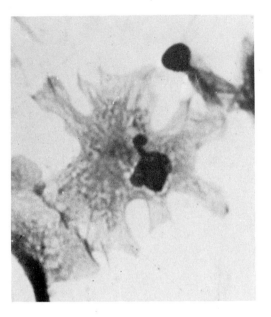

Fig. 8-5. Primary fibrocyte of *Crassostrea virginica*. Notice the lobate nucleus (N) and characteristic cytoplasmic extensions (glutaraldehyde fixation, Giemsa stain). After Foley and Cheng (1972).

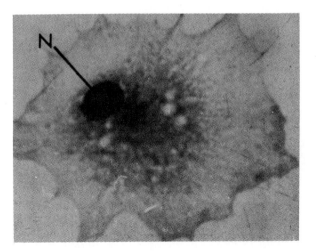

Fig. 8-6. Secondary fibrocyte of *Crassostrea virginica*. Notice the nonlobate nucleus (N) (glutaraldehyde fixation, May-Grunwald-Giemsa stain). After Foley and Cheng (1972).

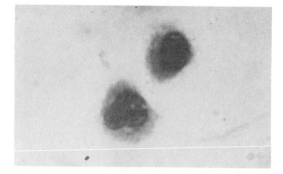

Fig. 8-7. Two hyalinocytes of *Crassostrea virginica* (methanol fixation, Giemsa stain). After Foley and Cheng (1972).

virginica. They have also been found in *Mercenaria mercenaria.* In the past these cells have been designated "lymphoid cells," or "lymphocytelike cells"; however, to avoid any suggestion that they are homologous or analogous to vertebrate lymphocytes, Foley and Cheng (1972) have designated them "hyalinocytes," although this is in part a misnomer since some may include a few, scattered cytoplasmic granules.

The nuclei of hyaline cells are comparatively large and range from subspherical to oval.

The staining characteristics of the granulocytes and hyalinocytes of the American oyster as related to different fixatives and stains are presented in Tables 8-2 and 8-3.

Large, multinucleated cells have been reported in histological sections of two species of mollusks associated with pathological conditions. Specifically, Sparks and Pauley (1964) have reported multinucleated cells, presumably hemolymph cells, designated "megakaryocytes," in moribund *Crassostrea gigas,* and Cheng and Galloway (1970) have found similar cells, which had been challenged with incompatible tissue grafts, in the pulmonate *Helisoma duryi normale.*

It is evident from the above that although several types of cells have been recognized in molluscan hemolymph, especially in the American oyster, *Crassostrea virginica* (Table 8-1), there is no concrete data yet to indicate whether these are all distinct terminal types of cells. In fact, as indicated,

TABLE 8-2

Staining Characteristics of *Crassostrea virginica* Granulocytes as Related to Different Fixatives and Stains[a]

	Granulocytes with predominantly acidophilic granules			Granulocytes with predominantly basophilic granules		
	Absolute methanol	2.5% Glutaraldehyde	10% Formalin	Absolute methanol	2.5% Glutaraldehyde	10% Formalin
May-Grunwald-Giemsa (pH 6.75)						
Granules	Pink, purple	Pink, purple	—	Dark blue	Dark blue	Dark blue
Cytoplasm	Pink	Pink	—	Light blue	Light purple or blue	Light blue
Nucleus	Magenta	Magenta	—	Magenta	Magenta	—
Vacuoles	Clear	Clear	—	Clear	Clear	—
Giemsa						
Granules	Pink, purple	Not well stained	—	Dark blue	Blue	—
Cytoplasm	Pink	Pink	—	Light blue	Pink	—
Nucleus	Magenta	Magenta	—	Magenta	Magenta	—
Vacuoles	Clear	Clear	—	Clear	Clear	—
Wright's						
Granules	Pink	—	Pink, purple	Blue	—	Dark blue
Cytoplasm	Pink	—	Pink or unstained	Light blue or unstained	—	Light blue
Nucleus	Light blue	—	Magenta	Light purple or magenta	—	Magenta
Vacuoles	Clear	—	Clear	Clear	—	Clear
Methylene blue–acid fuchsin						
Granules	—	Purple	Purple	Dark blue	Dark blue	Blue
Cytoplasm	—	Blue	Blue	Light blue	Light blue	Blue

TABLE 8-2 (continued)

	Granulocytes with predominantly acidophilic granules			Granulocytes with predominantly basophilic granules		
	Absolute methanol	2.5% Glutaraldehyde	10% Formalin	Absolute methanol	2.5% Glutaraldehyde	10% Formalin
Methylene blue–acid fuchsin (*continued*)						
Nucleus	—	Blue	Dark blue	Blue	Dark Blue	Blue
Vacuole	—	Clear	Clear	Clear	Clear	Clear
Harris' hematoxylin and eosine						
Granules	Intense red	—	—	—	—	—
Cytoplasm	Pink	Intense red	—	—	—	—
Nucleus	Purple	Purple	—	—	—	—
Vacuoles	Clear	Clear	—	—	—	—

[a]After Foley and Cheng (1972).

TABLE 8-3

Staining Characteristics of *Crassostrea virginica* Hyalinocytes and Fibrocytes as Related to Different Fixatives and Stains

	Hyalinocytes			Fibrocytes		
	Absolute methanol	2.5% Glutaraldehyde	10% Formalin	Absolute methanol	2.5% Glutaraldehyde	10% Formalin
May-Grunwald-Giemsa (pH 6.75)						
Cytoplasm	Blue	Light purple	—	Light blue	Light purple	—
Nucleus	Magenta	Deep purple	—	Magenta	Magenta	—
Vacuoles	Clear	Clear	—	Clear	Clear	—
Giemsa						
Cytoplasm	Blue	Deep pink	—	Clear	Pink	—
Nucleus	Deep purple	Dark magenta	—	Magenta	Magenta	—
Vacuoles	Clear	Clear	—	Clear	Clear	—
Wright's						
Cytoplasm	Light blue	—	Light blue	Clear or light blue	—	Light blue
Nucleus	Magenta	—	Magenta	Magenta	—	Magenta
Vacuoles	Clear	—	Clear	Clear	—	Clear
Methylene blue–acid fuchsin						
Cytoplasm	Dark blue	Blue	Dark blue	Light blue	Light blue	Light blue
Nucleus	Dark blue	Dark blue	Dark blue	Light blue	Light blue	Light blue
Vacuoles	Clear	Clear	Clear	Clear	Clear	Clear
Harris' hematoxylin and eosine						
Cytoplasm	Light blue	Light blue	—	Clear	Light blue	—
Nucleus	Light blue	Light purple	—	Light blue	Light purple	—
Vacuoles	Clear	Clear	—	Clear	Clear	—

[a] After Foley and Cheng (1972). [b] The few cytoplasmic granules present in some hyalinocytes and fibrocytes are either acidophilic or basophilic.

there is reason to believe that all the granulocytes, irrespective of the staining properties of their granules, represent stages in the development of a single cell lineage.

Cell Fragments

In addition to the true nucleated cells described above, Foley and Cheng (1972) have reported the presence of anucleate cell fragments in the hemolymph of *Crassostrea virginica*. These originate as the tips of the pseudopods of granulocytes that for some yet undetermined reason break off (Fig. 8-8). These fragments are capable of producing fine, elongate filopods along their periphery.

Fine Structure of Hemolymph Cells

The fine structure of molluscan hemolymph cells as determined by electron microscopy has been limited thus far to the cells of two species of

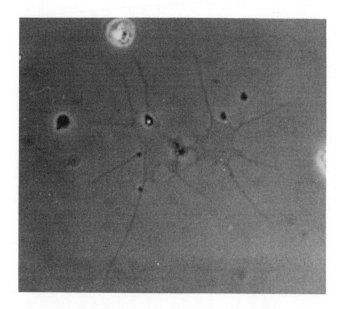

Fig. 8-8. Two anucleate cytoplasmic fragments of *Crassostrea virginica* with long cytoplasmic extensions (phase contrast). After Foley and Cheng (1972).

oysters, *Crassostrea virginica* and *C. gigas*. Rifkin *et al.* (1969) have studied the granulocytes of *C. virginica in situ* as constituents of the encapsulating cyst formed by the oyster against the larva of the cestode *Tylocephalum*. The more interesting cytological features reported by these investigators are the presence of lysosomes and dilated areas of the cisternae of the endoplasmic reticulum (Fig. 8-9). The latter suggests that these cells, when associated with capsules, are metabolically active in the synthesis of some proteinaceous material.

According to Ruddell (1971a), the granulocytes of *Crassostrea gigas* can be characterized into two distinct types, acidophils and basophils. Acidophils are reported to contain relatively small, spherical amorphous, osmiophilic cytoplasmic granules, each with a maximum dimension of 0.4–0.56 µm. On the other hand, basophils are reported to contain large, cytoplasmic granules each measuring 0.7–1.2 µm in diameter. Similarly, Feng *et al.* (1971) are of the opinion that the acidophilic, basophilic, and refractile granules of *C. virginica* can be distinguished in electron micrographs by their dimensions and the thickness of their cortical zones.

As the result of studying the cytoplasmic granules of *C. virginica*, Cheng

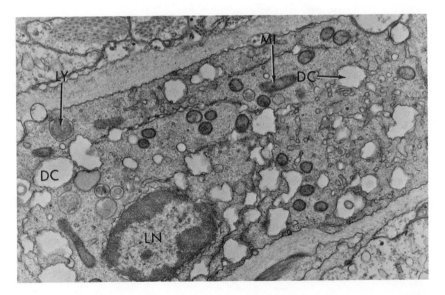

Fig. 8-9. Electron micrograph of a portion of a granulocyte of *Crassostrea virginica* (× 13,680). DC, Dilated cisternae; LN, nucleus of leukocyte; LY, lysosomelike body; MI, mitochondrion. After Rifkin *et al.* (1969).

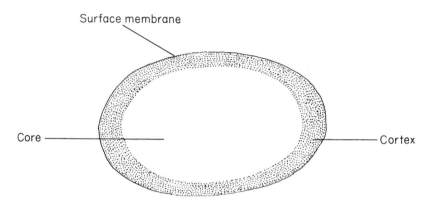

Fig. 8-10. Schematic diagram showing the shape and constituent parts of a cytoplasmic vesicle of *Crossostrea virginica* granulocytes.

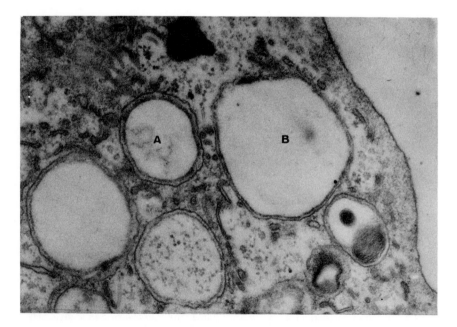

Fig. 8-11. Electron micrograph showing portion of the cytoplasm of a granulocyte of *Crassostrea virginica* and vesicles (the granules of light microscopy). Notice that the diameter of vesicle B is greater than that of vesicle A ($\times$ 72,450).

et al. (1974) have advanced the opinion that each granule is ovoid in shape (Fig. 8-10) and that differences in diameters as found by Ruddell (1971a) and Feng *et al.* (1972) can be attributed not to the type of granule but to the plane of section. Furthermore, Cheng *et al.* (1974) have postulated that the cortical region of each granule is thicker at the two poles of the ovoid body, and, therefore, one would expect to find the cross sections with smaller diameters to have thicker cortical zones (Fig. 8-11). Indeed, studies with the scanning electron microscope have revealed that each granule is ovoid (Cheng and Foley, 1972) (Fig. 8-12).

Since the hemolymph cells of *C. gigas* have not been subjected to detailed study with various stains, it cannot be stated with certainty whether distinct acidophils and basophils, as reported by Ruddell (1971a), truly exist. However, in view of the finding by Feng *et al.* (1971) and Foley and Cheng (1972) that the granulocytes of *C. virginica* may include a mixture of acidophilic, basophilic, and refractile granules, Ruddell's results are open to question from the standpoint of cell types, in addition to the classification of granulocytes based on the fine structure of their cytoplasmic granules.

It is of interest to note that Cheng *et al.* (1974) have found that the granules commonly include glycogen in the form of alpha rosettes (Fig. 8-13). Furthermore, evidence indicate that the so-called core of each granule (Fig. 8-10) is the site of glycogen synthesis (Cheng and Cali, 1974).

As the result of studying "agranular amoebocytes" associated with regenerating mantle wounds in *C. gigas*, Ruddell (1971b) has reported that those cells observed in amoebocytes plugs from early wounds may differentiate into fibroblasts and myoblasts typical of late wounds. Although this postulation is interesting, it is unfortunate that Ruddell has not ascertained whether his "agranular amoebocytes" are fibrocytes of hyalinocytes. Moreover, it should be cautioned that conclusions relative to the differentiation of one type of cell into another should be based on more dynamic, experimental studies, for example, tissue culture, labeling of stem cells, and so on, rather than on static electron micrographs.

The origins of all types of cytoplasmic granules is uncertain, although electron microscope studies have revealed a close association between granules and the smooth endoplasmic reticulum. Based on this type of morphological evidence, it has been suggested that these granules may be formed by dilation and/or coalescense of the vesicles of the endoplasmic reticulum (Feng *et al.*, 1971).

Brown Cells

In addition to leukocytes, another type of cell occurs in the hemolymph of certain mollusks. These have been observed in oysters and are designated

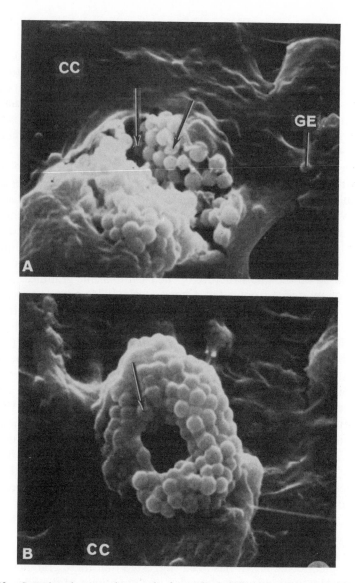

Fig. 8-12. Scanning electron micrograph of granules (vesicles) in granulocytes of *Crassostrea virginica*. (A) Micrograph of cell with membrane ruptured thus permitting direct view of the cytoplasmic granules. Notice that those granules visible from the lateral view are ovoid in shape (arrows) (× 4000). (B) Micrograph showing cytoplasmic granules in a cell the membrane of which had been removed. Notice the more or less concentric arrangement of the granules and the ovoid shape of those visible from the side (arrow) (× 4000). CC, Cortical cytoplasm; GE, cytoplasmic granule in ectoplasm or cortical cytoplasm. Parts A and B after Cheng and Foley (1972).

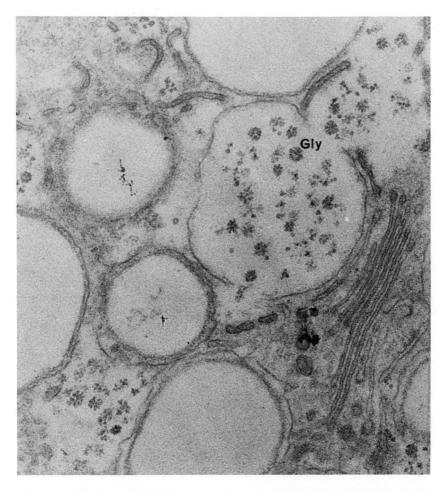

Fig. 8-13. Electron micrograph showing glycogen deposits (Gly) in cytoplasmic vesicle (granule of light microscopy) of *Crassostrea virginica* granulocyte (× 86,940).

as brown cells because of the presence of brown pigment globules in their cytoplasm. These cells measure from 4 to 18 μm in greatest diameter in *Crassostrea virginica* and occur both intravascularly and as free cells in tissues. According to Grobben (1888), they are formed in the *Pericardialdrüse* or pericardial glands, which are darkened areas not only on the pericardium but on the surfaces of the auricles and on the mantle of certain pelecypods (see reviews by White, 1942; Grassé, 1960). Brown cells are also amoeboid and capable of phagocytizing experimentally introduced carmine particles (Takatsuki, 1934b). They have been considered to be modified leukocytes, although this hypothesis is not widely accepted.

When observed with the light microscope, the cytoplasm of brown cells is usually so densely packed with yellowish brown to dark brown globules that the nucleus is normally masked, but it is present. These cells have been observed to undergo division in oyster tissue (Cheng and Burton, 1966).

When studied with the electron microscope, the globules appear as large, ovoid bodies of different textures and electron densities (Fig. 8-14) (Rifkin *et al.*, 1969). Many of the globules include well-defined crystals each portraying a periodicity of 200 Å (Fig. 8-14), which most probably represents proteins (Fawcett, 1966). These may be aggregates of enzymes and sphingomyelin, which have been reported from brown cells (Haigler, 1964; Cheng and Burton, 1966; Cheng, 1967).

The chemical composition of brown cells has attracted some attention. Letellier (1891), who studied these cells in *Cardium* and *Pecten*, was able to detect trace amounts of hippuric acid. Haigler (1964) has reported the presence of "granules of lipid and protein" in the brown cells of *Crassostrea virginica*. Furthermore, the fact that the globules give a positive test with Millon's reagent indicates that the protein is rich in tyrosine. Stein and Mackin (1955) and Haigler (1964) have also reported that the globules possess properties similar to those of lipofucsins, although, as Haigler has pointed out, the "lipofucsin" present in oyster brown cells is soluble in dilute acids and bases. Specifically, it is readily dissolved in 1 N solutions of NH_4OH, KOH, and NaOH, and in 1 N HCl. It is also readily dissolved in 6 N HNO_3 but not in a 1 N solution. A 10% perchloric acid solution will also cause an immediate discoloration of most globules. It is of interest to note that Stein and Mackin (1955) have reported that the brown cells in the same species of oyster are insoluble in dilute acids and bases as one would expect of true lipofucsins. Lipofucsins represent a class of lipogenous pigments derived from lipoid or lipoprotein sources (Pearse, 1961) or fatty acids (Gomori, 1952; Lillie, 1954).

The chemical complexity of the globules in brown cells is further indicated by Cheng and Burton (1966), who have found that only some of the brown cells in *C. virginica* are periodic acid-Schiff positive and diastase resistant. Thus, the chemical nature of the substrate could be a mucoprotein, a glycoprotein, a glycolipid, or a sphingolipid. Since Haigler has shown that brown cells include a complex of lipid and protein with properties similar to those of lipofucsins, it would appear that the periodic acid-Schiff positive and diastase resistant material could be classified as a sphingomyelin and the periodic acid-Schiff positive reac-

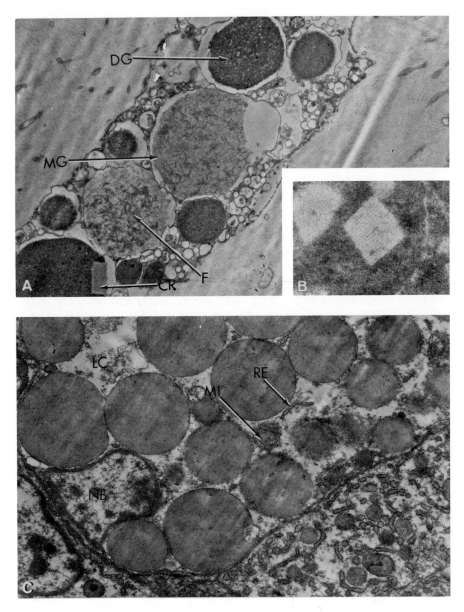

Fig. 8-14. Electron micrographs of portions of brown cells of *Crassostrea virginica*. (A) Portion of a brown cell showing presence of globules of varying densities ($\times$ 14,025). (B) Section of crystal found in a dense globule within brown cell ($\times$ 29,623). (C) Portion of brown cell showing conspicuous globules ($\times$ 11,305). CR, Intraglobular crystal in brown cell; DG, electron-dense globule; F, intraglobular fibrous material in brown cell; LC, leached cytoplasm; MG, moderately dense globule; MI, mitochondrion; NB, nucleus of brown cell; RE, rough endoplasmic reticulum. After Rifkin *et al.* (1969).

tion is not due to the presence of a 1:2-glycol-containing carbohydrate but to the presence of a primary acylated amine adjacent to a hydroxyl group that is capable of reacting with periodic acid. In addition to sphingomyelin, Cheng and Burton (1966) have also demonstrated the presence of acid mucopolysaccharides in brown cells of medium size, for example, those 6–12 μm in diameter, but not in smaller and larger ones.

Hemopoesis

Strange as it may seem, there is yet no definitive information pertaining to the site(s) of hemolymph cell formation in mollusks. Wandering phagocytic cells have been described as originating in connective tissues, from the epithelial layers of various tissues, and from other sources (see review by Wagge, 1955). Briefly, Wagge has reported that in *Helix pomatia* certain amoeboid cells originate from the mantle epithelium and others from the connective tissue of the mantle. Millott (1937) has described what he believed to be the formation of leukocytes by budding from the digestive gland of *Jorunna tomentosa*, and Potts (1923) has described a similar phenomenon in *Toredo*. More recently, Müller (1956) has reported that the hemolymph cells of *Lymnaea stagnalis* are formed continuously in connective tissue, particularly in the lung, and Pan (1958) has suggested that the leukocytes of *Biomphalaria glabrata* may be formed from fibroblasts situated in the trabeculae of the mantle blood sinuses and from the cellular reticulum occurring in the wall of the nephridium near the pericardium.

One of the major difficulties in determining the hemopoetic sites in mollusks by searching for concentrations of cells similar to those occurring in the vascular system is that mollusks have what is known as an open circulatory system, and the hemolymph, including its cellular constituents, is not limited to within the heart and vessels. In fact, hemolymph is continuously pumped into the hemolymph (or blood) sinuses and from there into tissues. Consequently, hemolymph cells are routinely found extravascularly in tissues, and, hence, concentrations of such cells observed in tissues need not indicate hemopoetic sites.

In addition to the studies cited, several earlier investigators have studied leukocyte production *in vitro*. Specifically, Gatenby and Hill (1934), Haughton (1934), Bourne (1935), and Crawford and Barer (1951), all of whom have examined tissues of *Helix aspersa* maintained in culture and have reported that leukocytes differentiate from connective tissue, particularly that located in the mantle. Such evidence, however, is open to question since certain types of molluscan cells round up, and even become phagocytic.

Consequently, free cells migrating from pieces of tissue maintained *in vitro* may well represent dedifferentiated tissue cells.

Cell Division

Hemolymph cells are known to divide. Earlier evidences for this phenomenon come from observations on tissues maintained *in vitro* (Bohuslav, 1933a,b; Gatenby, 1932; Gatenby and Hill, 1934; Gatenby *et al.*, 1934; Bourne, 1935). As stated earlier, there is an element of doubt whether free cells migrating from tissues *in vitro* are true hemolymph cells. On the other hand, Gresson (1937) has reported finding nuclei of leukocytes of *Modiolus* in early mitotic prophase, Fretter (1937) has described leukocytes of *Philine aperta* undergoing division, Cheng *et al.* (1969) have found leukocytes of *Littorina scabra* in what appeared to be division, and Feng (1967) has reported the rare occurrence of oyster (*C. virginica*) leukocytes undergoing mitosis. Fine structural evidence for leukocyte division has recently been provided by Feng *et al.* (1971) who found protocentrioles and associated microtubules in granulocytes of *C. virginica* (Fig. 8-15).

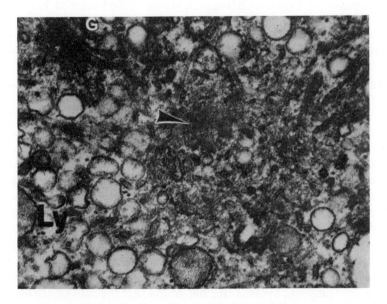

Fig. 8-15. Electron micrograph of a portion of a granulocyte of *Crassostrea virginica* showing a protocentriole (arrow) and associated microtubules ($\times$ 27,300). G, Golgi apparatus; Ly, lysosomelike bodies. After Feng *et al.* (1971).

It is of interest to note that there is no reason to believe that molluscan hemolymph cells can divide amitotically. Mitosis is the usual mechanism, although Bourne (1935) has described cytoplasmic fragmentation as another mechanism for the formation of new cells in *Helix aspersa*. Fragmentation of granulocytes of *C. virginica* also is known to occur (p. 166), and, although the fragments are capable of producing filopods, they are short-lived and presumably incapable of carrying on the normal functions of nucleated cells (Foley and Cheng, 1972).

Histochemistry and Biochemistry of Hemolymph Cells

As indicated in Chapter 9, at least certain types of leukocytes are extremely active in the phagocytosis and intracellular degradation of foreign meterials introduced into mollusks. Interest in the mechanisms involved in the chemical degradation of "nonself" molecules within phagocytic leukocytes has resulted in some studies on the enzymes occurring within these cells. Wagge (1951), by employing cytochemistry, has demonstrated alkaline phosphatase activity in the nuclei of "small amoebocytes" (presumably hyalinocytes) of *Helix aspersa*. This enzyme has also been detected in the cytoplasm of *Crassostrea virginica* (Eble, 1966; Eble and Tripp, 1968; Cheng and Rifkin, 1970; Feng *et al.*, 1971). According to Feng *et al.*, alkaline phosphatase constitutes 46.16% of the relative concentration of the enzymes examined (alkaline phosphatase, acid phosphatase, and nonspecific esterases) in these cells.

Acid phosphatase activity has also been demonstrated in oyster granulocytes (Feng *et al.*, 1971). It constitutes 16.99% of the three enzymes examined in these cells.

Esterases, including lipases, have been detected in leukocytes of several species of mollusks. Yonge (1926) and George (1952) have found that phagocytic leukocytes (most probably granulocytes) of *Crassostrea virginica*, *Ostrea edulis*, and *Modiolus demissus* can take up and hydrolyze fats. The occurrence of esterases has been cytochemically demonstrated by Feng *et al.* (1971), who found that these enzymes comprise 36.85% of the three categories of enzymes sought for in *C. virginica* granulocytes. Lipase activity in *Mercenaria mercenaria* leukocytes has been found by Zacks and Welsh (1953) and Zacks (1955) and in *Ostrea edulis* leukocytes by Takatsuki (1934a).

The occurrence of carbohydrases in molluscan leukocytes has been studied by Takatsuki (1934a). He has found that the cells of *Ostrea edulis* include carbohydrases that can reduce starch, glycogen, maltose, lactose, sucrose, and the glucosides, amygdaline and salicine. The hydrolysis of starch and glycogen is particularly evident, and the amylase has an optimum pH of about 7.0.

The occurrence of proteolytic enzymes in molluscan leukocytes is of particular interest since from the standpoint of public health it is essential to know if viruses, such as the hepatitis virus, can be rendered noninfective intracellularly within shellfish leukocytes after they are phagocytized as the result of the degradation of the protein coats of the virus. Despite the practical importance of this information, the only published study on proteinases to date is that of Takatsuki (1934a), who has found that the proteolytic enzyme in *Ostrea edulis* leukocytes can hydrolyze peptone and casein and has an optimum pH of about 8.0.

It is of interest to interject at this point that electron microscope studies of granulocytes of *Crassostrea virginica* that have been exposed to bacteria have revealed that, upon being phagocytized, the foreign cells are initially degraded within membrane-lined digestive vacuoles in the cytoplasm, with typical concentric lamellae forming around the partially digested bacteria. Subsequently, the partially digested material is transferred to the cytoplasmic vesicles (the granules of light microscopy) within which further digestion occurs, accompanied by the synthesis and laying down of concentric lamellae around the foreign material (Fig. 8-16). In time, the

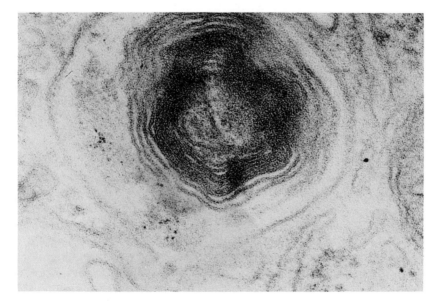

Fig. 8-16. Electron micrograph showing concentric digestive lamellae surrounding disintegrated bacterium within cytoplasmic vesicle (granule of light microscopy) of *Crassostrea virginica* granulocyte (× 62,790).

carbohydrate constituent of the bacteria is degraded to glucose and resynthesized as glycogen, and there is evidence that this intravesicular glycogen is released into the cytoplasm as the vesicular wall disintegrates and is eventually expelled through the cell membrane into the plasma where it presumably is degraded to glucose (Cheng and Cali, 1974).

In addition to the enzymes mentioned, a few other categories of enzymes have been demonstrated in molluscan hemolymph cells. Jatsenko (1928) has found an indigo carmine-reducing oxidase system in the cells of the freshwater clam *Anodonta*, and Takatsuki (1934b) has reported that a complete oxidase system occurs in *Ostrea edulis* leukocytes as revealed by the reduction of indigo carmine and by the guaiacum reaction method. More recently, Zacks and Welsh (1953) have demonstrated the presence of cholinesterase, and Zacks (1955) has found a dehydrogenase and cholinesterase in *Mercenaria mercenaria* leukocytes.

Composition of Plasma

Unlike the blood of vertebrates, molluscan hemolymph does not clot *in vitro*, and, hence, the fluid in which the cellular elements are suspended is more appropriately referred to as plasma. Very few studies have been made on the physical and chemical properties of molluscan plasma. Among the first were those by Deutsch and McShan (1949), Woods *et al.* (1958), Cheng and Sanders (1962), and Cheng (1964) who studied the plasma protein fractions in a variety of freshwater and marine species by employing a number of types of electrophoresis. Subsequently, similar studies have been carried out by Michelson (1966), Wright and Ross (1959, 1963), Targett (1963), Dusanic and Lewert (1963), Gress and Cheng (1973), and Lee and Cheng (1972b) on *Biomphalaria glabrata*. Such studies have revealed that molluscan plasma includes a number of protein fractions, although the exact nature of the proteins has not yet been ascertained. It is of interest to note that these earlier studies have essentially served as base line studies for subsequent investigations on quantitative fluctuations of plasma protein fractions as the result of antigenic challenge. This topic is discussed in Chapter 9.

The amino acid compositions of the plasma of a few species of mollusks have been determined. Cheng (1963) has reported that the plasma of *Physa gyrina* includes a free amino acid pool consisting of cystine, lysine, histidine, asparagine, serine, glutamic acid, threonine, alanine, proline, tyrosine, tryptophan, leucine, and isoleucine and that the bound amino acids are essentially the same except that tryptophan was not detected and cysteine, valine, and methionine were present. In the freshwater pelecypod

Musculium partumeium, Cheng (1963) has found the plasma free amino acid pool to consist of cysteine, arginine, aspartic acid, threonine, glutamic acid, alanine, tyrosine, cystine, lysine, asparagine, and proline. In addition to these, the bound amino acids also include valine, tryptophan, isoleucine, and serine. The same investigator has also studied the free and bound amino acids of the freshwater pulmonate *Helisoma trivolvis.* He found that the free amino acid pool consists of cysteine, tyrosine, tryptophan, leucine, and isoleucine. On the other hand, the bound amino acids are the same in addition to asparagine, glycine, alanine, valine, and methionine.

The free amino acids of *Biomphalaria glabrata* have been investigated by Gilbertson *et al.* (1967). They have reported the presence of sixteen amino acids (Table 8-4). Furthermore, they have found some differences in the amino acid concentrations in *B. glabrata* originating from Puerto Rico, Venezuela, Surinam, and Bahia (Fig. 8-17).

It is of interest to note that Cheng (1963), Dusanic and Lewert (1963), Gilberston *et al.* (1967), and Lee and Cheng (1972b) have all found a decrease not only in the total protein concentration but also in the constituents of the

TABLE 8-4

Comparison of Free Amino Acids of the Hemolymph of Uninfected *Biomphalaria glabrata* **and Those Infected with** *Schistosoma mansoni*[a,b]

	Uninfected	Infected 6 days	Infected 16 days	Infected 32 days
Lysine	0.020	0.014	ND[c]	0.014
Histidine	0.013	0.014	ND	0.007
Arginine	0.007	0.005	ND	0.004
Aspartic acid	0.021	0.022	0.015	0.008
Threonine	0.026	0.025	0.014	0.016
Serine	0.057	0.055	0.047	0.027
Glutamic acid	0.032	0.030	0.017	0.013
Proline	0.025	ND	ND	ND
Glycine	0.032	0.035	0.026	0.016
Alanine	0.027	0.029	0.031	0.013
Valine	0.014	0.014	0.016	0.007
Methionine	0.001	—	—	—
Isoleucine	0.008	0.007	0.006	0.003
Leucine	0.011	0.012	0.008	0.007
Tyrosine	Trace	—	—	—
Phenylalanine	0.006	0.005	Trace	0.003

[a]After Gilbertson *et al.* (1967).
[b]Amounts in μM/ml.
[c]Not determined.

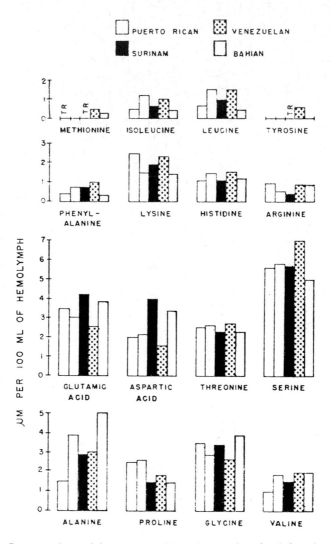

Fig. 8-17. Concentrations of free amino acids in four strains of uninfected *Biomphalaria glabrata*. Duplicated pools are represented for the Puerto Rican strain. Those amino acids present in amounts too small to calculate are designated as TR. After Gilbertson *et al.* (1967).

free amino acid pool in snails infected with larval trematodes. Although the decrease in total nitrogen concentration is attributable, in part, to utilization of amino acids by the parasites, some of it is also attributable to the utilization of the snail's hemoglobin in the case of *B. glabrata* (Lee and Cheng, 1972c).

In addition to amino acids and plasma protein fractions, other nitrogen-containing molecules also occur in molluscan plasma. Except for some pelecypods, all mollusks include a respiratory pigment. In most species this pigment is in the form of hemocyanin. In *Biomphalaria glabrata*, however, the respiratory pigment is hemoglobin. The characteristics of this hemoglobin have been studied by Figueiredo *et al.* (1966) and Lee and Cheng (1972b). It is very similar to all other hemoglobins known in its absorption spectra, including a Soret band and α and β fractions (Figs. 8-18 and 8-19). Lee and Cheng have found that starvation of *B. glabrata* causes a decrease in total protein concentration of hemolymph, and this is due partly to loss of hemoglobin and partly to loss of other proteins. The normal hemoglobin concentration in *B. glabrata* averages 0.956 g/100 ml of plasma.

In addition to *B. glabrata*, hemoglobin has been detected in several other species, including the pismo clam, *Tivella stultorum* (Fox, 1953); the quahog clam, *Mercenaria mercenaria* (Manwell, 1963); the venerid clam, *Saxidomus nuttalli* (Manwell, 1963); and certain members of the pelecypod families

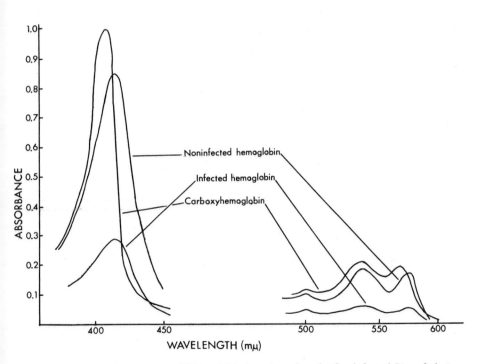

Fig. 8-18. Absorption spectra of hemoglobin from hemolymph of uninfected *Biomphalaria glabrata*, those infected with *Schistosoma mansoni*, and that of normal carboxyhemoglobin. The Soret bands have been reduced by one-half. After Lee and Cheng (1972b).

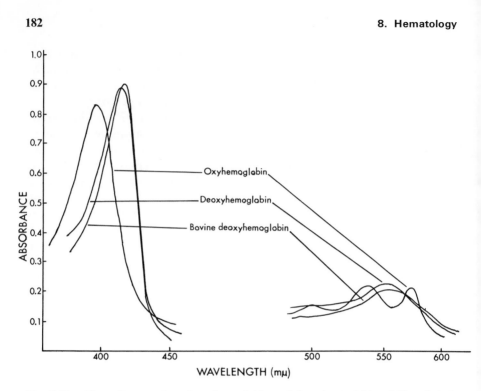

Fig. 8-19. Absorption spectra of oxyhemoglobin and deoxyhemoglobin of *Biomphalaria glabrata*. The absorption spectrum of bovine deoxyhemoglobin is included for comparison. The Soret bands have been reduced by one-half. After Lee and Cheng (1972b).

Carditidae and Astartidae (Nicol, 1960). It has also been reported in the bivalve *Phacoides pectinatus* (Read, 1962) and in the amphineuran *Cryptochiton stelleri* (Manwell, 1958). Except in the case of the carditids and astartids, the hemoglobin in the other species mentioned is restricted to specific tissues such as the muscles (as myoglobin) and the mantle. In still other species, such as several arcids, the hemoglobin is restricted to within erythrocytes (Nicol, 1960). For a good review of the possible functions of invertebrate hemoglobins and other pigments, see Manwell (1960).

Glucose

Hemolymph sugars in mollusks are primarily in the form of glucose. Quantitative determinations of glucose in the hemolymph of several species have been carried out (Table 8-5). Cheng and Lee (1971), as a result of studying glucose levels in *Biomphalaria glabrata* hemolymph, have pointed

TABLE 8-5
Glucose Concentrations in Hemolymph of Several Species of Mollusks

Molluscan species	Glucose concentration (mg/100ml)
Achatina fulica	8.30 ± 2.1
Agriolimax columbianus	27.90 ± 6.9
Cepaea nemoralis (= *Helix nemoralis*)	1.80–2.10
Biomphalaria glabrata	19.24–26.57

out that there is great variation in concentrations; however, it is quite evident that in those specimens infected with *Schistosoma mansoni*, there is a significant reduction in glucose levels after the third week of infection (p. 236). Available data suggest that this reduction may be attributed, at least in part, to uptake and utilization by the parasites.

pO_2, pCO_2, and pH

Little is known about the physical properties of molluscan hemolymph. Because of the public health importance of *Biomphalaria glabrata*, the intermediate host for *Schistosoma mansoni*, this aspect of its hematology has been studied to some extent. It is known that the pO_2 of its plasma averages 67.7 mm Hg, the mean pCO_2 is 12.3 mm Hg, and the mean pH is 7.6 (Lee and Cheng, 1972a).

References

Andrew, W. (1965). "Comparative Hematology." Grune & Stratton, New York.

Arby, L., and Gabe, M. (1949). Contribution à l'étude morphologique du sang des Polyplacophora. *Bull. Soc. Zool.* **74**, 173–179.

Arby, L., and Gabe, M. (1951). Données morphologiques sur le sang du *Dentale. Bull. Lab. Mar. Dinard* **35**, 15–22.

Bang, F. B. (1961). Reaction to injury in the oyster (*Crassostrea virginica*). *Biol. Bull.* **121**, 57–68.

Bohuslav, P. (1933a). Die Gewebezüchtung des postembryonalem Verdauungstraktus, der Glandula salivalis und des Receptaculum seminis bei Mollusken aus der Familie Helicidae, *Arch. Exp. Zellforsch. Besonders Gewebezüecht.* **13**, 673–708.

Bohuslav, P. (1933b). Die Explanation des reinen postembryonalen Herzbindegewebes aus *Helix pomatia. Arch. Exp. Zelforsch. Besonders Gewebzüecht.* **14**, 139–151.

Bourne, G. (1935). Notes on some experiments with snail tissue in culture. *Aust. J. Exp. Biol. Med. Sci.* **13**, 43–48.

Cheng, T. C. (1963). Biochemical requirements of larval trematodes. *Ann. N.Y. Acad. Sci.* **113**, 289–320.

Cheng, T. C. (1964). Comparative electrophoretic studies on the sera of marine and freshwater molluscs. *In* "Taxonomic Biochemistry, Physiology, and Serology" (C. A. Leone, ed.), pp. 659–666. Ronald Press, New York.

Cheng, T. C. (1967). Marine molluscs as hosts for symbioses: With a review of known parasites of commercially important species. *Advan. Mar. Biol.* **5**, 1–424.

Cheng, T. C., and Burton, R. W. (1966). Relationships between *Bucephalus* sp. and *Crassostrea virginica*: A histochemical study of some carbohydrates and carbohydrate complexes occurring in the host and parasite. *Parasitology* **56**, 111–122.

Cheng, T. C., and Cali, A. (1974). An electron microscope study of the fate of bacteria phagocytized by granulocytes of *Crassostrea virginica*. *Contemp. Top. Immunobiol.* **4**.

Cheng, T. C., and Foley, D. A. (1972). A scanning electrom microscope study of the cytoplasmic granules of *Crassostrea virginica* granulocytes. *J. Invertebr. Pathol.* **20**, 372–374.

Cheng, T. C., and Galloway, P. C. (1970). Transplantation immunity in mollusks: The histincompatibility of *Helisoma duryi normale* with allografts and xenografts. *J. Invertebr. Pathol.* **15**, 177–192.

Cheng, T. C., and Lee, F. O. (1971). Glucose levels in the mollusc *Biomphalaria glabrata* infected with *Schistosoma mansoni*. *J. Invertebr. Pathol.* **18**, 395–399.

Cheng, T. C., and Rifkin, E. (1970). Cellular reactions in marine molluscs in response to helmint parasitism. *In* "A Symposium on Diseases of Fishes and Shellfishes" (S. F. Snieszko, ed.). Spec. Publ. No. 5, pp. 443–496. Amer. Fisher. Soc., Washington, D.C.

Cheng, T. C., and Sanders, B. G. (1962). Internal defense mechanisms in molluscs and an electrophoretic analysis of a naturally occurring serum hemaglutinin in *Viviparus malleatus* Reeve. *Proc. Pa. Acad. Sci.* **36**, 72–83.

Cheng, T. C., Thakur, A. S., and Rifkin, E. (1969). Phagocytosis as an internal defense mechanism in the Mollusca: With an experimental study of the role of leukocytes in the removal of ink particles in *Littorina scabra* Linn. *In* "Mollusca," Part II, pp. 546–563. Mar. Biol. Ass., India.

Cheng, T. C., Cali, A., and Foley, D. A. (1974). Cellular reactions in marine pelecypods as a factor influencing endosymbioses. *In* "Symbiosis in the Sea" (W. Vernberg and F. J. Vernberg, eds.). pp. 61–91. Univ. of South Carolina Press, Columbia.

Crawford, G. N. C., and Barer, R. (1951). The action of formaldehyde on living cells as studied with phase-contrast microscopy. *Quart. J. Microsc. Sci.* **92**, 403–452.

Cuénot, L. (1891). Etudes sur le sang et les glandes lymphatiques dans le serie animale 2e partie: Invertébrés. *Arch. Zool. Exp. Gen.* **9**, 13–90.

Dawson, A. B. (1932). Supravital studies on the colored corpuscles of several marine invertebrates. *Biol. Bull.* **64**, 233–242.

de Bruyne, C. (1895). Contribution a l'étude de la phagocytose (1). *Arch. Biol.* **14**, 161–182.

Deutsch, H. F., and McShan, W. H. (1949). Biophysical studies of blood plasma proteins. XII. Electrophoretic studies of the blood proteins of some lower animals. *J. Biol. Chem.* **180**, 219–234.

Drew, G. H. (1910). Some points in the physiology of lamellibranch blood corpuscles. *Quart. J. Microsc. Sci.* **54**, 605–623.

Dundee, D. S. (1953). Formed elements of the blood of certain fresh-water mussels. *Trans. Amer. Microsc. Soc.* **72**, 254–264.

Dusanic, D. G., and Lewert, R. M. (1963). Alterations of proteins and free amino acids of *Australorbis glabratus* hemolymph after exposure to *Schistosoma mansoni* miracidia. *J. Infec. Dis.* **112**, 243–246.

Eble, A. F. (1966). Some observations on the seasonal distribution of selected enzymes in the American oyster as revealed by enzyme histochemistry. *Proc. Nat. Shellfish. Ass.* **56**, 37–42.

Eble, A. F., and Tripp, M. R. (1968). Enzyme histochemistry of phagosomes in oyster leucocytes. *Bull. N.J. Acad. Sci.*, *B* **13**, 93.

Fawcett, D. W. (1966). "An Atlas of Fine Structure: The Cell, its Organelles and Inclusions." Saunders, Philadelphia, Pennsylvania.

Feng, S. Y. (1967). Responses of molluscs to foreign bodies, with special reference to the oyster. *Fed. Proc., Fed. Amer. Soc. Exp. Biol.* **26**, 1685–1692.

Feng, S. Y., Feng, J. S., Burke, C. N., and Khairallah, L. H. (1971). Light and electron microscopy of the leucocytes of *Crassostrea virginica* (Mollusca: Pelecypoda). *Z. Zellforsch. Mikrosk. Anat.* **120**, 222–245.

Figueiredo, E. A., Gomez, M. V., Heneine, I. F., Hargreaves, F. B., and Sontos, I. O. (1966). Hemoglobina de *Biomphalaria glabrata*: purificacao e propriedades fisicoquimicas. III. *Simp. Bioquim. Planorbideos, Curitiba* **3**, 49–54.

Foley, D. A., and Cheng, T. C. (1972). Interaction of molluscs and foreign substances: the morphology and behavior of hemolymph cells of the American oyster, *Crassostrea virginica*, in vitro. *J. Invertebr. Pathol.* **19**, 383–394.

Fox, D. L. (1953). "Animal Biochromes and Structural Colours. "Cambridge Univ. Press, London and New York.

Fretter, V. (1937). The structure and function of the alimentary canal of some Polyplacophora (Mollusca). *Trans. Roy. Soc. Edinburgh* **59**, 119–164.

Gatenby, J. B. (1932). Absence of mitosis in tissue culture and regeneration in *Helix aspersa*. *Nature (London)* **130**, 628.

Gatenby, J. B., and Hill, J. C. (1934). Improved technique for nonaseptic tissue culture of *Helix aspersa*, with notes on molluscan cytology. *Quart. J. Microsc. Sci.* **76**, 331–352.

Gatenby, J. B., Hill, J. C., and MacDougald, T. J. (1934). On the behaviour of explants of *Helix aspersa* in aseptic and nonaseptic tissue culture. *Quart. J. Microsc. Sci.* **77**, 129–155.

George, W. C. (1952). The digestion and absorption of fat in lamellibranches. *Biol. Bull.* **102**, 118–127.

George, W. C. and Ferguson, J. H. (1950). The blood of gastropod molluscs. *J. Morphol.* **86**, 315–327.

Gilbertson, D. E., Etges, F. J., and Odle, J. D. (1967). Free amino acids of *Australorbis glabratus* hemolymph: Comparison of four geographic strains and effect of infection by *Schistosoma mansoni*. *J. Parasitol.* **53**, 565–568.

Gomori, G. (1952). "Microscopic Histochemistry." Univ. of Chicago Press, Chicago, Illinois.

Grassé, P. P., ed. (1960). "Traité de Zoologie," Vol. 5, Fasc. II. Masson, Paris.

Gress, F. M., and Cheng, T. C. (1973). Alterations in total serum proteins and protein fractions in *Biomphalaria glabrata* parasitized by *Schistosoma mansoni*. *J. Invertebr. Pathol.* **22**, 382–390.

Gresson, R. A. R. (1937). Studies on the cultivation of pieces of the mantle of *Modiolus modiolus*. *Quart. J. Microsc. Sci.* **79**, 659–678.

Griesbach, H. (1891). Beiträge zur Histologie des Blutes. *Arch. Mikrosk. Anat.* **37**, 22–99.

Grobben, C. (1888). Die Pericardialdrüse der Lamellibranchiaten. *Arb. Zool. Inst. Univ. Wien* **7**, 355–444.

Haigler, S. A. (1964). A histochemical and cytological study of the "brown cells" found in the "auricular pericardial gland" and other tissues of the oyster, *Crassostrea virginica* (Gmelin). M. S. thesis, University of Delaware, Newark.

Haughton, I. (1934). Note on the amoeboid elements in the blood of *Helix aspersa*. *Quart. J. Microsc. Sci.* **77**, 157–166.

Hill, R. B., and Welsh, J. H. (1966). Heart, circulation, and blood cells. *In* "Physiology of Mollusca" (K. M. Wilbur and C. M. Yonge, eds.), Vol. 2, pp. 125–174. Academic Press, New York.

Jatsenko, A. T. (1928). Die Bedeutung der Mantelhöhlenflussigkeit in der Biologie der Susswasserlamellibranchier. *Biol. Zentralbl.* **48**, 1–257.

Kollmann, M. (1908). Recherches sur les leucocytes et le tissu lymphoide des invertébrés.

Ann. Sci. Natur., Zool. [0] **8**, 1–240.

Lee, F. O., and Cheng, T. C. (1972a). *Schistosoma mansoni*: Respirometric and partial pressure studies in infected *Biomphalaria glabrata. Exp. Parasitol.* **30**, 393–399.

Lee, F. O., and Cheng, T. C. (1972b). *Schistosoma mansoni*: Alterations in total protein and hemoglobin in the hemolymph of infected *Biomphalaria glabrata. Exp. Parasitol.* **31**, 203–216.

Lee, F. O., and Cheng, T. C. (1972c). Incorporation of ^{59}Fe in the snail *Biomphalaria glabrata* parasitized by *Schistosoma mansoni. J. Parasitol.* **58**, 481–488.

Lemche, H., and Wingstrand, K. G. (1959). The anatomy of *Neophilina galatheae* Lemche (1957). *Galathea Rep.* **3**, 9–71.

Letellier, A. (1891). La fonction urinaire s'exerce chez les mollusques acephales, par l'organe de Bojanus et par les glandes de Keber et de Grobben. *C. R. Acad. Sci.* **112**, 56–58.

Lillie, R. D. (1954). "Histopathologic Technic and Practical Histochemistry." McGran-Hill (Blakiston), New York.

Manwell, C. (1958). The oxygen-respiratory pigment equilibrium of the hemocyanin and myoglobin of the amphineuran mollusc *Cryptochiton stelleri. J. Cell. Comp. Physiol.* **52**, 341–352.

Manwell, C. (1960). Comparative physiology: blood pigments. *Annu. Rev. Physiol.* **22**, 191–224.

Manwell, C. (1963). The chemistry and biology of hemoglobin in some marine clams. I. Distribution of the pigment and properties of the oxygen equilibrium. *Comp. Biochem. Physiol.* **8**, 209–218.

Michelson, E. H. (1966). Characterization of the hemolymph antigens of *Australorbis glabratus* by disk electrophoresis and immunoelectrophoresis. *Ann. Trop. Med. Parasitol.* **60**, 280–287.

Millott, N. (1937). On the structure and function of the wandering cells in the wall of the alimentary canal of nudibranch mollusca. *J. Exp. Biol.* **14**, 405–412.

Müller, G. (1956). Morphologie, Lebensablauf, und Bildungsort der Blutzellen von *Lymnaea stagnalis* L. *Z. Zellforsch. Mikrosk. Anat.* **44**, 519–556.

Nicol, J. A. C. (1960). "The Biology of Marine Animals." Wiley (Interscience), New York.

Pan, C. T. (1958). The general histology and topographic microanatomy of *Australorbis glabratus. Bull. Mus. Comp. Zool., Harvard Univ.* **119**, 237–299.

Pearse, A. G. E. (1961). "Histochemistry: Theoretical and Applied." Little, Brown, Boston, Massachusetts.

Potts, F. A. (1923). The structure of the liver of *Teredo*, the shipworm. *Biol. Rev. Cambridge Phil Soc.* **1**, 1–17.

Read, K. R. H. (1962). The hemoglobin of the bivalved mollusc, *Phacoides pectinatus* Gmelin. *Biol. Bull.* **123**, 605–617.

Rifkin, E., Cheng, T. C., and Hohl, H. R. (1969). An electron microscope study of the constituents of encapsulating cysts in *Crassostrea virginica* formed in response to *Tylocephalum* metacestodes. *J. Invertebr. Pathol.* **14**, 211–226.

Ruddell, C. L. (1971a). The fine structure of oyster agranular amebocytes from regenerating mantle wounds in the Pacific oyster, *Crassostrea gigas. J. Invertebr. Pathol.* **18**, 260–268.

Ruddell, C. L. (1971b). The fine structure of the granular amebocytes of the Pacific oyster, *Crassostrea gigas. J. Invertebr. Pathol.* **18**, 269–275.

Sato, T. (1931). Untersuchungen am Blut der geneinen japanischen Archemuskel (*Arca inflata* Rue). *Z. Vergl. Physiol.* **14**, 763–783.

Sparks, A. K., and Pauley, G. B. (1964). Studies of the normal postmortem changes in the oyster, *Crassostrea gigas* (Thunberg). *J. Insect Pathol.* **6**, 78–101.

Stein, J. E., and Mackin, J. G. (1955). A study of the nature of pigment cells of oysters and the relation of their numbers to the fungus disease caused by *Dermocystidium marinum. Tex. J. Sci.* **7**, 422–429.

Takatsuki, S. (1934a). On the nature and functions of the amoebocytes of *Ostrea edulis. Quart. J. Microsc. Sci.* **76**, 379–431.

Takatsuki, S. (1934b). Beiträge zur Physiologie des Austerhersens unter besonderer Beruck-cichtigung der vier physiologischen Reaktionen. *Sci. Rep. Tokyo Bunrika Daigaku, Sect. B* **2**, 56–62.

Targett, G. A. T. (1963). Electrophoresis of blood from intermediate and non-intermediate hosts of schistosomes. *Exp. Parasitol.* **14**, 143–151.

Tripp, M. R., Bisignani, L. A., and Kenny, M. T. (1966). Oyster amoebocytes in vitro. *J. Invertebr. Pathol.* **8**, 137–140.

Wagge, L. E. (1951). The activity of amoebocytes and of alkaline phosphatases during the regeneration of the shell in the snail *Helix aspersa. Quart. J. Microsc. Sci.* **92**, 307–321.

Wagge, L. E. (1955). Amoebocytes. *Int. Rev. Cytol.* **4**, 31–78.

White, K. M. (1942). The pericardial cavity and the pericardial gland of the Lamellibranchia. *Proc. Malacol. Soc. London* **25**, 37–88.

Woods, K. R., Paulsen, E. C., Engle, R. L., Jr., and Pert, J. H. (1958). Starch gel electrophoresis of some invertebrate sera. *Science* **127**, 519–520.

Wright, C. A., and Ross, G. C. (1959). Electrophoresis of snail blood. *Trans. Roy. Soc. Trop. Med. Hyg.* **53**, 308.

Wright, C. A., and Ross, G. C. (1963). Electrophoresis studies of blood and egg proteins in *Australorbis glabratus* (Gastropoda, Planorbidae). *Ann. Trop. Med. Parasitol.* **57**, 47–51.

Yonge, C. M. (1926). Structure and physiology of the organs of feeding and digestion in *Ostrea edulis. J. Mar. Biol. Ass. U. K.* **14**, 295–388.

Zacks, S. I. (1955). The cytochemistry of the amoebocytes and intestinal epithelium of *Venus mercenaria* (Lamellibranchiata), with remarks on a pigment resembling ceroid. *Quart. J. Microsc. Sci.* **96**, 57–71.

Zacks, S. I., and Welsh, J. H. (1953). Cholinesterase and lipase in the amoebocytes, intestinal epithelium and heart muscle of the quahog, *Venus mercenaria. Biol. Bull.* **105**, 200–211.

9 Internal Defense Mechanisms

When considering the phenotypic expressions of organisms that permit their survival through evolutionary time, biologists traditionally have given primary attention to morphological and physiological adaptive features, although in recent years it has become increasingly more apparent that the ability of an organism to confront and overcome invading foreign substances, including pathogenic organisms, is equally as important in this regard. If the animal under consideration is a vertebrate, both cellular and humoral immunological reactions within its body generally are operative against invading organisms and molecules. On the other hand, there is no clear-cut evidence yet that true immunity, that is, the synthesis of true antibodies in response to antigenic challenge, occurs in any group of invertebrates. This holds true for the Mollusca. Nevertheless, the mollusks must possess some mechanism(s) that would allow them to defend themselves against foreign substances or else these animals would not have survived through evolutionary time. Studies in this area of biology of mollusks have revealed that indeed this is the case, and the processes involved are preferably referred to as internal defense mechanisms since, as stated, the production of antibodies does not appear to be involved. Hence, immunity in the strict sense does not occur.

It should be pointed out that with the concern over biological and chemical pollution of our environment, including the estuarine niche where by far the majority of the economically important mollusks occur, an understanding of the internal defense mechanisms of mollusks is being recognized to be of critical importance. Specifically, there are evidences suggesting that if trace elements such as mercury, cadmium, and lead, which can be toxic to man and other vertebrates, are present in large quantities, they are concentrated by shellfish. The mechanism of concentration appears to be via phagocytosis. The trace-element-laden phagocytes can either transfer chemicals to other tissues within the mollusk, or the elements can remain for considerable periods within the body enclosed in phagocytes. Similarly, there is also evidence that such noxious molecules as DDT and other pesticides are concentrated in aquatic mollusks within phagocytes and may be transferred to other tissues from these cells.

Relative to biological pollutants, as is discussed in greater detail below, it is now well established that bacteria introduced into mollusks are readily phagocytized, and Fries and Tripp (1970) have demonstrated experimentally that a virus can be phagocytized by oyster leukocytes (Fig. 9-1). Thus, from the standpoint of shellfish sanitation, that is, the prevention of the transmission of pathogens and potential pathogens from shellfish to man, a thorough understanding of the role of molluscan hemolymph cells as concentrators of pathogens is essential if effective techniques are to be developed to cleanse shellfish of biotic pollutants.

From the standpoint of medical malacology, although definitive evi-

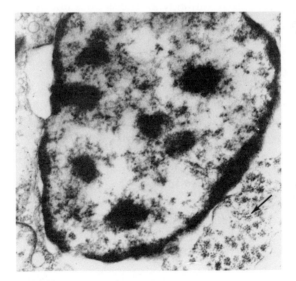

Fig. 9-1. Electron micrograph showing the occurrence of the blue–green algal virus LPP–1 (arrow) within the cytoplasm of the leukocyte of *Crassostrea virginica*. The oyster cell had been exposed to the virus for 2 hours (× 67,000). After Fries and Tripp (1970).

dence has yet to be contributed, it is possible that the entry of chemical molluscicides and potential viral and microbial biological control agents is in some way influenced by molluscan phagocytes.

The study of the internal defense mechanisms in mollusks had its origin with Haeckel (1862), who injected particulate dyes into specimens so that the distribution pattern of their circulatory systems might be determined. In so doing, he accidentally discovered that hemolymph cells phagocytized the dyes. As the result of this finding, it became apparent that molluscan leukocytes can arrest invading molecules.

Before going further, it would be desirable to define the categories of internal defense mechanisms in mollusks. Such mechanisms can be categorized into two types: innate and acquired. Innate mechanisms are those that are genetically controlled and are manifested in animals that have not been previously exposed to a specific foreign substance. Acquired mechanisms are those that only become apparent upon second or subsequent challenge with the foreign substance. In other words, the mollusk's ability to react is stimulated by the initial exposure to the foreign substance and becomes manifest upon subsequent challenge.

As indicated in Table 9-1, theoretically, both innate and acquired internal defense mechanisms may be of the cellular or humoral types in mollusks; however, as stated, acquired humoral reaction, for example, antibody production, has yet to be demonstrated unequivocally in mollusks. In fact, the current belief is that antibody synthesis does not occur in the phylum Mollusca.

Innate Cellular Internal Defense Mechanisms

Innate mechanisms are by far the most common type of reaction to foreign materials in mollusks. Information pertaining to this phenomenon has been comprehensively reviewed in recent years by Stauber (1961), Cheng

TABLE 9-1
Classification of Types of
Internal Defense Mechanisms

Innate internal defense mechanisms	{ Cellular Humoral
Acquired internal defense mechanisms	{ Cellular Humoral

and Sanders (1962), Cheng (1967), and Feng (1967) and need not be repeated in detail. In brief, if a foreign substance, whether it be an organism, a molecule, or even an element, invades or is experimentally introduced into a mollusk and is recognized as being "nonself," it elicits a rapid increase in the number of leukocytes within the animal. This phenomenon, known as leukocytosis, is appreciated by an increase in number of hemolymph cells both within the heart and vessels and extravascularly. Subsequent to leukocytosis, the foreign material elicits one of the three types of innate cellular internal defense mechanisms: phagocytosis, encapsulation, or nacrezation.

If physically small enough, the foreign material is arrested by the mollusk's hemolymph cells by phagocytosis. Although it was thought at one time that molluscan cells are all equally active in phagocytizing foreign materials, especially those of pelecypods, more recent studies by Cheng *et al.* (1973) have demonstrated that in the clam *Mercenaria mercenaria* it is the granulocyte (p. 159) that is actively phagocytic. The same has been suggested in the American oyster, *Crassostrea virginica*, by Galstoff (1964), Cheng and Rifkin (1970), and Foley and Cheng (1972). Experimental studies by a number of investigators have shown that India ink particles (Stauber, 1950; Cheng *et al.*, 1969), erythrocytes of fish, birds, and mammals (Tripp, 1958a,b, 1961), and bacteria, yeast cells, pollen, and polystyrene spheres (Tripp, 1961) are readily phagocytized by molluscan phagocytes (presumably granulocytes). In addition, Feng (1965) has demonstrated that nonparticulate materials, such as soluble starch, hemoglobin, serum albumin, diphtheria antitoxin, and rhodamine-labeled proteins, are pinocytized by these cells.

The fates of phagocytized and pinocytized molecules and organisms fall into three categories.

1. Usually the arrested materials are voided from the mollusk's body as the result of the migration of foreign-material-laden hemolymph cells across epithelial borders to the exterior. These epithelial borders are, as a rule, those associated with the alimentary tract, diverticula of the digestive gland, palps, mantle, heart, and pericardium in the case of the oyster *C. virginica* (see Stauber, 1950). In the case of *Biomphalaria glabrata*, Tripp (1961) has shown that the epithelial borders are those associated with the mantle, mantle collar, the rectal ridge bordering the mantle cavity, the digestive gland, the rectum, and that subjacent to the columellar muscle. In the case of the marine prosobranch *Littorina scabra*, Cheng *et al.* (1969) have shown that India ink particles are voided within granulocytes through the epithelial linings of the upper surfaces of the foot; the alimentary tract, particularly the intestinal wall; the ctenidial surfaces; and especially the nephridium. Although there are variations in the sites where the foreign-material-laden phagocytes cross to the exterior, the principle has been

established that the exomigration of these hemolymph cells occurs and represents a clearing mechanism. An analysis of the nature of the categories of foreign materials cleared by this mechanism has revealed that these are primarily indigestible substances, for example, India ink particles, polystyrene spheres, and malarial pigments.

2. Digestible foreign materials, particulate or soluble, are generally degraded intracellularly, presumably by enzymatic activity. Cheng *et al.* (1974), for example, have reported the erosion of the cell wall of the bacterium *Bacillus megaterium* that had been phagocytized by granulocytes of *Mercenaria mercenaria*.

3. The third possible fate of phagocytized materials is their retention within phagocytes where, as in the case of certain bacteria and other microorganisms, they may even multiply. For example, Michelson (1961) has reported that in planorbid snails acid-fast bacteria within phagocytes presumably can be carried to uninfected tissues. Similarly, Pan (1958) has reported viable yeastlike organisms within nerve cells and phagocytes of *Biomphalaria glabrata*.

The second type of innate cellular internal defense mechanism has been designated as encapsulation. This type of reaction is defined as the walling off of the "nonself" material by cells and/or fibers of the mollusk. From what is known, it is apparent that encapsulation occurs when the invading foreign material, usually a metazoan parasite, although incompatible tissue transplants also become encapsulated (Cheng and Galloway, 1970), is too large to be phagocytized. Malek (1967) agrees with earlier findings that *Schistosoma mansoni* miracidia, in nonsusceptible *Biomphalaria obstructa* from Louisiana, elicit a host reaction whereby the snail encapsulates the miracidium or the mother sporocyst.

Numerous examples of encapsulation of helminth parasites in mollusks are known (see Cheng and Rifkin, 1970, for review). Furthermore, the elements comprising the capsule appear to differ, depending on the host—parasite association and the position of the parasite within the mollusk. Examination of numerous examples of encapsulation has caused Cheng and Rifkin (1970) to propose the categories of encapsulation listed in Table 9-2.

It is of interest to note that encapsulation, and therefore the recognition of the foreign material as being nonself by the mollusk, appears to be dependent upon the recognition competence of specific tissues within the mollusk. In other words, the same species of parasite occurring at one location within a mollusk may not elicit encapsulation but will do so if for some reason it becomes lodged at a different site. For example, when sporocysts of the digenetic trematode *Glypthelmins pennsylvaniensis* are found in their natural habitat, the digestive gland of the pulmonate gastropod *Helisoma trivolvis*,

TABLE 9-2
Classification of Types of Encapsulation Presently Known[a]

Type of encapsulation	Description
Antiqufibrous	This type of encapsulation involves fibrous elements which are not formed *de novo* as the result of parasitic stimulation but represent preexisting fibers present in the immediate vicinity of the parasite. As more chemical information pertaining to the nature of the fibers become available, antiqufibrous encapsulation may be subcategorized as being collagenous, reticular, elastic, or of mixed antiqufibrous subtypes.
Novufibrous	This type of encapsulation involves fibrous elements which are formed *de novo* as the result of parasitic stimulation. As more evidence becomes available relative to the chemical nature of the fibers, novufibrous encapsulation could be subcategorized as collagenous, reticular, elastic or mixed subtypes.
Fibroblastic	Capsules resulting from this process are comprised of fibroblasts or fibroblastlike cells. No true fibers are involved. The origin of the fibroblasts is uncertain. Evidences presently available suggest that these represent metaplastic leukocytes.
Leukocytic	This type of encapsulation involves the aggregation of leukocytes to form a tunic surrounding the parasite.
Myofibrous	Capsules formed as the result of this process are comprised of preexisting muscle cells present in the immediate vicinity of the parasite.

[a]After Cheng and Rifkin (1970).

they are not encapsulated. However, if the sporocysts of this trematode are crowded out of the snail's digestive gland by large numbers, some migrate to and invade the reproductive system of the snail host. Cheng and Cooperman (1964) have shown that when these sporocysts occur in the albumin gland of *H. trivolvis*, a thin tunic of connective tissue is laid down by the host around the parasites.

The most extensive study of the origin and nature of the capsule formed by a mollusk in response to a parasite is that of the American oyster, *Crassostrea virginica*, when parasitized by a larva of the tapeworm *Tylocephalum* (Rifkin and Cheng, 1968; Rifkin *et al.*, 1969a,b). This is an example of novufibrous encapsulation (see Table 9-2).

As in the case of phagocytosis, the fates of encapsulated parasites differ. In some, for example, *Tylocephalum* larvae in the marine clam *Tapes semidecussata*, the parasite is rapidly destroyed and resorbed (Cheng and Rifkin, 1968) (Fig. 9-2), although the biochemical process has not been explored. On the other hand, other parasites, although encapsulated, remain viable

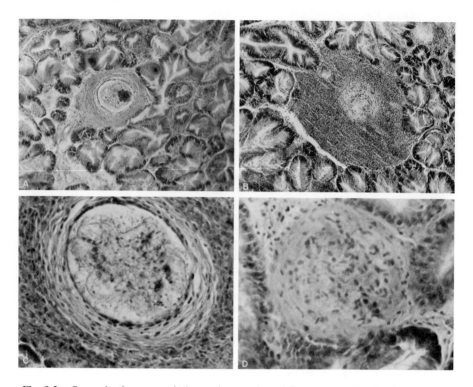

Fig. 9-2. Stages in the encapsulation and resorption of the metacestode of *Tylocephalum* in *Tapes semidecussata*. (A) Laying down of fibers around a metacestode situated in the digestive gland of the clam. (B) Heavy infiltration of the capsule by molluscan leukocytes and disintegration of the parasite. (C) Higher magnification showing disintegration of the encapsulated parasite. (D) Total disappearance of the parasite and replacement by an eosinophilic scar enclosing phagocytic leukocytes that have migrated in to remove the cellular debris. After Cheng and Rifkin (1968).

and are infective if ingested by the next host. An example of this is the third-stage larva of the nematode *Angiostrongylus cantonensis* encapsulated in the giant African snail, *Achatina fulica*. In this instance, when a foraging rat ingests a parasitized snail, the nematode escapes as the molluscan intermediate host's tissues are digested away, and it eventually develops to maturity.

An interesting feature of both encapsulation and phagocytosis is that the mollusk, for some yet undetermined reason, is capable of distinguishing "self" from "nonself." Specifically, if invaded by microorganisms or zooparasites, some are reacted against while others are not. As a rule of thumb, compatible parasites, for example, those naturally found in a particular mollusk, are neither phagocytized nor encapsulated. Exceptions to this rule do occur.

A great deal remains to be learned as to how molluscan cells are attracted to foreign materials. In a limited number of instances partial answers are available. For example, Cheng *et al.* (1973) have demonstrated that leukocytes of the oyster, *Crassostrea virginica*, are chemotactically attracted to the metacercarial cyst of the trematode *Himasthla quissetensis*, and Cheng (1966) has shown that when the nematode *Angiostrongylus cantonensis* is experimentally introduced into the same species of oyster, large numbers of leukocytes are attracted to the worm by the latter's molting fluid.

The third type of innate cellular response in mollusks, especially pelecypods, is designated as nacrezation. This is a rather specialized type of reaction involving the laying down of nacre around the invading material, biotic or abiotic. The process is specialized in that the foreign material must be situated on the surface of the nacre-secreting mantle. The process of nacrezation has been critically reviewed by Tsujii (1960). Apparently, it is the physical stimulus evoked by the foreign agent that causes the deposition of nacre around it. This natural phenomenon has been utilized with great efficiency, especially by the Japanese, to induce pearl formation in pearl oysters. In this case, sand grains or transplanted tissue is usually employed to induce nacrezation.

The fate of nacrezized biotic inducers is uniform. Such organisms are invariably killed and resorbed.

Innate Humoral Internal Defense Mechanisms

A number of investigators have reported the occurrence of innate humoral factors in mollusks; however, there is no chemical evidence that any of these are antibodylike. For example, a hemagglutinin occurs in the hemolymph of the cephalopod *Sepia* (Chanovitch, 1921) and in the "body fluids" of five marine gastropods (*Acmea digitalis*, *Lattia gigantia*, *Tegula galena*, *Astraea undosa*, and *Megathura crenulata*), and one pelecypod (*Mytilus californianus*) has been reported to include natural agglutinating activity when the blood cells and spermatozoa of a number of nonmolluscan invertebrates are placed therein (Tyler, 1946). Similarly, naturally occurring agglutinins have been found in saline extracts of the butter clam, *Saxidomus giganteus*, which will agglutinate human erythrocytes of the phenotypes A_1 and A_1B only. This agglutinin is nondialyzable and is thus probably a large molecule. Furthermore, it is inactivated when the extract is heated to 70°C for 20 minutes, thus indicating that it is probably a protein. Other natural molluscan agglutinins have been reported by Cheng and Sanders (1962), Cushing *et al.* (1963), Boyd and Brown (1965), Boyd *et al.* (1966), Tripp (1966), Li and Flemming (1967), McDade and Tripp (1967), Acton *et al.* (1969), Jenkin and Rowley (1970), and Pauley *et al.* (1971).

Cheng and Sanders (1962) have partially characterized the hemagglutinin in the plasma of the gastropod *Viviparus malleatus*, which is specific for
rabbit erythrocytes among five types of vertebrate erythrocytes tested
(*Coturnix* quail, *Rana pipiens*, rat, mice, and rabbit). Electrophoretic
fractionations of pre- and post-rabbit erythrocyte-adsorbed plasma have
revealed that the agglutinating property of the plasma is associated with all
of the five plasma fractions (Fig. 9-3). Confirmation of the proteinaceous
nature of the agglutinin was in the establishment of a linear correlation
between the agglutination titers of the plasma samples and their total
protein concentrations.

Among the more recent thorough characterizations of molluscan natural
hemagglutinins are those by Tripp (1966), Li and Flemming (1967), Acton
et al. (1969), and Pauley *et al.* (1971). The first three studies are concerned
with agglutinins in the American oyster, *Crassostrea virginica*, while that by
Pauley *et al.* is concerned with an agglutinin in the marine gastropod
Aplysia californica.

The agglutinin in *C. virginica* is unaffected by dialysis, although aging
renders it dialyzable. It exhibits cross reactivity, is heat labile, and has been
determined to be a protein with an extreme pH range of 6 to 9, breaking
down into subunits beyond pH 7 to 8. Furthermore, Li and Flemming (1967)
have reported that the oyster hemagglutinin activity is associated with two

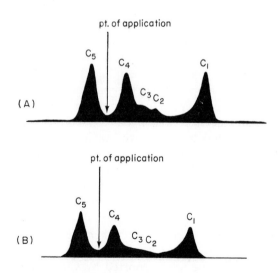

Fig. 9-3. Electrophoretic profiles of the serum protein fractions of *Viviparus malleatus*
before (A) and after (B) adsorption of the natural hemagglutinin by rabbit erythrocytes. After
Cheng and Sanders (1962).

distinct protein peaks after separation by Sephadex G-75 columns, thus indicating a molecular weight of less than 75,000. McDade and Tripp (1967) had estimated the molecular weight to be about 65,000. It has been suggested (Pauley *et al.*, 1971), however, that Li and Flemming and McDade and Tripp probably were working with subunits rather than the intact molecule since Acton *et al.* (1969) have reported that the oyster hemagglutinin is composed of noncovalently linked subunits, each with a molecular weight of 20,000, and that the entire molecule, with all its subunits intact, has a very high sedimentation coefficient of 33.4 S. It is also known that the oyster hemagglutinin is stabilized by calcium ions (McDade and Tripp, 1967; Acton *et al.*, 1969).

Pauley *et al.* (1971) have shown that the agglutinating activity of the hemolymph of *Aplysia californica* is due to a heterogeneous group of molecules of high molecular weight, about 130,000. The agglutinin shows two activity peaks with sedimentation coefficients around 18.5 S and 31.0 S. The molecule has a protein component associated with the active site since it is sensitive to heat, pH extremes, and extraction with 2-mercaptoethanol, phenol, chloroform, and trichloroacetic acid. It is not stabilized by calcium ions, and it is apparent from its physicochemical characteristics that this hemagglutinin is quite different from the classical vertebrate antibody.

The hemagglutinin in the mussel *Velesunio ambiguus* has been partially characterized by Jenkin and Rowley (1970). Its sedimentation coefficient is 28 S, and in the purified form it is a protein without sulfur-containing amino acids. In this respect it differs from the agglutinin of *Aplysia californica* since the latter has disulfide bonds.

It should be mentioned that naturally occurring humoral factors need not be or act like antibodies; they could prevent invasion and/or establishment by foreign organisms by some other means. This is especially true among mollusks. For example, it is known that the plasma of several species of marine pelecypods, namely, *Tapes semidecussata, Mytilus edulis, Modiolus demissus, Mercenaria mercenaria, Mya arenaria, Crassostrea virginica,* and *Crassostrea gigas*, will induce the encystment of the cercaria of the trematode *Himasthla quissetensis*, thus preventing it from penetrating and encysting *in vivo* (Cheng *et al.*, 1966).

Acquired Cellular Internal Defense Mechanisms

There is very little available information pertaining to acquired cellular reactions in mollusks. In fact, the only substantiated evidence is that reported by Barbosa and Coelho (1956). These investigators have found that *Biomphalaria glabrata* previously "cured" of *Schistosoma mansoni* infection can be reinfected; however, some tissue reaction, in the form of leukocytic encapsulation, is evoked in reinfected snails. This phenomenon is not usually associated with initial infections of *B. glabrata* with a compatible strain of *S. mansoni*.

Acquired Humoral Internal Defense Mechanisms

Although suggestions of acquired immunity, complete or partial, can be found in the literature (see Cheng, 1967, for review), there is no direct evidence that mollusks are capable of producing antibodies or antibodylike molecules. In fact, Cheng (1969), as the result of challenging the freshwater pulmonate *Helisoma duryi normale* with bacterial antigens followed by quantitative analysis of the protein fractions in the snail's hemolymph, has stated, "If, indeed, mollusks are capable of synthesizing antibodies, their occurrence continues to evade direct detection." This conclusion was based on the failure to detect an acquired agglutinin, a lysin, or hyperglobulinemia.

Two additional studies relative to acquired humoral internal defense mechanisms should be mentioned. Feng and Stauber (1968), as the result of finding a precipitous drop in numbers of the flagellate *Hexamita* (most probably *H. nelsoni*) intracardially inoculated into the oyster *Crassostrea virginica* and maintained at 18°C, have suggested the possible occurrence of "yet unidentified humoral elements" that may account for the disappearance of the flagellate, possibly by intravascular lysis. Such humoral factors, however, have not been demonstrated.

Feng and Canzonier (1970) have reported quantitative fluctuations in the hemolymph protein fractions of *C. virginica* parasitized with the trematode *Bucephalus* sp. and the haplosporidan *Minchinia nelsoni*. These investigators have interpreted this phenomenon "as evidence of host humoral responses to the infections." This is unquestionable; however, it remains unknown if these humoral responses serve any "immunological" function.

The two systems summarized above should prove to be extremely useful in future studies on possible acquired humoral factors; however, at this time the nature and function of the factors remain unknown.

Genetic Control of Internal Defense Mechanisms

It has been known for some time that certain parasites from one geographic area may not develop in snails from another area, even if the snails are of the same species. The best known example of this rests with the larval stages of the Puerto Rican strain of *Schistosoma mansoni*, which normally develop and multiply in *Biomphalaria glabrata* in its own area but will not survive in the Brazilian strains of *B. glabrata* (Newton, 1952). Earlier, Malek

(1950) had shown that Egyptian snails *Biomphalaria alexandrina* were insusceptible when they were exposed to a Puerto Rican strain of *Schistosoma mansoni*. They became infected, however, when they were reexposed to an Egyptian strain of the same species of schistosome. This and other examples of incompatibility of parasites of one strain with molluscan hosts of another strain have caused those working in this area of host–parasite relationship to suspect that the genetic compositions of both the parasites and the mollusks may play a major role in governing host–parasite compatibility. Although examples of the genetic basis of nonmolluscan invertebrate host compatibility or incompatibility with parasites are available, especially between mosquitoes and malarial parasites or filarial nematodes (Huff, 1940; Ward, 1963; Kartman, 1953; MacDonald, 1962), little is known about this aspect of the relationship between mollusks and their parasites. A brief review of what is known follows.

Newton (1953), by crossing a susceptible Puerto Rican strain of *Biomphalaria glabrata* with a nonsusceptible Brazilian strain, found that members of the subsequent generations revealed intermediate degrees of susceptibility to Puerto Rican *Schistosoma mansoni*. These results suggest that the incompatibility of the Brazilian snails and the compatibility of the Puerto Rican snails are genetically controlled and that several genetic factors are probably involved. In a later study (Newton, 1954) it was shown that the phenotypic manifestation of the genotypes governing incompatibility is in the form of a cellular reaction to the larval schistosomes. The cellular capsules formed around the parasites resulted in their death. Furthermore, hybrid snails revealed cellular reactions that were intermediate between the nonreaction of the susceptible parent and the severe reaction of the nonsusceptible parent.

More recently Richards (1970), as a result of selfing and cross-fertilization experiments with specimens of *Biomphalaria glabrata* that show differences in susceptibility to *Schistosoma mansoni*, has provided additional evidence for the genetic basis of susceptibility.

It is noted that among strains of *B. glabrata* established at the Laboratory of Parasitic Diseases, National Institute of Allergy and Infectious Diseases, Bethesda, Maryland, one strain is only susceptible to *S. mansoni* as juveniles, being refractory as adults; another strain is refractory at any age; and a third strain, like most wild-type snails, is susceptible at any age. Specimens of *Bulinus*, the intermediate host for *Schistosoma haematobium*, have also been reported to be refractory as juveniles (Sturrock, 1967). The same holds true for several other species of lymnaeid snails (Boray, 1966). Malek (1958), however, found that 2- to 4-week-old laboratory-reared *Bulinus truncatus* in the Sudan were the most susceptible to one strain of Sudanese *S. haematobium*.

Richards (1970) has suggested that stocks of *B. glabrata* refractory to

S. mansoni may be useful in the genetic control of this parasite. For example, the introduction of refractory snails into an endemic area could result in their hybridizing with the local susceptible population resulting in a range of susceptibility combinations in succeeding generations, thus reducing transmission of the parasite.

It should be noted that the refractiveness of snails to schistosome miracidia need not always be genetically controlled. Sturrock (1968), for example, has reported that specimens of *Bulinus (Physopsis) nasutus productus* collected in the field and specimens bred in the laboratory portray differences in their susceptibility to *Schistosoma haematobium*, with the laboratory-bred snails being resistant. The mechanism(s) responsible for this interesting phenomenon remains undetermined.

It is evident from the information presented in this chapter that mollusks depend primarily on innate cellular internal defense mechanisms in arresting and, in most cases, eliminating foreign materials naturally or experimentally introduced into their bodies. Moreover, there is some evidence, granted extremely limited and preliminary, suggesting that their ability to mount cellular reactions is genetically controlled. In some instances, however, a humoral substance of unknown nature, which causes the lysis of protozoan facultative parasites such as *Hexamita*, may be developed.

References

Acton, R. T., Bennett, J. C., Evans, E. E., and Schrohenloher, R. E. (1969). Physical and chemical characterization of an oyster hemaglutinin. *J. Biol. Chem.* **244**, 4128–4135.

Barbosa, F. S., and Coelho, M. V. (1956). Pesquisa de immunodade adquirida homologa em *Australorbis glabratus*, nas infestacoes por *Schistosoma mansoni*. *Rev. Brasil. Malariol. Doencas Trop.* **8**, 59–56.

Boray, J. C. (1966). Studies on the relative susceptibility of some lymnaeids to infection with *Fasciola hepatica* and *F. gigantica* and on the adaptation of *Fasciola* spp. *Ann. Trop. Med. Parasitol.* **60**, 114–124.

Boyd, W. C., and Brown, R. (1965). A specific agglutinin in the snail *Otala (Helix) lactea. Nature (London)* **208**, 583–594.

Boyd, W. C., Brown, R., and Boyd, L. G. (1966). Agglutinins for human erythrocytes in mollusks. *J. Immunol.* **96**, 301–303.

Chanovitch, X. (1921). Le pouvoir agglutinant du sang chez l'escargot en hibernation. *C. R. Soc. Biol.* **84**, 731–732.

Cheng, T. C. (1966). Perivascular leucocytosis and other types of cellular reactions in the oyster *Crassostrea virginica* experimentally infected with the nematode *Angiostrongylus cantonensis. J. Invertebr. Pathol.* **8**, 52–58.

Cheng, T. C. (1967). Marine molluscs as hosts for symbioses: With a review of known parasites of commercially important species. *Advan. Mar. Biol.* **5**, 1–424.

Cheng, T. C. (1969). An electrophoretic analysis of hemolymph proteins of *Helisoma duryi normale* experimentally challenged with bacteria. *J. Invertebr. Pathol.* **14**, 60–81.

Cheng, T. C., and Cooperman, J. S. (1964). Studies on host-parasite relationships between larval trematodes and their hosts. V. The invasion of the reproductive system of *Helisoma trivolvis* by the sporocysts and cercariae of *Glypthelmins pennsylvaniensis*. *Trans. Amer. Microsc. Soc.* **83**, 12–23.

Cheng, T. C., and Foley, D. A. (1972). A scanning electron microscope study of the cytoplasmic granules of *Crassostrea virginica* granulocytes. *J. Invertebr. Pathol.* **20**, 372–374.

Cheng, T. C., and Galloway, P. C. (1970). Transplantation immunity in mollusks: The histoincompatibility of *Helisoma duryi normale* with allografts and xenografts. *J. Invertebr. Pathol.* **15**, 177–192.

Cheng, T. C., and Rifkin, E. (1968). The occurrence and resorption of *Tylocephalum* metacestodes in the clam *Tapes semidecussata*. *J. Invertebr. Pathol.* **19**, 65–69.

Cheng, T. C., and Rifkin, E. (1970). Cellular reactions in marine molluscs in response to helminth parasitism. *In* "A Symposium on Diseases of Fishes and Shellfishes" (S. F. Snieszko, ed.), *Spec. Publ. No. 5*, pp. 443–496. *Amer. Fisher. Soc.*, Washington, D.C.

Cheng, T. C., and Sanders, B. G. (1962). Internal defense mechanisms in molluscs and an electrophoretic analysis of a naturally occurring serum hemagglutinin in *Viviparus malleatus* Reeve. *Proc. Pa. Acad. Sci.* **36**, 72–83.

Cheng, T. C., Shuster, C. N., Jr., and Anderson, A. H. (1966). Effects of plasma and tissue extracts of marine pelecypods on the cercaria of *Himasthla quissetensis*. *Exp. Parasitol.* **19**, 9–14.

Cheng, T. C., Thakur, A. S., and Rifkin, E. (1969). Phagocytosis as an internal defense mechanism in the Mollusca: With an experimental study of the role of leucocytes in the removal of ink particles in *Littorina scabra* Linn. *In* "Mollusca," Part II, pp. 546–563. Mar. Biol. Ass., India.

Cheng, T. C., Cali, A., and Foley, D. A. (1974). Cellular reactions in marine pelecypods as a factor influencing endosymbioses. *In* "Symbiosis in the Sea" (W. Vernberg and F. J. Vernberg, eds.) pp. 61–91. Univ. of South Carolina Press, Columbia.

Cushing, J. E., Calaprice, N. L., and Trump, G. (1963). Blood group reactive substances in some marine invertebrates. *Biol. Bull.* **125**, 69–80.

Feng, S. Y. (1965). Pinocytosis of proteins by oyster leucocytes. *Biol. Bull.* **128**, 95–105.

Feng, S. Y. (1967). Responses of molluscs to foreign bodies, with special reference to the oyster. *Fed. Proc., Fed. Amer. Soc. Exp. Biol.* **26**, 1685–1692.

Feng, S. Y., and Canzonier, W. J. (1970). Humoral responses in the American oyster (*Crassostrea virginica*) infected with *Bucephalus* sp. and *Minchinia nelsoni*. *In* "A Symposium on Diseases of Fishes and Shellfishes" (S. F. Snieszko, ed.), Spec. Publ. No. 5, pp. 497–510. Amer. Fisher. Soc., Washington, D.C.

Feng, S. Y., and Stauber, L. A. (1968). Experimental hexamitiasis in the oyster, *Crassostrea virginica*. *J. Invertebr. Pathol.* **10**, 94–110.

Foley, D. A., and Cheng, T. C. (1972). Interaction of molluscs and foreign substances: The morphology and behavior of hemolymph cells of the American oyster, *Crassostrea virginica*, in vitro. *J. Invertebr. Pathol.* **19**, 383–394.

Fries, C. R., and Tripp, M. R. (1970). Uptake of viral particles by oyster leukocytes in vitro. *J. Invertebr. Pathol.* **15**, 136–137.

Galtsoff, P. S. (1964). The American oyster, *Crassostrea virginica* Gmelin. *U.S., Fish Wildl. Serv.*, Fish. Bull. **64**. 1–480.

Haeckel, E. (1962). "Die Radiolarien." Geo. Reimer, Berlin.

Huff, C. G. (1940). Immunity in invertebrates. *Physiol. Rev.* **20**, 68–88.

Jenkin, C. R., and Rowley, D. (1970). Immunity in invertebrates. The purification of a haemagglutinin to rat and rabbit erythrocytes from the haemolymph of the murray mussel (*Velesunio ambiguus*). *Aust. J. Exp. Biol. Med. Sci.* **48**, 129–137.

Kartman, L. (1953). Factors influencing infection of the mosquito with *Dirofilaria immitis* (Leidy, 1856). *Exp. Parasitol.* **2**, 27–78.

Li, M. F., and Flemming, C. (1967). Hemagglutinin from oyster hemolymph. *Can. J. Zool.* **45**, 1225–1234.

McDade, J. E., and Tripp, M. R. (1967). Mechanism of agglutination of red blood cells by oyster hemolymph. *J. Invertebr. Pathol.* **9**, 523–530.

MacDonald, W. W. (1962). The genetic basis of susceptibility to infection with semiperiodic *Brugia malayi* in *Aedes aegypti*. *Ann. Trop. Med. Parasitol.* **56**, 373–382.

Malek, E. A. (1950). Susceptibility of the snail *Biomphalaria boissyi* to infection with certain strains of *Schistosoma mansoni*. *Amer. J. Trop. Med.* **30**, 887–894.

Malek, E. A. (1958). Natural and experimental infection of some bulinid snails in the Sudan with *Schistosoma haematobium*. *Proc. 6th Int. Congr. Trop. Med. Malaria, Lisbon* **2**, 5–13.

Malek, E. A. (1967). Susceptibility of tropicorbid snails from Louisiana to infection with *Schistosoma mansoni*. *Amer. J. Trop. Med. Hyg.* **16**, 715–717.

Michelson, E. H. (1961). An acid-fast pathogen of fresh water snails. *Amer. J. Trop. Med. Hyg.* **10**, 423–433.

Newton, W. L. (1952). The comparative tissue reactions of two strains of *Australorbis glabratus* to infection with *Schistosoma mansoni*. *J. Parasitol.* **38**, 362–366.

Newton, W. L. (1953). The inheritance of susceptibility to infection with *Schistosoma mansoni* in *Australorbis glabratus*. *Exp. Parasitol.* **2**, 242–257.

Newton, W. L. (1954). Tissue responses to *Schistosoma mansoni* in second generation snails from a cross between two strains of *Australorbis glabratus*. *J. Parasitol.* **40**, 352–355.

Pan, C. T. (1958). The general histology and topographic microanatomy of *Australorbis glabratus*. *Bull. Mus. Comp. Zool., Harvard Univ.* **119**, 237–299.

Pauley, G. B., Granger, G. A., and Krassner, S. M. (1971). Characterization of a natural agglutinin present in the hemolymph of the California sea hare, *Aplysia californica*. *J. Invertebr. Pathol.* **18**, 207–218.

Richards, C. S. (1970). Genetics of a molluscan vector of schistosomiasis. *Nature (London)* **227**, 806–810.

Rifkin, E., and Cheng, T. C. (1968). On the formation, structure, and histochemical characterization of the encapsulating cysts in *Crassostrea virginica* parasitized by *Tylocephalum* metacestodes. *J. Invertebr. Pathol.* **10**, 51–64.

Rifkin, E., Cheng, T. C., and Hohl, H. R. (1969a). An electron microscope study of the constituents of encapsulating cysts in *Crassostrea virginica* formed in response to *Tylocephalum* metacestodes. *J. Invertebr. Pathol.* **14**, 211–226.

Rifkin, E., Cheng, T. C., and Hohl, H. R. (1969b). The fine structure of the tegument of *Tylocephalum* metacestodes: With emphasis on a new type of microvilli. *J. Morphol.* **130**, 11–24.

Stauber, L. A. (1950). The fate of India ink injected intracardially into the oyster, *Ostrea virginica* Gmelin. *Biol. Bull.* **98**, 227–241.

Stauber, L. A. (1961). Immunity in invertebrates, with special reference to the oyster. *Proc. Nat. Shellfish. Ass.* **50**, 7–20.

Sturrock, B. M. (1967). The effect of infection with *Schistosoma haematobium* on the growth and reproduction rates of *Bulinus (Physopsis) nasutus productus*. *Ann. Trop. Med. Parasitol.* **61**, 321–325.

Sturrock, B. M. (1968). Resistance of *Bulinus (Physopsis) nasutus productus* to infection by *Schstosoma haematobium*. *Ann. Trop. Med. Parasitol.* **62**, 393–397.

Tripp, M. R. (1958a). Disposal by the oyster of intracardially injected red blood cells of vertebrates. *Proc. Nat. Shellfish. Ass.* **48**, 143–147.

Tripp, M. R. (1958b). Studies on the defense mechanism of the oyster. *J. Parasitol.*, **44**, Sect. 2, 35–36.

Tripp, M. R. (1961). The fate of foreign materials experimentally introduced into the snail *Australorbis glabratus. J. Parasitol.* **47**, 745–751.

Tripp, M. R. (1966). Hemagglutinin in the blood of the oyster *Crassostrea virginica. J. Invertebr. Pathol.* **8**, 478–484.

Tsujii, T. (1960). Studies on the mechanism of shell- and pear-formation in Mollusca. *J. Fac. Fish., Prefect. Univ. Mie* **5**, 1–70.

Tyler, A. (1946). Natural heteroagglutinins in the body-fluids and seminal fluids of various invertebrates. *Biol. Bull.* **90**, 213–219.

Ward, R. A. (1963). Genetic aspects of the susceptibility of mosquitoes to malaria infections. *Exp. Parasitol.* **13**, 328–341.

10　Parasite Induced Pathology

As indicated in Chapters 6, 7, and 8, mollusks are parasitized by a variety of organisms, ranging from viruses to arthropods. Irrespective of whether the mollusk is the intermediate, definitive, or only host in the developmental cycle of the parasite, one can expect to find pathological manifestations induced by the foreign organism. Such alterations from the normal can be appreciated as histopathological, physiological, as well as biochemical changes. Strange as it may seem, the impact of such alterations in parasitized mollusks remains unknown in most instances, although the presence of larval trematodes (sporocysts and/or rediae), especially the sporocysts of schistosomes, is known to result in reduced fecundity. This chapter presents some examples of the known pathological alterations one may expect to find in mollusks that are invaded by a variety of parasites.

Histopathology

The most commonly encountered histopathological changes in mollusks, especially gastropods, are those associated with the presence of larval trematodes. These range from extremely severe to minor alterations. This topic has been comprehensively reviewed by Cheng and Snyder (1962), and only a few additional studies have been reported since that review.

In considering histopathology induced by larval trematodes, it is extremely difficult to distinguish between the host's cellular reactions (see Chapter 9) and passive pathologic alterations. Only a thorough understanding and experience with the former will allow the investigator to distinguish between the two. Since the principles and selected examples of the various types of cellular reactions in mollusks have been considered in the previous chapter, they are not being reiterated here. Only what are considered to be passive pathologic alterations at the cellular and tissue levels are being reviewed.

DAMAGE TO THE DIGESTIVE GLAND

By far the majority of digenetic trematodes utilize their molluscan intermediate host's digestive gland as the primary site of infection, although if this organ becomes densely packed with sporocysts and/or rediae, some of these larvae may secondarily invade the adjacent gonads and other organs of the snail (Malek, 1952, 1955, 1958; Cheng and Cooperman, 1964; Pan, 1965; and others).

Usually there is very little, if any, cellular reaction in the digestive gland of mollusks harboring compatible larval trematodes, unless the parasites become moribund or are chemically altered for some other reason so that they become recognized as being "nonself." Consequently, histological and cytological changes associated with larval trematodes in this organ are what can be designated as the passive type, and several of these have been correlated with physiological and/or biochemical processes of the parasites.

As a rule, there is some degree of disarrangement of the acini comprising the digestive gland, when larval trematodes occur. This condition may be strictly mechanical displacement, with the acini being pushed to the periphery, as is the case in *Stagnicola emarginata angulata* parasitized by *Cercaria laruei, Plagiorchis muris, Cercaria vogena*, and *Diplostomum flexicaudum* (Pratt and Barton, 1941). Similarly, Pratt and Linquist (1943) have reported no destruction as well as no decrease in the number of acini in the same snail parasitized by *Cercaria laruei* or *Diplostomum flexicaudum*. On the other hand, Agersborg (1924), Dubois (1929), Cort *et al.* (1941), Malek (1952, 1958), Lal and Premvati (1955), Cheng and James (1960), James (1965), and others have reported the destruction of digestive gland acini in mollusks parasitized by larval trematodes. This destruction is of four types: (1) mechanical destruction due to pressure exerted by the parasites; (2) extracorporeal digestion by rediae and sporocysts and ingestion of rediae; (3) lysis due to the parasites' excreta; and (4) autolysis due to starvation.

Histologically, acinar cells affected by mechanical pressure appear extremely compressed, and, if ruptured, the fragments reveal jagged edges (Fig. 10-1). Furthermore, their nuclei are commonly not pycnotic, unless the nucleated fragments have persisted for some time, although this generally does not occur. Cells destroyed as the result of enzymes egested from the

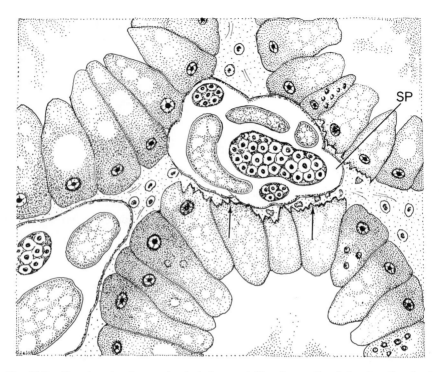

Fig. 10-1. Drawing showing mechanical damage inflicted on cells of the digestive gland (arrows) of a gastropod host by a sporocyst (SP) situated in the intertubular zone.

mouths of rediae or secreted from the tegument of sporocysts and rediae and those lysed by excreta are extremely difficult, if not impossible, to distinguish morphologically. Cell fragments usually possess eroded edges where the enzymes or excreta had acted upon them (Fig. 10-2). The nuclei of these cells are generally pycnotic. It is also of interest to note that because of the diffusibility of enzymes and soluble excreta, cells not in immediate contact with the parasites often show symptoms of destruction and/or necrosis, while in the case of mechanical damage, the compressed or cleanly ruptured cells usually occur in the immediate proximity of the parasites.

Cells destroyed as the result of starvation autolysis, when seen in histological sections, generally appear shriveled and with pycnotic nuclei. Comparatively large numbers of cytoplasmic vacuoles are present, but the cells are as a rule intact (Fig. 10-3).

In addition to the types of cell destruction discussed, another histopathological feature of parasitized digestive glands is the occurrence in large numbers of two types of globules of intracytoplasmic origin, especially if the

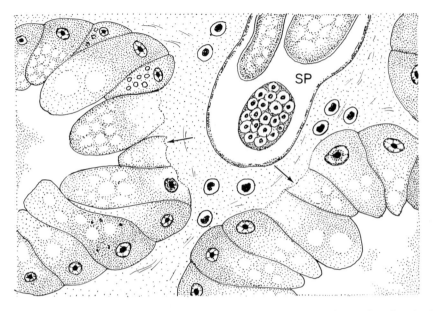

Fig. 10-2. Drawing showing lytic action of sporocyst-secreted material(s) on digestive gland cells of the gastropod host. The arrows indicate the eroded portions of the host's cells; SP, sporocyst.

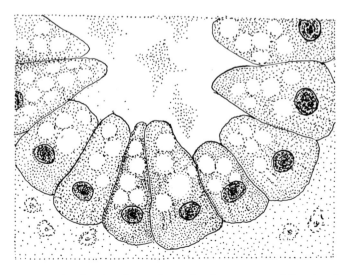

Fig. 10-3. Drawing showing shrunken and vacuolated appearance of digestive gland cells of a mollusk subjected to starvation.

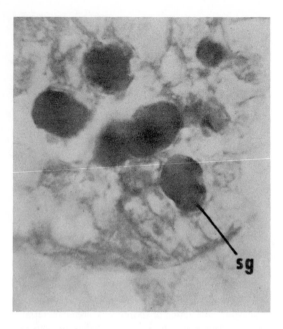

Fig. 10-4. Photomicrograph showing large numbers of ferment globules in cells of the digestive gland of *Nitocris dilatatus* parasitized by sporocysts of *Acanthatrium anaplocami* (Mallory's triple stain); sg, secretory or ferment globules (× 400). After Cheng (1971).

host–parasite association is of relatively long duration, that is, from more than a week to 10 days. The first type of globules, known as excretory or ferment globules, are yellowish brown, even in stained sections (Fig. 10-4). They are anucleate and represent accumulated metabolic wastes in hyperactive excretory or ferment cells of the digestive gland. As the cells become ruptured, digested, or lysed, the comparatively large excretory globules become dispersed throughout the tissues.

The second type of globules, known as calcium spherites (Fig. 10-5), originate in the so-called calcium cells of the digestive gland. These are usually lighter yellow in color and one-half to one-third the size of excretory globules. They are normal constituents of calcium cells and are composed of Ca^{2+} bound to a phosphate moeity (Aboliņš-Krogis, 1960, 1963a,b, 1968). In addition to calcium phosphate, these globules also include ionic calcium, an acid mucopolysaccharide, RNA, xanthine, probably hypoxanthine and pteridines, lipids, and proteins. When the mollusk becomes parasitized, for some yet undetermined reason, the number of calcium spherites becomes significantly increased in calcium cells (Cheng, 1971). As the duration of the

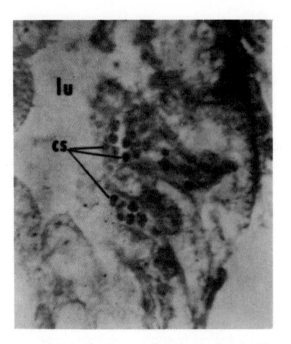

Fig. 10-5. Photomicrograph showing larger and greater number of calcium spherites (cs) in calcium cells of the digestive gland of *Nitocris dilatatus* parasitized by sporocysts of *Acanthatrium anaplocami* (oil red O stain); lu, lumen of digestive gland tubule (× 900). After Cheng (1971).

parasitization increases and the host cells become ruptured, large numbers of these globules also become intermingled with the cellular debris. Furthermore, there is a release of calcium spherites from intact cells, and, following this, the calcium ions become detached from the phosphate moeity. Consequently, significantly greater quantities of Ca^{2+} can be detected chemically in the digestive gland. Eventually, as reported by Cheng (1971), the calcium ions, carried in the hemolymph, become deposited in the nacre-secreting mantle and from there become incorporated in the shell. For this reason, Malek (1952), Etges (1961a,b), and Cheng (1971) have reported that parasitized snails have heavier shells than nonparasitized ones.

In pelecypods, a third type of yellowish brown bodies appear in fairly large numbers when the mollusk is parasitized. The parasite can be a fungus, a protozoan, a helminth, or an arthropod. These are the so-called brown cells (p. 169). They can be distinguished from the other types of yellowish bodies in that they are usually larger and nucleated, although their nuclei may be indistinct because of the pigment present in the cytoplasm.

The exact function(s) of brown cells deserves further attention, although some possible roles have been suggested. The most important attributed function is their role in the removal of degradation products of dead or moribund parasites and the metabolic by-products of successful parasites. Relative to this role, many investigators have noted increased pigmentation in *Crassostrea virginica* and other species of oysters infested with the annelids *Polydora* spp. or *Pinnotheres ostreum* (the oyster crab) and in *C. virginica* parasitized by the haplosporidan *Minchinia nelsoni*. In addition, Mackin (1951), who noted an increase in the number of brown cells in *C. virginica* parasitized by the fungus *Labyrinthomyxa marina*, has postulated that the increase may be indicative of an imbalance in lipid metabolism, possibly due to an increase in the oxidative and reductive processes resulting from disease. He has also noted an increase in the number of brown cells in *Macoma balthica* parasitized by *Labyrinthomyxa* and is of the opinion that the relative resistance of this clam to the fungus is the result of the large number of brown cells produced. Mackin's observations have been strengthened by the quantitative studies of Stein and Mackin (1955). Similarly, Cheng and Burton (1965, 1966) have noted that, although brown cells are present in nonparasitized *C. virginica*, their number is increased in oysters parasitized by sporocysts of the trematode *Bucephalus* sp.

Several cytopathological features have been reported associated with trematode parasitization of molluscan digestive glands. Hurst (1927) was the first to report an increase in the lipid content in the digestive gland cells of infected snails. Specifically, he has shown that the cells of *Physa occidentalis* include increased lipid droplets when parasitized by *Echinostoma revolutum* rediae. This initial observation has been subjected to modern cytochemical analysis by Cheng and Snyder (1962). They studied this phenomenon in *Helisoma trivolvis* parasitized by the sporocysts of *Glypthelmins pennsylvaniensis* and have found that not only is there an increase in the amount of neutral fats in the digestive gland cells of this pulmonate, but also that, as the duration of the parasitism increases, the accumulated neutral fats become degraded to fatty acids, and the latter pass from host cells into developing sporocysts and cercariae and are accumulated as a reserve nutrient source in their soma as long-chain fatty acids. Thus, there is a functional basis to the increased amount of lipids in the mollusk's digestive gland cells. It should be mentioned in conjunction with histopathology that sections of parasitized snail digestive glands usually reveal an increased number of cytoplasmic vacuoles as the fatty acids are passed from host to parasite in addition to the chemical alteration from neutral fats to fatty acids. The latter can be demonstrated by employing a cytochemical stain such as Nile blue sulfate.

The pathological effects of larval *Schistosoma mansoni* on the digestive gland of the snail *Biomphalaria pfeifferi* have recently been extensively studied by Meuleman (1972). This author also studied the normal structure of the digestive gland by histological, histochemical, and ultrastructural methods.

It is well known that the cells of the molluscan digestive gland, except those of prosobranchs, are primary sites for glycogen synthesis and storage. If these cells are treated with the periodic acid-Schiff procedure with appropriate controls, large accumulations of glycogen granules can be readily demonstrated. When mollusks become parasitized, especially by helminths, there is a marked reduction in the amount of stored glycogen in the cells of their digestive glands. This phenomenon, first reported by Faust (1920), has been confirmed by a number of investigators in a variety of mollusk–helminth associations by employing histochemistry and biochemistry (Hurst, 1927; von Brand and Files, 1947; Malek, 1952, 1958; Cheng and Snyder, 1962; Zischke and Zischke, 1965; James, 1965; and others). It should be noted that the reduction in glycogen is not limited to the digestive gland. All the glycogen in the body is reduced.

The loss of glycogen in the digestive gland cells of *Helisoma trivolvis*, a freshwater gastropod, parasitized by the larvae of the trematode *Glypthelmins pennsylvaniensis*, and in those of the oyster *Crassostrea virginica*, parasitized by the larvae of another trematode, *Bucephalus* sp., has been attributed to the breakdown of this polysaccharide to glucose, apparently stimulated in some yet undertermined manner by the presence of the parasites, and the glucose molecules are taken up and utilized for energy production and/or resynthesized as glycogen by the parasites.

Another striking cytopathological feature commonly encountered in digestive gland cells of mollusks infected with larval trematodes is the reduction of the normally columnar epithelial cells of each acinus to cuboidal or even squamous epithelium. This phenomenon, which has been reported by Cheng and Snyder (1962), has been confirmed by James (1965). This morphological change can be attributed to the starvation of cells as the result of the blockage of the hemolymph channels by the parasites (Rees, 1936; James, 1965).

Although not readily appreciated in routinely stained histological preparations, critical cytological examination of sections of molluscan digestive glands harboring trematodes stained with nuclear stains (Heidenhain's hematoxylin, Feulgen reaction, etc.) may reveal abnormal mitotic figures involving multipolars spindle fibers (Faust, 1920).

If the digestive gland becomes packed with larval trematodes, the thin layer of connective tissue, known as the tunica propria, enveloping the gland is commonly ruptured. This condition was observed in the snail *Helisoma corpulentum* infected with the rediae of *Petasiger chandleri* (Malek, 1952).

In summary, histopathological features associated with the digestive glands of mollusks parasitized by larval trematodes include the following:

1. Disarrangement of the acinar tubules
2. Mechanical compression and rupturing of cells
3. Lysing of cells by enzymes and excreta from parasites
4. Starvation autolysis of cells
5. Presence of large numbers of ferment globules
6. Increase in number of calcium spherites
7. Presence of large numbers of brown cells in pelecypods
8. Increase in lipid content in cells
9. Increase in number of cytoplasmic vacuoles
10. Reduction in amount of stored glycogen in cells
11. Alteration from columnar to cuboidal or squamous epithelium
12. Possible occurrence of abnormal mitotic figures
13. Rupturing of the tunica propria

DAMAGE TO GONADS

It has been noted earlier that a reduction in the fecundity of mollusks parasitized by larval trematodes is known. This information is the result of studies by Hurst (1927), Rees (1936), Malek (1952), Coelho (1954), Pan (1965), Etges and Gresso (1965), and Sturrock (1967) who have found that the number of eggs produced by the hermaphroditic snail hosts of human-infesting schistosomes and other trematodes is reduced. Among economically important mollusks, it is known that the presence of the dendritic sporocysts of *Bucephalus* spp. in the gonads of the American oyster, *Crassostrea virginica*, results in a decrease in the number of ova produced (Galtsoff, 1964; Cheng and Burton, 1965). As the result of such information, a limited number of studies have been carried out to ascertain the cause(s) of the reduced egg production. Incidentally, the total or partial elimination of gamete formation in hosts by parasites is known as parasitic castration.

From what is known, parasitic castration appears to be the result of two sets of processes, one mechanical and the other physiological. What has been reported about the first is summarized below. The physiological suppression of gamete production and/or development is considered in the following section.

It is now apparent that if the molluscan host's digestive gland becomes filled with trematode sporocysts and/or radiae, the enveloping tunica propria usually become ruptured, and the larval trematodes may invade the abutting gonad (Pan, 1965; Cheng and Cooperman, 1964; and others). This is usually the mechanism for invasion of the reproductive system in gastropods, although a few species of trematodes utilize the gonads as the primary site of infection. In *C. virginica*, the dendritic *Bucephalus cuculus* sporocysts utilize the gonads as the primary site of infection, although a northern species of *Bucephalus*, yet unnamed, which occurs in Rhode Island, utilizes the oyster's digestive gland as the primary site of infection, but, as the sporocysts grow, their branches are extended into the adjacent gonadal tissue (Cheng and Burton, 1965).

Upon entering the gonad, be it an ovotestis, an ovary, or a testis, the larval trematodes, if they are rediae, can actively ingest gonadal tissue. Such is the case when rediae of *Petasiger chandleri* or *Clinostomum marginatum* invade the ovotestis of *Helisoma corpulentum* (Malek, 1958), or the rediae of *Parorchis acanthus* invade the gonads of the southern oyster drill, *Thais haemastoma* (Cooley, 1962) (Fig. 10-6). Gross manifestations of parasitized gonads are in the form of color changes. For example, Cooley has reported that the gonads of uninfected *T. haemastoma* are usually brownish in males and yellow to orange in females; however, if *P. acanthus* rediae are present,

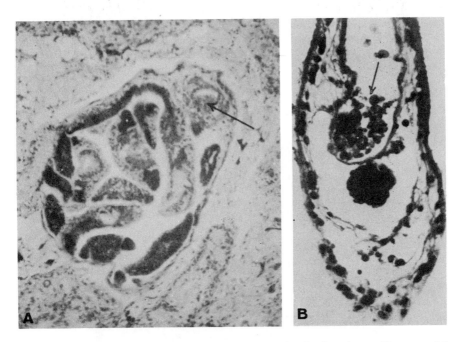

Fig. 10-6. Photomicrographs of rediae of *Parorchis acanthus* that have ingested host material. (A) Section of a redia showing yolk platlets of host origin situated in posterior end of its intestinal cecum (arrow) ($\times$ 450). (B) Longitudinal section of a redia showing ingested yolk platlets (arrow) ($\times$ 215). Parts A and B after Cooley (1962).

the thin and patchy gonads are cream to brown in males and may be oyster white in females.

If parasitic castration is caused by sporocysts, as in the case of *Biomphalaria glabrata*, parasitized by *Schistosoma mansoni*, or *Crassostrea virginica*, parasitized by *Bucephalus* spp., the suppression of egg production is primarily physiological, although morphological evidence of abnormal ova can be appreciated. In the oyster, for example, Cheng and Burton (1965) have reported that the ova of infected specimens appear degenerate and are smaller, being similar in appearance to those undergoing resorption after the normal spanning period and to those undergoing autolysis during post-mortem changes (Fig. 10-7). In addition to the abnormal appearance of the ova, the integrity of the oyster's gonadal lobes are partially or completely destroyed. It was reported by Malek (1952, 1955) that in the case of *Biomphalaria alexandrina* infected with *Schistosoma mansoni* sporocysts invaded the connective tissue around and between the acini of the ovotestis, but none of them were found inside any acini. He concluded that the effect of parasitisim on the gonad by this schistosome or by other trematodes having a daughter sporocyst stage, for example, the strigeid *Uvulifer ambloplitis*, is not the result of mechanical influence of the parasite but rather by induced physiological conditions that tend to disturb the metabolism of the snail host.

It is of interest to note that parasitic castration has been suggested as a method, combined with others, to control certain species of undesirable

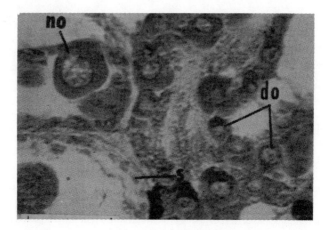

Fig. 10-7. Photomicrograph of a section of the gonad of *Crassostrea virginica* parasitized by sporocysts of *Bucephalus* sp. showing smaller, degenerate ova (Mallory's stain). do, Degenerate ova; no, normal ovum; s, sporocyst ($\times$ 400). After Cheng and Burton (1965).

mollusks (p. 315). For example, Cooley (1962) has suggested that *Parorchis acanthus* might be used to control oyster drills, and, in the area of medical malacology, Cheng *et al.* (1973) have suggested that another trematode, *Zoogonus rubellus*, might be employed to control the incidence of swimmer's itch (cercarial dermatitis) caused by the avian schistosome *Austrobilharzia variglandis*. This latter idea is based on the finding that the sporocysts of *Z. rubellus* will cause the parasitic castration of the mudflat snail, *Nassarius obsoletus*, which is also the intermediate host for *A. variglandis*. Thus, if *Z. rubellus*, as the result of inducing parasitic castration, reduces the *N. obsoletus* population, it would follow that less snails would be available to transmit the avian schistosome.

DAMAGE TO CONNECTIVE TISSUE

The only detailed study to date of histopathological changes in connective tissue other than those associated with innate cellular reactions to foreign agents (p. 190) is that by Pan (1965). Even then, the changes reported by Pan are probably associated with cellular reactions.

Pan has studied changes in the structure of the connective tissue constituents of *Biomphalaria glabrata* infected with *Schistosoma mansoni*. He has reported that, when large numbers of escaping cercariae occur in connective tissue, especially in loose vascular connective tissue, characteristic of the mollusk's rectal ridge, pseudobranch, and mantle collar, there is a marked hyperplasia of fibroblasts. Furthermore, the hemolymph lacunae, crystalline concretions, and myofibers normally associated with connective tissue diminish in number and size. The hyperplastic fibroblasts eventually become hypertrophic, and their nuclei are pycnotic, oval, clearly vesicular, and rich in chromatin. An accumulation of cytoplasm occurs around each nucleus, and the fibroblasts become spindle-shaped (Fig. 10-8). Eventually, the hypertrophic fibroblasts occupy whole areas so that the normal architecture of the connective tissue is lost (compare Fig. 10-9 with Fig. 10-8). Pan is of the opinion that these hypertrophic fibroblasts can transform into amoebocytes.

It is of interest to note that these alterations associated with connective tissue only occur if escaping cercariae are present. Migrating daughter sporocysts en route to the digestive gland do not elicit such histopathologic changes.

It should be noted at this point that there are some structural as well as chemical changes in the loose areolar connective tissue of the oyster *Crassostrea virginica* associated with the presence of metacestodes of the tapeworm *Tylocephalum*. Rifkin and Cheng (1968) have reported that prior to the deposition of fibers to form the capsule surrounding each parasite, the

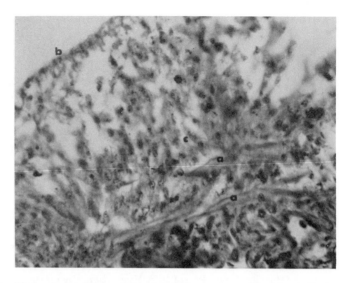

Fig. 10-8. Photomicrograph showing early cellular response of the hyperactive loose connective tissue in the rectal ridge of *Biomphalaria glabrata* infected with *Schistosoma mansoni*. a, Myofibers; b, respiratory epithelium; c, hypertrophic fibroblasts (× 585). After Pan (1965).

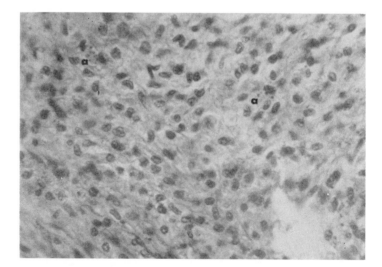

Fig. 10-9. Photomicrograph showing mobilization of amoebocytes in *Biomphalaria glabrata* infected with *Schistosoma mansoni* at the height of hyperactivity. a, Fragments of degenerated cercarial tissue containing pycnotic nuclei. Most of the cells are hypertrophic amoebocytes, fibroblasts, and cells intermediate between these two types (× 500). After Pan (1965).

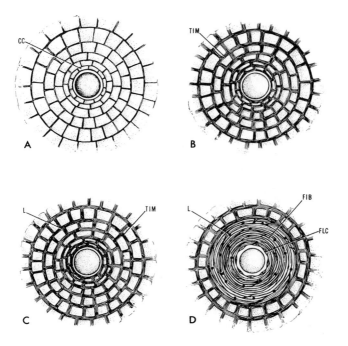

Fig. 10-10. Diagrammatic drawings showing steps involved during the formation of fibrous capsule surrounding *Tylocephalum* metacestode in *Crassostrea virginica*. (A) Appearance of compressed Leydig cells around metacestode; (B) appearance of thickened intercellular material between Leydic cells; (C) infiltration of leukocytes into the area; (D) deposition of more or less concentric lamellae of fibers, originating as thickened intercellular material, around metacestode and the appearance of innermost layer of fibroblastlike cells. CC, Compressed host cell; FIB, fibrous capsule; FLC, fibroblastlike cell; L, leukocyte; TIM, thickened intercellular material. After Rifkin and Cheng (1968).

Leydig (connective tissue) cells in the immediate proximity of the metacestode are mechanically compressed (Fig. 10-10).

Our knowledge of chemical changes in molluscan connective tissue elements associated with parasites is limited to the glycogen and lipid contents of Leydig cells in oysters. Cheng and Burton (1966) have reported that there is a significant reduction in the amount of stored glycogen in these cells of *C. virginica* parasitized by *Bucephalus* sp. This reduction is not limited to those host cells situated in the immediate proximity of the parasites but occurs throughout the host. Relative to lipids, Cheng (1965) has found that there is a reduction of total lipids in the same species of oyster harboring the same parasite. This reduction in total fats reflects the concurrent reduction of both neutral fats and fatty acids in the same cells. The reduction of neutral fats is believed to have resulted from their being hydrolyzed by lipase of parasite origin.

DAMAGE TO HEMOLYMPH VESSELS

There is only limited information available on histopathological changes in molluscan hemolymph vessels as the result of the presence of helminth parasites.

Pan (1965) has demonstrated that the walls of the aorta and arteries of *Biomphalaria glabrata* infected with *Schistosoma mansoni* become thickened after the sixth week postinfection. The cells lining these vessels are hypertrophic and hyperplastic, and some undergo division. The muscular tunic of the arteries and aorta is thickened and is intensely eosinophilic. In addition, the cells comprising the vessels' connective tissue tunics are usually hypertrophic and contain lightly basophilic, abundant cytoplasm and oval, chromatin-rich nuclei. These changes are most conspicuous in small arteries.

The second piece of information pertaining to histopathologic changes of molluscan hemolymph vessels associated with helminth parasitism has been contributed by Cheng (1966). He has reported that, if larvae of the nematode

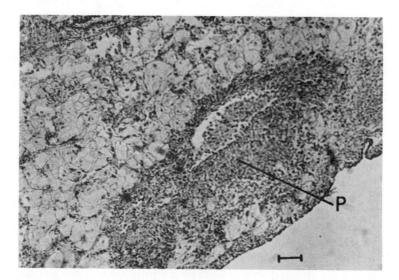

Fig. 10-11. Photomicrograph showing typical perivascular leukocytosis in *Crassostrea virginica* experimentally infected with *Angiostrongylus cantonensis* larvae. Notice the heavy tunic of leukocytes surrounding a blood vessel (P) and the large number of leukocytes in the lumen. This oyster was examined 10 days after infection. After Cheng (1966). Bar = 50 μm.

Angiostrongylus cantonensis are experimentally introduced into *Crassostrea virginica* and find their way into hemolymph vessels, in time, a tunic of hemolymph cells is formed around the vessels (Fig. 10-11). Cheng has proposed that these cells, free in the oyster's tissues, are attracted to the vessel walls by the molting fluid of the intravascular nematodes when the latter molt.

DAMAGE TO NERVOUS TISSUE

Our knowledge of histopathological alterations in mollusks due to parasites is limited to the single observation by Pan (1965) who has reported that the central ganglia of *Biomphalaria glabrata* are sometimes invaded by the mother sporocysts and cercariae of *Schistosoma mansoni*. In any case, the deeply basophilic plaques, or granules, in the cytoplasm of the ganglionic cells become confluent, thus forming large masses. These stain poorly and are pale blue. The nuclei of the host's cells become poorly defined and pale. Nerve fibers compressed by mother sporocysts are sometimes locally constricted and stain poorly with eosin. The pale pink fibers include few or no recognizable neurofibrils.

Pathophysiology

Studies of the effects of invading organisms on the physiological well-being of molluscan hosts have been relatively recent. As one would expect, most of these studies have been limited to the medically or economically important species, although a few exceptions exist.

EFFECT ON FECUNDITY

It has been stated that the presence of certain helminth parasites, especially larval trematodes, is known to eliminate or reduce the production of eggs by mollusks. If the larval trematodes are rediae, available evidences already cited indicate that the host's gonadal tissues are totally or partially destroyed as the result of direct ingestion. On the other hand, if the larval trematodes are sporocysts, parasitic castration apparently is due to physiological stress. In addition to the above findings, Malek (1952, 1955) has also shown, based on morphological and histological studies, that sporocysts and rediae of trematodes affect other parts of the genitalia, especially the albumin gland, the prostate, the uterus and the sperm duct, and thus indirectly affect the reproductive capacity of the parasitized snail. Evidences for the belief that parasitic castration by sporocysts is apparently due to physiological stress are presented at this point.

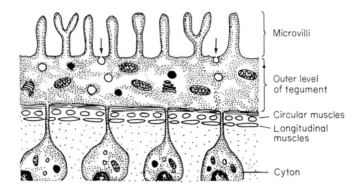

Fig. 10-12. Diagrammatic drawing of the fine structure of the surface of a sporocyst showing vesicles associated with the surface (arrows).

Trematode sporocysts are without a mouth and hence are incapable of actively ingesting host cells as can rediae. Yet, these saccular larvae are not passive organisms. Recent chemical and electron microscope studies have revealed that the sporocyst tegument is a dynamic structure that is metabolically active (for reviews, see Lee, 1966, Cheng 1973). Fine structural studies have revealed vesicles associated with the microvilli-bearing outer surface of sporocysts, and some of these vesicles may be secretion containing and are en route to the exterior (Fig. 10-12). Thus, it is possible that sporocysts may secrete enzymes that would have a deleterious physiological effect on germinal epithelia and on developing and fully developed gametic cells in molluscan gonads. It should be mentioned in passing that rediae, at least those of *Philophthalmus gralli* in the snail *Tarebia granifera*, are known to secrete a nonspecific aminopeptidase from their tegument that can cause the lysin of adjacent host cells (Cheng and Yee, 1968).

Physiological inhibition and/or retardation of egg formation in parasitized mollusks (as opposed to mechanical destruction, including ingestion by rediae) due to the presence of sporocysts is exemplified by Pan's (1965) data on egg production in *Biomphalaria glabrata* parasitized by *Schistosoma mansoni*. From his data, presented in Table 10-1, it is evident that, not only is there a significant decline in egg masses laid by the third week postinfection, but there is a cessation of egg production by the fifth week. Similarly, Etges and Gresso (1965) have reported that egg laying in *B. glabrata* parasitized by the same schistosome is reduced, but according to these investigators it is never permanently inhibited. Evidence other than Pan's for total cessation of egg production has been contributed by Sturrock (1966), who has found that egg laying in *Biomphalaria pfeifferi* parasitized by

TABLE 10-1

Comparison of the Fecundity of *Biomphalaria glabrata* Infected with *Schistosoma mansoni* and Uninfected Snails[a]

Week post-infection	Infected snails[b]		Uninfected snails	
	No. of egg masses laid	No. of eggs	No. of egg masses laid	No. of eggs
0				
1	148	2,618	110	2,066
2	444	8,299	365	5,889
3	247	4,238	329	6,311
4	2	20	466	10,472
5	0	0	497	11,617
6	0	0	431	10,927
7	0	0	545	13,919
8	0	0	285	7,285
9	0	0	204	5,273

[a]After Pan (1965).
[b]Each infected snail had been exposed six times to miracidia during the first 12 days of the experiment.

S. mansoni is completely suppressed. On the other hand, Chu *et al.* 's (1966) data on *Bulinus truncatus* infected with *Schistosoma haematobium* support the contention of Etges and Gresso that, although egg production is dramatically reduced, it is never totally suppressed. In addition, McClelland and Bourns (1969) have reported a reduction of egg laying by *Lymnaea stagnalis* parasitized by *Trichobilharzia ocellata*.

Of particular interest relative to reduced egg production in mollusks parasitized by trematode sporocysts is the study by Hosier and Goodchild (1970). These investigators have found that, when the snail *Menetus dilatatus* is experimentally infected with the larval stages of a Georgian strain of the turtle lung fluke, *Spirorchis scripta*, egg laying is reduced by the third day postinfection and completely suppressed in about 7 days (Table 10-2). On the other hand, if Georgian *M. dilatatus* are experimentally infected with a Minnesota strain of *S. scripta*, egg laying is reduced after 9 days of infection but never permanently suppressed (Table 10-3). Since the same number of miracidia was used to infect each snail of each experimental group, these results suggest that whether complete suppression occurs or not may be due to the strain of parasite involved.

Another important observation contributed by Hosier and Goodchild (1970) is that histological examinations of parasitized *M. dilatatus* have

TABLE 10-2

Number of Eggs Laid by Uninfected *Menetus dilatatus* **and**
M. dilatatus **Infected with a Georgian Strain of** *Spirorchis scripta*[a]

Days postexposure	No. of eggs laid[b]	
	Uninfected snails (34 specimens)	Infected snails (38 specimens)
1	3.5 ± 0.35	3.8 ± 0.35
2	3.1 ± 0.33	3.1 ± 0.30
3	2.1 ± 0.30	1.3 ± 0.19[c]
4	2.3 ± 0.27	0.2 ± 0.10[c]
5	3.0 ± 0.33	0.1 ± 0.08[c]
6	3.0 ± 0.36	0.1 ± 0.05[c]
7	3.1 ± 0.36	0[d]

[a]After Hosier and Goodchild (1970).
[b]Mean ± standard errors.
[c]Significantly less than uninfected.
[d]No eggs were laid by infected snails through day 20 in one experiment and through day 228 in another experiment.

TABLE 10-3

Number of Eggs Laid by Uninfected *Menetus dilatatus* **and**
M. dilatatus **Infected with a** (Georgian) **Strain of** *Spirorchis scripta*[a]
MINNESOTA

Days postexposure	No. of eggs laid[b]	
	Uninfected snails (83 specimens)	Infected snails (15 specimens)
1	1.88 ± 0.23	2.73 ± 0.33
2	2.12 ± 0.40	2.07 ± 0.53
3	2.00 ± 0.60	2.00 ± 0.47
4	2.25 ± 0.16	1.60 ± 0.31
5	2.00 ± 0.53	1.67 ± 0.36
6	1.75 ± 0.49	1.27 ± 0.25
7	1.25 ± 0.37	0.60 ± 0.19
8	0.50 ± 0.38	0.20 ± 0.11
9	3.12 ± 0.48	0.47 ± 0.19[c]
10	2.38 ± 0.46	0.33 ± 0.21[d]

[a]After Hosier and Goodchild (1970).
[b]Means ± standard errors.
[c]Significantly less than uninfected.
[d]Reduced egg laying continued through day 53.

revealed that there was no invasion of nor damage to the snail's reproductive system during the first 3 days of infection; however, some of the parasitized snails had usually small, abnormally stained albumin glands, oviducts, or sperm ducts after the fourth day, although no parasites were present in the reproductive systems. This information suggests that the histopathological changes associated with the reproductive system and the suppression of egg production are due to indirect involvement, possibly some secreted material. Indirect, physiological disruption of the normal function of the molluscan host's reproductive system by sporocysts has also been suggested by Pan (1965) and McClelland and Bourns (1969), and Cheng and Burton (1965) have found abnormal appearing ova in the ovaries of *Crassostrea virginica* associated with *Bucephalus* sporocysts.

CHANGES ASSOCIATED WITH PARASITIC CASTRATION

In addition to reduction or cessation of egg laying, several other interesting manifestations of parasitic castration have been reported. Wesenberg-Lund (1934) appears to be the first to have reported that mollusks parasitized by larval trematodes become abnormally large. Specifically, he found that parasitized *Lymnaea auricularia* become larger. A more detailed discussion of this phenomenon, sometimes designated as gigantism, is presented in the following subsection (p. 224). It is being mentioned briefly here because Rothschild (1936, 1938, 1941a,b) and Rothschild and Rothschild (1939) have studied this phenomenon extensively (for a review, see Cheng, 1967) and have expressed the opinion that the abnormal increase in size of parasitized snails is "... brought about by the destruction of the gonads and other glands" (Rothschild, 1936). The physiological basis for her suggestion remains uninvestigated. Furthermore, there is some doubt whether true enhanced growth, involving soft tissues, does occur (Cheng, 1971).

Sex reversal is another phenomenon that has been associated with parasitic castration. Pelseneer (1906, 1928) was the first to point out that the penes of snails harboring larval trematodes are reduced. This, in his opinion, is due to partial or complete castration of the host. It was Wesenberg-Lund (1931), however, who first proposed the theory that changes in sex in mollusks might be directly the result of parasitization by larval trematodes. He arrived at this hypothesis after finding that in the hermaphroditic snail *Succinea putris*, after the female organs are completely destroyed, sperm are produced for some time before complete castration. Wesenberg-Lund's contention is that a hermaphrodite has been altered to a male. As to whether this is indeed a case of sex reversal is questionable since what could have happened is that the ovarian tissue was destroyed before the testicular tissue of the ovotestis.

Krull (1935), who studied the morphology of a number of snails, including the estuarine snail *Hydrobia ulvae*, has reported that the size of the penis in specimens harboring larval trematodes is reduced and that the mollusks represent "sex-reversed" females. The conclusion was based on anatomical studies, which had revealed that the snails were unquestionably females but, as the result of parasitization, had developed nonfunctional penes. Krull did not suggest that these snails had ever functioned as males; therefore, "sex reversal" is an unsatisfactory term in this instance.

Rees (1936) has also studied sex reversal of parasitized snails. He has demonstrated that there are definite reductions in the size and prominence of the accessory sex organs (penis and vas deferens in males, oviduct in females) in the prosobranch *Littorina littorea* harboring the larval stages of either *Himasthla leptosoma* or *Cercaria lophocerca* in the gonads. In fact, the accessory organs become invisible. A partial reduction of this type also occurs in *L. littorea* parasitized by *Cercaria emasculans*. According to Rees, the reason for only a partial reduction of the accessory organs in snails parasitized by *C. emasculans* is that this trematode never completely destroys the host's gonads. Although Rees has found no transitional stages from male to female or vice versa, he has suggested that there is the possibility of sex reversal, since among the individuals recovering from parasitization all were females while among the older, nonparasitized snails there was only a slight preponderance of females. As to whether this indirect evidence is reliable is open to question.

Finally, Rothschild (1938) has also studied the manifestations of gonadal destruction in *Hydrobia ulvae*. She has found that the penes of all parasitized snails are abnormal, usually being reduced in size. She has expressed the opinion that in some of the specimens loss of the penis was caused by the complete destruction of the testes. In one infected female she found a small penis; however, Rothschild has stated that it is highly improbable that all infected snails with reduced penes are sex-reversed females.

From the available information, it appears inconclusive that true sex reversal occurs in mollusks suffering from parasitic castration. At best, the only conclusion that can be drawn is that the development of secondary sex characteristics in mollusks is governed by gonadal hormones, and, if the gonads are destroyed, there may be a reduction in size of the external genitalia.

EFFECT ON GROWTH

The literature pertaining to the influence of parasites on the growth of hosts has been critically reviewed by Cheng (1971). Among mollusks, there are several reports that enhanced growth occurs, at least temporarily, if larval trematodes are present (Wesenberg-Lund, 1934; Rothschild, 1936, 1938, 1941a,b; Rothschild and Rothschild, 1939; Lysaght, 1941; Hoshina and Ogino, 1951; Menzel and Hopkins, 1955a,b; de Andrade, 1962; Chernin, 1960; Pan, 1962, 1965). Contrary to this, Pesigan *et al.* (1958), Moose (1963), and Zischke and Zischke (1965) have reported that there is a retardation in the growth of snails harboring larval trematodes.

   The most detailed study to date on possible enhanced growth of parasitized snails is that by Pan (1965). He has shown that adolescents of *Biomphalaria glabrata* (7.3 mm in shell diameter) mass infected with *Schistosoma mansoni* have greater shell diameters than uninfected snails between the second and sixth weeks after infection (Fig. 10-13). However, as the result of studying *Nitocris dilatatus*, parasitized by *Acanthatrium anaplocami* and *Physa sayii* parasitized by *Echinostoma revolutum*, Cheng (1971) has indicated that, although there are greater amounts of calcium deposited in the shells of parasitized snails, there is no increase in soft tissue weight (Tables 10-4 and 10-5), and, hence, true enhanced growth may not occur or at least not as a consistent phenomenon. Thus the greater weights of parasitized snails (Malek, 1952; Cheng, 1971) are not due to true enhanced growth but to heavier shells. This could account for the greater shell sizes as reported by Chernin (1960) and Pan (1962, 1965). Relative to this point, it is of interest to point out that Wesenberg-Lund (1934) has reported that parasitized *Lymnaea auriculata* often have "ballooned" shells. This phenomenon could also account for greater shell diameters, at least in part. The hypercalcifica-

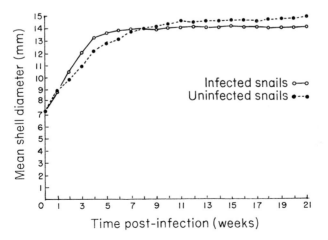

Fig. 10-13. Comparative growth of *Biomphalaria glabrata* infected and uninfected with *Schistosoma mansoni*. Data from Pan (1965).

TABLE 10-4

Mean Weights of Nonparasitized *Nitocris dilatatus*, **Those Parasitized by** *Acanthatrium anaplocami*, **and Sporocysts Removed from the Latter**[a]

Mean weights	Parasitized snails (35 specimens)	Nonparasitized snails (45 specimens)	Sporocysts	Statistical significance at 5% level
Whole snails (g ± SD)	0.396 ± 0.144	0.329 ± 0.137		+
Soft tissues (g ± SD)	0.126 ± 0.055	0.114 ± 0.45		−
Dried shells (g ± SD)	0.221 ± 0.084	0.162 ± 0.071		+
Each para-sitized snail (g ± SD)			0.024 ± 0.011	

[a]After Cheng (1971).

TABLE 10-5

Weights of Nonparasitized *Physa sayii*, **Those Parasitized by** *Echinostoma revolutum*, **and Rediae Removed from the Latter**[a]

Mean weights	Parasitized snails (33 specimens)	Nonparasitized snails (25 specimens)	Rediae	Statistical significance at 5% level
Whole snails (g ± SD)	0.335 ± 0.016	0.217 ± 0.090		+
Soft tissues (g ± SD)	0.085 ± 0.030	0.086 ± 0.024		−
Dried shells (g ± SD)	0.156 ± 0.002	0.085 ± 0.040		+
Each para-sitized snail (g ± SD)			0.031 ± 0.012	

[a]After Cheng (1971).

tion of the shell of *Helisoma anceps* parasitized by the rediae of *Cercaria reynoldsi* has been noted by Etges (1961a) in nature. The source of the extra calcium in parasitized snails has been discussed earlier (p. 208).

EFFECT ON SHELL MORPHOLOGY

In addition to differences in the degree of calcification and the dimensions of the shells of parasitized and nonparasitized mollusks, another type of abnormality is known. Specifically, Sturrock and Sturrock (1970, 1971) have reported that the shell of *Biomphalaria glabrata* is commonly distorted when infected with *Schistosoma mansoni*. Their observations have been confirmed by one of us (T. C. C.). This distortion (Fig. 10-14) is due to a reversal of the lip deflection found in uninfected snails from ventral to dorsal. Sturrock and Sturrock (1971) have demonstrated that this shell distortion in infected snails first appears at about the time when cercarial shedding begins and increases as the infection progresses. The cause of this phenomenon is not completely known; however, as the result of finding granulomata in histo-

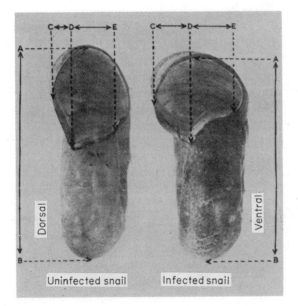

Fig. 10-14. Photographs of two shells of *Biomphalaria glabrata*, one with a 20-week-old *Schistosoma mansoni* infection, the other uninfected, showing the location of the maximum diameter (AB), the dorsal deflection (CD), and the height of the inner lip (DE). After Sturrock and Sturrock (1971).

logical sections in the mantle collar on the side opposite the pseudobranch, for example on the side on which the distortion occurs, it has been suggested that it may be caused by a disturbance of the hemolymph supply or composition, which, in turn, could affect the normal function of the pseudostratified epithelium. It has also been suggested that hypertrophy of the underlying tissues could be responsible for the development of the distorted shell.

As the result of the finding that the shell distortion begins when infected snails commence to shed cercariae, Sturrock and Sturrock (1971) have proposed that an analysis of the degree of distortion may be useful in determining how long an infected snail had been shedding.

EFFECT ON LONGEVITY

Despite extremely severe histopathological alteration in parasitized mollusks, especially in instances of trematode parasitization, from what is known helminthic diseases of mollusks may be considered chronic rather than virulent and/or acute. In other words, the molluscan host is not killed in a short period of time. Quantitative information on the effect of parasitization on the longevity of mollusks is still scanty and is almost exclusively limited to the species harboring schistosomes.

Pan (1965), as a part of his comprehensive report on the pathobiology of *Biomphalaria glabrata* parasitized by *Schistosoma mansoni*, has reported that among 150 snails "... of various sizes (that) were exposed (in lots of 50) en masse (to an undetermined number of miracidia) for 3 hours in finger bowls (21 × 6 cm) containing about 100 ml of charcoal-filtered water," a 6.7% mortality rate occurred during the first 6 weeks as opposed to 3% among 100 control snails. During this period of time the parasites are maturing. Mortality rose sharply during the second 6 week period, increasing from 6.7% to 44.7%, and continued into the third and fourth 6 week periods. The cumulative mortality among infected snails was 89.3% for the first 24 weeks postinfection while that of the controls for the same period was 35%. The mortality rate among the controls would have been lower except that 21 snails were killed in a laboratory accident during the twenty-second week of the experiment.

Pan has also reported that if relatively old, sexually mature *B. glabrata* (13.0–20.5 mm in shell diameter) were mass exposed to "large numbers of miracidia," high mortality also commenced when heavy emergence of cercariae began during the sixth week postinfection. Earlier, Ritchie *et al.* (1963) had reported survival of 29% of *B. glabrata* infected with *S. mansoni* during 26 weeks under favorable conditions, and Sturrock and Sturrock (1970) have since shown that infected snails have a median life expectancy of 6 months in the laboratory. This bears out the field and laboratory observations by Barbosa (1963) in Brazil, although it is at variance with the results of Chu and Dawood (1970) for *Biomphalaria alexandrina* infected with *S. mansoni* in Egypt. The latter investigators have reported a much shorter median life span.

It is apparent from the information reviewed that the longevity of *B. glabrata* is reduced when infected with *S. mansoni*. Whether this is the case in other mollusk–parasite associations remains to be studied.

EFFECT ON HEART RATE AND RESPIRATION

Lee and Cheng (1970) were the first to report that the heart rate of *Biomphalaria glabrata* is significantly increased as the result of parasitization by *Schistosoma mansoni*. A more detailed analysis (Lee and Cheng, 1971a) has revealed that when the heart rates of snails (NIH albino strain, 10 mm in shell diameter) exposed to ten miracidia are compared to those of uninfected controls over a period of 8 weeks postinfection, there is a significant decrease from the fourth week on in the former (Fig. 10-15). If similar infected snails and controls are maintained at temperatures ranging between 24° and 33°C, with the exception of 33°C, the heart rates of infected snails are consistently greater than those of control snails.

It is of interest to note that the metabolic rate of mollusks, as reflected by their heart rates, has proven to be a useful tool in the bioassay of molluscicides (Cheng and Sullivan, 1973).

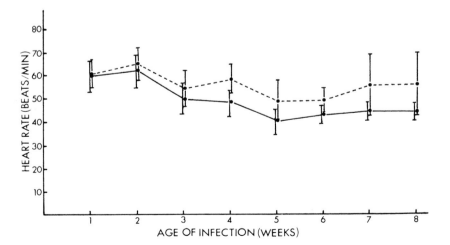

Fig. 10-15. Comparison of heart rates of noninfected *Biomphalaria glabrata* (———) and those infected with *Schistosoma mansoni* (-----) at different time intervals postinfection. Vertical lines represent standard deviations. After Lee and Cheng (1971a).

EFFECT ON RESPIRATION

Since von Brand *et al.* (1950) have demonstrated that there is a correlation between the heart rate of *Biomphalaria glabrata* and oxygen consumption, Lee and Cheng (1971b) have conducted studies to ascertain the oxygen consumption of snails uninfected and infected with *Schistosoma mansoni.* Earlier studies by von Brand and Files (1947) and Edwards *et al.* (1951) have suggested that there is no significant difference; however, Lee and Cheng (1971b) have found that although the oxygen uptake by infected snails is only statistically greater during the sixth and eighth weeks postinfection (Fig. 10-16), regression analysis has indicated that the rates of oxygen uptake by infected snails increase as a function of time while those of the control snails decrease. Furthermore, as the result of determining uptake rates for *S. mansoni* sporocysts and cercariae, it has been concluded that the increased oxygen consumption by infected snails is due primarily to the increased oxygen utilization of host tissues and secondarily to that by parasites, and a possible relationship between increased oxygen uptake and increased heart rate in infected snails is indicated.

EFFECT ON THERMAL TOLERANCE

Vernberg and Vernberg (1963) have established the principle that mollusks infected with larval trematodes have a lower maximum thermal tolerance limit. They investigated *Nassarius obsoletus* parasitized by either

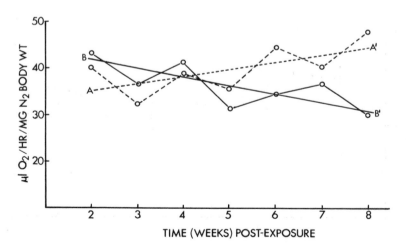

Fig. 10-16. Rates of oxygen uptake by noninfected *Biomphalaria glabrata* (----) and those infected with *Schistosoma mansoni* (————). The lines AA' and BB' are the regression lines of the oxygen uptake by infected and noninfected snails, respectively. After Lee and Cheng (1971b).

Lepocreadium ovalis sporocysts or *Zoogonus rubellus* sporocysts. Similarly, Etges and Gresso (1965) have noted that specimens of *Biomphalaria glabrata* infected with *Schistosoma mansoni* died at higher temperatures* while uninfected ones survived.

Lee and Cheng (1971a) subjected uninfected *B. glabrata* and those infected with ten *S. mansoni* miracidia each to temperature stress and determined their thermal tolerances on a quantitative basis. They have found that infected snails demonstrate a lower maximum thermal tolerance limit than uninfected ones, with 40% dying within 5 days when maintained at 33°C. When maintained at 28°C for 10 weeks, 75% mortality occurred among the infected snails while only 40% mortality occurred among the uninfected controls.

EFFECT ON PARTIAL PRESSURE OF HEMOLYMPH

Possible alterations in the pO_2, pCO_2, and pH of the hemolymph of *Biomphalaria glabrata* infected with *Schistosoma mansoni* have been investigated by Lee and Cheng (1971b). As indicated in Table 10-6, no statistically significant differences occur in the hemolymph of infected and noninfected snails.

TABLE 10-6

pO_2, pCO_2, and pH Values of the Hemolymph of Uninfected *Biomphalaria glabrata* and Those Infected with *Schistosoma mansoni*[a]

Parameter measured	No. of determinations	Hemolymph of				*t* test
		Nonparasitized snails		Parasitized snails		
		Mean	Range	Mean	Range	
pO_2	3	67.7[b]	60.5–80.8	72.7[b]	68.3–77.8	$P < 0.05$[c]
pCO_2	3	12.3[b]	11.7–13.2	12.8[b]	12.2–13.2	$P < 0.05$[c]
pH	3	7.6	7.52–7.65	7.54	7.5–7.6	$P < 0.05$[c]

[a]After Lee and Cheng (1971b).
[b]Given as mm Hg.
[c]Not statistically significant.

*Etges and Gresso (1965) did not give the ambient temperatures. The infected snails died when their air-conditioning system failed.

EFFECT ON HEMOLYMPH OSMOLARITY

Measurements of the osmolarity of the hemolymph of *Biomphalaria glabrata* parasitized by *Schistosoma mansoni* have revealed that there is generally a drop. Lee and Cheng's (1972a) data based on determinations made on snails 8–10 mm in shell diameter, each infected with 10 miracidia, indicate that the osmolarity drops from 107.9 milliosmoles (mOsm)/liter to 97.6 mOsm/liter. This decrease can be explained by the reduction in the levels of total protein and glucose in the hemolymph of infected snails (p. 000); however, because of the size of the hemoglobin molecule of this snail—it has a molecular weight of 1.69×10^6 (Figueiredo *et al.*, 1966)—its removal would not seriously alter the colloidal osmotic pressure of the hemolymph.

Pathobiochemistry

Little has been done in the area of pathobiochemistry of parasitized mollusks. There is ample histochemical evidence, however, that mollusks infected with larval trematodes have severely depleted carbohydrate stores. For example, among medically and economically important species, it is known that the stored glycogen in the American oyster, *Crassostrea virginica*, is severely depleted when parasitized by the sporocysts of *Bucephalus* sp. (Cheng and Burton, 1966), and the same occurs in *Biomphalaria glabrata* parasitized by the sporocysts of *Schistosoma mansoni* (von Brand and Files, 1947). It is also known that there is a reduction of lipids in *C. virginica* parasitized by *Bucephalus* (Cheng, 1965).

Biochemical studies to date have been almost exclusively limited to quantitative changes in certain macromolecules in the molluscan host. Targett (1962), Senft (1967), and Gilbertson *et al.* (1967) have studied alterations in the amino acid composition of different tissues of *B. glabrata* harboring *S. mansoni*. Targett has found that infected snails have an overall reduction in their free amino acid contents. Certain amino acids, such as methionine, are quantitatively reduced more than others. The seventeen amino acids that occur in the snail host, including methionine, have been detected in the proteins of *S. mansoni* cercariae, and Targett has suggested that the parasite obtains at least part of its amino acid requirements from the free amino acids of its host.

Gilbertson *et al.* have shown that the levels of all free amino acids of the hemolymph of infected snails decrease during the course of the infection and that in snails with mature infections, the concentration of amino acids drops to about one-half that of control snails. A striking reduction in the hemolymph protein of these infected snails has also been demonstrated. This finding is in contrast to the work of Wright and Ross (1963), who have reported that they have been unable to reveal any qualitative or quantitative changes in the protein pattern of *B. glabrata* infected with *S. mansoni.*

The proteins and free amino acids of the hemolymph of *B. glabrata* have been studied by Dusanic and Lewert (1963) using starch zone electrophoresis and paper chromatography. They have reported that one hour after exposure to miracidia, a difference in the number and relative concentrations of the protein and free amino acids can be discerned but are no longer detectable after 20 hours. They have suggested that such changes may be the result of pathological changes induced by miracidial penetration and migration.

Quantitative changes in the hemolymph proteins of *B. glabrata* infected with *S. mansoni* have also been investigated by Lee and Cheng (1972a). They have demonstrated that the total protein concentration in snails (8–10 mm in shell diameter), each infected with ten miracidia, averages 0.96 g/100 ml after 62 days of infection while that of matched uninfected snails averages 1.42 g/100 ml.

Biomphalaria glabrata, like other planorbid snails, includes the respiratory pigment hemoglobin in its hemolymph. Lee and Cheng (1972a) have established the fact that the reduction in total hemolymph protein concentration in this gastropod parasitized by *S. mansoni* is due largely to reduction in the hemoglobin concentration. As the result of employing ^{59}Fe as a tracer, it has been shown that the host's hemoglobin, at least the heme-including moeity, is taken up and utilized by the schistosome larvae (Lee and Cheng, 1972b). That the hemoglobin content of *B. glabrata* infected with *S. mansoni* is reduced has also been reported by Coles (1971).

Relative to changes in tissue protein concentrations in *B. glabrata* parasitized by *S. mansoni*, Christie and Foster (1970) have demonstrated that there is a drop in the relative dry weights of the albumin gland of parasitized snails from the fifteenth day to the fiftieth day postinfection, when the experiment was terminated. On the last day, the mean dry weight of this gland of infected snails was about one-third that of the control, and they have shown that this is due to the depletion of the proteins. They have suggested that since the egg protein levels are almost the same in both the infected and control groups, the depletion in albumin protein levels is due primarily to the presence of the parasite and secondarily to the drain resulting from egg laying.

Recently, Gilbertson and Michelson (1969) have studied the *in vitro* incorporation of precursors of RNA into the digestive gland of uninfected *B. glabrata* and those infected with *S. mansoni*. They have found that the digestive gland from infected snails includes higher quantities of labeled

RNA than that from uninfected controls. Such accelerated incorporation occurs even before the sporocysts reach the digestive gland. They have suggested that infection in the anterior organs of the snail may decrease the rate of RNA breakdown, decrease the host's uridine pool, or increase the rate of RNA synthesis in the still nonparasitized digestive gland.

By subjecting cell-free hemolymph samples from uninfected *B. glabrata* and those infected with *S. mansoni* to polyacrylamide-disc gel electrophoresis, Lee and Cheng (1972a) have detected twenty protein fractions in the samples from uninfected snails, but an additional fraction with an R_f value between 0.8260 and 0.8305 commonly occurs in the hemolymph of snails harboring older infections (Fig. 10-17; Table 10-7). As indicated in Table 10-7, of the twenty bands present in each of the two gels of noninfected hemolymph, twelve have R_f values with less than 1% difference from the homologous sample in the corresponding infected hemolymph. The remaining comparable bands have R_f values differing from 1.1 to 4.2%.

The finding of an additional fraction in snails harboring older infections is unusual, since no such fraction has been detected in *Helisoma duryi normale*, another subtropical planorbid gastropod, when challenged with bacterial antigens (Cheng, 1969), and, although there are quantitative changes in certain hemolymph protein fractions of the oyster, *Crassostrea virginica*, parasitized by the trematode *Buecephalus* sp. and the haplosporiadan protozoan *Minchinia nelsoni*, no additional fraction occurs (Feng and Canzonier, 1970). The nature of the additional fraction in parasitized *B. glabrata* remains undetermined.

As stated, Feng and Canzonier (1970) have demonstrated quantitative changes in the hemolymph protein fractions of parasitized *C. virginica*. Specifically, they have found that among four fractions resolvable by polyacrylamide-disc electrophoresis (one fast migrating anodal fraction designated as fraction I, and three slow moving cathodal fractions designated as fractions II, III, and IV) there is a significant increase in fraction II and a concurrent decrease in fraction IV in oysters infected with *Bucephalus* sp. and *M. nelsoni*.

It is known that oysters include lysozymes in their hemolymph. Feng and Canzonier (1970) have shown that there is an increase of this enzyme in *C. virginica* infected with *Bucephalus* sp. and *M. nelsoni*.

In a more recent study, Gress and Cheng (1973) have reported a total of thirty-four serum protein fractions in uninfected *Biomphalaria glabrata*, although all these fractions usually do not occur in every snail. In snails exposed to five *Schistosoma mansoni* miracidia there is a reduction in the amount of the individual fractions, especially after 35 days postexposure to the miracidia. However, three of the serum protein fractions, designated as 7, 9, and 10, do not appear to be reduced in quantity as a result of the infection. These remain essentially unaltered in quantity for up to 70 days,

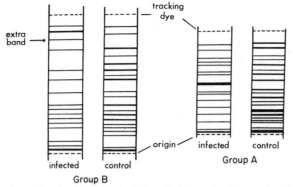

Fig. 10-17. Tracings of stained polyacrylamide gel electrophorigrams showing the relative positions of the hemolymph protein fractions of uninfected *Biomphalaria glabrata* and those infected with *Schistosoma mansoni*. The infected snails of group A has been infected for 35 days while that of group B had been infected for 60 days. After Lee and Cheng (1972a).

TABLE 10-7

Comparison of Protein Bands of Hemolymph of Uninfected *Biomphalaria glabrata* and Those Infected with *Schistosoma mansoni* Separated by Polyacrylamide Gel Electrophoresis[a,b]

Band No.	Pair I Infected R_f	Pair I Control R_f	Pair II Control R_f	Pair II Infected R_f	Additional band R_f
1	0.018	0.020	0.020	0.027	
2	—	0.048	0.037	0.035	
3	—	0.111	0.131	—	
4	0.120	0.125	0.155	—	
5	—	0.152	0.184	0.188	
6	—	0.181	0.209	0.221	
7	0.200	0.218	0.239	0.252	
8	0.264	0.274	0.273	0.287	
9	—	0.306	0.306	0.323	
10	0.334	0.340	0.345	0.351	
11	0.398	0.404	0.406	—	
12	0.412	0.429	0.443	0.441	
13	0.504	0.520	0.530	0.537	
14	0.588	0.577	0.556	—	
15	0.616	0.612	0.601	0.606	
16	0.685	0.669	0.640	—	
17	0.729	0.721	0.704	—	
18	0.760	0.751	0.756	0.755	0.829
19	0.831	0.857	0.864	0.880	
20	0.894	0.873	0.916	0.921	

[a]After Lee and Cheng (1972a).

[b]The infected snail of Pair I had been infected for 35 days while that of Pair II had been infected for 60 days.

the duration of the experiment. It is also noted that by day 70 postexposure to miracidia, the total protein concentration in the plasma had declined to one-third of that in uninfected snails.

Practically nothing is known about the pathobiochemistry of parasitized mollusks as related to carbohydrates other than the histochemical information referred to earlier (p. 211). Furthermore, the chemical studies have been limited to determinations of quantitative changes in the hemolymph glucose concentrations of *Biomphalaria glabrata* infected with *Schistosoma mansoni* (Cheng and Lee, 1971). These investigators have reported that although great variations in glucose concentration occur in noninfected and infected snails, it is quite evident that beyond the third week, snails measuring 8–10 mm in shell diameter each infected with ten miracidia, include significantly reduced hemolymph glucose levels. The reduction in glucose can be attributed, at least in part, to utilization by the parasites.

Relative to alterations in enzyme levels of parasitized mollusks, Michelson and Dubois (1973) have reported that there is an increase in alkaline phosphatase in both the hemolymph and digestive gland extracts of *Biomphalaria glabrata* parasitized by *Schistosoma mansoni*. In addition, Manohar *et al.* (1972) have reported that the level of aspartate aminotransferase in the "body fluid" of *Lymnaea luteola* is increased significantly when parasitized by *Prosthogonimus* sp., *Schistosoma incognitum*, and *Cercaria pigmentata*; however, the alanine transferase level is only elevated when parasitized by *Prothogonimus* sp. These investigators have suggested the increases in transferase activity may be associated with the replenishment of metabolites lost to the parasites.

It is apparent from this brief review of the pathobiochemistry of medically and economically important mollusks that this area of molluscan pathobiology is in its infancy.

References

Abolinš-Krogis, A. (1960). The histochemistry of the hepatopancreas of *Helix pomatia* (L.) in relation to the regeneration of the shell. *Ark. Zool.* **13**, 159–201.

Abolinš-Krogis, A. (1963a). The morphological and chemical basis of the initiation of calcification in the regenerating shell of *Helix pomatia* (L.) *Acta Univ. Stockholm.* **20**, 1–22.

Abolinš-Krogis, A. (1963b). Some features of the chemical composition of isolated cytoplasmic inclusions from the cells of the hepatopancreas of *Helix pomatia* (L.). *Ark Zool.* **15**, 393–429.

Abolinš-Krogis, A. (1968). Shell regeneration in *Helix pomatia* with special reference to the elementary calcifying particles. *In* "Studies in the Structure, Physiology and Ecology of Molluscs" (V. Fretter, ed.). pp. 75–92. Academic Press, New York.

Agersborg, H. P. K. (1924). Studies on the effects of parasitism upon the tissues. I. With special reference to certain gastropod molluscs. *Quart. J. Microsc. Sci.* **68**, 361–401.

Barbosa, F. S. (1963). Survival in the field of *Australorbis glabratus* infected with *Schistosoma mansoni. J. Parasitol.* **49**, 149.

Cheng, T. C. (1965). Histochemical observations on changes in the lipid composition of the American oyster, *Crassostrea virginica* (Gmelin), parasitized by the trematode *Bucephalus* sp. *J. Invertebr. Pathol.* **7**, 398–407.

Cheng, T. C. (1966). Perivascular leucocytosis and other types of cellular reactions in the oyster *Crassostrea virginica* experimentally infected with the nematode *Angiostrongylus cantonensis. J. Invertebr. Pathol.* **56**, 111–122.

Cheng, T. C. (1967). Marine molluscs as hosts for symbioses: With a review of known parasites of commercially important species. *Advan. Mar. Biol.* **5**, 1–424.

Cheng, T. C. (1969). An electrophoretic analysis of hemolymph proteins of *Helisoma duryi normale* experimentally challenged with bacteria. *J. Invertebr. Pathol.* **14**, 60–81.

Cheng, T. C. (1971). Enhanced growth as a manifestation of parasitism and shell deposition in parasitized mollusks. *In* "Aspects of the Biology of Symbiosis" (T. C. Cheng, ed.), pp. 103–137. Univ. Park Press, Baltimore, Maryland.

Cheng, T. C. (1973). "General Parasitology." Academic Press, New York.

Cheng, T. C., and Burton, R. W. (1965). Relationships between *Bucephalus* sp. and *Crassostrea virginica*: Histopathology and sites of infection. *Chesapeake Sci.* **6**, 3–16.

Cheng, T. C., and Burton, R. W. (1966). Relationships between *Bucephalus* sp. and *Crassostrea virginica*: A histochemical study of some carbohydrates and carbohydrate complexes occurring in the host and parasite. *Parasitology* **56**, 111–122.

Cheng, T. C., and Cooperman, J. S. (1964). Studies on host-parasite relationships between larval trematodes and their hosts. V. The invasion of the reproductive system of *Helisoma trivolvis* by the sporocysts and cercariae of *Glypthelmins pennsylvaniensis. Trans. Amer. Microsc. Soc.* **83**, 12–23.

Cheng, T. C., and James, H. A. (1960). The histopathology of *Crepidostomum* sp. infection in the second intermediate host, *Sphaerium striatinum. Proc. Helminthol. Soc. Wash.* **27**, 67–68.

Cheng, T. C., and Lee, F. O. (1971). Glucose levels in the mollusc *Biomphalaria glabrata* infected with *Schistosoma mansoni. J. Invertebr. Pathol.* **18**, 395–399.

Cheng, T. C., and Snyder, R. W., Jr. (1962). Studies on host-parasite relationships between larval trematodes and their hosts. I. A review. II. Host glycogen utilization by the intramolluscan larvae of *Glypthelmins pennsylvaniensis* Cheng and related phenomena. *Trans. Amer. Microsc. Soc.* **81**, 327–331.

Cheng, T. C., and Sullivan, J. T. (1973). The effect of copper on the heart rate of *Biomphalaria glabrata* (Mollusca: Pulmonata). *Comp. Gen. Pharmacol.* **4**, 37–41.

Cheng, T. C., and Yee, H. W. F. (1968). Histochemical demonstration of aminopeptidase activity associated with the intramolluscan stages of *Philophtalmus gralli* Mathis and Léger. *Parasitology* **58**, 473–480.

Cheng, T. C., Sullivan, J. T. and Harris, K. R. (1973). Parasitic castration of the marine prosobranch *Nassarius obsoletus* by sporocysts of *Zoogonus rubellus* (Trematoda): Histopathology. *J. Invertebr. Pathol.* **21**, 183–190.

Chernin, E. (1960). Infection of *Australorbis glabratus* with *Schistosoma mansoni* under bacteriologically sterile conditions. *Proc. Soc. Exp. Biol. Med.* **105**, 292–296.

Christie, J. D., and Foster, W. B. (1970). Effect of larval stages of *Schistosoma mansoni* on the albumen gland of *Biomphalaria glabrata. J. Parasitol.* **56**, Sect. II, Part 1, 55–56.

Chu, K. Y., Sabbaghian, H., and Massoud, J. (1966). Host-parasite relationship of *Bulinus truncatus* and *Schistosoma haematobium* in Iran. *Bull. W. H. O.* **34**, 121–130.

Chu, K. Y., and Dawood, I. K. (1970). Cercarial transmission seasons of *Schistosoma mansoni* in the Nile Delta area. *Bull. W. H. O.* **42**, 575–580.

Coelho, M. V. (1954). Acao des formas larvarias de *Schistosoma mansoni* sobre a reproducao de *Australorbis glabratus. Publ. Avulsas Inst. Aggeu Magalhaes Recife, Brasil* **3**, 39–53.

Coles, G. C. (1971). Haemoglobin changes in infected *Biomphalaria glabrata*. *Trans. Roy. Soc. Trop. Med. Hyg.* **65**, 686–687.

Cooley, N. R. (1962). Studies on *Parorchis acanthus* (Trematoda: Digenea) as a biological control for the southern oyster drill, *Thais haemastoma. Fish. Wildl. Serv., Fish. Bull. U. S.*, **62**, 77–91.

Cort, W. W., Olivier, L., and McMullen, D. B. (1941). Larval trematode infection in juveniles and adults of *Physa parkeri* Currier. *J. Parasitol.* **27**, 123–141.

De Andrade, R. M. (1962). Ecologia de "Australorbis glabratus" em Belo Horizonte, Brasil. III. Indices de infeccao natural por "Schistosoma mansoni" segundo os diametros dos caramujos. *Rev. Brasil Biol.* **22**, 383–390.

Dubois, G. (1929). Les cercaires de la région de Neuchâtel. *Bull. Soc. Neuchatel. Sci. Natur.* [N. S.]**53**, 3–177.

Dusanic, D. G., and Lewert, R. M. (1963). Alterations of proteins and free amino acids of *Australorbis glabratus* hemolymph after exposure to *Schistosoma mansoni* miracidia. *J. Infec. Dis.* **112**, 243–246.

Edwards, G. A., Neto, B. M., and Dobbin, J. E., Jr. (1951). Influence of infestation and other factors upon the respiration of the snail, *Australorbis glabratus. Publ. Avulsas Inst. Aggeu Magalhaes Recife, Brazil* **1**, 9–26.

Etges, F. J. (1961a). *Cercaria reynoldsi* n. sp. (Trematoda: Echinostomatidae) from *Helisoma anceps* (Menke) in Mountain Lake, Virginia. *Trans. Amer. Microsc. Soc.* **80**, 221–226.

Etges, F. J. (1961b). Contributions to the life history of the brain fluke of newts and fish, *Diplostomulum scheuringi* Hughes, 1929 (Trematoda: Diplostomatidae). *J. Parasitol.* **47**, 453–458.

Etges, F. J., and Gresso, W. (1965). Effect of *Schistosoma mansoni* infection upon fecundity in *Australorbis glabratus. J. Parasitol.* **51**, 757–760.

Faust, E. C. (1920). Pathological changes in the gastropod liver produced by fluke infection. *Bull. Johns Hopkins Hosp.* **31**, 79–84.

Feng, S. Y., and Canzonier, W. J. (1970). Humoral responses in the American oyster (*Crassostrea virginica*) infected with *Bucephalus* sp. and *Minchinia nelsoni*. *In* "A Symposium on Diseases of Fishes and Shellfishes" (S. F. Snieszko, ed.), Publ. No. 5, pp. 497–510. Amer. Fisher. Soc. Washington, D.C.

Figueiredo, E. A., Gomez, M. V., Heneine, I. F., Hargreaves, F. B., and Santos, I. O. (1966). Hemoglobina de *Biomphalaria glabrata*: purificacao e propriedades fisicoquimicas. III. *Simposio de Bioquimica de Planorbideos, Curitiba*, **3**, 44–54.

Galtsoff, P. S. (1964). The American oyster, *Crassostrea virginica* Gmelin. *U.S., Fish Wildl. Serv., Fish. Bull.* **64**, 1–480.

Gilbertson, D. E., and Michelson, E. H. (1969). *In vitro* incorporation of precursors of RNA into the digestive gland of normal and of *Schistosoma*-infected *Biomphalaria glabrata. J. Parasitol.* **55**, 276–278.

Gilbertson, D. E., Etges, F. J., and Odle, J. D. (1967). Free amino acids of *Australorbis glabratus* hemolymph: Comparison of four geographic strains and effect of infection by *Schistosoma mansoni. J. Parasitol.* **53**, 565–568.

Gress, F. M., and Cheng, T. C. (1973). Alterations in total serum proteins and protein fractions in *Biomphalaria glabrata* parasitized by *Schistosoma mansoni. J. Invertebr. Pathol.* **22**, 382–390.

Hoshina, T., and Ogino, C. (1951). Studien ueber *Gymnophalloides tokiensis* Fujita, 1925. I. Ueber die einwirkung der Larvalen Trematoda auf die chemische Komponente und das Wachstum von *Ostrea gigas* Thunberg. *J. Tokyo Univ. Fish.* **38**, 335–350.

Hosier, D. W., and Goodchild, C. G. (1970). Suppressed egg-laying by snails infected with *Spirorchis scripta* (Trematoda: Spirorchiidae). *J. Parasitol.* **56**, 302–304.

Hurst, C. T. (1927). Structural and functional changes produced in the gastropod mollusk, *Physa occidentalis*, in the case of parasitism by the larvae of *Echinostoma revolutum*. *Univ. Calif., Berkeley, Publ. Zool.* **29**, 321–404.

James, B. L. (1965). The effects of parasitism by larval Digenea on the digestive gland of the intertidal prosobranch, *Littorina saxatilis* (Olivi) subsp. *tenebrosa* (Montagu). *Parasitology* **55**, 93–115.

Krull, H. (1935). Anatomische Untersuchungen an einheimische Prosobranchieren und Beiträge zur Phylogenie der Gastropoden. *Zool. Jahrb., Abt. Anat. Ontog. Ticic* **60**, 399–464.

Lal, M. B., and Premvati. (1955). Studies in histopathology. Changes induced by larval monostome on the digestive gland of the snail, *Melanoides tuberculatus* (Müller). *Proc. Indian Acad. Sci., Sect. B*, No. 2, 193–299.

Lee, D. L. (1966). The structure and composition of the helminth cuticle. *Advan. Parasitol.* **4**, 187–354.

Lee, F. O., and Cheng, T. C. (1970). Increased heart rate in *Biomphalaria glabrata* parasitized by *Schistosoma mansoni*. *J. Invertebr. Pathol.* **16**, 148–149.

Lee, F. O., and Cheng, T. C. (1971a). *Schistosoma mansoni* infection in *Biomphalaria glabrata*: Alterations in heart rate and thermal tolerance in the host. *J. Invertebr. Pathol.* **18**, 412–418.

Lee, F. O., and Cheng, T. C. (1971b). *Schistosoma mansoni*: Respirometric and partial pressure studies in infected *Biomphalaria glabrata*. *Exp. Parasitol.* **30**, 393–399.

Lee, F. O., and Cheng, T. C. (1972a). *Schistosoma mansoni* infection in *Biomphalaria glabrata*: Alterations in total protein and hemoglobin concentrations in the host's hemolymph. *Exp. Parasitol.* **31**, 203–216.

Lee, F. O., and Cheng, T. C. (1972b). Incorporation of ^{59}Fe in the snail *Biomphalaria glabrata* parasitized by *Schistosoma mansoni*. *J. Parasitol.* **58**, 481–488.

Lysaght, A. M. (1941). The biology and trematode parasites of the gastropod *Littorina neritoides* (L.) on the Plymouth breakwater. *J. Mar. Biol. Ass. U.K.* **25**, 481–488.

Manohar, L., Rao, P. V., and Swami, K. S. (1972). Variations in aminotransferase activity and total free amino acid in the body fluid of the snail *Lymnaea luteola* during different larval trematode infections. *J. Invertebr. Pathol.* **19**, 36–41.

McClelland, G., and Bourns, T. K. R. (1969). Effects of *Trichobilharzia ocellata* on growth, reproduction, and survival of *Lymnaea stagnalis*. *Exp. Parasitol.* **24**, 137–146.

Mackin, J. G. (1951). Histopathology of infection of *Crassostrea virginica* (Gmelin) by *Dermocystidium marinum* Mackin, Owen and Collier. *Bull. Mar. Sci. Gulf Carib.* **1**, 72–87.

Malek, E. A. (1952). Morphology, bionomics and host-parasite relations of Planorbidae (Mollusca: Pulmonata). Ph.D. thesis, University of Michigan, Ann Arbor.

Malek, E. A. (1955). Anatomy of *Biomphalaria boissyi* as related to its infection with *Schistosoma mansoni*. *Amer. Midl. Natur.* **54**, 394–404.

Malek, E. A. (1958). Factors conditioning the habitat of bilharziasis intermediate hosts of the family Planorbidae. *Bull. W.H.O.* **18**, 785–818.

Menzel, R. W., and Hopkins, S. H. (1955a). Effects of two parasites on the growth of oysters. *Proc. Nat. Shellfish. Ass.* **45**, 184–186.

Menzel, R. W., and Hopkins, S. H. (1955b). The growth of oysters parasitized by the fungus *Dermocystidium marinum* and by the trematode *Bucephalus cuculus*. *J. Parasitol.* **41**, 333–342.

Meuleman, E. A. (1972). Host-parasite interrelationships between the freshwater pulmonate *Biomphalaria pfeifferi* and the trematode *Schistosoma mansoni*. *Netherlands J. Zool.* **22**, 355–427.

Michelson, E. H., and Dubois, L. (1973). Increased alkaline phosphatase in the tissues and hemolymph of the snail *Biomphalaria glabrata* infected with *Schistosoma mansoni. Comp. Biochem. Physiol.* **44B**, 763–767.

Moose, J. W. (1963). Growth inhibition of young *Oncomelania nosophora* exposed to *Schistosoma japonicum. J. Parasitol.* **49**, 151–152.

Pan, C. T. (1962). The course and effect of infection with *Schistosoma mansoni* in *Australorbis glabratus. J. Parasitol.* **48**, Sect. 2, 20.

Pan, C. T. (1965). Studies on the host-parasite relationship between *Schistosoma mansoni* and the snail Australorbis glabratus. *Amer. J. Trop. Med. Hyg.* **14**, 931–976.

Pelseneer, P. (1906). Trématodes parasites de mollusques marins. *Bull. Sci. Fr. Belg.* **40**, 161–186.

Pelseneer, P. (1928). Les parasites des mollusques et les mollusques parasites. *Bull. Soc. Zool. Fr.* **53**, 158–189.

Pesigan, T. P., Hairston, N. G., Tauregui, J. J., Garcia, E. G., Santos, A. T., Santos, B. S., and Besa, A. A. (1958). Studies on *Schistosoma japonicum* infection in the Philippines. 2. The molluscan host. *Bull. W. H. O.* **18**, 481–578.

Pratt., I., and Barton, G. D. (1941). The effects of four species of larval trematodes upon the liver and ovotestis of the snail, *Stagnicola emarginata angulata* (Sowerby). *J. Parasitol.* **27**, 283–288.

Pratt, I., Lindquist, W. D. (1943). The modification of the digestive gland tubules in the snail *Stagnicola* following parasitization. *J. Parasitol.* **29**, 176–181.

Rees, W. G. (1936). The effect of parasitism by larval trematodes on the tissues of Littorina littorea (Linne). *Proc. Zool. Soc. London* 357–368.

Rifkin, E., and Cheng, T. C. (1968). On the formation, structure, and histochemical characterization of the encapsulating cysts in *Crassostrea virginica* parasitized by *Tylocephalum* metacestodes. *J. Invertebr. Pathol.* **10**, 51–64.

Ritchie, L. S., Berrios-Duran, L. A., Frick, L. P., and Fox, I. (1963). Molluscicide qualities of bayluscide (Bayer 73) revealed by 6-hour and 24-hour exposures against representative stages and sizes of *Australorbis glabratus. Bull. W. H. O.* **29**, 281–286.

Rothschild, A., and Rothschild, M. (1939). Some observations on the growth of *Peringia ulvae* (Pennant, 1777) in the laboratory. *Novitates Zool.* **41**, 240–247.

Rothschild, M. (1936). Gigantism and variation in *Peringia ulvae* Pennant, 1777, caused by infection with larval trematodes. *J. Mar. Biol. Ass. U.K.* **30**, 537–546.

Rothschild, M. (1938). Further observations on the effect of trematode parasites of *Peringia ulvae* (Pennant, 1777). *Novitates Zool.* **41**, 84–102.

Rothschild, M. (1941a). The effect of trematode parasites on the growht of *Littorina neritoides* (L.). *J. Mar. Biol. Ass. U.K.* **25**, 84–102.

Rothschild, M. (1941b). Observations on the growth and tematode infections of *Peringia ulvae* (Pennant, 1777) in a pool in the Pamar Saltings, Plymouth. *Parasitology* **33**, 406–415.

Senft, A. W. (1967). Studies in arginine metabolism by schistosomes. II. Arginine depletion in mammals and snails infected with *S. mansoni* or *S. haematobium. Comp. Biochem. Physiol.* **21**, 299–306.

Stein, J. E. and Mackin, J. G. (1955). A study of the nature of pigment cells of oysters and the relation of their numbers to the fungus disease in the oyster, *Ostrea lurida. Proc. Nat. Shellfish. Ass.* **50**, 67–81.

Sturrock, B. M. (1966). The influence of infection with *Schistosoma mansoni* on the growth rate and reproduction of *Biomphalaria pfeifferi. Ann. Trop. Med. Parasitol.* **60**, 187–197.

Sturrock, B. M. (1967). The effect of infection with *Schistosoma haematobium* on the growth and reproduction rate of *Bulinus (Physopsis) nasutus productus. Ann. Trop. Med. Parasitol.* **61**, 321–000.

Sturrock, B. M., and Sturrock, R. F. (1970). Laboratory studies of the host-parasite relationship of *Schistosoma mansoni* and *Biomphalaria glabrata* from St. Lucia, West Indies. *Ann. Trop. Med. Parasitol.* **64**, 357.

Sturrock, R. F., and Sturrock, B. M. (1971). Shell abnormalities in *Biomphalaria glabrata* infected with *Schistosoma mansoni* and their significance in field transmission studies. *J. Helminthol.* **45**, 201–210.

Targett, G. A. T. (1962). The amino-acid composition of blood from snail hosts of schistosomiasis. *Ann. Trop. Med. Parasitol.* **56**, 61–66.

Vernberg, W. B., and Vernberg, F. J. (1963). Influence of parasitism on thermal resistance of the mud-flat snail. *Nassarius obsoleta* Say. *Exp. Parasitol.* **14**, 330–332.

von Brand, T., and Files, V. S. (1947). Chemical and histological observations on the influence of *Schistosoma mansoni* on *Australorbis glabratus*. *J. Parasitol.* **33**, 476–482.

von Brand, T., Baernstein, H. D., and Mehlman, B. (1950). Studies on the anaerobic metabolism and the aerobic carbohydrate consumption of some fresh water snails. *Biol. Bull.* **98**, 266–276.

Wesenberg-Lund, C. J. (1931). Contributions to the development of the Trematoda Digenea. Part I. The biology of *Leucochloridium paradoxum*. *Kgl. Dan Vidensk. Selsk., Skr.* **4**, 89–142.

Wesenberg-Lund, C. J. (1934). Constribution to the development of the Trematoda Digenea. Part II. The biology of the freshwater cercariae in Danish waters. *Kgl. Dan. Vidensk. Selsk. Skr.* **5**, 1–223.

Wright, C. A., and Ross, G. C. (1963). Electrophoretic studies of blood and egg proteins in *Australorbis glabratus* (Gastropoda, Planorbidae). *Ann. Trop. Med. Parasitol.* **57**, 47–51.

Zischke, J. A., and Zischke, D. P. (1965). The effects of *Echinostoma revolutum* larval infection on the growth and reproduction of the snail host *Stagnicola* palustris. *Amer. Zool.* **5**, 707–708.

11   Tissue and Organ Culture

Tissue Culture

Interest in molluscan tissue culture stems from four interrelated but recognizable areas of research.

1. The potentiality of employing microorganisms, especially viruses, as biological control agents against species of mollusks that transmit pathogens to man and animals, for example, *Lymnaea truncatula*, one of the intermediate hosts of the sheep and cattle liver fluke, *Fasciola hepatica*, *Biomphalaria glabrata* and *Bulinus truncatus*, the most common intermediate hosts of *Schistosoma mansoni* and *S. haematobium*, respectively, or against species that are deleterious to economically important mollusks and other animals, for example, the southern oyster drill, *Thais haemastoma*, can only become a reality if the promising candidate viruses can be cultured in the laboratory and harvested in large numbers. Since viruses are obligatory intracellular parasites, compatible molluscan cells must be cultured in order to achieve this goal.

2. Attempts to produce vaccines against trematode-caused diseases, especially schistosomiasis, although not yet a reality, is a possibility. However, in order to produce the large quantities of cercariae to use in the preparation of antigens, an efficient *in vitro* culture system must be developed. One possibility that has been advocated is to culture cercariae-producing sporocysts *in vitro* in the presence of compatible molluscan cells. This approach is physiologically sound since larval trematodes are known to depend on molluscan cells, at least in part, for nutrients (see Cheng, 1963,

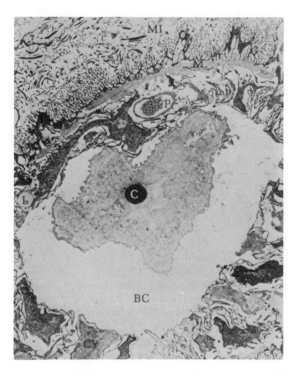

Fig. 11-1. Electron micrograph of cross section of a daughter sporocyst of *Schistosoma mansoni* embedded in intertubular space of the digestive gland of *Biomphalaria glabrata*. Notice branched microvilli arising from the surface of the sporocyst. BC, Brood chamber of sporocyst; C, section of cercaria; CY, cyton of inner layer of sporocyst tegument; L, lipid material; M, muscle layer; MI, microvilli; P, protonephridum (flame cell) ($\times$ 8500). After Rifkin, in Cheng (1973).

1967, for reviews), and electron microscope studies have revealed that the daughter sporocysts of *S. mansoni* are intimately associated with the digestive gland cells of *B. glabrata*, with branched microvilli of parasite origin infiltrating host cells (Figs. 11-1 and 11-2). Ideally, of course, the schistosomes should be axenically cultured in a chemically defined medium from miracidium to cercaria, but this is in the distant future. In the meantime molluscan cells must be cultured in order to sustain daughter sporocysts.

3. As discussed in Chapter 9, a thorough understanding of the cellular internal defense mechanisms of mollusks is essential if we are to elucidate in detail the phenotypic expression on the genetic basis of compatibility and/or incompatibility of mollusks and invading organisms. Increased knowledge in this area of molluscan pathobiology is not only useful in developing refractile strains of mollusks that normally harbor pathogens of man and

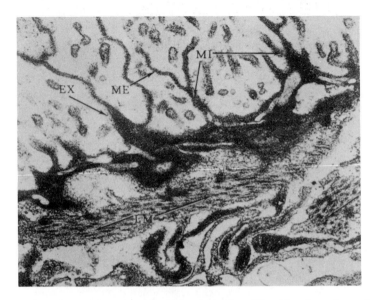

Fig. 11-2. Electron micrograph showing branched microvilli arising from the surface of a daughter sporocyst of *Schistosoma mansoni*. EX, Extracellular material adhering to microvillar surface; LM, longitudinal muscles; ME, surface membrane; MI, microvilli (× 25,000). After Rifkin, in Cheng (1973).

animals but also important from the standpoint of developing economically important mollusks, such as various species of clams and oysters that are resistant to natural pathogens such as *Minchinia nelsoni* (p. 148). In order to achieve a more sophisticated understanding of the cellular internal defense mechanisms of mollusks, these cells and the mollusk's hematopoetic tissues must be cultured *in vitro* so that sufficiently large numbers can be obtained for biochemical and other types of studies.

4. Comparative oncology, for example, the study of the development of neoplasms, including true carcinomas, on a comparative basis, is increasing in emphasis (Dawe, 1969), and, since the viral etiology of certain vertebrate cancers has been fairly well established, there is some interest as to whether a similar etiology occurs among the lower animals, including mollusks. Although a variety of neoplasms is known among mollusks (see Pauley, 1969, for review), only two viruses from mollusks have thus far been reported (Rungger *et al.*, 1971; Farley *et al.*, 1972). Even in this instance, the virus was detected in static electron micrographs, and, hence, in accordance with the accepted practice of virologists, its true viral nature remains to be determined through infectivity studies. However, before this can be accom-

plished, molluscan cell lines must be established for the maintenance and characterization of the virus. Consequently, the successful development of molluscan tissue culture is imperative if true comparative oncology is to progress.

Although molluscan tissue culture is still in its infancy and no completely satisfactory method(s) has yet been developed, a review of what has been done is useful in that it points out what mistakes others have made in methodology and interpretation and at the same time provides pieces of foundation upon which future attempts can be made. It should be cautioned at this point that the review by Flandre (1971) should be accepted with caution since it is at best misleading.

A Critical Review

Orton (1922), in his pioneering attempt to maintain molluscan cells *in vitro*, placed oyster hemolymph cells in dishes of seawater and reported that they survived for 3–4 days. According to Gresson (1973), Zweibaum, in 1925, attempted to maintain the ciliated epithelium of the ctenidia of the freshwater clam *Anodonta* in a modified Ringer's solution and found that those kept in a dilute (?) solution survived for 63 days. Furthermore, it was reported that the excised epithelia tended to fragment into two or three smaller pieces, and each piece became spherical after 4–6 days. A multiplication of epithelial cells is said to have occurred toward the center of each sphere for 6–10 days, and leukocytes were observed migrating from each mass. From the evidence provided, however, it remains a moot point whether Zweibaum actually saw cell division.

Cary (1931) attempted to culture the gonad, kidney, and gills of the oyster *Ostrea edulis* and the cerebral and pleural ganglia as well as the mantle edge of *Strombus gigas*. The medium used consisted of seawater or Goldschmidt's medium fortified with 5–10% *Strombus* hemolymph. He reported the survival of these tissues for a limited period.

The most extensive studies on molluscan tissue culture during the early period have been those of Gatenby and his associates employing *Helix aspersa*. Gatenby (1931) attempted to maintain pieces of the mantle and hemolymph cells of *H. aspersa* in a sealed, hollow slide chamber in homologous hemolymph maintained at 15°, 25°, and 30°C. The only sterile precaution taken was flaming the slides and coverslips. The tissue fragments were washed in Ringer's solution prior to being placed in the hemolymph-filled chambers. Gatenby reported the exomigration of amoebocytes shortly thereafter, followed by epithelial cells in about 24 hours. Gatenby (1932a) maintained gonadal, foot, "visceral hump," and mantle of *H. aspersa* in similar hemolymph-filled chambers and reported that mantle tissue gave the best results. Specifically, he reported that 50% of the mantle preparations revealed growth in 2 days when maintained at 25°–30°C. Activity of the mantle tissue was manifested as exomigration of amoebocytes and epithelial cells in addition to the development of a pulsating "bladderlike growth" onto which the epithelial cells wandered. Since no mitotic figures were observed, Gatenby concluded that amitosis was the mechanism of cell division, if this indeed did occur. In addition to maintaining tissue explants in hemolymph, media consisting of mixtures of hemolymph and albumin gland and ovotestis and Ringer's solution were tried with less success.

Gatenby and Duthie (1932) repeated Gatenby's (1932a) work and reported that amitosis was most probably the mechanism for cell division in *H. aspersa* and that explants of mantle tissue survived for as long as 60 days in homologous hemolymph. The occurrence of amitosis was reiterated by Gatenby (1932b) since he could not account for "growth" through mitosis. It should be noted that since his criterion for growth, for example, exomigration of cells and the development of a "bladderlike growth," is open to question, it may be that he never attained true growth, and, hence, it is not surprising that mitosis was not observed. It is of interest to note that Hillman (1963) has demonstrated mitotic division of molluscan cells *in vivo*. This finding lends credence to the doubt as to whether true growth was attained by Gatenby. It is important to note, however, that Gatenby (1932a) did find that tissues maintained in a confined area, for example, in a double-mount preparation, survived better than in the comparatively more spacious hanging drop mounts.

Gatenby and Hill (1934) maintained *H. aspersa* mantle tissue in Hédon-Fleig's Ringer solution adjusted to pH 7.2, and the results were comparable to those reported earlier.

The next attempt at molluscan tissue culture was that of Federow (1933), who reported an outgrowth of nerve fibers from fragments of the optic lobe of the cephalopod *Rossia glaucopias*. It is doubtful, however, whether what was observed was true growth, as cytological evidence was not provided.

Haughton (1934) also studied the fate of *Helix aspersa* tissues in homologous hemolymph hanging drop preparations as well as in the Hédon-Fleig medium. The tissue employed was fragments of the atrium. He reported that growth(?) and exomigration of amoebocytes occurred in less than 24 hours and produced a network, which survived for 3–6 days. It is of interest to note that Haughton found growth and migration of cells were more certain if the snail's heart was injured with a needle 4–5 hours prior to removal of the atrium. In view of our present knowledge of reaction to injury in mollusks

(Pauley and Sparks, 1967; Armstrong *et al.*, 1971), what Haughton had observed could be interpreted to be leukocytosis followed by the exomigration of leukocytes, rather than multiplication of amoebocytes *in vitro*.

Bourne (1935) repeated Gatenby's earlier experiments, also using *Helix aspersa*. He found that sterile saline alone maintained pulmonary tissue for one month while hemolymph cells did not survive. He also reported the absence of mitosis but noted the fragmentation of cells. That the latter occurs with molluscan granulocytes *in vitro* is now known to be an expected process (Foley and Cheng, 1972). Because of the absence of mitosis, it can also be argued that Bourne did not succeed in truly culturing *H. aspersa* tissues. In the same paper, Bourne reported that myofibers from the foot of *H. aspersa* placed in a mixture of commercial meat extract and 0.65% saline remained for 2 months without exhibiting any degenerative changes. If the medium was changed, the life span of the muscles was extended for another 2 months.

Gresson (1937) attempted to culture mantle tissue from the marine pelecypod *Modiolus modiolus*. His medium consisted of seawater and 10% extract of the gonad and muscle of *Modiolus* maintained at pH 8.0. He reported growth of shell-secreting epithelium; however, the relationship of this epithelium to ciliated epithelium was found to be important. Specifically, if the shell epithelium was placed next to the cover slip, it grew between 24–72 hours postpreparation; however, if placed next to ciliated epithelium it did not grow. Like all previous investigators, he observed the exomigration of amoebocytes. No mitotic figures or amitosis were observed. Because of this, it is again questionable if true growth was experienced.

In an abstract, Cameron (1949) claimed to have cultured "clam" mantle and gill and squid chromatophores. This report cannot be critically evaluated since the details were not presented nor subsequently published. Similarly, Bevelander and Martin (1949) maintained mantle tissue of *Pintata radiata*, a marine pelecypod, in homologous plasma and reported that the cells migrated from the explant and clumped. These cells were identified as epithelial, "pigment", and hemolymph cells. No cell division was observed, and, hence, true culture was not achieved.

Vago and Chastang (1958), in their attempts to develop a culture medium for the honeybee, *Bombyx mori*, and other insects, also attempted to grow cells from the gastropods *Helix aspersa* and *H. pomatia*. Like all the earlier investigators, they reported the exomigrating of cells, primarily fibroblast-like cells, but, in addition, they reported the occurrence of mitosis. No indication, however, was given as to the transferability of the cells or the longevity of the primary culture. Again, it is our opinion that the cells observed by these French workers are hemolymph cells migrating from the explants and were not cells proliferating *in vitro*. Mature molluscan hemolymph cells are known to undergo mitosis as well as take on fibroblastlike shapes (Tripp *et al.*, 1966).

In attempts to study shell formation *in vitro*, Hirata (1953) suspended the mantle of oysters in running seawater and inserted fragments of glass cover slips on the mantle. The deposition of birefringent crystals on the cover slips occurred, and an organized shell was recognizable after 2.3 days. This experiment suggests that oyster mantle tissue, and possibly that of other mollusks, can be maintained and is metabolically active in a nonnutrient medium for a few days.

Up until 1963, aside from Vago and Chastang (1958), the only investigators to have observed mitosis of molluscan tissue maintained *in vitro* are Necco and Martin (1963a,b). The latter investigators cultured cells of the so-called white body of *Octopus vulgaris* in various modifications of commercial media and found that one cell per thousand entered mitosis per hour when cultured in tubes containing 1 ml of Difco TC 199 medium with the addition of 26.833 g/liter of NaCl and with the temperature maintained at 18°C. In view of Cowden's (1972) finding that *Octopus* white bodies are actually a type of hematopoetic tissue, the question can be raised as to whether Necco and Martin actually cultured cells from this organ or merely provided a sustaining medium in which normal activity, for example, production of hemocytes, was sustained, and at a lower rate at that.

Working with *Biomphalaria glabrata*, but also with *Helix pomatia* and *Pomatiopsis lapidaria*, Burch and Cuadros (1965) maintained gonadal tissue that portrayed meiosis I prophase nuclei for up to 60 days at pH 7.0 in their medium. Furthermore, after 14 days, many mitotic metaphase cells were seen in one primary explant culture of *H. pomatia*, and as many as three successful subcultures were made. Foot muscle was maintained at pH 8.5 for 45 to 60 days, and mantle, oviduct, and esophagus tissues were successfully maintained for 45 days.

The meiotic figures found by Burch and Cuadros in gonadal tissue need not indicate that the culture medium was sustaining cell division. It could mean that the medium was maintaining the gonadal tissue at such a physiologic level that gametic cells committed to differentiating into mature gametes were not sufficiently arrested in their development but were progressing toward their commitment. It is interesting, however, that Burch and Cuadros have observed mitotic figures, but, unfortunately, their occurrence was extremely limited. There is no doubt that their medium is a good one for maintenance, but the generally accepted criteria among tissue culture experts for successful establishment of a cell line have not been met. These criteria are as follows. (1) The cultured cells must be replicating (usually ascertained by the criteria of cell counts, occurrence of mitotic figures, and the uptake of radioactively labeled thimidine). (2) The cells

must have passed through at least seventy subcultures (Federoff, 1966).*
(3) The molluscan origin of the cells in culture must be ascertained [usually by the cytotoxicity test of Green *et al.* (1964)].

Ebstein *et al.* (1965), working with embryonic blastomeres of *Nassarius obsoletus*, were able to observe fibroblastlike cells emigrating in a medium consisting of 5% Eagle's HeLa, 1% horse serum, and 94% pasteurized sea-water and antibiotics maintained at 24°C.

Because of considerable interest in understanding the reaction of shell-fish (primarily oyster) cells to foreign agents, several investigators have attempted to culture oyster tissues and/or cells. Perkins and Menzel (1964) maintained mantle tissue from *Crassostrea virginica* for 42 days in hanging drop preparations consisting of a coagulum of Millipore-filtered crab plasma and a pH 7.2–7.4 salt solution. Rosenfield (1965) maintained cells of *C. virginica* up to 10.5 months in a medium consisting of 10% oyster serum, 100 units of pencillin/ml, and 100 mg of streptomycin/ml maintained at 20°C. The medium was changed weekly during the initial 4 weeks and monthly thereafter.

Li *et al.* (1966) attempted to culture heart explants of *C. virginica* in six test media and found that the tissues survived best, from 6 days to 2 weeks, in a medium consisting of 50% salt solution, 10% bovine amniotic fluid, and 10% human serum. In this medium, they reported the exomigration of cells as well as "proliferation" by amitosis. Evidence for the latter, however, was not convincingly presented. Tripp *et al.* (1966) tested 250 different media for the culture of *C. virginica* cells. Furthermore, plastic flasks, Leighton tubes, hanging drops, petri dishes, and Sykes-More perfusion chambers were all tested. It was found that the cells (mostly amoebocytes and fibroblastlike cells) survived for 7–10 days in a balanced salt solution (BSS) while they survived for 70 days in Scherer's media diluted with BSS and supplemented with chicken serum. No mitotic figures were reported.

The only investigator to have claimed totally successful primary culture of cells from a marine pelecypod, *Spisula solidissima*, is Cecil (1969). He has reported growing monolayers of cells for extended periods. The original cells were disaggregated cells (with 0.25% trypsin-EDTA) from pooled cardiac tissue, and the medium employed consisted of salts, glucose, tre-halose, galactose, Eagle's minimum essential amino acids, nonessential amino acids, fetal calf serum, and whole egg ultrafiltrate. According to Cecil, all stages of mitosis were observed in the monolayers from days 11–60, although second-generation cell passage has not been shown to proliferate.

---

*The paper by Federoff (1966) should be consulted for the proper usage of terms employed in tissue culture.

Consequently, the true establishment of a cell line has not been achieved based on the criteria given earlier.

It is noted that Cheng and Arndt (1973) have devised a medium (p. 256) in which intestinal cells of *Biomphalaria glabrata* have been maintained for 15 days, the longest record to date for any molluscan cell. This medium has now been successfully used to passage cells through eighteen transfers.

From this review, it is apparent that no one has yet succeeded in establishing a cell line from any mollusk. Furthermore, it is quite apparent that what most previous investigators have observed is the maintenance of molluscan tissues and concurrent with this is the exomigration of hemolymph cells and/or fibroblastlike cells.

PHYSICAL AND CHEMICAL CONDITIONS OF HEMOLYMPH

One of the major drawbacks in molluscan tissue culture in the past has been the apparent lack of concern, at least in some instances, for simulating the precise physical and chemical parameters of the hemolymph in which tissues are bathed *in vivo*. Consequently, the initial objective for prospective tissue culturists should be to define these parameters, primarily the physical conditions, of the hemolymph of the molluscan species to be cultured. The osmolality of freshly drawn hemolymph can be determined by the use of the Fiske osmometer (based on freezing point depression) and could be confirmed by use of the Mechrolub vapor pressure esmometer. The pO_2, pCO_2, and pH of molluscan hemolymph samples can be ascertained by use of a radiometer, following the technique of Lee and Cheng (1971). The relative ionic concentrations of K, Ca, Mg, Na, and chlorides can be ascertained by use of atomic absorption spectrometry.

The availability of the information emphasized above will permit the composition of a basic salt solution (BSS) for the molluscan species from which tissues and/or cells are to be cultured.

Further analysis of hemolymph must include total protein concentration determinations either by use of the method of Lowry *et al.* (1951) or by some other method. The technique of Lowry *et al.* has been applied with success to *Biomphalaria glabrata* hemolymph by Lee and Cheng (1972). Specifically, 0.04 ml of hemolymph is diluted with 4 ml of distilled water and thoroughly mixed. Subsequently, 0.5 ml aliquots are used for protein determination using a Spectronic 20 spectrophotometer read at 600 μm. A known standard and a control are concurrently analyzed with the test samples, and the protein concentrations are read off a previously established standard curve.

Qualitative amino acid determinations can be achieved by thin-layer chromatography while both qualitative and quantitative determinations can be done with an automated amino acid analyzer or by some other method.

The total carbohydrate content of the hemolymph can be determined colorimetrically by the anthrone procedure (Oser, 1965) while the reducing sugar content can be determined colorimetrically by the Nelson (1944) method or some other test.

It is being emphasized that the osmolality and ion concentrations of the hemolymph are of immediate importance since this information is essential to the design of a balanced salt solution (BSS).

Measurements of the physical and chemical properties of the hemolymph of medically and economically important mollusks remains scanty. What is known about the hemolymph of *Biomphalaria glabrata*, the intermediate host for *Schistosoma mansoni*, is presented on p. 183.

Despite the lack of success up to this time in establishing a molluscan cell line, several important technical advances relative to the establishment of several basic salt solutions and maintenance media have been made, and these are presented below.

Review of Useful Techniques

BASIC SALT SOLUTION

Several basic salt solutions (BSS) have been devised for inclusion in culture (or maintenance) media. The formulations of the most useful are as shown in the following tabulations.

Bohuslav's (1933a) BSS[a,b]

Ingredient	Concentration (g/1000 ml of distilled H_2O)
NaCl	7.40
KCl	0.45
$CaCl_2$	0.50
$MgCl_2$	0.02
$NaCHO_3$	0.15
Na_2HPO_4	0.05

[a]Used for maintenance of tissues from *Helix aspersa*, *H. austriaca*, *H. obvia*, and *Arion empiricorum*.
[b]At pH 8.8.

Vago and Chastang's (1958) BSS[a,b]

Ingredient	Concentration (g/1000 ml of distilled H_2O)
NaCl	6.50
KCl	0.14
$CaCl_2$	0.12
NaH_2PO_4	0.01
CO_3NaH	0.20

[a]Used for maintenance of tissues from *Helix aspersa* and *H. pomatia.*
[b]At pH 7.6–7.9.

Chernin's (1963) BSS[a,b]

Ingredient	Concentration (g/1000 ml of distilled H_2O)
NaCl	2.80
KCl	0.15
Na_2HPO_4 (anhydrous)	0.07
$MgSO_4 \cdot 7H_2O$	0.45
$CaCl_2 \cdot 2H_2O$	0.53
$NaHCO_3$	0.05

[a]Used for maintenance of organs of *Biomphalaria glabrata.*
[b]At pH 7.3–7.5.

Tripp *et al.'s* (1966) BSS[a,b]

Ingredient	Concentration (g/1000 ml of distilled H_2O)
NaCl	23.50
KCl	0.67
$CaCl_2$ (anhydrous)	1.10
$MgCl_2$ (anhydrous)	2.03
$MgSO_4$ (anhydrous)	2.94
$NaHCO_3$	0.02
K_2HPO_4 (anhydrous)	0.19
Glucose	0.50
Trehalose	0.50
Phenol red	0.05

[a]Used for maintenance of cells of *Crassostrea virginica.*
[b]At pH 7.2–7.4.

MAINTENANCE MEDIA

As stated, a totally satisfactory true culture medium is still unavailable for molluscan cells and/or tissues; however, the selected media given in the following tabulations have been used with some success at maintaining molluscan tissues.

Vago and Chastang's (1958) Medium[a,b]

Ingredient	Concentration
Glucose	1.0 g/1000 ml
Casein hydrolysate	0.5 g/1000 ml
Glutamine	0.1 g/1000 ml
Choline	0.002 g/1000 ml
Yeast extract	2 ml
Homologous hemolymph	10%
Penicillin	200,000 units
Streptomycin	50 mg/1000 ml
Vago and Chastang's (1958) BSS	1000 ml

[a]Used for maintenance of foot, mantle, and heart of *Helix aspersa* and *H. pomatia*.
[b]At pH 7.6–7.9.

Chernin's (1963) Medium[a,b]

Ingredient	Concentration
Glucose	1.00 g/1000 ml
Trehalose	1.00 g/1000 ml
Bovine amniotic fluid	110.00 ml/1000 ml
Beef embryo extract	12.5 ml/1000 ml
Horse serum	12.5 ml/1000 ml
Lactalbumin hydrolysate (5%)	10.0 ml/1000 ml
Yeast extract (10%)	5.0 ml/1000 ml
Penicillin	100 units/ml
Streptomycin sulfate	100 μg/ml
Phenol red (0.4%)	5 ml/ 100 ml
Chernin's (1963) BSS	850 ml

[a]For maintenance of heart of *Biomphalaria glabrata*.
[b]At pH 7.3–7.5.

Tripp *et al.'s* **(1966) Medium**[a,b]

Ingredient	Concentration
Casaamino acids (5%)	1.0 ml/1000 ml
Yeast extract (10%)	10 ml/1000 ml
Lactalbumin hydrolysate (5%)	10 ml/1000 ml
Calf serum	10 ml/1000 ml
Tripp *et al.'s* (1966) BSS	969 ml

[a] For maintenance of heart of *Crassostrea virginica*.
[b] At pH 7.2–7.4.

Burch and Cuadros's (1965) Medium[a]

Ingredient	Concentration
Part I (snail medium)[b]	
Distilled water[c]	480 ml
Medium 199 + 0.5% peptone	500 ml
BHI bacteriological broth	20 ml
S. L. broth[d]	20 ml
M-9 stock solution A	4 ml
M-9 stock solution B	8 ml
Calf fetal serum	40 ml
Snail extract[e]	40 ml
Antibiotic mixture	8 ml
Part II (S. L. broth)	
Trypticase	10 g
Yeast extract	5 g
K_2HPO_4	6 g
Ammonium citrate	2 g
Glucose	20 g
Sodium acetate	25 g
Glacial acetic acid	1.32 ml
Salt solution	5 ml
Tween 80	1 g
Distilled water	500 ml
Part III (salt solution)	
$MgSO_4·7H_2O$	11.5 g
$MnSO_4·H_2O$	2.86 g
Distilled water	100 ml
Part IV (stock solutions)	
Solution A[f]	
Na_2HPO_4 (anhydrous)	150 g
K_2HPO_4 (anhydrous)	75 g
Distilled water	1000 ml

Burch and Cuadros's (1965) Medium[a] (*continued*)

Ingredient	Concentration
Solution B[f]	
MgSO$_4$	20 g
NaCl	50 g
NH$_4$Cl	1 g
Distilled water	1000 ml
Antiobiotic mixture	
Fungizone	50 mg
Penicillin	1,000,000 units
Streptomycin	1 g
Distilled water	100 ml

[a] For maintaining limited culturing of gonads, foot muscle, mantle, oviduct, and esophagus of *Biomphalaria glabrata*, *Helix pomatia*, and *Pomatiopsis lapidaria*.

[b] Preparation of snail medium. All components are pooled and mixed in a 2-liter flask. The pH is adjusted to the desired value (7 for gonadal tissue, 8.5 for foot muscle) by adding steam-sterilized 0.3 N NaOH. The indicator (phenol red) contained in the 500 ml of Medium 199 is sufficient to indicate the pH. The medium is filtered through a Millipore filter, dispensed in 100-ml Pyrex bottles, and stored at $-5°C$.

[c] Burch and Cuadros used triple-distilled water throughout

[d] Preparation of snail extract. The shells were sterilized with 70% ethanol prior to removal. The soft tissues are minced in a Waring blender suspended in a volume of distilled water equal to the weight of the tissues for 30 minutes at 0°C. The homogenate is centrifuged for 10 minutes at 2000 rpm at 10°C. The supernatant is the "snail extract."

[e] Preparation of S. L. broth. The ingredients are dissolved in 500 ml of sterile distilled water before the volume is adjusted to 1 liter with distilled water.

[f] Preparation of stock solutions A and B. Stock solutions A and B are prepared separately then each is made up to 1 liter with distilled water.

EMPLOYING HOMOLOGOUS HEMOLYMPH

Short of a satisfactory culture medium, homologous hemolymph, for example, hemolymph from the same species of mollusk, can be employed to at least maintain tissues and/or cells. Furthermore, homologous hemolymph has been employed by several investigators as a supplemental nutritive to media (Bohuslav, 1933a; Haugton, 1934; Vago and Chastang, 1958; Chernin, 1963).

Cheng and Arndt's (1973) medium[a]

Ingredient	Concentration
Chernin's (1963) BSS	18.5 ml
5% Lactalbumin hydrolysate	0.1 ml
10% Yeast extract	0.05 ml
Fetal bovine serum, inactivated	0.125 ml
Bovine hemoglobin	0.1 ml of a 10 mg/ml aqueous solution
Tissue culture vitamins, Eagle	0.2 ml
Lysine	0.151 mg
Histidine	0.104 mg
Arginine	0.063 mg
Aspartic acid	0.145 mg
Threonine	0.160 mg
Serine	0.310 mg
Glutamic acid	0.244 mg
Proline	0.148 mg
Alanine	0.125 mg
Glycine	0.124 mg
Valine	0.085 mg
Methionine	0.007 mg
Isoleucine	0.054 mg
Leucine	0.074 mg
Phenylalanine	0.051 mg
Penicillin G (10,000 units/ml)	0.2 ml (final concentration = 104 units/ml)
Tris (hydroxymethyl) aminomethane	0.0388 g

[a]The pH of the medium is 7.6 and the osmolarity is 117 mOsm/ liter.

A variety of methods can be employed to collect molluscan hemolymph. Among pelecypods, the insertion of a hypodermic needle into the adductor muscle sinus through a notch filed at the shell edge is quite satisfactory (Fig. 11-3). In the case of large gastropods, such as *Achatina fulica* and a number of species of viviparous snails, a considerable amount of hemolymph can be obtained by use of a syringe and hypodermic needle inserted into the cephalopedal sinus. In the case of the so-called albino strain of *Biomphalaria glabrata*, Lee and Cheng (1971) have been successful in collecting hemolymph by use of a glass capillary tube inserted into the heart through the transparent shell. Also, if all else fails, the shell of the mollusk can be gently cracked and the seeping hemolymph can be collected with a tuberculin

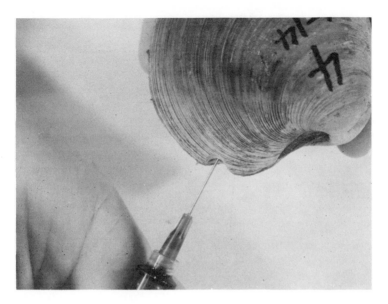

Fig. 11-3. Technique for bleeding clam by inserting needle through a notch cut on the valves.

syringe and needle from the edge of a Stendor dish or small petri dish in which the mollusk had been placed (Fig. 11-4). The main drawback with this method is maintaining aseptic conditions.

PREPARATION OF TISSUES

In order to obtain small pieces of molluscan tissue for explant studies, aseptic procedures involving a pair of fine irridectomy scissors is recommended. This method has the distinct advantage that the cells toward the center are surrounded by their natural environment and are not exposed to chemical or mechanical injury. The disadvantage of this method in molluscan tissue culture is the fact that the exomigration of hemolymph cells occurs, and, as stated, this may be interpreted to be new cells migrating from the explant.

A variety of techniques have been employed to dissociate small pieces of tissue to obtain isolated cells. The preferred technique, if chemical procedures are to be avoided, is mincing followed by passing the small pieces through a fine-mesh stainless steel screen fitted in the nozzle of a syringe.

A number of enzymes are now available for dissociating cells. Among these are trypsin, pronase, and versene. Trypsin has been successfully

Fig. 11-4. Technique for collecting hemolymph from small gastropods. The shell of the snail is gently crushed, and the hemolymph seeping from the sinuses and tissues is pooled along the edge of a dish and taken up with a syringe.

employed on molluscan tissues by Chardonnet and Peres (1963) and Chernin (1963). The technique involves placing tissue fragments in a 25% trypsin solution in an appropriate basic salt solution at pH 7.6–7.9 for 50–60 minutes with gentle stirring. The enzyme action can be stopped by either placing the preparation in melted ice or by blocking with an inhibitor. The common inhibitor employed is a pancreatic inhibitor (Santucci *et al.*, 1962); however, the action of trypsin is irreversibly blocked by this method.

Cecil (1969) has successfully utilized a 0.25% solution of trypsin-EDTA in a 2.6% NaCl solution to dissociate the cardiac cells of the surf clam, *Spisula solidissima*.

CULTURE VESSELS

Although the hanging drop method originally designed by Harrison (1907) is useful in invertebrate tissue and cell culture, especially if the tissue is small, it is impractical if large numbers of cells are to be harvested. Similarly, the cover slip method is useful for preliminary, short-term studies. This involves placing a tissue fragment in a drop of medium on a cover slip, inverting the cover slip over a depression slide, and sealing.

For larger scale cultures, the usual vessels used for vertebrate tissue and cell culture may be used. These include glass or plastic Carrel D_5 and D_3 flasks, roller tubes with flattened surfaces, T-flasks, and Leighton tubes.

Studies on insect cells have indicated that they adhere more readily to plastic vessels. Whether this is also true of molluscan cells has not been ascertained.

LIQUID MEDIUM

Vago and Chastang (1958) have been successful in maintaining tissues of *Helix aspersa* and oysters in a liquid medium. This technique involves placing tissue fragments, 1 mm in diameter, in the medium in contact with a glass slide. Cells migrating from the explant are either attached to the slide or are freely suspended in the liquid medium. Suspended cells are readily transferred with a pipette.

TEMPERATURE

Although most attempts at molluscan tissue or cell culture have been carried out at 20°–25° C, Burch and Cuadros (1965) have observed that cultures of *Helix, Biomphalaria*, and *Pomatiopsis* tissues appear to do better at 15° C.

GAS PHASE

A gas phase has not yet been employed in molluscan tissue culture since the use of an O_2 gas phase in tissue culture is usually necessary as the result of the presence of a bicarbonate buffer, which is not recommended for molluscan tissue culture. If another type of buffer is used, there may be no need to use a gas phase other than air. In the case of digestive gland tissue, it may be necessary to use a gas phase of O_2 and H_2, predominantly the latter, since indirect evidences suggest that trematode larvae embedded in this gland are unable to metabolize fat as an energy source, possibly because of the absence of O_2 (Cheng, 1963). If this is truly the case, a minimum of O_2 may be more conducive to cell growth.

Organ Culture

Technically, organ culture is distinguished from tissue or cell culture in that whole organs are maintained *in vitro*; however, in many instances the line of demarcation between tissue and organ culture is hazy at best. The rationale generally used for organ culture in medical malacology is to maintain host organs in suitable media so that parasites can be sustained in the organs where they are more readily available for study than they are within the entire host organism. A few investigators have attempted molluscan organ culture with varying success. The following is a brief review. Interested readers are referred to the more extensive review by Gomot (1971).

Bohuslav (1933a,b) apparently was the first to attempt molluscan organ culture. He maintained several postembryonic organs and explants of *Helix aspersa*, *H. pomatia*, *H. austriaca*, *H. obvia*, and *Arion empiricorum* in a medium composed of a homologous or heterologous peptone solution in which hearts of *H. aspersa* pulsated for 39 days. In addition, seminal vesicles were reported to have grown, although salivary glands degenerated. Various ducts were reported to develop thickened epithelial walls (metaplasia?), and the stomach wall developed metaplastic epithelioid cysts.

Konicek (1933) attempted to culture the atrium and ventricle, as well as other tissues, of *Helix pomatia*. The medium employed consisted of 0.45% agar containing peptone broth, glucose, and Ringer's salt solution. The organs were transplanted every 5–7 days, and the only success achieved was the finding of amoebocytes migrating from the atrial explants, although the atria pulsated for 3 weeks and the ventricles pulsated for a few hours.

Sengel (1961) attempted the culture of gill filaments and digestive gland of the marine pelecypod *Barnea candida* with limited success. He employed two modifications of the medium devised by Wolff and Haffen (1952). One of these, Medium M, consisted of a mixture of 1% agar and seawater, while the other, Medium St M, consisted of 1% agar, seawater, and chick embryo extract. On both media the organs survived for 7 days, with the gills undergoing no structural change, including active ciliary activity; however, the digestive gland became moribund.

Chernin (1963) has been successful at maintaining heart explants of *Biomphalaria glabrata* in flasks for up to 47 days. He developed a balanced salt solution (p. 253) and nutrient medium and amoebocyte and epithelial cell exomigration occurred from the hearts placed therein. Furthermore, 50% of the hearts pulsated between the second and fifth days *in vitro*.

The most recent attempt at molluscan organ culture has been that of Hollande (1968) who maintained the multifide glands of *Helix pomatia* for 33 days in dilute Eagle's liquid medium with antibiotics added.

In addition to the studies mentioned, some interesting information has been made available from peripheral studies. Specifically, Ripplinger and Joly (1961) have reported that if crushed nerves from a mollusk are added to a maintenance medium for excised hearts, the heart beats are sustained longer. Along similar lines, Benex (1964) has reported that tentacles of *Biomphalaria glabrata*, including nerve ganglia, survive longer *in vitro* than tentacles without these nerve cells.

It is also of interest to note that Benex (1967a) has reported that the respiratory rates of excised mantle and gill filaments of *Mytilus* placed in a balanced salt solution with glucose added is elevated if vitamin C is provided. On the other hand, vitamins B_1, B_2, B_6, and B_{12} have no effect. In addition, Benex has found that the survival of these tissues of *Mytilus* is enhanced if sulfamides (1162 F and sulfadiazine) or *p*-aminobenzoate is added. In a later report, Benex (1967b) has provided evidence that molecules with a benzene nucleus and an NH_2 group at the para position enhances the survival of organs and tissues of *Mytilus*. The reason for this remains unknown.

In conclusion, it should be noted that molluscan organ culture, or at least short-term maintenance, has been carried out by a number of investigators interested in comparative endocrinology. The main objective of these studies has been to study the effects of hormones and related compounds on mature and immature organs *in vitro*. These studies have involved media suitable for short-term maintenance. Interested persons should consult the review by Gomot (1971) for leads to the primary literature.

References

Armstrong, D. A., Armstrong, J. L., Krassner, S. M., and Pauley, G. B. (1971). Experimental wound repair in the black abalone, *Haliotis cracherodii*. *J. Invertebr. Pathol.* **17**, 216–227.

Benex, J. (1964). Sur la dédifférenciation des tentacules de planorbes en survie: Rôle de la présence d'éléments nervaux sur le retard de cette dédifférenciation. *C. R. Acad. Sci.* **258**, 2193–2196.

Benex, J. (1967a). Substances susceptibles d'augmenter la survie d'explants maintenus en culture organotypique. *C. R. Acad. Sci.* **265**, 571–574.

Benex, J. (1967b). Importance de la structure chimique et de la configuration stérique dans l'augmentation de la survie d'explants maintenus en culture organotypique. *C. R. Acad. Sci.* **265**, 631–634.

Bevelander, G., and Martin, J. (1949). Culture of mantle tissue of marine molluscs. *Anat. Rec.* **105**, 614.

Bohuslav, P. (1933a). Die Gewebezuchtung des postembryonalen Verdavungstraktus, der Glandula salivalis und des Receptaculum Sominis bei Mollusken aus der Familie Helicidae. *Arch. Exp. Zellforsch. Besonders Gewebezuecht.* **13**, 673–708.

Bohuslav, P. (1933b). Die Explantation des reinen postembryonalen Herz-bindegewebes aus *Helix pomatia. Arch. Exp. Zellforsch. Besonders Gewebezuecht.* **14**, 139–151.

Bourne, G. (1935). Notes on some experiments with snail tissue in culture. *Aust. J. Exp. Biol. Med. Sci.* **13**, 43–48.

Burch, J. B., and Cuadros, C. (1965). A culture medium for snail cells and tissues. *Nature (London)* **206**, 637.

Cameron, G. (1949). Cultivation of tissues from cold blooded animals. *Anat. Rec.* **103**, 431.

Cary, L. R. (1931). Report on tissue culture. Year book Carnegie Inst. Washington **31**, 282–283.

Cecil, J. T. (1969). Mitoses in cell cultures from cardiac tissue of the surf clam *Spisula solidissima. J. Invertebr. Pathol.* **14**, 407–410.

Chardonnet, Y., and Peres, G. (1963). Essai de culture de cellules provenant d'un mollusque: *Mytilus galloprovincialis* L. *C. R. Soc. Biol.* **157**, 1593–1595.

Cheng, T. C. (1963). Biochemical requirements of larval trematodes. *Ann. N.Y. Acad. Sci.* **113**, 289–320.

Cheng, T. C. (1967). Marine molluscs as hosts for symbioses: With a review of known parasites of commercially important species. *Advan. Mar. Biol.* **5**, 1–424.

Cheng, T. C., and Arndt, R. J. (1973). Maintenance of cells of *Biomphalaria glabrata* (Mollusca) in vitro. *J. Invertebr. Pathol.* **22**, 308–310.

Chernin, E. (1963). Observations on hearts explanted in vitro from the snail *Australorbis glabratus. J. Parasitol.* **49**, 353–364.

Cowdsen, R. R. (1972). Some cytological and cytochemical observations on the leucopoeitic organs, the "white bodies", of *Octopus vulgaris. J. Invertebr. Pathol.* **19**, 113–119.

Dawe, C. J. (1969). Phylogeny and oncology. *Nat. Cancer Inst.., Monogr.* **31**, 1–39.

Ebstein, B. S., Rosentral, M. D., and De Haan, R. L. (1965). Cells from isolated blastomeres of *Ilyanassa obsoleta* in tissue culture. *Exp. Cell. Res.* **40**, 174–177.

Farley, C. A., Banfield, W. G., Kasnic, G., Jr., and Foster, W. S. (1972). Oyster herpes-type virus. *Science* **178**, 759–760.

Federoff, S. (1966). Proposed usage of animal tissue culture terms. *In Vitro* **2**, 155–159.

Federow, B. G. (1933). Über die In vitro-kultur des Nervengewebes der Cephalopoden. *Biol. Zentralb.* **53**, 41–49.

Flandre, O. (1971). Cell culture of mollusks. *In* "Invertebrate Tissue Cutlure" (C. Vago, ed.), Vol. 1, pp. 361–383. Academic Press, New York.

Foley, D. A., and Cheng, T. C. (1972). Interaction of molluscs and foreign substances: The morphology and behavior of hemolymph cells of the American oyster, *Crassostrea virginica*, in vitro. *J. Invertebr. Pathol.* **19**, 383–394.

Gatenby, J. B. (1931). Outgrowths from pieces of *Helix aspersa*, the common snail. *Nature (London)* **128**, 1002–1003.

Gatenby, J. B. (1932a). A technique for studying growth and movement in explants from *Helix aspersa. Arch. Exp. Zellforsch. Besonders Gewebezuecht.* **13**, 665–671.

Gatenby, J. B. (1932b). Absence of mitosis in tissue culture and regeneration in *Helix aspersa. Nature (London)* **130**, 628.

Gatenby, J. B., and Duthie, E. S. (1932). On the behaviour of small pieces of the pulmonary cavity wall of *Helix aspersa* kept in blood. *J. Roy. Microsc. Soc.* [3] **52**, 395–403.

Gatenby, J. B., and Hill, J. C. (1934). Improved techniques for nonaseptic tissue culture of *Helix aspersa*, with notes on molluscan cytology. *Quart. J. Microsc. Sci.* **76**, 331–352.

Gomot, L. (1971). The organitypic culture of invertebrates other than insects. *In* "Invertebrate Tissue Culture" (C. Vago, ed.), Vol. 2, pp. 41–136. Academic Press, New York.

Green, A. E., Coriell, L. L., and Charney, J. (1964). A rapid cytotoxic antibody test to determine species of cell cultures. *J. Nat. Cancer Inst.* **32**, 779–786.

Gresson, R. A. R. (1937). Studies on the culturation of pieces of the mantle of *Modiolus modiolus. Quart. J. Microsc. Sci.* **79**, 659–678.

Harrison, R. G. (1907). Observations on the living developing nerve fiber. *Anat. Rec.* **7**, 116–118.

Haughton, I. (1934). Note on the amoeboid elements in the blood of *Helix aspersa. Quart. J. Microsc. Sci.* **77**, 157–166.

Hillman, R. E. (1963). An observation of the occurrence of mitosis in regenerating mantle epithelium of the eastern oyster, *Crassostrea virginica. Chesapeake Sci.* **4**, 172–174.

Hirata, A. A. (1953). Studies on shell formation. II. A mantle shell preparation for *in vitro* studies. *Biol. Bull.* **104**, 394–397.

Hollande, E. (1968). Evolution des grains de sécrétion dans le cellules des glandes multifides d'*Helix pomatia*, maintenus en surne expérimentale. *C.R. Acad. Sci.* **267**, 2054–2057.

Konicek, H. (1933). Über die Züchtung des Lungensack-und Herzgewebes bei *Helix pomatia* (Vorläufige Mitteil.). *Arch. Exp. Zellforsch. Besonders Gewebezuecht.* **13**, 709–716.

Lee, F. O., and Cheng, T. C. (1971). *Schistosoma mansoni*: Respirometric and partial pressure studies in infected *Biomphalaria glabrata*. *Exp. Parasitol.* **30**, 393–399.

Lee, F. O., and Cheng, T. C. (1972). *Schistosoma mansoni*: Alterations in total protein and hemoglobin in the hemolymph of infected *Biomphalaria glaborata*. *Exp. Parasitol.* **31**, 203–216.

Li, M. F., Stewart, J. E., and Drinnan, R. E. (1966). *In vitro* cultivation of the oyster, *Crassostrea virginica*. *J. Fish. Res. Bd. Can.* **23**, 545–599.

Lowry, O., Rosenbrough, N., Farr, A., and Randall, R. (1951). Protein measurement with the Folin phenol reagent. *J. Biol. Chem.* **193**, 265–275.

Necco, A., and Martin, R. (1963a). Behavior and estimation of the mitotic activity of the white body cells in *Octopus vulgaris* cultured *in vitro*. *Exp. Cell Res.* **30**, 588–623.

Necco, A., and Martin, R. (1963b). The mitotic activity of the white body cells of *Octopus vulgaris in vitro*. *Ann. Epiphyt.* [2] **14**, 23–25.

Nelson, N. (1944). A photometric adaption of the Somogyi method for the determination of glucose. *J. Biol. Chem.* **153**, 275–300.

Orton, J. H. (1922). The blood cells of the oyster. *Nature (London)* **109**, 612–613.

Oser, B. L., ed. (1965). "Physiological Chemistry," 14th ed. McGraw-Hill (Blakiston), New York.

Pauley, G. B. (1969). A critical review of neoplasia and tumor-like lesions in mollusks. *Nat. Cancer Inst., Monogr.* **31**, 509–539.

Pauley, G. B., and Sparks, A. K. (1967). Observations on experimental wound repair in the adductor muscle and the Leydig cell of the oyster *Crassostrea gigas*. *J. Invertebr. Pathol.* **9**, 298–309.

Perkins, F. O., and Menzel, R. W. (1964). Maintenace of oyster cells *in vitro*. *Nature (London)* **204**, 1106–1107.

Ripplinger, J., and Joly, M. (1961). Role of constituents of the hemolymph in the activity of the heart of *Helix pomatia*. *C.R. Soc. Biol.* **155**, 825–827.

Rosenfield, A. (1965). Maintenance of oyster tissue *in vitro*. *Amer. Malacol. Un. Bull.* **32**, 30.

Rungger, D., Rastelli, M., Braendle, E., and Malsberger, R. G. (1971). A viruslike particle assiocated with lesions in the muscles of *Octopus vulgaris*. *J. Invertebr. Pathol.* **17**, 72–80.

Santucci, J., Haag, J., Choay, J., and Thely, M. (1962). Culture cellulaire: Inhibition de la trypsine cristallisée par les inhibeteurs naturels. *C.R. Acad. Sci.* **254**, 955–957.

Sengel, P. (1961). Survie en culture *in vitro* de divers organes d'invertébrés marine adultes. *C.R. Acad. Sci.* **252**, 3666–3668.

Tripp, M. R., Bisignani, L. A., and Kenny, M. T. (1966). Oyster amoebocytes in vitro. *J. Invert. Pathol.* **8**, 137–140.

Vago, C., and Chastang, S. (1958). Obtention de lignées cellulaires en culture de tissus d'invertébrés. *Experientia* **14**, 110–111.

Wolff, E., and Haffen, K. (1952). Sur une méthode de culture d'organes embryonnaires *in vitro*. *Tex. Rep. Biol. Med.* **10**, 463–472.

12 Aquaculture

With the world's ever increasing population comes the problem of providing adequate nutrition. More specifically, new methods must be found to satisfy the protein requirements of three-quarters of the world's population. One of the proposed methods is aquaculture, that is farming the world's waters to raise fish and shellfish. Relative to mollusks, the raising of shellfish up to now has been almost exclusively limited to waters along the coasts of several northern European countries, especially Holland, and Japan, although mariculture, that is farming in marine waters, has been started in other nations, including the United States. It may be debated whether shellfish and fish would help alleviate the nutritional problem; however, together with other new approaches, aquaculture must be considered a plus factor.

As one would expect, the mariculture of mollusks has been primarily concentrated on oysters (several species) and the hard clam, or quahog clam, *Mercenaria mercenaria*, the latter in the United States, although the blue mussel, *Mytilus edulis*, is being farmed in Holland, parts of Britain, and elsewhere in Europe.

It is not the intent in this chapter to present a comprehensive review of this aspect of applied malacology. Rather, certain principles, efficient practices, and those aspects of the biology of oysters and clams that are essential to mariculture are presented.

Oysters

SPECIES OF OYSTERS

What are commonly called "oysters" actually represent several species, each with its own characteristics. Among the commercially important are (1) the American oyster, *Crassostrea virginica* (Fig. 12-1), a native of eastern

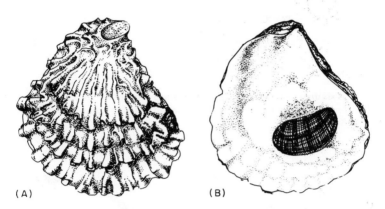

Fig. 12-1. *Crassostrea virginica*, the American oyster. (A) Lower (left) valve. (B) Inside of upper (right) valve. Specimen from Wellfleet Harbor, Massachusetts. After Galtsoff (1964).

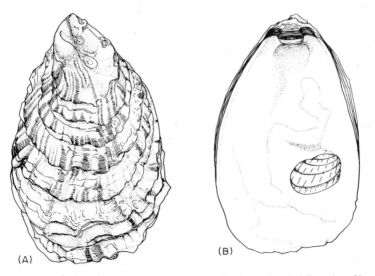

Fig. 12-2. *Crassostrea gigas*, the Japanese, or West Coast, oyster. (A) Exterior of lower (left) valve. (B) Interior of upper (right) valve. Specimen from Willapa Harbor, Washington, grown from seed imported from Japan. After Galtsoff (1964).

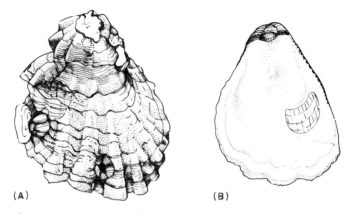

Fig. 12-3. *Crassostrea commercialis*, the New Zealand rock oyster. (A) Exterior of lower (left) valve. (B) Interior or upper (right) valve. Specimen collected in Kaneohe Bay, Oahu, Hawaii. After Galtsoff (1964).

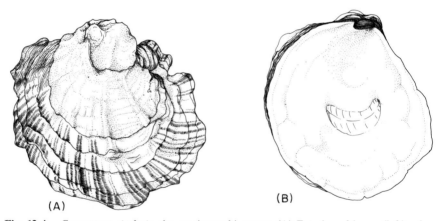

Fig. 12-4. *Crassostrea rivularis*, the suminoegaki oyster. (A) Exterior of lower (left) valve. (B) Interior of upper (right) valve. Specimen from Puget Sound, Washington. After Galtsoff (1964).

North America; (2) the Japanese oyster, *Crassostrea gigas* (Fig. 12-2), a native of the Orient that has been introduced into the waters of British Columbia in Canada, the western states of the United States, including Alaska, and a few colonies have been transplanted in Mobile Bay, Alabama, and in Massachusetts; (3) *Crassostrea commercialis* (Fig. 12-3), the Sydney rock oyster or commercial oyster, a native of Australia that has been introduced to various islands of the Pacific Basin, including Hawaii, and (4)

Crassostrea rivularis (Fig. 12-4), the "suminoegaki" oyster, a native of Japan and China that has been planted in Puget Sound by accident with the seed of *C. gigas*.

Also included among the more important oysters from the commercial viewpoint are two members of the genus *Ostrea*. These are (1) *Ostrea edulis* (Fig. 12-5), the European flat oyster, which is the species of primary commercial value in northern Europe; and (2) *Ostrea lurida* (Fig. 12-6), the lurida oyster, which inhabits the tidal waters of the Pacific Coast of North America,

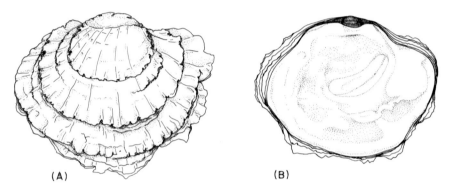

(A)   (B)

Fig. 12-5. *Ostrea edulis*, the European oyster. (A) Exterior of the left (lower) valve. (B) Interior of the right (upper) valve. Specimen from Boothbay Harbor, Maine. After Galtsoff (1964).

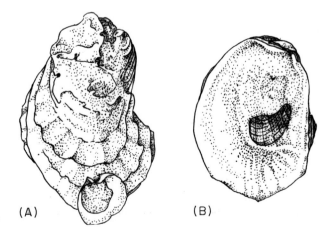

(A)   (B)

Fig. 12-6. *Ostrea lurida*, the lurida oyster. (A) Left valve. (B) Right valve. Specimen from Puget Sound, Washington. After Galtsoff (1964).

extending from Alaska to lower California. This genus also includes *O. equestris*, the horse or crested oyster; *O. frons*, the frons oyster; and *O. permollis*, an extremely small oyster that lives in sponges. These three species of *Ostrea*, however, are of no commercial importance.

In addition to *Crassostrea* and *Ostrea*, a third genus of oysters, *Pycnodonte*, exists; however, it is not of commercial importance.

The primary reason for listing those species of commercial importance is that there is a striking difference between the species of *Crassostrea* and *Ostrea* from the standpoint of development. Members of *Crassostrea*, like all oysters, are protandric hermaphrodites, that is, they are initially functional males and later become females. However, the sperm and ova are discharged into water where fertilization occurs. The release of gametes is commonly referred to as "spawning." In the case of members of the genus *Ostrea*, spermatozoa are discharged by males and taken into the inhalant chamber of the gills of females and fertilization occurs at this site. Furthermore, the larvae develop and are incubated in the gill cavity (or chamber). It is only after the embryo develops into a veliger larva that it is "spawned." Thus, spawning is different among members of *Crassostrea* and *Ostrea*, with the former involving the release of gametes and the latter involving the release of larvae. Relative to this phase of the biology of oysters, the common belief has persisted that oysters should be eaten only during the eight "R" months—January, February, March, April, September, October, November, and December—since in the case of *Ostrea edulis* it is during the four "non-R" months, May through August, that the shell-bearing larvae occur in adults and, consequently, oysters have a gritty texture when eaten. Among members of *Crassostrea*, as stated, fertilization is external, and, hence, these oysters are not incubators and can be eaten during May through August without being unpalatable.

DEVELOPMENT OF OYSTERS

The ovum is fertilized by a sperm and irrespective of whether this occurs internally or externally in seawater, the embryo undergoes cleavage and passes through the blastula and gastrula stages. It then differentiates into a ciliated larva, known as the trochophore (Fig. 12-7), which escapes from the egg and differentiates into a second larval form, the veliger (Fig. 12-8). This larva usually develops on about the fifth day postfertilization in the case of *Ostrea edulis* and slightly longer in the case of *Crassostrea* spp., but in both cases the developmental time is influenced by the ambient temperature.

As stated, in the case of *Ostrea* spp. the veligers developing from trochophores are maintained in the parent's inhalant gill chamber and are eventually discharged into seawater while in the case of *Crassostrea* spp. both the trochophore and veliger larvae are free-swimming.

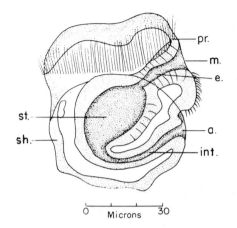

Fig. 12-7. Trochophore of *Ostrea edulis*. a., Anus; e., esophagus; int., intestine; m., mouth; st., stomach; sh., shell; pr., prototroch. After Pelseneer (1906).

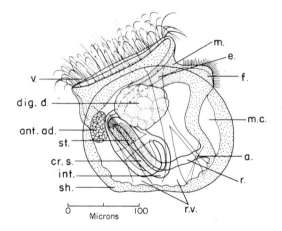

Fig. 12-8. Early free-swimming veliger of *Ostrea edulis*. a., Anus; ant. ad., anterior adductor muscle; cr.s., crystalline style sac; dig. d., digestive diverticula; e., esophagus; f., rudiment of foot; int., intestine; m., mouth; m.c., mantle cavity; r., rectum; r.v., velar retractor muscles; sh., shell; st., stomach; v., velum. After Yonge (1926).

In both genera the fully formed veliger is about 0.2 mm long. It remains as a part of the zooplankton for 1–2.5 weeks and during this time feeds primarily, if not exclusively, on algal cells that measure less than 0.01 mm in diameter. The veliger reaches a maximum size of about 0.3 mm in length during this period.

After its free-swimming period, during which approximately 90% of the veligers die as the result of predation, environmental stress, and other reasons, the remaining commence to settle. This is a highly complex process that is beyond the scope of this chapter. Interested readers are referred to the highly readable account by Yonge (1960). In brief, after settling on a solid substrate, each veliger undergoes a predictable behavioral pattern (Fig. 12-9) and finally secretes an adhesive substance from its byssus gland situated in the base of its foot (Fig. 12-10). Soon after secreting this substance, the byssus gland degenerates, although in certain other pelecypods, such as mussels, the gland persists.

There is some evidence that oyster veligers prefer to settle on the under-surfaces of substrates (Korringa, 1940), and experiments involving placing tiles and slates at various angles in water have revealed that the number of settling veligers decreases as the position of the substrate approaches the verticle. In addition, veligers tend to settle on substrates near the bottom (in shallow areas), probably because the water currents are less active at this level.

After settling and becoming attached, the veliger commences to metamorphose into the young adult, or spat. This involves a series of interesting and highly complex processes that will not be considered here. Again, interested persons are referred to the account by Yonge (1960) or to the detailed account by Galtsoff (1964). It is noted that attached spat that have grown approximately 2 cm in length are commonly referred to as "seed oysters." This is the stage that is usually transferred and replanted at different geographic sites. For example, seed oysters of *Crassostrea gigas* are shipped annually from Japan and Korea to the states of Oregon and Washington where they are placed in suitable sites and allowed to grow to commercial size.

INDUCED SPAWNING

Crassostrea virginica can be induced to spawn throughout the year and, if necessary, several times a year (Loosanoff and Davis, 1952). This can be accomplished by raising the ambient temperature to 22°–32°C, depending on the previous environmental temperature. In addition, adding homologous sperm and ova into the water helps to stimulate spawning.

Information pertaining to the sexuality and propagation of *Ostrea edulis*, including the induction of spawning, has been reviewed by Orton (1937), Korringa (1940), Walne (1956), and Yonge (1960). Interested readers are referred to these accounts. In brief, the European flat oyster can also be induced to spawn by raising the ambient temperature by a few degrees; the addition of homologous gonadal material to the water also enhances induced spawning.

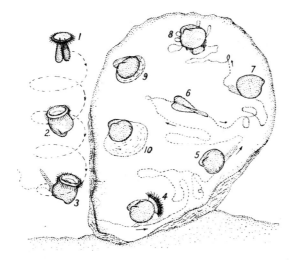

Fig. 12-9. Diagrammatic representation of the process of settling by the American oyster, *Crassotrea virginica*. 1 and 2. Swimming larvae with protruding velum, end and side views. 3 and 4. "Searching" phase with foot also protruded. 5–7. Crawling phase, with velum withdrawn. 8. Fixation. 9 and 10. Spat 1 and 2 days old. After Prytherch (1934).

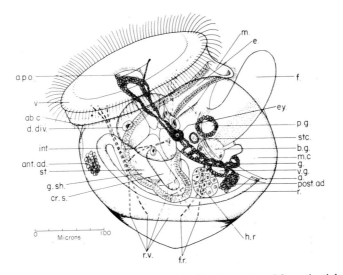

Fig. 12-10. Fully developed larva of *Ostrea edulis*. Specimen viewed from the right side with velum and foot at the ventral side in the uppermost position, which is typical during swimming. a., Anus; ab.c., aboral belt of cilia; ant. ad., anterior adductor muscle; a.p.o., apical sense organ and ganglion; b.g., byssus gland; cr. s., crystalline style sac; d. div., digestive diverticula; e., esophagus; et., ete; f., foot; f.r., foot retractor muscles; g., gill rudiment; g. sh., gastric shield; h.r., heart and kidney rudiment; int., intestine; m., mouth; m.c., mantle cavity; p.g., pedal ganglion; post. ad., posterior adductor muscle; r., rectum; r.v., velar retractor muscles; st., stomach; stc., statocyst; v., velum; v.g., visceral ganglion. After Erdmann (1934).

In the case of *Ostrea lurida*, gonadal development and spawning can be induced out of season by maintaining them at room temperature (21°–22°C) for several weeks. In nature, Coe (1931) has reported that spawning commences when the ambient temperature reaches 16°C.

As stated, oyster embryos first develop into trochophore larvae, with those of *C. virginica* and the other species of *Crassostrea* being free-swimming and those of *Ostrea edulis* and the other species of the genus being incubated in the parent. The trochophore larva develops into the veliger larva.

ARTIFICIAL REARING OF VELIGERS

In consideration of the development of oysters outlined above, it follows that the primary method of maintaining oysters in culture is to raise veliger larvae. Research in this area commenced with Wells in 1920; however, it has only been since the late 1930's, particularly in the 1950's, that any substantial progress has been made (for reviews, see Galtsoff, 1964; Loosanoff and Davis, 1963). As a result, it is now known that in order to rear veligers in holding tanks, flagellated algal cells must be added. Furthermore, organic enrichment of the water may be necessary.

Relative to algae, which are fed upon by veligers, "naked" flagellated cells serve as better food than those with heavy cell walls. The latter can be utilized only by older larvae. In the case of *C. virginica*, Davis (1953) has established that *Dicrateria inornata, Chromulina pleiades, Isochrysis galbana, Hemiselmis rufescens*, and *Pyramimonas grossi* can be utilized as food by veligers of all ages and *Chlorella* sp. can be utilized by older veligers only. In addition, *Monochrysis lutheri* is known to be a suitable food (Loosanoff and Davis, 1963). The utilizable flagellates are added to rearing tanks at a rate of 15,000 to 25,000 cells/ml per day with no toxic effects when the larval oyster population is approximately 5000/liter.

The addition of organic enrichment to rearing tanks is to provide nutrients for the algae, although some are undoubtedly also utilized by the oyster larvae. Thus, if fresh algal cells are continuously being added to the water, the addition of organic nutrients is unnecessary. On the other hand, if static tanks are employed and fresh algae are not added, organic enrichment must be introduced. Cole (1939), for example, has reported that the addition of the meat of the crab *Carcinus* ground with sand and heated to boiling was satisfactory as a nutrient for algae. The crab additive was added to a 90,000-gallon tank at a rate corresponding to 12.5 medium-sized crabs per day for a period of 3 to 4 weeks. With the advent of suitable culture media for algal cells, and the development of circulating tanks, the necessity to add organic enrichment is no longer a necessity.

It is noted that according to Loosanoff and Davis (1963), when pro-

vided with a satisfactory algal died and maintained at 30°C, the larvae of
C. virginica begin settling between the tenth and twelfth days postfertilization. If the temperature is lowered to 24°C, the larvae being settling on
the twenty-fourth day, and at 20°C, only a few veligers settle by the thirty-
eighth day.

The techniques described for *C. virginica*, are also applicable to the other
species of commercially important oysters. Only the optimal temperature
requirements and time of settling differ. Such information can be found in
the review of Loosanoff and Davis (1963) along with noted to the basic
biology of veligers maintained in artifical rearing tanks.

COLLECTING SPAT IN NATURE

Although it is not only possible but practical to cause spawning and rear
veligers in the laboratory, commercial oyster farming has not yet adopted
this practice on a large scale. Rather, spat is collected in oyster-growing areas
on several types of substrates and subsequently transferred to growing areas.
This is the common practice both in Japan and in northern Europe where
oyster culture is far ahead of the rest of the world. This is also the preferred

Fig. 12-11. Strips of used tires with young oysters, *Crassostrea virginica*, attached. The strips
of rubber were placed in water for the settling larvae to become attached to.

method in North America where controlled oyster rearing occurs on a limited scale. The primary reason for this is the apparent expense of setting up tanks for veligers and culturing algae for their food.

Although laboratory studies indicate that settling veligers prefer certain types of substrates, in practice, these larvae will settle on a variety of materials, including strips of used automobile tires (Fig. 12-11). In fact, the use of pieces of old tires strung on ropes to "catch" settling larvae is being employed on a private basis in some areas of the Atlantic Seaboard of the United States.

The practice developed in Japan of stringing the shells of large species of pelecypods and attaching them to poles in oyster-growing areas (Fig. 12-12) has now become the preferred method. Along the northeastern Atlantic coast of North America, shells of the large surf clam, *Spisula solidissima*, are readily available and serve as an ideal substrate for settling oyster larvae (Fig. 12-13). Of course, the shells of any pelecypod will do, including that of the quahog clam, *Mercenaria mercenaria*, and the American oyster itself.

The main obstacle for collecting spat in North America, especially the United States, with this manner is the limited amount of shoreline available for stringing out substrates. The affluent American society, where protein

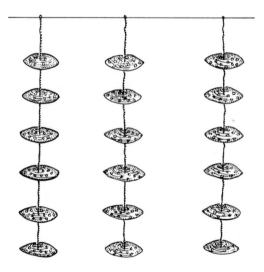

Fig. 12-12.   Drawing showing shells strung on string to catch the settling larvae of oysters.

Fig. 12-13. A shell of *Spisula solidissima* with young oysters, *Crassostrea virginica*, attached. The shell of the surf clam had been in water when the oyster larvae were settling.

deficiency is still not a dietary problem, would rather use areas where spat could be collected for recreational boating. Nevertheless, it is possible that such areas as the lower Delaware River basin in New Jersey, especially along the shoreline, could be used for this purpose. In fact, it is being used to a limited extent and within a very limited range in this manner by the Rutgers University Experiment Station.

There is little doubt that the Pacific Northwest in the United States is a more productive area for the farming of oysters at the present time than the Atlantic Seaboard. However, the favored *Crassostrea virginica* does not grow satisfactorily in the Pacific Northwest, although *Crassostrea gigas* and *Ostrea lurida* will grow in that area. If *C. virginica* is to be grown in sufficient quantities along the Atlantic Coast under controlled conditions, for example, by mariculture, artificial ponds need to be constructed since much of the Atlantic Coast is now polluted. For example, at least 80% of the shoreline of Connecticut has been condemned for the harvesting of oysters by the state and the U.S. Public Health Service because of biological pollution. The building of artificial ponds, however, does present an economic problem since real estate along waterfronts is at a premium.

Clams

The controlled culturing of clams in the United States has been limited primarily to the quahog, or hard clam, *Mercenaria mercenaria* (Fig. 12-14), even then, it is on a very limited basis. Clam farming is negligible in other parts of the world.

SPECIES OF CLAMS

What are commonly designated as "clams," as in the case of "oysters," actually represent several species of pelecypods. In fact, there are far more different species of clams than oysters. Listed in Table 12-1 are the taxonomic and common names of some of the economically important species.

In North America, the most important clams from the standpoint of commercial fisheries are *Mercenaria mercenaria*, *M. campechiensis*, *Mya arenaria*, *Arca transversa*, *Spisula solidissima*, *Tapes semidecussata*, and *Pitar morrhuana*. Among these, only *M. mercenaria* has been cultured to any extent under controlled conditions.

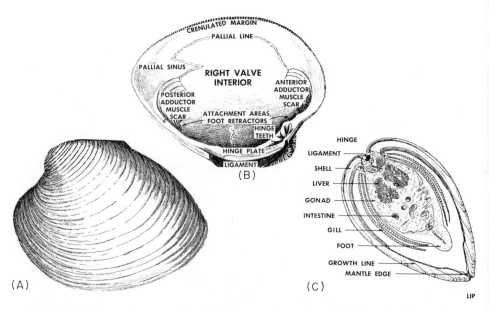

Fig. 12-14. *Mercenaria mercenaria*, the hard, or quahog, clam. (A) View of exterior of left valve; (B) view of interior of right valve; (C) cross section of whole specimen. Courtesy of Dr. C. N. Shuster, Jr.

TABLE 12-1
Scientific and Common Names of Some Clams of Commercial Value

Scientific name	Common name
Mercenaria mercenaria (Linn.)	Quahog, or hard, clam
Mercenaria campechiensis (Gmelin)	Southern hard clam
Mya arenaria Linn.	Soft-shell clam
Spisula (= *Mactra*) *solidissima* Dillwyn	Surf clam
Tapes semidecussata Reeve	Japanese littleneck clam
Arca transversa Say	Transverse ark clam
Anomia simplex D'Orbigny	Anomia clam
Laevicardium mortoni (Conrad)	Morton's cockle
Cardium edule Linn.	Common cockle
Pitar (= *Callocardia*) *morrhuana* Gould	Pitar clam
Petricola pholadiformis Lamarck	False angel wing clam
Ensis directus (Conrad)	Razor clam

DEVELOPMENT OF CLAMS

As in the case of oysters, a brief description of the development of clams, especially *M. mercenaria*, is being presented to acquaint the beginning student of applied malacology with the essentials so that what is known about clam farming can be explained more readily.

Unlike oysters, clams are dioecious. During the spring the ovaries or testes of *M. mercenaria* enlarge in preparation for spawning, and the visceral mass becomes plump due to the accumulation of numerous eggs and sperm.

Spawning in clams is identical to that in *Crassostrea virginica* in that the ova and sperm are discharged into the water and fertilization occurs externally. In the case of *M. mercenaria*, found along the northern Atlantic Seaboard of North America, this occurs from the middle of June to the middle of August. It occurs a few weeks earlier in the case of *M. campechiensis*, which is found along the southern range of the Atlantic Seaboard.

The fertilized zygote undergoes a series of developmental changes, and by the time the embryo is able to break out of its gelatinous membrane case in 12–14 hours postfertilization, it is known as a trochophore larva (Fig. 12-15); This larva, which bears cilia, swims through water with a spiral movement upon hatching. In the course of the next 24 hours a thin transparent shell is developed (Fig. 12-16), and, when this occurs, the trochophor has become a veliger (Fig. 12-17). The development from fertilization to veliger takes about 36 hours.

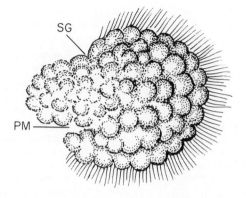

Fig. 12-15. Trochophore larva of *Mercenaria mercenaria*. This stage of development is reached 12 to 14 hours after fertilization. The body is elongate, and the cilia are confined to the front end. The opening of the primitive mouth (PM) is on the lower side and a slight indentation on the upper side represents the beginning of the shell gland (SG).

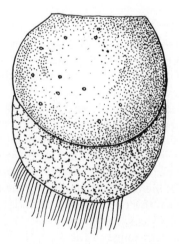

Fig. 12-16. Shell formation in the larva of *Mercenaria mercenaria*. The shell arises at two symmetrical points of calcification to the left and right of the midline.

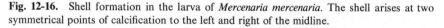

The veliger is also an active swimmer, but it eventually settles down to the substrate and crawls for a brief period before becoming attached by an elastic thread secreted by the byssal gland situated in the foot, which has developed by this time. This attachment, which is commonly to sand grains but could be to practically any solid substrate, prevents at least some of the young clams from being swept away by the water currents. Unlike oysters, clams, including *M. mercenaria*, are not attached as adults but are buried in sand and mud; therefore, sometime during the growth of the young clam, which takes on adult characteristics soon after the veliger becomes attached, it becomes dislodged from the attached substrate, burrows into the sand, and continues to increase in size.

INDUCED SPAWNING

Mercenaria mercenaria can be conditioned and induced to spawn throughout the year. The simplest method in the laboratory is to elevate the ambient temperature.

ARTIFICIAL REARING OF VELIGERS

Veligers of *Mercenaria mercenaria* (Fig. 12-17) can be reared under confined conditions with relative ease since their food requirements are not as rigid as those of *C. virginica* veligers. According to Loosanoff and Davis (1963), these larvae can be grown to metamorphosis on a diet consisting almost exclusively of the alga *Chlorella* sp.; however, such species as *Isochrysis galbana, Monochrysis lutheri, Chlorococcum* sp., *Platymonas* sp., and *Dicrateria* sp., promote better growth.

The temperature requirements of *M. mercenaria* veligers is broad since they will grow between 15° C and 33° C. At the latter temperature settling occurs from 6 to 8 days postfertilization.

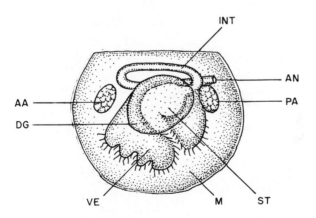

Fig. 12-17. Veliger larva of *Mercenaria mercenaria.* AA, Anterior adductor muscle; AN, anus; DG, digestive gland; INT, intestine; M, mantle; PA, posterior adductor muscle; ST, stomach; VE, velum.

Settling veligers are not very selective as far as the substrate is concerned. They will metamorphose into young adults in containers with a substrate of glass, plastic, earthenware, Plexiglas, and concrete. These larvae are also apparently not affected by light as far as settling is concerned.

POND CULTURE

As stated, a limited amount of commercial farming of *Mercenaria mercenaria* is now in practice, especially along the Atlantic Coast of the United States. In these instances veligers are placed in artificial ponds and permitted to settle and grow, embedded in sandy bottoms. The price of clams raised in this manner is higher than that of clams harvested in nature. Most of the pond-cultured clams are sold as "littlenecks" for the steam clam market.

Mussels

Although mussels, both *Mytilus edulis* (the blue mussel) (Fig. 12-18) and *Modiolus demissus* (the ribbed mussel), are not sold extensively in North America as a commercial shellfish, except in Italian grocery stores in the

Fig. 12-18.   Specimens of the blue mussel, *Mytilus edulis*, from Delaware Bay.

larger cities, these mussels are important commerically in Europe and England. *Mytilus edulis* is being cultured in these areas, especially in Holland.

The life histories of both *Mytilus edulis* and *Modiolus demissus* parallels those of *Crassostrea virginica* and *Mercenaria mercenaria* in that fertilization is external, and there is both a trochophore and veliger stage. The latter, when fully developed, is the settling form; however, unlike the other two species mentioned, the byssal gland of mussels is a permanent structure, and these bivalves are permanently attached to the substrate throughout life by extremely strong byssal threads.

INDUCED SPAWNING

Mytilus edulis cannot be induced to spawn either by raising the ambient temperature or by adding sex products to the water. However, if the adductor muscle is stimulated, specimens with ripe gonads will spawn readily. The stimulation can be in the form of (1) rupturing the muscle by prying the valves open; (2) stretching the muscle by inserting a wooden wedge between the valves; or (3) pricking the muscle with a probe. Loosanoff and David (1963) have suggested that the induction of spawning of both males and females by stimulating the adductor muscles indicates that stimulating centers, which induce discharge of sperm or ova, are probably located in these muscles. The artificial spawning of *Modiolus demissus* has not yet been accomplished.

ARTIFICIAL REARING OF VELIGERS

Veligers of both *Mytilus edulis* (Fig. 12-19) and *Modiolus demissus* (Fig. 12-20) have been successfully reared in the laboratory by providing algae as a food source. Although *Chlorella* will sustain veligers of *M. edulis, Monochrysis lutheri* and *Isochrysis qalbana* are better. *Isochrysis qalbana* is a suitbale food for *Modiolus demissus* veligers in the laboratory although the full development of these larvae is far from completely satisfactory, even when maintained at an optimum temperature of 22°C (Loosanoff and Davis, 1963).

The culture of mussels, particularly *Mytilus edulis*, in Europe and Britain is still primarily in natural estuaries rather than in man-made ponds. Furthermore, except on an experimental basis, the settling veligers are the result of natural spawning rather than induced spawning. Thus, the commercial mussel beds do not represent true mariculture in the restricted sense, that is, rearing mussels from veligers resulting from artificially spawned gametes. There are controlled farming areas where spawning, growth, and settling of veligers and the subsequent development and growth of adults are de-

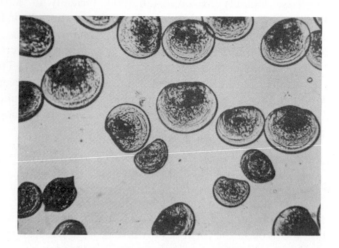

Fig. 12-19. Larvae of *Mytilus edulis*. The largest larvae are approximately 170 μm long. Several small, abnormal individuals are seen in the lower left corner. After Loosanoff and Davis (1963).

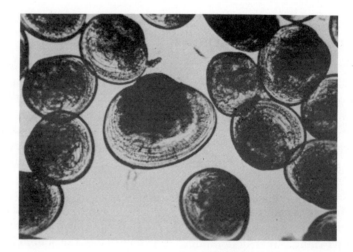

Fig. 12-20. Larvae of *Modiolus demissus*. Notice the difference in the sizes of larvae that have developed from the same group of eggs and were reared in the same vessel. The largest larva in the center is about 300 μm long. After Loosanoff and Davis (1963).

pendent on the natural reproductive processes of the adults and the natural occurrence of nutrients.

Compared to fish farming, the aquaculture of mollusks is still in its infancy, especially in the United States. Nevertheless, this represents an underdeveloped area of marine biology that deserves increased attention in view of the potential. It should be borne in mind, however, that aquaculture (or mariculture) involves more than inducing spawning, rearing veligers, and providing suitable environments for the growth of adult mollusks. As in agriculture, the health of the product, edible mollusks in this case, must be taken into consideration. In other words, much work is needed in advancing our knowledge of the prevention of epizootic diseases among shellfish, the specific nutrient requirements, and the most effective usage of the estuarine environment for mariculture. In addition, from the standpoint of public health, increased consideration must be given to potential and real human pathogens transmissible by shellfish. It is known, for example, that viral hepatitis can be transmitted to man by shellfish grown in polluted waters (Mason and McLean, 1962; Dougherty and Altman, 1962), and a number of potentially pathogenic zooparasites are transmissible by shellfish as well (Cheng, 1973). In addition, shellfish are known to transmit toxins of algal origin that cause paralytic shellfish poisoning (Ray, 1971). The public health aspects of applied malacology pertaining to aquaculture is an area that is poorly staffed by competent scientists.

References

Cheng, T. C. (1973). Human parasites transmissible by seafood – and related problems. *In* "Microbiological Quality of Seafood" (C. O. Chichester and H. Graham, eds.), pp. 163–189. Academic Press, New York.

Coe, W. R. (1931). Sexual rhythm in the California oyster (*Ostrea lurida*). *Science* **74**, 247–249.

Cole, H. A. (1939). Further experiments in breeding of oysters (*Ostrea edulis*) in tanks. *Fish. Invest., London, Ser.* 2 **16**, 64.

Davis, H. C. (1953). On food and feeding of larvae of the American oyster, *Crassostrea virginica*. *Biol. Bull.* **104**, 334–350.

Dougherty, W. J., and Altman, R. (1962). Viral hepatitis in New Jersey 1960–61. *Amer. J. Med.* **32**, 704–736.

Erdmann, W. (1934). Uber die Entwicklung und die Anatomie der "ansatzreifen" Larve von *Ostrea edulis*, mit Bemarkungen uber die Lebensgeschichte der Auster. *Wiss. Meeresunters. Abt. Helgoland, N.F.* **19**, 1–25.

Galtsoff, P. S. (1964). The American oyster *Crasostrea virginica* Gmelin. *U.S., Fish. Wild. Serv., Fish. Bull.* **64**, 1–480.

Galtsoff, P. S. (1964). The American oyster *Crassostrea virginica* Gmelin. *U.S., Fish. Wild. Serv., Fish. Bull.* **64**.

Korringa, P. (1940). Experiments and observations on swarming, pelagic life and settling in the European flat oyster, *Ostrea edulis* L. *Arch. Neer. Zool.* **5**, 1–249.

Loosanoff, V. L., and Davis, H. C. (1952). Temperature requirements for maturation of gonads of northern oysters. *Biol. Bull.* **103**, 80–96.

Loosanoff, V. L., and Davis, H. C. (1963). Rearing of bivalve mollusks. *Advan. Mar. Biol.* **1**, 1–136.

Mason, J. O., and McLean, W. R. (1962). Infectious hepatitis traced to the consumption of raw oysters. *Amer. J. Hyg.* **75**, 90–111.

Orton, J. H. (1937). "Oyster Biology and Oyster Culture. The Buckland Lectures for 1935." Arnold, London.

Pelseneer, P. (1906). Trematodes parasites de mollusques marins. *Bull. Sci. Fr. Belg.* **40**, 161–186.

Prytherch, H. F. (1940). The life cycle and morphology of *Nematopsis ostrearum* sp. nov., a gregarine parasite of the mud crabs and oysters. *J. Morphol.* **66**, 39–65.

Ray, S. M. (1971). Paralytic shellfish poisoning: a status report. *Curr. Top. Comp. Pathobiol.* **1**, 171–200.

Walne, P. R. (1956). Experimental rearing of larvae of *Ostrea edulis* L. in the laboratory. *Fish. Invest., London, Ser.* 2 **20**, 1–23.

Yonge, C. M. (1960). "Oysters." Collins, London.

13 Control of Economically and Medically Important Snails

Terrestrial Snails and Slugs

According to Burch (1960), fifty-five species (forty-four snails and eleven slugs) of nonnative gastropods have been introduced into the United States either accidentally or intentionally. These are the dangerous species as they are destructive agricultural pests that cause damage to vegetables, ornamentals, and other plants. The garden slugs *Deroceras reticulatum*, *Limax maximus*, and *L. flavus* and the terrestrial snails *Helix aspersa and Otala lactea* have become well established in the United States and are of considerable economic importance. In recent years one of the most dangerous terrestrial snails that has been introduced is the giant African snail, *Achatina fulica*, which is a voraceous eater and reproduces prolifically. It has been introduced from East Africa into many parts of the Orient and the Pacific Islands. In Hawaii this snail was introduced in 1936 and has been destructive to plants. The cost thus far for its control has been estimated to be about a quarter of a million dollars. Fortunately, its menace was stopped in California when it was introduced after World War II. Concentrated control efforts saved that state and probably many other states from this agricultural pest. Recently, it appeared in Florida but is believed to be under control. A detailed account of the biology, dispersal, and control of *A. fulica* has been contributed by Mead (1961).

Although in certain areas control of destructive snails and slugs is not possible, in other areas a certain degree of control can be accomplished, whereby their danger is lessened and the economic loss due to them is reduced considerably.

Certain physical methods have been employed with great success in some places. Hand picking and crushing, although tedious, have considerably reduced the population of several species of undesirable mollusks. For the large edible snails, their collection for local human and animal consumption as well as their shipment to other places have been advocated as a means of control. These practices serve a multiple purpose. They control the molluscan population, provide food, and serve as the basis for a new industry for the stricken area.

Certain chemical methods have been used for the control of land snails and slugs. These are usually categorized as attractants, contact poisons, or repellents. Care must be taken, however, in the use and handling of certain types of chemicals because they may be poisonous to man and animals and may be injurious to certain plants.

Potassium aluminum sulfate and several arsenical compounds have been commonly used as molluscicides against terrestrial mollusks. In addition, a bait of calcium arsenate prepared according to the following formulation has been reported to be very effective against land snails:

```
Bran  ................................ 25 lb
Calcium arsenate  ...................... 2 lb
Molasses  ............................ 3/4 gallon
Water  ............................... 1 gallon
```

Sodium arsenite ("penite" is a 40% commercial solution) has been used as a spray in the form of a 0.5–1.0% solution. It is, however, expensive and is poisonous to vegetation.

One of the most effective chemicals against land snails and slugs is "metaldehyde," an inflammable polymerized form of acetaldehyde that is known commercially under several names of which "Meta Fuel" is the most common. It is a contact and a stomach poison and, in the case of slugs, it has anesthetic, toxic, and irritating effects that cause an excessive secretion of mucus. It is used as a bait prepared according to several formulas, one of which includes metaldehyde, bran, flour, mucilage, lard, and a leavening agent, baked at about 64.5°C, and formed as a biscuit. It is also used as a liquid spray (20% metaldehyde by dry volume) or as a dust (15% metaldehyde by weight). Metaldehyde baits are often mixed with calcium arsenate or sodium fluosilicate to make the product more effective, especially when used during wet weather and periods of high humidity. Metaldehyde has been reported to be very effective when applied on clear, dry, warm days because its efficacy apparently is enhanced when sprayed snails are exposed to the sun.

Land snails and slugs can also be controlled by employing mechanical devices or by a combination of these and chemical means. For example, barriers of closely placed bamboo sticks have been effective in some areas of Southeast Asia and the Pacific. Barriers of coal tar, ash, soot, lime, salt, and other substances have been used alone or together with kerosene or phenol.

The biological control of terrestrial snails and slugs by using their natural enemies and predators has been advocated for their eradication. However, to import natural enemies of an introduced, undesirable snail in a geographic area can be in itself a dangerous and unwise action. Moreover, although the natural enemy preys freely on the young and sometimes the adults, they have not proven to be highly effective in the control of terrestrial mollusks. For example, the carnivorous predatory snail *Gonaxis* (= *Streptaxis*) *kibweziensis*, a natural enemy of *Achatina fulica* in East Africa, has been observed to kill the latter species when the two species occur together; however, there has been no evidence that *G. kibweziensis* causes any real control of the achatinid. *Euglandina rosea* is another snail that preys on *Achatina* but has never produced any noticeable control of the prey species where both occur together. The American carnivorous snail *Haplotrema concavum* and several other species of this genus, for example, *H. minima* in California, also have no noticeable effect on the introduced snail *Helix aspersa*.

Freshwater and Amphibious Snails

As indicated in Chapter 5, many freshwater and amphibious snails are of medical and economical importance as they are obligatory intermediate hosts for many species of trematodes of man and domestic animals.

To prevent the spread of trematode infections, several methods have been suggested to break the parasite's life cycle at one or more stages. Thus, human schistosomiasis could be controlled by treating infected individuals with one of a few known chemotherapeutic agents known to kill the adult schistosomes occurring in the circulatory system. This procedure, however, is unrealistic when one considers the fact that there are about three hundred million cases of human schistosomiasis in the world, and a significant percentage of the infection occurs in individuals, such as numerous African tribesmen, who would not subject themselves to treatment. Furthermore, the total safety of the currently available drugs against human schistosomiasis is questionable. Some are highly toxic while others have other undesirable effects such as being mutagenic.

Another method for controlling human schistosomiasis is to prevent excreta from infected individuals from reaching the water through the provision of latrines, adequate domestic water supply, and proper sewage disposal methods. This method of interrupting the life cycle of schistosomes, that is, by preventing the parasite's eggs from reaching natural bodies of water and hatching into snail-infecting miracidia, also has its drawbacks. It is expensive, and, even if they are provided, there is no assurance that egg-passing individuals will break from ethnic practices of long standing and utilize modern sanitary facilities. The construction of waterworks and sewage treatment plants, as one can imagine, presents logistic as well as economic problems in parts of Africa, Asia, and South America (Malek, 1961a, 1961b).

Because of the difficulties encountered in the chemotherapeutic and sanitation approaches, plus the fact that a satisfactory vaccine is not yet available as a prophylaxis against schistosomiasis, the only feasible method for control at this time is mollusk control. This topic is discussed at a later point.

For the control of human trematode infections other than schistosomiasis, health education methods aimed at preventing the public from eating raw or inadequately cooked crabs, crayfish, fish, and vegetation are among the most important. In certain areas where fascioliasis is highly prevalent in cattle and man, control efforts in the form of moving cattle to higher and drier areas from marshy and overflow areas, digging wells to provide drinking water for cattle, avoiding the use of grass from marshy areas as fodder, and treatment of cattle with one of the known chemotherapeutic agents have been implemented with considerable success.

One of the problems that confront policy makers who are responsible for outlining control measures for parasitic diseases is that these are correlated with dietary and other habits that form an integral part of the culture of the populations involved and are very difficult to change. To bring about marked changes in the habits of these populations will require at least several decades of intense education. In the case of schistosomiasis, the habit of indiscriminate pollution of waters; in opisthorchiasis and clonorchiasis, the habit of eating raw or inadequately cooked fish; and in fascioliasis, the habit of eating raw watercress and other vegetation grown near water where cattle and sheep are reared, must be altered. The habit of eating raw crabs and crayfish results in paragonimiasis due to the lung fluke *Paragonimus westermani* in many parts of the Orient. In addition, other cultural and sociological factors aid to perpetuate the spread of lung fluke infections; for example, the belief held by inhabitants of certain communities in Korea that crushed raw crayfish has medicinal value in the treatment of measles and the belief held among certain tribes in the Cameroons in Africa that raw crabs increase the fertility of women (also see Malek, 1970).

Some economical factors also contribute to the spread of trematode infections. For example, the use of night soil as fertilizer in the Orient ensures that the parasites' eggs pollute irrigation canals and ponds containing the snail hosts. Agricultural development under irrigation and fish farming intended for the welfare of the country involved have increased the incidence of trematode infections, especially schistosomiasis (Malek, 1972).

The occurrence of reservoir hosts of trematode infections to man in certain areas creates another problem to be considered in the control of trematode diseases since these hosts directly or indirectly pollute the water containing the snail hosts with the parasites' eggs, even more than humans do, and thus maintain a high level of endemicity or enzooticity.

Another problem in the control of trematode infections is the lack of satisfactory drugs. This is especially true in the case of schistosomiasis, but also applies to fascioliasis, paragonimiasis, clonorchiasis, and opisthorchiasis.

Mollusk Control

Because of the economic, sociological, as well as scientific difficulties discussed, snail control is regarded by many experts as the best means of control of trematode infections at the present. This widely accepted practice is based on the following facts: (1) the mollusk represents the weakest link in the life cycle of trematodes; (2) control can be carried out without the regimented cooperation of the population; and (3) in certain areas satisfactory results have been obtained at much less expense than with other means of control. Added to these facts is the advantage of controlling more than one economically important trematode infection in the same area as the result of killing several species of molluscan hosts.

Approaches to snail control can be grouped under the following headings: ecological, chemical, and biological.

ECOLOGICAL CONTROL

Ecological control is effected through altering the habitat necessary for the establishment of snail colonies and thus either eradicating them or considerably reducing the size of the population. Some of the methods employed are the dessication of the habitat by intermittent use of canals and the clearance of mud and vegetation. Some of the aquatic mollusks, however, can withstand desiccation and are able to repopulate the habitat within a short period after the water has returned. For example, in northeastern Brazil the snails, *Biomphalaria glabrata*, may attain a saturation density within 50 days if there are a few survivors in the habitat after desiccation (Barbosa and Olivier, 1958). Similar observations have been made in several other areas in the Middle East and Africa (van der Schalie, 1958; Malek, 1958).

The lining of the streams with concrete or the implementation of other engineering methods by which the banks of the streams are made steeper and the water current swifter have been advocated and actually employed as ecological measures of control (W.H.O., 1965b). Proper drainage, clearance of vegetation, and improved farming methods have also been effective measures where amphibious snails are involved.

CHEMICAL CONTROL

At the beginning of the century the Japanese recommended the use of calcium cyanamide as a combined cercaricide and molluscicide. Copper sulfate was later found to possess molluscicidal properties, and it was and still is widely used in many parts of the world, especially in Egypt, the Sudan, and the Middle East. After World War II, as a result of screening of several thousands of chemicals, two phenol derivatives, sodium pentachlorophenate (NaPCP) and dinitro-*o*-cyclohexylphenol (DCHP), were found to be very effective against both amphibious and aquatic snails (McMullen *et al.*, 1951; Kuntz and Wells, 1951). The first compound has been used with success in Egypt, Brazil, and Venezuela for the control of mollusks that transmit schistosomiasis, especially *Biomphalaria glabrata* and *B. alexandrina*. A number of recently developed molluscicides are now available, and some of these are being employed in increasing quantities for the control of schistosomiasis and bovine fascioliasis in endemic areas. In order to acquaint those interested with this aspect of medical malacology, the following is a brief review of what is known about the molluscicides used most extensively against amphibious and aquatic snails that transmit schistosomes and other pathogenic trematodes (also see Malek, 1961a, 1961b; W.H.O., 1965b; Ritchie and Malek, 1969; Ritchie, 1973).

Copper Sulfate.   Very low concentrations of copper sulfate are lethal to *Biomphalaria* spp. and *Bulinus* spp. in the laboratory (Table 13-1). Higher concentrations (30 ppm) have been found to be effective under field conditions. Even at these high concentrations, copper sulfate is neither lethal nor deleterious to man or domestic animals, but it does kill fish and aquatic vegetation. In fact, copper sulfate is used to abate algal and other types of plant growth in water reservoirs and other bodies of water where plant growth is not desired. For example, in the Lombard Valley in northern Italy, a copper compound is added to the water in rice fields not only to kill fungi that are pathogenic to young rice plants but also to kill several species of aquatic mollusks that feed on rice seedlings. Surprisingly, the presence of copper in the water has been reported to enhance the growth of the rice plants. Thus, the addition of copper is beneficial in several ways: it serves as a fungicide, it kills deleterious mollusks, and it enhances rice production.

It is noted, however, that several factors in natural waters are known to

TABLE 13-1

Effect of CuSO$_4$ at Low Concentrations on *Biomphalaria glabrata*

Snail size (mm)	Cu concentration[a] (ppm)	Exposure period (hours)	State at termination of exposure period	State at termination of recovery period in distilled H$_2$O		
				24 Hours	48 Hours	72 Hours
4–12	0.07	24	All alive	All dead	—	—
4–12	0.07	48	<10 mm Dead	>10 mm Dead	—	—
4–12	0.07	72	All dead	—	—	—
4–12	0.7	24	All alive	<12 mm Dead	>12 mm Dead	—
4–12	0.7	48	All dead	—	—	—

[a] The copper was dissolved in deionized water.

deter the effectiveness of the copper ion as a molluscicide. Specifically, the occurrence of certain organic and inorganic substances results in the absorption or adsorption of the copper ion, and it is precipitated in the form of insoluble compounds (Malek, 1962). Because of this feature, copper sulfate should not be applied during flood periods in large rivers with high amounts of silt; vegetation, if possible, should be removed before application; and the bottom should not be disturbed during the process.

Since copper has proven to be such an effective molluscicide and since it is relatively inexpensive when compared with most of the other more popular synthetic compounds, research is underway in several laboratories in the United States and Europe to develop copper compounds that do not portray the undesirable characteristics and, as a part of this effort, to find copper compounds that are specific as a lethal agent against *Biomphalaria glabrata* and other species of disease-transmitting snails and those that are agricultural pests. As a first step in this direction, studies have been conducted to ascertain in what stereochemical form the copper-containing molecule must occur to be effective as a molluscicide. Such studies have revealed that copper in the form of copper(II)-bis-N,N-dihydroxyethylglycine [Cu(DEG)$_2$] is equally as effective as a cidal agent against *Biomphalaria glabrata* as copper sulfate. On the other hand, copper(II)-ethylenediamine-N, N, N', N'-tetraacetic acid (CuEDTA) has no cidal property (Cheng and Sullivan, 1973a). The basis for this difference is readily revealed when one considers the stereochemistry of CuEDTA and Cu(DEG)$_2$. Specifically, it is known that DEG forms a 1:1 tridentate complex with copper when dissociated in solution and forms a square planar configuration. When in the dissociated form (Fig. 13-1), the copper moeity, although stereochemically encapsulated, is bonded in part to H$_2$O, and, since this bonding has a low stability, that is, the H$_2$O can be displaced by ligands with greater electronegative charges, the copper is in essence biologically exposed. Thus, it is not surprising that

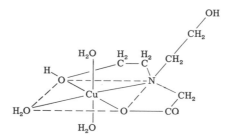

Fig. 13-1. Structural formula of copper(II)-bis-N,N-dihydroxyethylglycine [Cu(DEG)$_2$]. After Cheng and Sullivan (1973a).

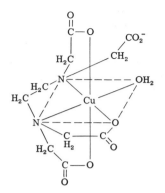

Fig. 13-2. Structural formula of copper(II)-ethylenediamine-*N*,*N*,*N'*,*N'*-tetraacetic acid (CuEDTA). After Cheng and Sullivan (1973a).

Cu(DEG)$_2$ is capable of killing *B. glabrata* since Hopf *et al.* (1963) have demonstrated that it is the Cu ion per se that is the cidal agent.

On the other hand, the copper moeity of CuEDTA is also stereo-chemically encapsulated but differs from that of Cu(DEG)$_2$ in that it is not aquated except at one position (Fig. 13-2). Consequently, it is considerably less exposed biologically. It is known that EDTA forms a 1:1 quinquedentate complex with copper when dissociated in solution. Thus, it is apparent that the chemical basis for the toxicity of Cu(DEG)$_2$ rests with the fact that its copper moeity is biologically exposed while the nontoxicity of CuEDTA is due to the nearly total encapsulation of its copper moeity. This finding has permitted a more rational approach to the synthesis of new copper-containing molluscicides as a substitute for copper sulfate.

It is also of interest to note that slow-release copper compounds are now available on an experimental basis. These are in the form of copper compounds, primarily copper sulfate, embedded in a rubber base. Such preparations have been reported to release toxic copper ions into water for as long as 65 days.

Sodium Pentachlorophenate (NaPCP). This compound is effective in flowing waters for about 8 hours at a concentration of 5 to 10 ppm. It has the advantage of being lethal to snails and their eggs for long distances downstream from the place of application. For example, Wright *et al.* (1958) have reported the effectiveness of NaPCP 32 km down river in one operation in Egypt. This compound, however, has disappointed many workers because it is photosensitive and is readily broken down by sunlight, especially in alkaline waters. Another disadvantage of NaPCP is that when used in certain areas, it is irritating to the snails, forcing them to crawl out of the water and thus escape the lethal effect of the molluscicide.

It should be noted that NaPCP, which has been widely used in Japan, is extremely toxic to handlers. In fact, deaths among handlers are known to have occurred. Its toxicity, however, can be reduced if it is used in the briquet form (a solid formulation that allows transfer to metal baskets without removal from shipping containers) or as a solid formulation.

Satisfactory results have been obtained by combining both copper sulfate and NaPCP to form copper pentachlorophenate, which is not irritating to the snails and has a residual effect.

Aqualin. This compound is produced by the Shell Company as a herbicide. It contains acrolein. It is also effective against snails, their eggs, and cercariae at 3 ppm. The disadvantages, however, are that this liquid is irritating to the eyes, and it is inflammable and highly volatile. Proper equipment, including special pumps, would have to be employed for the spraying of aqualin.

Bayluscide (Niclosamide). This commercial product is produced by the Bayer Company in Germany. It is the ethanolamine salt of 5,2'-dichloro-4'-nitrosalicylanilide and is formulated as a 70% wettable powder. The compound is lethal to snails and their eggs at 1 ppm under field conditions. It is sparingly soluble in water but forms a stable suspension. Bayluscide has proven to be a very effective molluscicide. Its degree of activity exceeds that of other available molluscicides by 10 or more times. It is ovicidal and of low toxicity for mammals. It has been repeatedly observed, however, that the wettable powder is not a satisfactory formulation because it has to be continually stirred when admixed with water, and nozzles of dispensing equipment become clogged by the sediment. An emulsifiable concentrate has been formulated and has overcome the difficulty in applying the wettable powder formulation.

A laboratory evaluation of the emulsifiable concentrate (25% active ingredient) was carried out (Malek, 1971).

Frescon (WL 8008). This compound is produced by the Shell Company in England. It is N-triphenylmethylmorpholine (N-tritylmorpholine). A liquid formulation in tetrachloroethylene provides good performance and is easily handled in the field. It is stable to heat, sunlight, and alkalis. Frescon has been tested and proven very effective against the intermediate hosts of schistosomes (*S. mansoni* and *S. haematobium*) in storage dams, ponds, irrigation canals, and natural water courses in Brazil, Tanzania, and Rhodesia. It has also been reported to be effective against *Oncomelania nosophora* and *O. quadrasi*, intermediate hosts for *S. japonicum* in the Orient.

For irrigation systems it has been recommended to use very low concentrations continuously for 7 days and to repeat the treatment every month. This schedule is to compensate for the disadvantage of the molluscicide being nonovicidal. Very good results have also been obtained with Frescon for the control of the amphibious snail *Fossaria (= Lymnaea) truncatula*, the intermediate host of *Fasciola hepatica* in Europe.

Organotin Compounds. Several organotin compounds are known to exhibit molluscicidal activities. These compounds have a wide commercial use as fungicides in hospitals and in the paper, textile, and wood industries. Triphenyltin acetate and bis(tri-*n*-butylin) oxide are examples of organotin compounds that hold promise as molluscicides. Several laboratory evaluations have been performed, but only limited information is available on field evaluations. It is noted, however, that Webbe and Sturrock (1964) have reported that tri-*n*-phenyltin acetate and tri-*n*-butyltin acetate are about equally effective against both *Bulinus* and *Biomphalaria*, ranking with niclosamide and Frescon. These organotin compounds, however, are not as effective against *Oncomelania quadrasi*.

It is noted that the organotin compounds are somewhat toxic to mammals. For example, the single oral LD_{50} concentration for rats is 200 mg/kg or less. For guinea pigs and rabbits, the LC_{50} dosage is approximately 30 mg/kg. In addition, these tin compounds should be considered as potential skin irritants to handlers.

Yurimin (P-99) (3,5-Dibromo-4-hydroxy-4′-nitrobenzene). This is a highly insoluble compound that is prepared as a 5% granular formulation. This suspension becomes miscible in water, and, if stirred regularly during application, it will become stable. It is 16 to 18 times as active as sodium pentachlorophenate against *Oncomelania nosophora* but not as effective against *Biomphalaria glabrata*. The compound is more effective in alkaline than in acid waters. It is not affected by photochemical action, and its lethal concentration is a little higher for fish than for snails. Yurimin, in concentrations normally used for the control of mollusks, has no effect on plants. It is safe for handling, although it is somewhat toxic if ingested. The LC_{50} for mice by oral testing is 167.9 mg/kg.

Endod. Many plants have been reported from various parts of the world to possess molluscicidal properties. Among these is Endod (*Phytolacca dodecandra*). The crude ground berries of Endod are used as soap by the local population in Ethiopia. Lemma (1970) evaluated an aqueous extract of the berries in Ethiopia under laboratory and field conditions and has reported good results against several species of snails including *Biomphalaria glabrata*. A methanol extract of the berries has been reported to be even more effective as a molluscicide.

TABLE 13-2

Common name	Niclosamide	N-Trityl-morpholine	NaPCP	Copper sulfate	ZDC	Yurimin	Copper oxide
Physical form of technical material	Crystalline solid	Crystalline solid	Crystalline solid	Crystalline solid	Amorphous solid	Crystalline solid	Amorphous solid
Active ingredient	Ethanol-amine salt of 2′5-dichloro-4′-nitrosalicyl-anilide	N-Trityl-morpholine	Sodium pentachloro-phenate	Copper ion	Zinc di-methyldithio-carbamate	3,5-Dibromo-4-hydroxy-4′-nitroazo-benzene	Copper ion
Solubility in water	230 ppm (pH dependent)	—	33%	32%	65 ppm	Very slight	—
Stability, affected by UV light	Yes	—	Yes	No	—	No	No
Mud, turbidity	Yes	No	No	Yes	No	Yes	Yes
pH	Optimum 6–8	Yes	No	Yes	—	Slight	Yes
Algae, plants	No	No	No	Yes	No	—	Yes
Storage	No	No	No	No	No	—	Yes
Handling qualities Safe	Yes	Yes	Varies	Yes	Yes	Yes	Yes
Simple	Yes	Yes	Yes	Yes	Yes	Yes	Yes
Toxicity Snail LC_{90} (ppm × h)	3–8	0.5–4	20–100	20–100	25–60	4–5	7–100
Snail eggs LC_{90} (ppm × h	2–4	240	3–30	50–100	50–100	—	50–100
Cercaria LC_{90} (ppm)	0.3	—	—	—	—	—	—
Fish LC_{90} (ppm)	0.05–0.3 (LC_{50})	2–4	—	—	—	0.16–0.83 (LC_{50})	—
Rats, acute oral, LD_{50} (mg/kg)	5,000	1,400	40–250	—	1,400	168 (Mice)	2,000
Herbicidal activity	None	None	None	Yes	None	None	None
Formulations	70% W.P. 25% E.C.	16.5% E.C.	75% Flakes 80% Pellets 80% Briquettes		50% Gran-ules 90% Powder	50% Gran-ules	Powder
Field dosage Aquatic snails (ppm × h)	4–8	1–2	50–80	20 +	100	—	60
Amphibious snails on moist soil (g/m²)	0.2	—	0.4–10	—	10	5	Not effective

A List of Available Molluscicides for the Control of the Molluscan Vectors of Schistosomiasis and Their Properties[a]

PTA	TBTO	TBTA	TPLA	TBS	Endod	Nicotin anilide
rystalline lid	Liquid	Crystalline solid	Crystalline solid	Crystalline solid	Powdered berries	Amorphous solid
iphenyltin etate	Tri-n-butyltin oxide	Tri-n-butyltin acetate	Triphenyl lead acetate	3,4′,5-Tribromo-salicyl anilide	—	—
500 ppm	10–30 ppm	80–150 ppm	1.5%	—	High	> 100 ppm
ght	No	No	Slight	Yes	No	No
s	Yes	Yes	Yes	No	No	
	No	No		No	No	
s	Yes	Yes	Slight		No	Slight
	No	No	Slight	No	No	No
s	Yes	Yes	No	—	Yes	Yes
	Yes	Yes	No		Yes	Yes
	0.9–1.3	7.2	> 3.6	2–4	240–480	4–6
	0.55	0.55	—	0.2	10,000	1–2
.05	> 0.001	> 0.05	> 0.07	—	100	
-4.8	1–3	> 2			1,200	> 10–100
00	> 250	> 250	12.3	—	220	2 g/kg (Mice)
s	No	Yes	—	—	No	No
wder	6–10% Slow release pellets 95% Liquid	6–10% Slow release pellets Powder	Powder	Powder	Powder	Powder
0	4–20	10–15	—	20–30	300–600	20 +
g/m²	—	—	—	—	86 ppm (Laboratory)	—

[a] Modified after the World Health Organization (1965a).

Listed in Table 13-2 are the known properties and characteristics of the available molluscicides.

Application of Molluscicides

Chemical molluscicides are usually applied either as solids or as liquids in solution or suspension. Muslin or jute bags are filled with the molluscicide, which may be crystalline, for example, copper sulfate; powdered; or in the form of briquettes, for example, NaPCP. These bags are placed in running water or are pulled along the margin of the water. Molluscicides in liquid form may be applied to streams by compression sprayers, or the solution is allowed to drip from special boxes or barrels. The size and the frequency of the drops are adjusted to maintain the desired concentrations.

The incorporation of a molluscicide in an elastomeric matrix for slow release is an effective method. Solid formulations of molluscicides that are durable and remain active for long periods should be ideal for prolonged and continuous treatments. Both copper-containing and organotin molluscicides have been prepared in this manner. Berrios-Duran and Ritchie (1968) have found in the laboratory that bis(tri-*n*-butyltin) oxide (TBTO) formulated in rubber was effective against *Biomphalaria glabrata* and *Bulinus* (*Physopsis*) *globosus* for long periods. Bayluscide (Niclosamide) has also been found to be soluble in specific elastomeric formulations as has copper sulfate. Such molluscicides incorporated in an elastomeric matrix could make possible the interruption of transmission of schistosomiasis by destroying not only snails but also the miracidia and cercariae when applied continuously for long periods.

Prior to the mass application of any molluscicide, adequately controlled laboratory and field tests are essential in order to facilitate the choice of the most appropriate compound and the timing of the operation. Survey studies (p. 379) should reveal information pertaining to the hydrography of the area, the ecology and distribution of the target mollusk in the area, seasonal fluctuations in the population density of the snail, and similar fluctuations in infection rates in the snail and in humans and animals. The susceptibility of the local snails of various ages to various molluscicides should also be tested, with emphasis on such local conditions as the composition of the water and the particular strain or strains of snails present. Postcontrol evaluation of the results is essential but, unfortunately, is not always carried out. Criteria for the evaluation of a specific molluscicide should include its effects on the snail population and on the infection rates among humans and other vertebrates (Malek, 1962).

Bioassay of Molluscicides

Medical malacologists are often called upon to test the effectiveness of existing and new molluscicides. Existing molluscicides require testing if they are to be employed in waters different from that in which they have been proven to be effective. The necessity of screening new potential molluscicides is obvious. To familiarize the reader with the standard methods for bioassaying molluscicides, the following procedures, which are recommended by the World Health Organization (1965a), are being presented.

Immersion Test
(For Aquatic and Amphibious Snails)

Snails to be used: If the snails are aquatic, they should be laboratory-reared and/or uninfected local vector snails. The former is preferred. Ideally, the snails to be used for bioassaying molluscicides in all laboratories should be of the same strain; however, this is usually not feasible. Furthermore, the same strain of snail maintained differently in different laboratories may react differently to the candidate molluscicide. Consequently, each laboratory should use its own strain, and differences portrayed by the various strains should be confirmed.

Container: The containers employed should be no less than 1 liter vessels in which ten snails are exposed to the test solution at 100 ml per snail. Vessels made of glass or some other nonporous material are recommended. Should snails show a tendency to crawl out of the test solution, a glass cover must be inserted just above the water line. If the solution level is too low to permit the placement of an effective cover, it can be raised by adding glass beads. If desired, the trap system depicted in Fig. 13-3 can also be used to prevent the snails from crawling out of the test solution.

Number of replicates: A minimum of three containers at each concentration with ten snails each should be used. As an alternative, the use of five snails per test with four containers at each concentration is acceptable.

Number and age of snails: Thirty snails should be exposed to each of at least three concentrations that lie between the levels resulting in 5% and 95% mortality. These snails should be young but mature and relatively uniform in age and size. In the case of *Biomphalaria glabrata*, snails with a shell diameter of 6–8 mm are well suited.

Water: Deionized water should be used to make up the test solutions and for the controls. Aeration is not necessary during the exposure and recovery periods.

Concentration of molluscicide: A tenfold dilution (solution, suspension, emulsion, etc.) series of 0.1, 1.0, and 10 ppm of the candidate molluscicide is generally employed. In some cases a twofold series is further used after the critical range is ascertained. Mixing during the exposure period is not considered to be necessary.

Light: Conventional laboratory lighting with normal diurnal alternations should be used.

Fig. 13-3. Apparatus used to keep test snails submerged. The snails are maintained in an open petri dish covered with cheesecloth.

pH: The pH of the test solution should be determined at the beginning of the exposure period.

Temperature: Temperature is an important ambient factor. The recommended temperature is $25° \pm 1°C$ for those species that harbor the human-infecting schistosomes.

Food: Snails need not be fed during the exposure and recovery periods.

Exposure period: Generally an exposure period of 24 hours is adequate. Other exposure periods may be used for the comprehensive evaluation of candidate molluscicides and in experiments involving operculated amphibious snails.

Observations on behavior: Behavior of snails that may be protective is important, but these must be subjected to experimental testing to indicate their consistency.

Recovery period: After the snails have been exposed to the candidate molluscicide, they are washed in three changes of deionized water to remove traces of the molluscicide from their shells and transferred to a vessel containing deionized water for recovery. The usual recovery period is 24 hours.

Criteria of death: Snails that had been killed during the exposure or recovery period can be recognized by discoloration, absence of muscle contractions, and/or crushing in order to examine for signs of life. The so-called National Institutes of Health's (NIH) albino strain of *Biomphalaria glabrata* is especially useful for bioassaying molluscicides since it has an unpigmented mantle, and the criterion of absence of heart beats is a most reliable one for death. Certain strains of *Bulinus*, such as one of Rhodesian origin, also have a similar mantle, and hence their heart beats can be observed. Snails that are obviously dead in the exposure or recovery tanks should be removed to prevent fouling.

LC_{50} *determination*: LC_{50} and LC_{90} values should be computed, especially if the test is used in comprehensive evaluations.

Controls: Two types of controls should be carried out with this bioassay method. (1) A minimum of two identical containers containing ten snails in 1 liter of water should be used to ascertain the "normal" mortality rate. (2) Trials using a reference molluscicide (such as those listed in Table 13-2) should be repeated regularly.

Plate Test
(For Amphibious Snails)

Snails to be used: The snails should be active, freshly collected (24–48 hours) field snails or laboratory-reared specimens.

Container: The test container should be a 15 × 1 cm petri dish (glass or plastic). The bottom of the dish should be covered with a sheet of fine-grained filter paper, and a lid is necessary.

Number of replicates: If a single concentration of the candidate molluscicide is to be tested, at least two replicates must be carried out. If more than two concentrations are to be tested, one or more containers for each concentration are to be used.

Water: Deionized water should be used to make up the test solutions and for the controls.

Concentration of molluscicide: If a single concentration is to be tested, the concentration of the candidate molluscicide should be 100 ppm. However, if multiple concentrations are to be tested, 10, 100, and 1000 ppm dilutions are recommended. Furthermore, a twofold series can be used after the critical range is determined. Two ml of the dilutions should be evenly distributed on the filter paper, and the solvent should be allowed to evaporate. If the molluscicide is not soluble in water, a volatile solvent should be used if possible. If it is insoluble, use finely divided material to achieve an even distribution over the filter paper. Three ml of deionized water are added at the time the snails are placed in the dish.

Light: Conventional laboratory lighting with normal diurnal alterations should be used.

Temperature: The recommended ambient temperature is 26°–28°C.

Food: Snails need not be fed during the exposure period.

Exposure period: The snails are maintained in the petri dishes for 4 days.

Observations on behavior: First day—make three observations, note reactions, place the snails in the center of the dish, add water as required to keep the filter paper moist. Second day—observe once, note reactions, place the snails in the center of the dish, add water if required. Third day—observe once, note reactions, place the snails in the center of the dish, add water if required. Fourth day—note reactions and prepare for final examination.

Criteria of death: At the time of the final examination, all the snails should be rinsed in a small strainer, and the washed snails should be placed in the respective petri dish lid and covered with water. The usual procedure is to crush all snails showing no activity and examine for signs of life, such as muscle contractions and so on.

LC_{50} *determination*: LC_{50} and LC_{90} values are computed.

Controls: Two types of controls should be carried out in conjunction with the Plate Test. The first involves placing ten snails in each of five identically prepared petri dishes except that the candidate molluscicide is not added to the filter paper bottoms. This set of controls will reveal what the "normal" mortality rate is among nonexposed snails.

The second set of controls involves determining the LC_{50} with niclosamide at concentrations of 20, 50 and 100 ppm, two plates for each concentration, once a month to check the reproducibility of the obtained values.

Lehigh Molluscicide Test
(For *Biomphalaria* spp.)

In addition to the bioassay methods presented, a method that offers several advantages over the more established procedures has been developed at the Institute for Pathobiology of Lehigh University. This method is more expedient, since the evaluation of a compound can be completed within hours; more sensitive, since the tests are able to distinguish between different molecular configurations of the same toxic substance; and more accurate. This method involves measuring the respiration and heart rates of snails exposed to the candidate molluscicide as well as making observations on their behavior. The respiratory rate is determined by use of a differential respirometer (Cheng and Sullivan, 1973a); heart rates are quantified by examining specimens of the NIH albino strain of *Biomphalaria glabrata* with a dissection microscope (Cheng and Sullivan, 1973b); and the behavior pattern of the snail immediately withdrawing into its shell when confronted

with a toxic substance is readily appreciated. The specific procedures to be
followed are presented below.

Respirometry: We use a Model GRP 14 Gilson differential respirometer
(Middletown, Wisconsin), although practically any differential respirometer
can be substituted.

Ten specimens of *Biomphalaria* of identical size (9 mm in shell diameter
in our case, but any size of mature snails will do) are blotted dry and placed
in the individual reaction vessels containing 6 ml of the test molluscicide.
Two-tenths of 1 ml of potassium hydroxide is placed in the center well of
each flask together with a filter paper fan (Whatman No. 2) for the absorption
of the CO_2 evolved. The reaction vessels are submerged in the water bath
maintained at 27°C and allowed to equilibrate for 15 minutes with shaking
at 80 oscillations per minute. After this period, the respirometric readings
are recorded at 20-minute intervals for a 2-hour period.

At the conclusion of the 2-hour period the snails are dissected from their
shells, dried overnight at 78°C, and weighed. The raw respirometric data are
converted to microliters of O_2 per gram of dry weight. Identically obtained
respirometric data on two snails immersed in deionized water are obtained

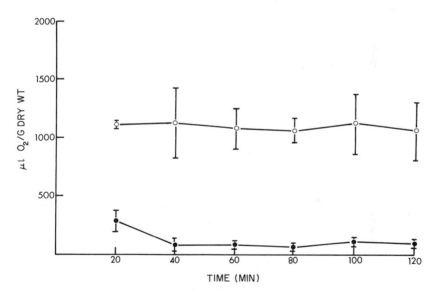

Fig. 13-4. Oxygen consumption of *Biomphalaria glabrata* exposed to 12.5 ppm of copper as
Cu(DEG)$_2$ as a function of time. Control ($O - O$) experimental ($\bullet - \bullet$). The vertical lines represent standard deviations. After Cheng and Sullivan (1973a).

simultaneously, and these serve as the controls. By following this procedure, the respirometric data obtained for the control snails can be compared with those of the test snails with greater reliability than if the determinations of oxygen consumption of the two categories of snails are determined separately.

Figures 13-4 and 13-5 depict the results of Cheng and Sullivan (1973a) on the effect of 12.5 ppm of copper(II)-bis-*N*,*N*-dihydroxyethylglycine [Cu(DEG)$_2$ and copper(II)-ethylenediamine-*N*,*N*,*N'*,*N'*-tetraacetic acid (CuEDTA) on the oxygen consumption of *Biomphalaria glabrata*, respectively. The Cu(DEG)$_2$ is cidal to the snail while CuEDTA is not. Thus, it is evidence from these data that respirometry is an effective method for quantifying molluscicidal activity.

Determination of heart rate: Seven mature *Biomphalaria glabrata* of the NIH albino strains of equal size are placed in 250 ml of deionized water in a 250 ml beaker immersed in a water bath maintained at $27° \pm 1°C$. Subsequent to a 15-minute acclimation period at this temperature, the time required for ten ventricular contractions is recorded for each snail as the control, or preexposure time. This is accomplished by examining the transparent snails

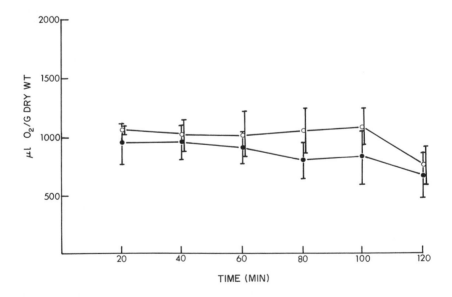

Fig. 13-5. Oxygen consumption of *Biomphalaria glabrata* exposed to 12.5 ppm of copper as CuEDTA as a function of time. Control (O – O); experimental (● – ●). The vertical lines represent standard deviations. After Cheng and Sullivan (1973a).

with a dissection microscope suspended over the snails in the beaker partially submerged in the water bath (Fig. 13-6).

After ascertaining the preexposure time, the snails are removed from the 250-ml beaker, individually blotted dry, and placed in separate Stendor dishes containing 10 ml of the dilution of the candidate molluscicide. The Stendor dishes containing the snails are then placed in the 27° ±1°C water bath, and the heart rate of each snail is recorded at 20-minute intervals for 2 hours.

The recorded time required for ten ventricular contractions in the control and experimental snails are converted to beats/minute.

Figure 13-7 depicts the mean heart rates of *B. glabrata* exposed to 20 ppm and 0.05 ppm of Cu as $CuSO_4$ as reported by Cheng and Sullivan (1973b). It is evident from these data that not only is the monitoring of heart rates an effective quantitative method for determining the effects of candidate molluscicides but also serves as a method for estimating the concentration of the molluscicide if not known. It is noted that 20 ppm of Cu as $CuSO_4$

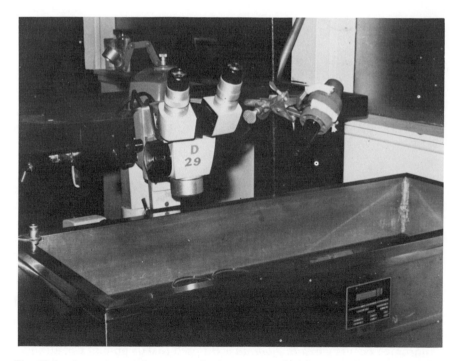

Fig. 13-6. Apparatus used to count the heart rates of snails exposed to candidate molluscicides.

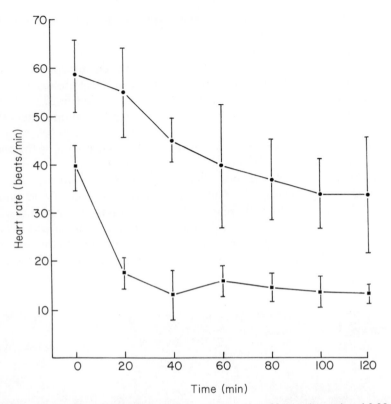

Fig. 13-7. Heart rates of *Biomphalaria glabrata* exposed to 20 ppm (■ – ■) and 0.05 ppm (● – ●) of copper as copper sulfate as functions of time. The verticle lines represent standard deviations. After Cheng and Sullivan (1973b).

in deionized water will kill *B. glabrata* after a 2-hour exposure, and 0.05 ppm Cu as $CuSO_4$ in similar water will kill the snails after a 24-hour exposure.

Behavior studies: Harry and Aldrich (1963) have reported that *B. glabrata* will react to toxic concentrations of metallic ions in terms of the "distress syndrome." In this condition, which is evoked at concentrations of metallic ions below those causing complete retraction into the shell, the snail's cephalopedal mass is partially to fully extended from the shell aperture, and, since the mollusk is not able to attach its foot to the substratum, its crawling attempts are ineffectual. According to Harry and Aldrich this "distress syndrome" occurs when *B. glabrata* is exposed to 0.05 ppm of Cu, although Cheng and Sullivan (1973b) have reported its occurrence when exposed to as low as 0.01 ppm of Cu.

By using a combination of respirometry, heart rate determinations, and the occurrence of the "distress syndrome," the activity of potential molluscicides can be tested on a more rapid and quantitative basis.

Test for Slow-Release Molluscicides

As stated earlier, copper and organotin molluscicides have been formulated as slow-release molluscicides by embedding the cidal metals in a rubber matrix. The testing of this category of molluscicides necessitates a modification in the procedure, and the one currently being used at the Institute for Pathobiology at Lehigh University is described below.

Snails: In each test ten snails are placed in a finger bowl (6 cm in diameter) the top of which is secured with a piece of cotton gauze. All the mature snails

Fig. 13-8.   Apparatus used to test slow-release candidate molluscicides.

are of the same size, measuring between 5 and 8 mm in shell diameter in the case of *Biomphalaria* spp.

Apparatus: As depicted in Fig. 13-8, the bowl containing the snails is placed in the center of a round glass dish (15 cm in diameter, 11 cm deep), which is fitted with the outlet from an aeration pump and a thermometer. One thousand ml of deionized water is placed in this dish, and the slow-release pellet is placed in the water.

Temperature: The ambient temperature should be maintained at a constant 25°C if *Biomphalaria* spp. and *Bulinus* spp. are exposed. If other aquatic snails are used, the ambient temperature should be similar to that in their natural habitats.

Amount of test material: The pellet of slow-release material placed in the test system should weigh about 0.03 g.

Procedure: For "initial exposure" tests, the snails comprising each experiment are exposed to a fresh pellet and examined at 12-hour intervals for up to 4 days. If the snails have not all been killed within that period, they are removed to a container of deionized water and permitted to recover for 48 to 72 hours. The number of deaths, as determined by the absence of muscular movement, heart beats, and so on, during both the exposure and recovery periods, are recorded.

For "second exposure" tests, the pellet is presoaked in 1 liter of deionized water for 1 week before it is transferred to the test system. As in the case of the "initial exposure" tests, the mortality rate among snails during the exposure and recovery periods is recorded.

For "third exposure" tests, a fresh pellet is presoaked in 1 liter of deionized water for 2 weeks before it is transferred to the test system. The mortality rate among the test snails is recorded as previously.

Subsequent "fourth exposure," "fifth exposure," and so on, tests are similarly carried out with the fresh pellet presoaked for an additional week each time. By comparing the mortality rates resulting from a series of exposure tests, the effectiveness of the slow-release material is determined.

Control: As a control, an identically structured system should be maintained except that no slow-release pellet is introduced. By checking the "natural" mortality rate among the control snails, actual percent mortality attributable to the slow-release substance is ascertained.

Observations on behavior: The behavior pattern of snails exposed to pellets should be recorded.

LC_{50} and LC_{90} Determinations

The potency of a candidate molluscicide is quantified as LC_{50} or as LC_{90}. The definition of LC_{50} is the lethal concentration of the compound required to kill 50% of the mollusks per specified unit time, while LC_{90} is the lethal concentration of the compound required to kill 90% of the mollusks per specified unit time.

The most commonly employed method to calculate the LC_{50} and LC_{90} values for a candidate molluscicide is that developed by Litchfield and Wilcoxon (1949), although in recent years the probit analysis method (Finney, 1952) is gaining popularity.

By the Litchfield and Wilcoxon method for determining LC_{50} and LC_{90} values, concentrations of the molluscicide are plotted along the x axis while the observed percent mortality is plotted along the y axis on logarithmic–probability paper, leaving space for, but not plotting, the 0% and 100% mortality points (see the procedure for plotting the 0% and 100% mortality values presented below under "A working example.") At least two points above 50% mortality and two points below this value are recommended. With these values plotted, a temporary straight line is drawn through the points, which represents the expected mortalities over the concentration range of the molluscicide being tested. It is noted that concentrations that predict a mortality of greater than 99.99% or less than 0.01% are eliminated. Zero and 100% mortality values are corrected according to the graphic expected value for those concentrations by employing the accompanying tabular material (Table 13-3). No more than two 0% and 100% mortality values are to be included. This procedure may have to be repeated until the temporary line satisfactorily fits all the plotted data (see specific example given below).

TABLE 13-3
Corrected Values of 0 to 100% Effect (Body of Table) Corresponding to Expected Values (Margins)[a, b]

Expected	0	1	2	3	4	5	6	7	8	9
0	—	0.3	0.7	0.1	1.3	1.6	2.0	2.3	2.6	2.9
10	3.2	3.5	3.8	4.1	4.4	4.7	4.9	5.2	5.5	5.7
20	6.0	6.2	6.5	6.7	7.0	7.2	7.4	7.6	7.8	8.1
30	8.3	8.4	8.6	8.8	9.0	9.2	9.3	9.4	9.6	9.8
40	9.9	10.0	10.1	10.2	10.3	10.3	10.4	10.4	10.4	10.5
50	—	89.5	89.6	89.6	89.6	89.7	89.7	89.8	89.9	90.0
60	90.1	90.2	90.3	90.5	90.7	90.8	91.0	91.2	91.4	91.6
70	91.7	91.9	92.2	92.4	92.6	92.8	93.0	93.3	93.5	93.8
80	94.0	94.3	94.5	94.8	95.1	95.3	95.6	95.9	96.2	96.5
90	96.8	97.1	97.4	97.7	98.0	98.4	98.7	99.0	99.3	99.7

[a] After Litchfield and Wilcoxon (1949).
[b] These values are derived from the maximal and minimal corrected probits of Bliss (1938).

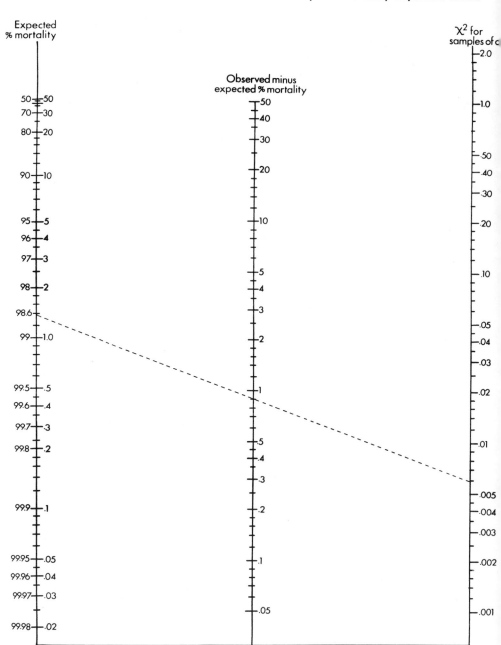

Fig. 13-9. Nomograph for determining LC_{50} and LC_{90} values.

TABLE 13-4
Hypothetical Data upon Which the Accompanying Working Example is Based

1	2	3	4	5	6
Molluscicide concentration (ppm)	Killed/tested	Observed % mortality	Expected % mortality (Fig. 13-10)	Observed minus expected	Contribution to x^2 (Fig. 13-9)
10.00	8/8	99.5	98.6	0.9	0.006
5.00	7/8	88.0	90.5	2.5	0.007
2.50	4/8	50.0	67.0	17.0	0.110
1.25	4/8	50.0	34.0	16.0	0.105
0.62	1/8	12.0	9.5	2.5	0.007

After the fit of the line has been checked by use of the x^2 test for n degrees of freedom (n = number of concentrations plotted minus 2), by employing the accompanying nomograph (Fig. 13-9), LC_{50} and LC_{90} values can be determined from the line of the graph.

A working example: Suppose the testing of a candidate molluscicide resulted in the set of data presented in Table 13-4, then the following steps, which correspond to and explain the six columns in Table 13-4, must be followed.

1. *Molluscicide concentration in parts per million (ppm).* A tenfold dilution series is recommended until less than 100% mortality is obtained, after which a twofold series is standardly used. A more narrow dilution range may be required. In the case of heavy metal-containing molluscicides, the concentration of the molluscicide is expressed as parts per million of the metal and not of the compound.

2. *Killed/tested.* This is the number of mollusks killed as the result of exposure to the molluscicide divided by the number of mollusks tested. Although eight snails per test are employed in the example presented in Table 13-4, thirty snails per test are recommended.

3. *Observed percent mortality.* These values represent the quotients from step 2. Note that eight killed divided by eight tested is expressed as 99.5% mortality. This value is obtained by reading the expected percent mortality at 10 ppm from the straight line obtained by plotting all the percent mortalities (column 3 of Table 13-4), except for the first value, against concentrations of 0.62, 1.25, 2.5, and 5.0 ppm (Fig. 13-10). It is noted that 0% and 100% mortality cannot be plotted on logarithmic–probability paper. The value thus obtained, which is the expected percent mortality at 10 ppm, is then converted to the observed percent mortality by employing Table 13-3. In the example given, the plotted line intersects a value of 98.6% mortality on

Percent mortality

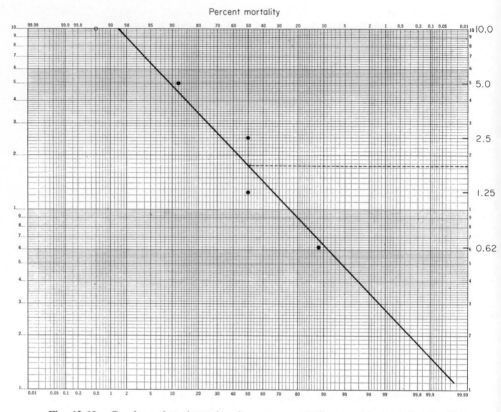

Fig. 13-10. Graph used to determine the percent mortality as a function of molluscicide concentration.

the *y*-axis at 10 ppm (Fig. 13-10). The value of 98.6 (the expected mortality) corresponds to an observed percent mortality of 99.5% in Table 13-3. Once this value of 99.5 is derived, it is also plotted on the graph of percent mortality versus molluscicide concentration (shown as an open circle in Fig. 13-10). Now that all the data have been plotted, the line may, but rarely, require adjusting for a better fit. If an adjustment is made, a new set of expected and corrected values must be obtained by repeating the foregoing procedure. In the example given, no such adjustment is required.

    4. *Expected percent mortality.* The values are read directly from the final plot of percent mortality versus molluscicide concentration (Fig. 13-10). Concentrations for which percent mortality is expected to be greater than 99.9 or less than 0.01 are omitted.

    5. *Observed minus expected.* This is the absolute difference between steps 3 and 4.

6. *Contribution to* X^2. Using the accompanying nomograph (Fig. 13-9), connect a value on the expected percent mortality scale with a value on the observed minus expected percent mortality scale with a straight line (dotted line on Fig. 13-9). The intersection of this line on the X^2 scale is the contribution to X^2, which is 0.006 for an expected percent mortality of 98.6 and an observed minus expected percent mortality of 0.9.

If the data are significantly heterogeneous, then the line is still not a good fit. In order to determine whether or not the data are significantly heterogeneous, use the following procedure.

1. Sum the contributions to X^2 (column 6, Table 13-4)

$$
\begin{array}{l}
0.006 \\
0.007 \\
0.110 \\
0.105 \\
\underline{0.007} \\
0.235 = \text{total contribution to } X^2
\end{array}
$$

2. Divide the total number of snails exposed to the molluscicide by the number of concentrations tested, as follows,

Total number of animals = 40 (column 2, Table 13-4)
Number of concentrations = 5 (column 1, Table 13-4)
Animals/concentration = 40/5 = 8

3. Multiply the total contributions to X^2 (step 1) by animals/concentration (step 2). The product equals X^2. Or,

$$X^2 = 0.235 \times 8 = 1.88$$

4. Determine the degrees of freedom (n), which is 2 less than the number of concentrations tested, as follows,

$$n = \text{degrees of freedom} = 5 - 2 = 3$$

5. Consult a X^2 table (Table 13-5) to determine the maximum permissable X^2 for the degrees of freedom determined in step 4. In the present example, X^2 for n of 3 = 7.82.

6. If the X^2 value determined in step 3 is less than that determined in step 5, the data are not significantly heterogeneous, and the line is a good fit. LC_{50} and LC_{90} values may now be read directly from the graph (Fig. 13-10). In the present example, 1.88 is less than 7.82, and the LC_{50} for this molluscicide is 1.75 ppm (dotted line on Fig. 13-10).

7. If the X^2 value determined in step 3 is more than that determined in step 5, the data are significantly heterogeneous, and the line is not a good fit. If the X^2 of the line cannot be reduced below the maximum permissable X^2 by refitting the line and recalculating X^2, the t value in the X^2 table for n degrees of freedom should be stated.

TABLE 13-5
Values of t and X^2 for $P = 0.05$

Degrees of freedom	t	X^2
1	12.7	3.84
2	4.3	5.99
3	3.18	7.82
4	2.78	9.49
5	2.57	11.1
6	2.45	12.6
7	2.36	14.1
8	2.31	15.5
9	2.26	16.9
10	2.23	18.3

Sequence of Tests

The World Health Organization has recommended that the screening of candidate molluscicides be carried out in three sequential steps. (1) Preliminary screening during which the potential toxicity of the candidate molluscicide is tested; (2) definitive screening during which the LC_{50} (and usually also the LC_{90}) values are determined; and (3) comprehensive laboratory evaluation during which the molluscicidal activity of the compound is tested against a number of variables prior to field testing. The following specific phenomena are to be tested during phase three.

1. Time-concentration relationships plus any protective behavior displayed by the snail
2. Chemical stability of the molluscicide at working dilutions
3. Stage-size array susceptibilities
4. The effect of pH on the activity of the molluscicide
5. Stability of the molluscicide in sunlight
6. The effect of temperature on the activity of the molluscicide
7. Mammalian toxicity and phytotoxicity tests
8. Residual properties of the molluscicide
9. Inactivating properties of minerals in natural waters where the molluscicide is to be used
10. Inactivating effects of physicochemical adsorption in the environment
11. Stability of the molluscicide in storage

BIOLOGICAL CONTROL

A number of competitors, predators, and parasites have been advocated as agents for the biological control of the medically important snails. These contentions have been mostly based on the results of laboratory experiments. Under laboratory conditions, however, the biological balance is disturbed to the disadvantage of the snail, and, therefore, in nature, where this imbalance does not occur, it seems unlikely that these parasites and predators are effective in exterminating the snails. There may be, however, some reduction in the population density. In many bodies of water all over the world mollusks are parasitized by leeches, oligochaetes, trematodes, nematodes, fungi, and bacteria, and some of these may be pathogenic (Chapter 7). Mollusks are also preyed upon by certain species of insects, arachnids, crustaceans, fishes, amphibians, reptiles, birds, and mammals. Accounts of these parasites and predators are included in articles by Michelson (1957), Malek (1958, 1961a, 1961b), and Berg (1964). In Table 13-6 are listed the known macroinvertebrate and vertebrate predators.

In the case of the ampullarid *Marisa cornuarietis*, laboratory and field observations have shown that it will devour both the egg masses and young of *Biomphalaria glabrata*. This is not due to predation but because young snails occur on the vegetation on which *M. cornuarietis* feeds voraciously. The reduction or extermination of *Biomphalaria glabrata* in the presence of *M. cornuarietis* apparently results from great depletion of the common food supply in the habitat, in addition to ingestion of eggs and the young. Apparently some success has been obtained using *M. cornuarietis* for control of *B. glabrata* under field conditions in certain situations. Field studies in Puerto Rico have shown that such control can be achieved at a very low cost, and the procedure is simple (Ruiz-Tiben *et al.*, 1969). This study was carried out in a large number of irrigation ponds in the Guayama–Arroyo irrigation project.

The control of natural populations of the medically important snails by infecting them with noneconomically important trematodes has been suggested as another approach to biological control. Actually, this approach is based on two fundamental biological phenomena that are quite different. First, it is known that certain species of trematodes will cause the castration of their molluscan hosts. The condition is known as "parasitic castration" (p. 212). If the castration of mollusks that can also serve as the intermediate hosts of medically important parasites can be totally or even partially effected in a population, then one would expect the number of mollusks available in the transmission of the parasites pathogenic to humans to be reduced. Hence, the desired reduction in the frequency of contact between the infective form of the parasite and man would take place. Although

TABLE 13-6

A List of Invertebrate and Vertebrate Predators That Have Been Reported to Attack Mollusks

Predator	Molluscan prey
Annelida	
Helobdella (= *Glossosiphonia*) spp.	*Biomphalaria glabrata*
Rotifera	
Proales gigantea	Eggs of pulmonates
Arthropoda	
Dytiscus marginalis (beetle)	*Lymnaea stagnalis*
	Planorbarius corneus
Larva of *Luciola cruciata* (beetle)	*Lymnaea, Planorbis,*
	Melania, Oncomelania
Larva of *Luciola lateralis* (beetle)	*Lymnaea, Planorbis,*
	Melania, Oncomelania,
	Thiara libertina
Larvae of beetles of the family Lampyridae	*Galba*
Flies of the family Sciomyzidae	Various aquatic snails
Larvae of tabanid flies	Aquatic mollusks
Chironomus	*Lymnaea peregra*
	Lymnaea limosa
Astacus (crayfish)	*Physopsis[a], Bulinus[a],*
	Planorbis[a]
Cambarus (crayfish)	*Physopsis[a], Bulinus[a],*
	Planorbis[a]
Cypridopsis hartwigi (ostracod)	*Biomphalaria glabrata[a],*
	Bulinus contortus[a]
Mollusca	
Physa hypnorum	*Lymnaea auricularia[a]*
Marisa cornuarietis	Eggs and young of
	Biomphalaria glabrata
Lymnaea stagnalis lillianae	*Helisoma campanulatum*
Fish	
Serranochromis macrocepha	*Lymnaea, Biomphalaria*
Umbra pygmaea	Planorbids
Cichlasoma biocellatum	Planorbids
Tetradon schontedeni	Planorbids
Pelmatochromis kribensis	Planorbids
Tilapia sp.	Planorbids
Clarias gariepinus	*Physopsis globosa*
Birds	
Aramus solopaceus	*Pomacea*
Aramus pictus pictus	*Pomacea*
Rostrahamus sociabilis	*Pomacea*

[a] Observed under laboratory conditions only.

theoretically a highly desirable method for the biological control of schisto-somes, liver flukes, and other trematode-caused diseases, the employment of the principle of parasitic castration as an effective control method has not been highly successful. Nevertheless, it may play a part in an integrated control program involving chemical as well as several types of biological and environmental control methods.

The second biological basis for utilizing a nonmedically important species of trematode as a biological control agent is based on the knowledge that interspecific competition between intramolluscan larval trematodes occurs, and this, at least in the case of certain combinations, leads to the death and/or retarded growth of the medically important species and, hence, the failure to produce cercariae, which is the infective form to man in the case of the schistosomes. This topic has been comprehensively reviewed by Lim and Heyneman (1972), and interested readers are referred to that account. Presented below is an abbreviated review of the principles involved.

When two species of larval trematodes occur within the same molluscan host, antagonism occurs. This may be in the form of direct and/or indirect antagonism. Direct antagonism usually involves a redia, commonly that of an echinostome, and a sporocyst, with the former activity devouring the latter. Since the original report by Wesenberg-Lund (1934) of this pheno-menon, the extensive investigations by Lie, Lim, Heyneman, and their associates* on direct antagonism between echinostome rediae and schisto-some sporocysts have resulted in the belief that this phenomenon holds promise for the biological control of schistosomes. A list of those species of parasites that have been tested for antagonism by the staff of the Hooper Foundation is presented in Table 13-7.

Indirect antagonism is also manifested by the retardation and/or death of the subordinate (or recessive) species, but the result is not due to direct ingestion by the dominant species. The exact cause(s) remains uncertain, although it is believed to be due to either the toxic effects of the secretions of the dominant species or competition for nutrients and other metabolic requirements, with the dominant species being successful. Of course, a combination of these two causes is possible. It is, however, no longer general-ly believed that immunological response on the part of the molluscan host plays any role during indirect antagonism since antibody synthesis does not appear to occur in mollusks.

In summary, the present status of the control of medically important mollusks is still primarily dependent on chemical and environmental control,

*The numerous publications by the G. W. Hooper Foundation group have been reviewed by Lim and Heyneman (1972).

TABLE 13-7

Intramolluscan Intertrematode Antagonism[a, b]

Gastropod host	Dominant parasite	Subordinate parasite
Lymnaea rubiginosa	*Echinostoma audyi* (r)	Unindentified strigeid (s)
L. rubiginosa	*E. audyi* (r)	Unidentified xiphidiocercaria (s)
L. rubiginosa	*E. audyi* (r)	*Trichobilharzia brevis* (s)
L. rubiginosa	*E. audyi* (r)	*Fasciola gigantica* (r)
L. rubiginosa	*Echinoparyphium dunni* (r)	Unidentified xiphidiocercaria (s)
Indoplanorbis exustus	*Echinostoma malayanum* (r)	*Schistosoma spindale* (s)
Biomphalaria straminea	*Paryphostomum segregatum* (r)	*Echinostoma barbosai* (r)
B. straminea	*P. segregatum* (r)	*Ribeiroia marini* (r)
Biomphalaria glabrata (originally from St. Lucia)	*P. segregatum* (r)	*R. marini* (r)
B. glabrata	*Ribeiroia marini* (r)	*Schistosoma mansoni* (s)
B. glabrata (from NIH)	*Echinostoma barbosai* (r)	*S. mansoni* (s)
	Paryphostomum segregatum (r)	*S. mansoni* (s)
B. glabrata (from NIH)	*P. segregatum* (r)	*Echinostoma lindoense* (r)
B. glabrata (from NIH)	*P. segregatum* (r)	*Echinostoma paraensei* (r)
B. glabrata (from NIH)	*P. segregatum* (r)	*Ribeiroia marini* (r)
B. glabrata (from NIH)	*P. segregatum* (r)	*Echinostoma liei* (r)
B. glabrata (from NIH)	*Schistosoma mansoni* (s)	*Cotylurus lutzi* (s)
B. glabrata (from NIH)	*Ribeiroia marini* (r)	*Schistosoma mansoni* (s)
B. glabrata (from NIH)	*Echinostoma liei* (r)	*S. mansoni* (s)

[a] These combinations have been studied by the personnel of the G. W. Hooper Foundation.
[b] Redia (r); sporocyst (s).

although biological control is gaining in popularity but has yet to be proven to be effective in nature. We predict that as more biochemical and physiological information becomes available relative to the nature of both direct and indirect antagonism, especially the latter, interspecific competition between intramolluscan trematode larvae could well be employed as a control program limited to restricted bodies of water such as subsections of rice paddies and ponds. We would also like to call the reader's attention to the fact that simultaneous infection of the same individual snail with certain combinations of two, and sometimes three, larval trematodes (sometimes schistosome sporocysts and other trematode rediae) is not uncommon in nature (also see p. 107).

References

Barbosa, F. S., and Olivier, L. (1958). Studies on the snail vectors of bilharziasis mansoni in north-eastern Brazil. *Bull. W.H.O.* **18**, 895–908.

Berg, C. O. (1964). Snail control in trematode diseases: The possible value of sciomyzid larvae snail-killing Diptera. *Advan. Parasitol.* **1**, 259–309.

Berrios-Duran, L. A., and Ritchie, L. R. (1968). Molluscicidal activity of Bis(tri-n-butyltin) oxide formulated in rubber. *Bull. W.H.O.* **39**, 310–312.

Bliss, C. I. (1938). Determination of dosage-mortality curve for small numbers. *Quart. J. Pharm. Pharmacol.* **11**, 192–216.

Burch, J. B. (1960). Some snails and slugs of quarantine significance to the United States. *U.S. Dep. Agr., Agr. Res. Serv. Plant Quarantine Div., Publ. ARS* **82–1**.

Cheng, T. C., and Sullivan, J. T. (1973a). A comparative study of the effects of two copper compounds on the respiration and survival of *Biomphalaria glabrata* (Mollusca: Pulmonata). *Comp. Gen. Pharmacol.* **4**, 315–320.

Cheng, T. C., and Sullivan, J. T. (1973b). The effect of copper on the heart rate of *Biomphalaria glabrata* (Mollusca: Pulmonata). *Comp. Gen Pharmacol.* **4**, 37–41.

Finney, D. J. (1952). "Probit Analysis: A Statistical Treatment of the Sigmoid Response Curve," 2nd ed. Cambridge Univ. Press, London and New York.

Harry, H. W., and Aldrich, D. V. (1963). The distress syndrome in *Taphius glabratus* (Say) as a reaction to toxic concentrations of inorganic ions. *Malacologia* **1**, 283–289.

Hopf, H. S., Duncan, J., and Wood, A. B. (1963). Molluscicidal activity of copper compounds of low solubility. *Bull. W.H.O.* **29**, 128–130.

Kuntz, R. E. and Wells, W. H. (1951). Laboratory and field evaluation of two dinitrophenols for control of schistosomiasis vectors in Egypt with emphasis on importance of temperature. *Amer. J. Trop. Med.* **31**, 784–824.

Lemma, A. (1970). Laboratory and field evaluation of the molluscicidal properties of *Phytolaca dodecandra*. *Bull. W.H.O.* **42**, 597–612.

Lim, H. K., and Heyneman, D. (1972). Intramolluscan inter-trematode antagonism: A review of factors influencing the host-parasite system and its possible role in biological control. *Advan. Parasitol.* **10**, 191–268.

Litchfield, J. T., and Wilcoxon, F. (1949). A simplified method of evaluating dose-effect experiments. *J. Pharmacol. Exp. Ther.* **96**, 99–113.

McMullen, D. B., Komyama, N., Ishi, N., Endo-Itabashi, T., and Mitoma, Y. (1951). Results obtained in testing molluscicides in field plots containing *Oncomelania nosophora*, an intermediate host of *Schistosoma japonicum. Amer. J. Trop. Med.* **31**, 583–592.

Malek, E. A. (1958). Factors conditioning the habitat of bilharziasis intermediate hosts of the family Planorbidae. *Bull. W.H.O.* **18**, 785–818.

Malek, E. A. (1961a). The ecology of schistosomiasis. Chapter 10. *In* "Studies in Disease Ecology" (J. M. May, ed.), pp. 261–327; 553–568. Hafner Co., New York.

Malek, E. A. (1961b). Public health importance of helminthic diseases and basic principles for their control. V. Helminthic infections transmitted by snails. World Health Organization Document, WHO/Helminth/8. pp. 1–98.

Malek, E. A. (1962). Bilharziasis control in pump schemes near Khartoum, Sudan and an evaluation of the efficacy of chemical and mechanical barriers. *Bull. W.H.O.* **27**, 41–58.

Malek, E. A. (1970). Diseases of the respiratory system: Paragonimiasis (Endemic Haemoptysis). Chapter 9. *In* "Diseases of Children in the Subtropics and Tropics." (D. B. Jelliffe, ed.), pp. 242–248. Edward Arnold, Ltd., London.

Malek, E. A. (1971). Laboratory evaluation of an emulsifiable concentrate formulation of niclosamide. World Health Organization Document. WHO/Schisto/71.9. pp. 1–3.

Malek, E. A. (1972). Environmental control: Snail ecology and man-made habitats. *In* "Proceedings of a Symposium on the Future of Schistosomiasis Control". (M. J. Miller, ed.), pp. 57–60. Tulane University, New Orleans, Louisiana.

Mead, A. R. (1961). "The Giant African Snail: A Problem in Economic Malacology." Univ. of Chicago Press, Chicago, Illinois.

Michelson, E. H. (1957). Studies on the biological control of schistosome-bearing snails. Predators and parasites of freshwater Mollusca: A review of the literature. *Parasitology* **47**, 413–426.

Ritchie, L. S. (1973). Chemical control of snails. *In* "Epidemiology and Control of Schistosomiasis (Bilharziasis)." (N. Ansari, ed.), pp. 458–532. S. Karger, Basel and University Park Press, Baltimore.

Ritchie, L. S., and Malek, E. A. (1969). Molluscicides: Status of their evaluation, formulations and methods of application. World Health Organization Document, PD/MOL/69.1. pp. 1–16.

Ruiz-Tiben, E., Palmer, J. R., and Ferguson, F. F. (1969). Biological control of *Biomphalaria glabrata* by *Marisa cornuarietis* in irrigation ponds in Puerto Rico. *Bull. W.H.O.* **41**, 329–333.

van der Schalie, H. (1958). Vector snail control in Qalyub, Egypt. *Bull. W.H.O.* **19**, 263–283.

Webbe, G., and Sturrock, R. F. (1964). Laboratory tests of some new molluscicides in Tanganyika. *Ann. Trop. Med. Parasitol.* **58**, 234–239.

Wesenberg-Lund, C. J. (1934). Contributions to the development of the Trematoda Digenea. Part II. The biology of the freshwater cercariae in Danish freshwaters. *Kgl. Dan. Vidensk. Selsk., Skr.*, 9R, **5**, 1–223.

World Health Organization. (1965a). Molluscicide screening and evaluation. *Bull. W.H.O.* **33**, 567–581.

World Health Organization (1965b). "Snail Control in the Prevention of Bilharziasis" W.H.O. Monograph Series, No. 50.

Wright, W. H., Dobrovolny, C. G., and Berry, E. G. (1958). Field trials of various molluscicides (chiefly sodium pentachlorophenate) for the control of aquatic intermediate hosts of human bilharziasis. *Bull. W.H.O.* **18**, 963–974.

14 Laboratory Techniques and Exercises

MORPHOLOGY OF MOLLUSKS

Morphology of a Snail

Early descriptions of snails were based almost solely on shell characteristics and, hence, by modern standards do not provide satisfactory bases for distinguishing between species. In fact, the shells of gastropods do not represent good taxonomic criteria since they exhibit individual variations due to the age of the snail, the type of habitat, and in the case of aquatic snails, the quality of the water in which they live.

Modern systematists now recognize that there are several anatomical features of gastropods that provide adequate bases for differentiating between species. Even then, because of differences in methodology during the preparation of specimens for anatomical studies and in interpretation, there are discrepancies in identification.

The use of chromosome morphology and number has been recommended in taxonomic studies of snails, but this is not a totally satisfactory criterion since Burch (1960a) has shown that the chromosome number is the same for nearly all species of aquatic pulmonate snails. The limited value of chromosome numbers as a taxonomic tool has been discussed by Burch (1960b) who has recommended karyotype studies. It is of interest to note that Burch (1967) and Brown and Burch (1967) have suggested that the occurrence of polyploidy among various races or populations of snails may reflect strain differences in susceptibility to infection with schistosomes.

In addition to the morphological criteria mentioned for distinguishing between species of snails, some biological methods have been also employed. These include such biochemical techniques as paper chromatography and electrophoresis, genetical methods such as crossbreeding experiments, and comparative susceptibility studies involving exposure to the infective stages of trematodes and nematodes. Among these, chromatographic analyses of hemolymph and somatic proteins have been attempted, but their value as taxonomic tools has not yet been conclusively demonstrated. Wright and Ross (1965, 1966) have reported that the egg proteins of planorbid gastropods, when subjected to electrophoresis, are sensitive indicators of differences at the populational level. Recently, studies on the enzyme systems of adult planorbid snails (Wright *et al.*, 1966; Malek and File, 1971) have been carried out to elucidate phylogenetic relationships and to uncover possible biochemical factors that may influence the capacity of these snails to act as hosts for certain trematodes, especially the schistosomes. It has been established by these investigators that the esterases of the digestive gland from mature snails are useful for comparative purposes.

The natural occurrence of albino specimens among certain colonies of the hermaphroditic planorbid gastropods, where albinism is determined by a single recessive gene and, therefore, can be used as a genetic marker, made crossbreeding among these snails recognizable. The crossbreeding of members of different species has been accomplished in the case of the bisexual hosts of certain trematodes; for example, *Oncomelania* spp., which are intermediate hosts for *Schistosoma japonicum* in the Orient.

Serological techniques have been used to compare the precipitating activity of the various hemolymph antigens in the presence of specific snail "antisera." Genera and some congeneric species have been differentiated by gel diffusion methods (Michelson, 1966; Wright and Klein, 1967; Davis, 1968; Burch and Lindsay, 1970).

The intent of this chapter is to familiarize the reader with those aspects of the morphology of the shell and of the animal that serve as the bases for the classification of snails. In addition, a number of laboratory exercises and certain commonly employed experimental procedures are presented.

THE SHELL

Shell Structure and Characteristics

The shell consists of three strata: the periostracum, the prismatic layer, and the nacreous layer.

The periostracum, or epidermis, is a thin, outer protective layer comprised of conchiolin, which is constituted of calcium embedded in an organic matrix and which is similar to chitin. The prismatic layer constitutes the main portion of the shell. It is comprised primarily of calcium carbonate, although a small amount of calcium phosphate is also present in some shells. The nacre is the innermost layer. It is smooth, shiny, and is adherent to the animal located inside the shell.

The prismatic and nacreous layers are soluble in acids, but the periostracum is resistant. Thus, when a snail is left for some time in Bouin's fluid (p. 367), only a thin membranous periostracum remains covering the animal.

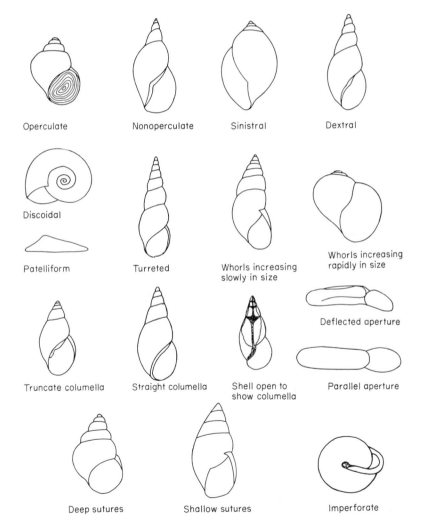

Operculate   Nonoperculate   Sinistral   Dextral

Discoidal

Patelliform   Turreted   Whorls increasing slowly in size   Whorls increasing rapidly in size

Deflected aperture

Truncate columella   Straight columella   Shell open to show columella   Parallel aperture

Deep sutures   Shallow sutures   Imperforate

Fig. 14-1. Shell characteristics of snails. After Malek (1962).

Paucispiral
(*Oncomelania*)

Multispiral
(*Brotia*)

Concentric
(*Bulimus*)

Fig. 14-2. Types of shell opercula.

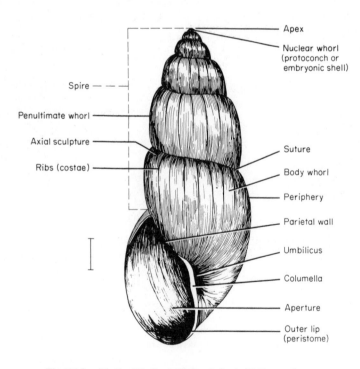

Fig. 14-3. Shell of *Bulinus* (*Bulinus*) *forskalii*. Bar = 1 mm.

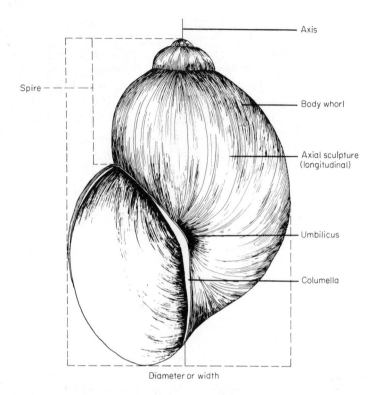

Fig. 14-4.   Shell of *Bulinus (Bulinus) truncatus.*

Laboratory Exercise

You are provided with a number of shells. Record their specific characteristics, proceeding according to the following outline. Refer to Figs. 14-1, 14-3, 14-4, 14-5, and 14-6.

1. *Operculate or nonoperculate.* An operculate shell has its aperture covered with a horny or calcareous plate known as the operculum. This structure is attached to the foot of the animal and fits closely into the aperture. The growth lines of the operculum are of taxonomic importance. An operculum (Fig. 14-2) may be concentric, that is with circular growth lines revolving around a central point, or spiral, in which case there may be a large number of whorls in the spire (multispiral) or a few whorls (paucispiral). Also record the shape of the operculum. It may be round, oval, or spindle-shaped.

2. *Spiral coiling.* To determine whether the shell is dextral (right-handed

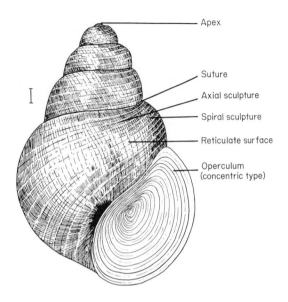

Fig. 14-5. Shell of *Viviparus* sp. Bar = 1 mm.

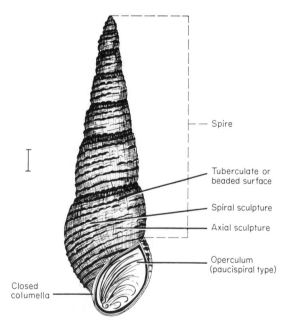

Fig. 14-6. Shell of *Thiara tuberculata*. Bar = 1 mm.

coiling), or sinistral (left-handed coiling), hold the shell in your hand with the aperture facing you and the apex directed upwards (upright).

3. *General shape of the shell.* A shell may be flat discoidal, elevated (conical, globose, or turrete), or patelliform.

4. *Whorls.* Record the number of whorls and whether they increase in size slowly or rapidly. Are their periphery carinate (keeled), angular, or rounded? Are the sutures between the whorls deep or shallow?

5. *Outline of aperture.* The aperture may be parallel with the body whorl or it may be deflected. It may be narrow, wide, round, oval, lunate, or ovate–lunate.

6. *The peristome.* The peristome is the entire lip of the aperture. Its outer edge may be thickened and reflected, curved, or straight and sharp. The shell may be armed with teeth, known as parietal teeth, on the parietal wall of the aperture or with teeth, known as palatal and basal teeth, on the outer lip of the aperture. If it is dentate, it may be unidentate, bidentate, or tridentate, depending on the number of teeth. The shell may be edentate, that is, with no teeth.

7. *Dimensions.* Record the width or diameter of the shell, the height or length of the shell, and the height of both the aperture and the spire.

8. *Markings on surface.* Shell markings are in the form of both sculpture and color. A shell may be smooth or the surface of the whorls may include obvious or fine striations, both axial (growth lines) and spiral. One of the following structures may be present on the surface of some of the shells: ribs (costae), striae, tubercles, papillae, and hairs. If the spiral lines are raised, the shell is described as being lirate. Record other markings on the shell surfaces as color bands or spots.

9. *The columella.* The columella is a centrally situated projection oriented along the longitudinal axis inside the shell and cannot be observed from the exterior. Its basal segment, however, is observable through the aperture, and it may be straight, twisted, or abruptly terminated. If the latter is the case, it is designated as being truncate. A fold called a "plait" may be present on the columella.

10. *The umbilicus.* The umbilicus is the opening of the central axis of the shell, that is the columella. The umbilicus may be closed (imperforate shell) or open (umbilicate shell).

Terms Used in Describing Gastropod Shells

Aperture	Opening of shell through which animal extrudes and retracts itself
Apex	The tip of the shell
Body whorl	The last whorl, usually the longest and largest
Callus	Calcareous deposit, sometimes thick, at the base of the columella near the shell aperture

Carinate	Keeled or ridged
Columella	The internal axial column around which the whorls are coiled
Concentric	With circular growth lines revolving around a central point (relative to opercula)
Corneous	Hornlike, as are the opercula of some snails
Costate	With riblike ridges
Dentate	Possessing teeth on parietal wall at aperture
Depressed	Flattened, as are the spires of some shells
Dextral	Right-hand shell
Discoidal	Round and flat like a disc
Edentate	Shell without teeth at aperture
Epiphragm	A hardened mucous covering that seals off the aperture in terrestrial and some freshwater snails for protection against desiccation
Globose	Spherical or subspherical in shape
Imperforate	Shell in which the umbilicus is closed
Lamellae	Calcareous barriers inside the shell of some planorbids, for example *Segmentina*
Lip	Edge of the aperture; also known as the peristome
Lirate	A shell with raised spiral lines or ridges on its surface
Multispiral	An operculum with many spirals or whorls
Nuclear whorls	Terminal part of the spire is the embryonic shell that the snail possesses when it hatches; also see protoconch
Operculum	"Trapdoor" attached to foot of some snails; it closes the aperture when the animal withdraws into shell
Operculates	Snails with operculum
Ovately conic	Shell oval, but with a somewhat conical spire
Parietal wall	Lateral side of body whorl at aperture
Patelliform	Caplike or limpet-shaped; with flattened out cone
Paucispiral	Operculum with few rapidly enlarging whorls
Penultimate whorl	The whorl next to the last whorl
Periostracum	The epidermal horny layer of a shell
Peristome	The entire lip of the aperture
Plait	A fold on the columella
Plicate	Folded, costate
Protoconch	Embryonic shell; also known as nuclear whorls
Reflexed	Bent backward; also described as reflected, for example, the lip in some snails
Sculpture	Surface impressions on a shell
Sinistral	Left-hand shell, that is, aperture is on left if the shell is held with apex upright and aperture facing examiner
Spire	That part of the shell from above aperture to apex
Subcarinate	Moderately carinate
Subcentral	Not quite in the center
Subconical	Moderately conical
Suture	The line where one whorl of the shell makes contact with another
Tortuous	Twisted or winding
Truncate	Having the end cut off, for example, the columella
Tuberculate	Covered with tubercles or rounded knobs
Turrete	Towerlike

Umbilicus	Basal end of columella
Umbilicate	Having an umbilical opening, which is moderate to wide
Whorl	One complete revolution around shell axis; counting of whorls starts at apex and proceeds to shell aperture

THE ANIMAL (SOFT PARTS)

As an introduction to the anatomy of the animal, study the anatomy of a planorbid snail, specifically that of *Biomphalaria*.

Procedure for Dissection and Study of Gross Structures

The animal is firmly connected to its shell by a tendonlike columellar muscle. An animal that has been relaxed prior to fixation can sometimes be pulled out of the shell. It can also be pulled out easily if it is first killed in hot water. An alternative is to dissolve the shell by placing the snail in either hot Bouin's or alcohol–formalin–acetic acid fixative for an hour. The shell can also be removed by breaking it into small pieces. The best procedure for doing this is as follows: by using a needle make fine holes a few millimeters apart along the sutures of both sides starting at either the aperture or the nuclear whorl. Be careful not to pierce the animal within. Remove the pieces of shell between each two holes with a pair of forceps. Place the animal in either water or 30% ethanol and examine it from the left side (Fig. 2-8).

Planorbid snails show the divisions of the gastropod body—a head, a foot, a pallial region, and a visceral mass. The head and foot are fused to form a somewhat triangular head–foot region or mass. The pallial region is enclosed in a membranous, partly pigmented mantle, which has a thick fleshy flap, the mantle collar, along the edge of the shell aperture. This collar is attached to the columellar muscle. On the left side, the mantle collar embraces the "neck" and pseudobranch of the snail. The latter is a conspicuous structure that functions as a gill in that it permits the animal to utilize the oxygen dissolved in the water. The visceral mass is enclosed in a transparent nonpigmented tunica propria, which is an extension of the mantle.

A pair of tentacles, with an eye at the base of each, protrude from the upper surface of the head–foot region. Situated near the base of the left tentacle is the male genital aperture. Lift the pseudobranch and observe the female genital aperture. Notice the mouth opening on the anteroventral surface of the head–foot region. It is surrounded by a jaw comprised of three brown horny plates, one upper and two laterals. A small opening, the pneumostome, is situated in the region of the mantle collar near the pseudobranch, and it is connected with the pulmonary cavity (or lung). The anus is also situated in this region. Although the mantle is pigmented above the pulmonary cavity, the internal organs are still visible as depicted in Fig. 2-8.

To open the animal, rupture the mantle with a pair of forceps in the region of the mantle collar, where it is attached to the columellar muscle. Fold the mantle back. The pulmonary cavity is now exposed. Notice the kidney adhering to the roof of the mantle and extending distal to the pericardium. The pericardium envelops the heart, which is situated on the right side of the animal and consists of an auricle (or atrium) and a ventricle. The kidney is connected anteriorly* with a short, thick, tubular ureter, which curves on itself and opens into the respiratory cavity near the mantle collar.

On the ventral surface of the pulmonary cavity can be seen the male and female genital tracts and the esophagus lying adjacent to one another. Trace these structures as they extend to the region of the posterior end of the lung. Also observable on the ventral surface of the pulmonary cavity is the rectum, which is directly above the columellar muscle. Notice the ridge above the rectum. Trace the rectum to its anterior end, which is the anal pore, situated at the base of the pseudobranch.

Remove the pseudobranch to expose the female genital pore. Clean the epidermal tissues in this region to expose the vas deferens. Make an incision close to the middorsal line of the head and locate the penial complex, which leads anteriorly to the male genital pore located at the base of the left tentacle. Trace the vas deferens and note the V-shaped loop that it forms before joining the penial complex. Carefully detach the penial muscles from the surrounding tissues. Locate the buccal mass, which encloses a radular ribbon; the elongated and fringed salivary glands, which are connected to the buccal mass at its junction with the esophagus; and a ring of nerve ganglia (eleven in number) joined together by circumesophageal commissures. These eleven ganglia include two cerebral, two buccal, two pedal, two pleural, two visceral, and one abdominal ganglia. Nerves projecting from these ganglia supply the various organs of the body.

Turning now to the distal portion of the animal, remove the enveloping tunica propria and connective and muscular tissues to expose the stomach and the intestine. The stomach consists of a crop, receiving the esophagus, a large muscular gizzard, and a pylorus. The intestine emerges from the pylorus, curves around the stomach, and then passes through the concavity of a cup-shaped gland, the albumin gland, and continues posteriorly as a loop through a large, tubular digestive gland (also known as the liver or hepatopancreas). The intestine then proceeds forward on the left side of the animal, located close to the columellar muscle. Also found in the distal portion of the animal is an ovotestis, or hermaphroditic gland, comprised of several follicles, or acini, situated at the terminal of the spiraled body. A herma-

---

*Proximal and distal or anterior and posterior are in relation to the head–foot region.

phroditic duct, with seminal vesicles, extends between the ovotestis and genital tracts. Carefully remove a part of the digestive gland to expose this duct. Having completed the dissection to this point, make a labeled sketch of your dissected animal (Fig. 2-9) (also see Malek, 1955).

The genital tracts, both male and female, are situated adjacent to each other above the columellar muscle and are both parallel to the esophagus. Separate the genital tracts from the esophagus by removing the connective tissue and membranes that hold them together. Also remove the digestive gland tubules covering parts of the ovotestis and free the penial complex from the head–foot region. The genitalia with its three portions, that is, the ovotestis and hermaphroditic duct, the genital tracts, and the penial complex and vas deferens, is now exposed and free.

Make a labeled sketch of the genitalia and note that the sperm duct arises as a bifurcation of the hermaphroditic duct. After receiving secretion from the prostate gland, it becomes the vas deferens, which joins the penial complex. In the female tract the oviduct arises as a bifurcation of the hermaphroditic duct, leads to a uterus that adheres to the prostate gland, and continues as the vagina, which opens at the female genital aperature. There is a globular spermatheca whose duct opens into the vagina.

The radular ribbon is enclosed in a radular sac situated within the muscular buccal mass. It is a membranous ribbon with a large number of transverse rows of teeth that overlap. The central tooth, or rachidian, is bicuspid in members of the family Planorbidae, and there is a series of duplicating teeth on each side of the central tooth (Fig. 14-7). Note the division on each side of the central tooth into laterals, intermediates, marginals, and outer marginals. The lateral tooth is tricuspid. The three daggerlike cusps are in the form of an inner short endocone, a large median mesocone, and a small outer ectocone.

The intermediate teeth are located between the typical laterals and marginals. The ectocone and endocone may show some splitting in the intermediate teeth, but this splitting is more obvious on the marginals. The mesocone is unsplit or it may be split on the outer marginals.

The radular formula of *Biomphalaria* is expressed as 24–1–24, which means that in each transverse row there are 24 teeth on each side of the central tooth.

Characteristics of Importance in Taxonomy

Different features in different regions of the gastropod's body are of taxonomic importance. Specifically, in the head–foot region, the texture of body surface, the position of the eyes, the shape of the tentacles, and the structure of the radula serve as taxonomic characteristics. In the pallial region, the mantle edge, the pseudobranch, the kidney, and the ridges on the

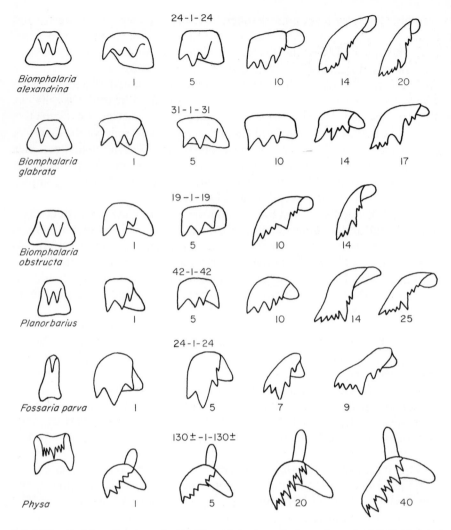

Fig. 14-7. Radulae of gastropods. (A) The radular formula for each species is indicated, and the central tooth, representatives of the laterals, marginals, and outer marginals of the right side of a row are shown. The number indicates the tooth number.

kidney and rectum are of taxonomic significance; and in the visceral region, the morphology of various parts of the digestive system and genitalia serves this function.

Presented below are the major features of each of the three regions of gastropods that are employed as taxonomic criteria.

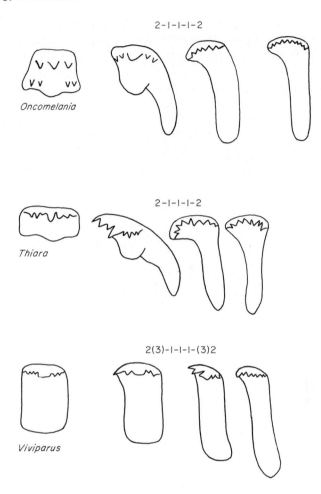

Fig. 14-7. (B) In the case of *Oncomelania*, *Thiara*, and *Viviparus* the single lateral and the two marginals of the right side are shown. After Malek (1962).

Head–Foot Region. The surface of the body of terrestrial snails is covered with scales while that of aquatic species is smooth.

EYES. The eyes are located on the tips of the posterior pair of tentacles in land snails and at the base of the single pair of tentacles in freshwater snails.

TENTACLES. The tentacles are long, filiform, and cylindrical (round in cross section) in members of the Planorbidae, Physidae, and in many species of hydrobiids. Flattened triangular tentacles of medium length characterize the members of the family Lymnaeidae. Members of the family Ancylidae have short, blunt, and cylindrical tentacles. Members of the family Viviparidae have long and slender tentacles. In males of this family the right tentacle is shorter than the left and forms a sheath for the verge. Long, slender eyes carried on peduncles situated at the external base of the tentacles characterize members of the Neritidae.

RADULA (Fig. 14-7). The number, shape, size, and position of the cusps on the central, lateral, and marginal teeth are important taxonomic characteristics. In pulmonates the rows of teeth on the lingual ribbon may be V-shaped, as in members of the Physidae, or in a straight line as in the other families.

In members of the Planorbidae the central tooth is bicuspid, the lateral teeth are large and either bi- or tricuspid, and the marginals are long, narrow, and multicuspid or serrated. In members of the Lymnaeidae the central tooth is unicuspid, and in members of the Ancylidae the central tooth is uni- or bicuspid. In members of the Physidae the central tooth is multicuspid while the laterals and marginals are obliquely bent, comblike, and multicuspid, with a process at their external angle.

In members of the families of operculate snails the basal denticles on the central tooth are either present or absent. In members of the Hydrobiidae the central tooth is multicuspid, with basal denticles; the laterals are hatchet-shaped and multicuspid; and the marginals are slender and multicuspid. Members of the family Thiaridae have a small, central multicuspid, which is without basal denticles, and one lateral and two marginals each with few or many cusps.

Pallial Region. MANTLE EDGE. The mantle edge is plain and smooth in members of the Planorbidae, Lymnaeidae, Ancylidae, and Hydrobiidae. It is plain or with digitiform processes in members of the Physidae and Thiaridae.

PSEUDOBRANCH. The pseudobranch, which is present only in members of the Planorbidae and Ancylidae, may be simple, branched, or folded.

KIDNEY. In members of the Planorbidae the kidney is elongated and is as long as the respiratory cavity. The ureter is short and tubular, curving on itself, and it opens near the mantle collar. In members of the Lymnaeidae the kidney is large, wide, and pear-shaped, and the ureter proceeds directly forward without bending. Genera, subgenera, and species show such variations as the presence or the absence of a ridge of the ventral surface of the kidney. In *Bulinus (Physopsis)* a ridge is present while in *Bulinus (Bulinus)* it is absent. A ridge is present in *Biomphalaria glabrata*, absent or rudimentary in *B. nigricans (=B. tenagophila)*, and absent in other *Biomphalaria* spp. (Fig. 14-8) (Malek, 1969).

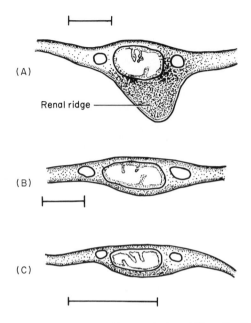

Fig. 14-8. Transverse sections through kidneys of planorbid snails. (A) *Biomphalaria gla-brata.* Note renal ridge. (B) *Biomphalaria alexandrina.* (C) *Biomphalaria obstructa.* Bars = 1 mm. After Malek (1962).

Genitalia. The operculates are dioecious while the pulmonates are hermaphroditic. Among the latter, the land snails (Stylommatophora) have male and female tracts that unite near their proximal ends and discharge ova and sperm through a common aperture. In freshwater snails (Basommato-phora) the male and female genital pores are separate. Apparently no males occur among the Thiaridae, and the females are parthenogenetic. Many are ovoviviparous and show variations of taxonomic significance in the positions and the shapes of their brood pouches (Fig. 14-9).

COPULATORY ORGAN. In members of the Hydrobiidae the verge, or penis, has a characteristic shape and a definite structure in each species. It may be simple exserted, for example, in *Oncomelania* and *Pomatiopsis*, bifid as in *Amnicola* and *Bulimus*, or with five or six small digitate processes as in *Littoridina* (Fig. 14-10).

Among the Basommatophora the following characteristics of the penial complex are of taxonomic value: the shape and relative size of the preputium and the vergic sac, the length and shape of the verge in specimens that had been relaxed before fixation, and the presence or absence of a stylet on the

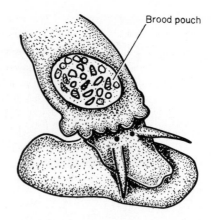

Fig. 14-9. Anterior portion of *Thiara* sp. showing brood pouch.

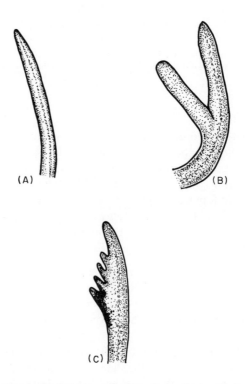

Fig. 14-10. Verge of some hydrobiid snails. (A) *Oncomelania*. (B) *Bulimus* (= *Bithynia*). (C) *Littoridina*. After Malek (1962).

verge. It is also taxonomically significant as to whether the verge is simple and filiform as in *Biomphalaria* or is coiled and inverted as an ultrapenis as in *Bulinus*. In addition, the presence or absence of flagella where the vas deferens joins the vergic sac; the number, shape, and arrangement of the penial muscles; and the presence or absence of a preputial gland and duct are of taxonomic importance. If present, examine the shape and size of the preputial gland and the length and position of its duct. If absent, examine the characteristics of the pilasters on the inner wall of the preputium (Fig. 14-11).

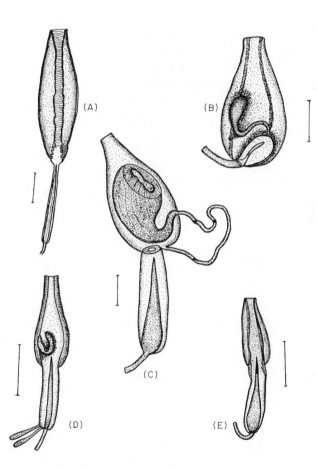

Fig. 14-11. Penial complexes of some planorbid snails. (A) *Biomphalaria glabrata*. (B) *Planorbarius corneus*. (C) *Helisoma trivolvis*. (D) *Segmentina hemisphaerula*. (E) *Gyraulus parvus*. Bars = 1 mm. After Malek (1962).

In *Biomphalaria*, the vergic sac is thinner than the preputium. Species of this genus show variations as to the relative length of both the preputium and vergic sac.

In *Segmentina* and *Hippeutis* there are two short flagella on the vergic sac, and in *Drepanotrema* there are usually two long flagella.

Members of the subfamily Helisomatinae have a well-developed, cup-shaped preputial gland from which a long duct extends. Such is the case in *Helisoma*, but in *Planorbarius* this gland is small, situated at the base of the preputium, and tapers into an appendage but is without a duct. In *Biomphalaria* there is no preputial gland, only pilasters occur (Malek, 1952b, 1954a, 1954b).

In *Gyraulus* there is a conspicuous stylet at the tip of the verge.

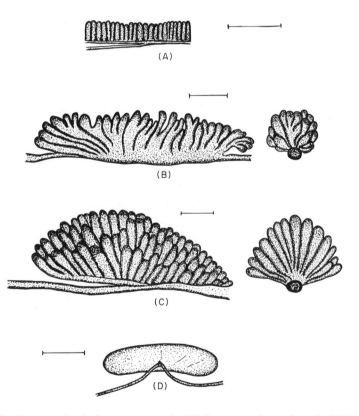

Fig. 14-12.   Prostate gland of some gastropods. (A) *Segmentina hemisphaerula*. (B) *Biomphalaria glabrata*. The figure on the right is a transverse section through the gland. (C) *Helisoma trivolvis*. The figure on the right is a transverse section through the gland. (D) *Pomatiopsis lapidaria*. Bars = 1 mm. After Malek (1962).

PROSTATE GLAND. In members of the Planorbidae the prostate gland may be multiply diverticulated, fan-shaped in cross section, and with a duct, as in *Helisoma* (Fig. 14-12). The prostate diverticula are simple sacs arranged in a single row along the prostate duct as in *Segmentina* and *Hippeutis*. However, in *Biomphalaria* the prostate diverticula are branched, and there is no prostate duct. Species of *Biomphalaria* show considerable variation as to the number and branching of the diverticula. In members of the Lymnaeidae the prostate is commonly bulbous and long; it may be ovate or cylindrical.

SPERM DUCT AND SEMINAL VESICLES. The length and shape of the sperm duct and the number of the seminal vesicles are of taxonomic value.

SEMINAL RECEPTACLE. The shape and size of the seminal receptacle and the length of its duct are also taxonomically important.

OVIDUCT. The length of the oviduct is of significance in taxonomy.

VAGINA. The vagina may be provided with a pouch that is visible externally. The surface of the vagina may be corrugated or it may be smooth.

The ratios of the length of the female tract (from the point of bifurcation of the hermaphroditic duct to the female opening) to oviduct, penial complex, hermaphroditic duct, spermathecal duct and sac, and prostate are of importance at the species and populational levels (Malek, 1969).

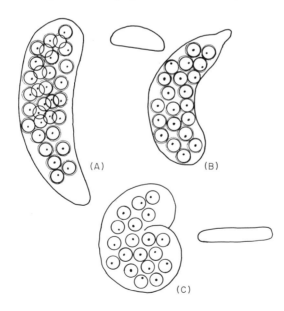

Fig. 14-13. Egg masses of some basommatophorans. (A) Lymnaeid. (B) Physid. (C) Planorbid. Outlines of cross sections are shown.

EGG MASSES (Fig. 14-13).   In members of the Lymnaeidae and Physidae the egg capsule is gelatinous, convex, elongate, cylindrical, and may be straight or somewhat curved. The eggs possess internal and external membranes and attached to each mass is a free terminal "tail." The egg mass is twisted to the left (counterclockwise) in the case of the Lymnaeidae and to the right (clockwise) in the case of the Physidae.

Egg masses deposited by planorbid and ancylid gastropods are firm, somewhat flattened, and portray spiral torsion. Furthermore, planorbid egg masses are markedly yellow and do not bear a free "tail." The eggs possess no external membranes.

Laboratory Exercise: Microanatomy of Organ Systems

This exercise is to acquaint the student with the normal histology of the organ systems of a snail. Such information is essential to the malacologist who intends to study pathological changes in parasitized snails or identify sites within snails where larval trematodes occur.

The reports of Baecker (1932), Malek (1952a,b, 1954a,b), and Pan (1958) on the normal histology of gastropods should be used as references during this exercise.

Serial cross and sagittal sections through the planorbid snails *Biomphalaria alexandrina* and/or *B. glabrata* will be provided by the instructor. To determine the interrelationship of the various organs refer to Figs. 2-7, 2-8, and 2-9.

Foot. The foot is surrounded by an epithelial layer of columnar cells. The goblet cells, which secrete mucus, are found beneath and intermingled with the columnar cells and communicate with the exterior via cytoplasmic ducts situated between the epithelial cells. The matrix of the foot consists of a large number of thin myofibers that are oriented in various directions throughout the dense vascular connective tissue.

Tentacles. When viewed in cross section, each tentacle is almost round, and it is enveloped by a layer of ciliated columnar epithelial cells. The core consists of connective tissue and myofibers, which are more dense near the base of the tentacle. In this core are embedded a nerve trunk and an artery. Pigment cells also occur in the core. Hemolymph sinuses occur in the zone between the core and the epithelial surface, and these are connected with the central artery.

Digestive system. Examine histological sections of the esophagus, intestine, and rectum and notice the general structure of the digestive tract. The architecture is generally the same throughout except for the sizes and shapes of the different segments of the alimentary tract. The lumen is lined with simple columnar epithelium resting on a basement membrane and is supported by two layers of myofibers: an inner longitudinal and an outer circular layer. The muscle layers are enveloped by connective tissue. Many of the lining columnar epithelial cells bear cilia. The cells include oval, chromatin-rich nuclei. Goblet cells embedded deep in the muscle layer secrete into the lumen via cytoplasmic ducts.

The crop and pylorus of the stomach are histologically similar and differ from the rest of the wall of the alimentary canal in possessing a conspicuous tunic of mesenchymal tissue and myofibers, the latter oriented in various directions in the mesenchyme. The wall of the gizzard is even richer in muscle tissue.

The digestive gland, also known as the "liver" or hepatopancreas, is a compound acinar gland that is connected to the alimentary tract by a duct that is connected with the latter at the junction of the intestine and the stomach. The acinar lobules of the digestive gland are separated from each other by a loose, vascular connective tissue, which also covers the entire gland and is continuous with that of the neighboring ovotestis. In some species this tunic of connective tissue is extremely thin or nonexistant, and, consequently, the digestive gland is almost directly enveloped by the tunica propria.

The cells comprising each acinus consist mainly of columnar digestive cells, which vary in shape according to their physiological condition. In addition, there are a few lime or calcium cells intermingled among the digestive cells. These calcium cells are usually pyramidal in shape, with the apex directed toward the lumen of the acinus (Fig. 2-10). Furthermore, calcium cells include small, spherical calcium spherites, which, according to Abolinš-Krogis (1963a,b), are comprised of calcium phosphate, ionic calcium, an acid mucopolysaccharide, RNA, xanthine, probably hypoxanthine and pteridines, lipids, and proteins. It is of interest to note that Abolinš-Krogis (1960) has demonstrated that the deposition of these spherites is increased if the mollusk is placed under stress, and Cheng (1971) has found that there is a similar increase in the number of calcium spherites in mollusks parasitized by larval trematodes, at least during the initial stages of parasitism.

Some investigators are of the opinion that a third type of cells, known as excretory cells, occur in the digestive gland acinus. These cells, characterized by the presence of large cytoplasmic vacuoles, are believed to be involved in the excretion of metabolic wastes. It remains doubtful, however, if the excretory cells actually constitute a distinct type of cell. They probably represent an alternate phase in the metabolic cycle of digestive cells. In fact, the generally held opinion at this time is that the cells of the digestive gland pass through a cycle of several phases including digestion, excretion, absorption, phagocytosis, and food storage.

Nerve ganglia. The center of each ganglion contains bundles of neurofibrils (Fig. 14-14). Ganglionic cells are located on the periphery except at

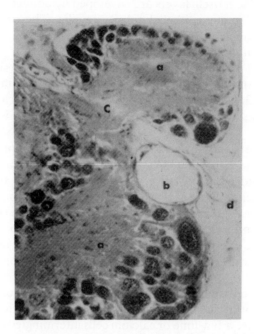

Fig. 14-14. Photomicrograph showing pedal ganglion and statocyst of *Biomphalaria glabrata*; a, ganglion; b, statocyst; c, commissure; d, epineurium. After Pan (1958).

the sites where a nerve fiber or a commissure arises from the ganglion. The ganglion is covered by a thin sheath called the "perineurium," outside of which there is a relatively thick layer, the epineurium, which contains arteries and hemolymph spaces.

Statocyst. This is a paired organ associated with each pedal ganglion. Its function is to maintain equilibrium. It consists of an outer connective tissue sheath, which is fused to the epineurium of the pedal ganglion, and an inner epithelial layer, in the form of a one-cell-thick membrane, lining the lumen. A statolith occurs in the lumen of each statocyst.

Osphradium. This olfactory organ is elongate, pear-shaped, and saccular. It is located at the junction of the mantle collar and the neck. The lumen of the organ is lined with a layer of tall, columnar epithelial cells which are covered with dense cilia.

Eye. In a histological section of the eye identify the following structures: optic capsule, cornea, retina, lens, vitreous humor, and optic nerve.

Heart. The heart of *Biomphalaria* is comprised of two chambers, an auricle and a ventricle. The wall of both chambers is muscular. The ventricular wall is thick while the auricular wall is thin. In both cases the myofibers are both longitudinally and circularly oriented, and those in the ventricular wall are branched and anastomosed. The heart is covered with a thin epicardium in the form of a continuous layer of small oval cells.

Circulatory system. The complete circulatory system of *Biomphalaria* spp. has yet to be elucidated, although the studies of Malek (1955), Basch (1969) and Pan (1971) on the circulatory system of *Biomphalaria* spp. have provided anatomical information. There are two aortic trunks that arise from the heart (Figs. 14-15, 14-16). The posterior aorta serves the intestine and digestive gland area and terminates as the gonadal artery in the ovotestis. The anterior aorta gives off the cecal axis, renal artery, and smaller vessels to the anterior reproductive glands and columellar muscle before terminating at the buccal vascular aborescence. From this point, near the circumeso-

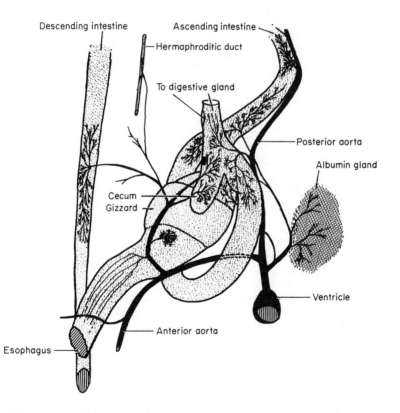

Fig. 14-15. A portion of the digestive system of *Biomphalaria glabrata* showing typical pattern of arterial distribution. After Basch (1969).

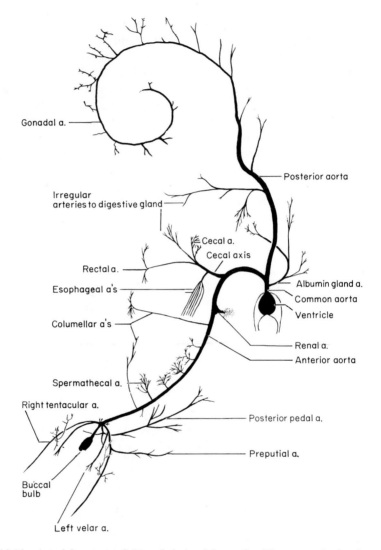

Fig. 14-16. Arterial system of *Biomphalaria glabrata*. Semidiagrammatic drawing of primary branches of the entire arterial system. After Basch (1969).

phageal ganglia, the buccal, pedal, and paired tentacular arteries arise and supply hemolymph to the head–foot region.

It is not possible to trace even the major portions of the arterial system of *B. glabrata* as a laboratory exercise; however, by studying the accompanying illustrations, the student should become familiar with this system.

Lung. The lung is enveloped by the mantle. The mantle is comprised of low columnar to cuboidal cells each with a rounded nucleus and brownish black cytoplasmic pigment. It is this pigmentation of the mantle surface covering the pulmonary cavity that can be observed through the shell. On the other hand, the tunica propria covering the digestive gland and the ovotestis is not pigmented and is made of flat or squamous epithelial cells.

The pulmonary cavity is lined with squamous epithelium but the cells may be cuboidal or even columnar. Between the mantle covering and the pulmonary epithelium there is a layer of vascular connective tissue.

Kidney. The kidney is situated dorsal to and slightly to the right of the pulmonary cavity. The epithelial portion of the kidney consists of columnar to cuboidal cells resting on a basement membrane, which, in turn, is supported by a layer of connective tissue and muscle fibers. Vacuoles are found in the epithelial kidney cells.

Ovotestis. The ovotestis consists of a large number of vesicles known as acini. Each acinus is enveloped in a sheath of squamous epithelium and thin connective tissue. Large vascular connective tissue cells lie between the acini and the covering tunica propria.

Larval trematodes commonly occur in this area and in a continuous and similar tissue around and between the digestive gland tubules.

In each acinus of the ovotestis there is a number of immature oocytes, a few mature ova, and bundles of sperm.

Female genital tract. The female tract is mostly glandular, consisting of the muciparus gland, the uterus, and the oöthecal gland. In the epithelium lining the cavity of the female tract there are, in addition to glandular cells, cells whose cilia move eggs down the tract or convey sperm upwards. At the base of the epithelium there is a thin layer of connective tissue and a few muscle fibers. In the wall of the vagina muscle fibers predominate.

Male genital tract. The sperm duct and the prostate are glandular but the vas deferens and the penial complex are muscular, and there are a few secretory cells intermingled among the myofibers. A section of the prostate or of the sperm duct will reveal the lining epithelium to be of secretory columnar cells with some nonsecretory cells intermingled among them. Peripheral to the lining epithelium is a thin layer of connective tissue and muscle fibers.

A cross section of the verge or of the vas deferens will reveal the circular outline and the lining epithelium of cuboidal ciliated cells. Peripheral to these cells is a tunic of longitudinally oriented muscle fibers.

The preputial cavity is H-shaped because of the presence of two longitudinal ridges known as pilasters. The wall is supported by bundles of longitudinal fibers separated by radial fibers.

Glossary of Anatomical Terms

Hemolymph (or blood) sinuses	Large sinuses or spaces that form part of the circulatory system (the open part of the system) where the hemolymph bathes the organs and tissues
Buccal mass	Heavily muscular structure containing the radular ribbon
Columellar muscle	A shiny elastic muscle by which the animal is attached to its shell
Digestive gland	A compound tubular gland, also called liver or hepatopancreas, which communicates with the alimentary tract via a duct connected at the junction of the stomach and the intestine
Ectocone	The outer cusp or cone on a tooth of a radula; it may be split into a few small cusps on marginal teeth
Endocone	The inner cusp or cone on a tooth of a radula, usually split on marginal teeth
Eye	Well-developed in pulmonates, comparable in structure to those of vertebrates; consisting of an optic capsule, cornea, retina, lens, vitreous humor, and optic nerve
Exserted	Brought out, as is the verge of members of the Hydrobiidae
Head–foot region	A triangular portion of the body consisting of the head and foot fused together
Heart	This major part of the circulatory system usually consists of a pear-shaped muscular ventricle and a thin-walled auricle, with a pair of muscular valves in between; these, together with an aorta and a few arteries and veins, constitute the closed part of the circulatory system
Hemolymph	The "blood" of mollusks
Mesocone	The middle cusp on a radular tooth
Ovotestis	Reproductive organ in hermaphroditic snails, producing both ova and sperm in compartments known as acini
Pallium	Mantle
Penial complex	In basommatophorans this complex consists of a verge inside a vergic sac, a preputium, and the penial muscles
Perineurium	Thin sheath surrounding a nerve ganglion
Pneumostome	Opening of the pulmonary cavity (lung) to the outside at the mantle collar
Preputium	Portion of penial complex opening at male genital aperture
Preputial gland	Gland inside the preputium of certain planorbids
Pseudobranch	An accessory gill developed in planorbids and ancylids to make use of oxygen in the water
Pulmonary cavity	Mantle cavity or lung in pulmonates
Rachidian tooth	Central tooth in each row of teeth on the radular ribbon
Radula	A lingual ribbon in the buccal mass for rasping food stuff, consists of several horizontal rows of teeth on a lingual membrane

Reno-pericardial canal	Passage between pericardial cavity and kidney
Tentacle	A tactile sensory organ that is richly innervated and very flexible
Verge	Penis or copulatory organ; enclosed in a vergic sac in the basommatophorans; naked in operculates
Vergic sac	Sheath enclosing verge and is continuous with preputium in basommatophorans

MORPHOLOGY OF A BIVALVE

Laboratory Exercise

The bivalves are of various shapes; they may be oval, elongate, sub-circular, quadrate, subtriangular, rhomboidal, or elliptical. The outer layer of the shell, or periostracum, exhibits various coloration. The two valves are quite securely attached to each other by means of an elastic hinge ligament.

Examine the exterior of each valve of a bivalve and notice the beak or umbo. This is the point at which growth begins in the young bivalve. The beak is surrounded by concentric lines, known as growth lines, which extend to the edge of the valve. The beak may portray fine, coarse, or tuberculated sculpture. Furthermore, it may be subcentral or subterminal in position. The outer surface of the valve may be either smooth, tuberculous, or in some cases even spiny.

Examine the inside of a valve and note the smooth, shiny nacreous layer which may be silvery, purple, or gray. Notice the hinge and the impressions of the animal on the shell. There are a series of projecting and interlocking hinge teeth in the form of the small, pseudocardinal teeth in the anterior part of the valve below the beak, and the long, narrow ridgelike lateral teeth in the posterior part. The impressions of the anterior and the posterior adductor muscles are obvious. In addition, there are scars of three foot muscles, the anterior retractor, the posterior retractor, and the protractor. The mantle is adhered to each valve and its lower edge forms a scar, known as the pallial line, on the inside of the valve.

Some anatomical features of a bivalve are shown in Figs. 3-1, 3-2, and 3-3. The foot is a hatchet- or ax-shaped muscular structure at the anterior end of the animal. An anal (or dorsal) and a branchial (or ventral) siphon are located at the posterior margin of the foot. There is no head, tentacles, eyes, or buccal mass. There are two long gills or ctenidia on each side of the animal, an outer and an inner. Note the muscles that leave their scars on the valves; namely, the posterior adductor, the posterior retractor, the anterior adductor, the posterior retractor, and the protractor. When the gills on one side are totally or partly removed, other structures become visible. These include the digestive gland, stomach, intestine, kidney, reproductive organs, and heart.

Family Unionidae.   In members of the family Unionidae the valves are large, smooth, course, or tuberculated. The beak sculpture is of fine or course concentric ridges, and the hinge has pseudocardinals, which may be vestigial or are totally absent. Lateral teeth are present. The sexes are separate although a few species are hermaphroditic. Representative genera of this family include *Anodonta, Anodontoides, Lasmigona, Gonidia, Fusconia, Elliptio, Lampsilis*, and *Eurynia*. Examine and draw a specimen of *Anodonta grandis*.

Family Corbiculidae.   *Corbicula* spp. have a wide distribution in Africa and Asia where they occur on the muddy bottoms of various types of bodies of water, especially creeks, ponds, and irrigation canals. *Corbicula fluminea* is a species that has been introduced into the United States. It occurs primarily in irrigation canals and reservoirs in Arizona, California, Washington, and a few other states. It is rapidly becoming established in the Mississippi River drainage.

Family Rangiidae (= Mactridae).   The members of this family are brackish water forms. Their shells are thick and of medium size. They are usually subtrigonal and with prominent beaks. The hinge is armed with cardinal and anterior and posterior lateral teeth. *Rangia cuneata* is a representative species which occurs in brackish waters of the Gulf of Mexico.

Family Sphaeriidae.   The Sphaeriidae consists of the finernail clams. The shell of these is thin, fragile, and small. Few are more than 10 mm in length and the concentric growth rings are not prominent. The cardinal teeth are minute, and the lateral teeth are present anterior and posterior to the cardinals. The species are hermaphroditic.

Key to Common Genera of Sphaeriidae

1. Beaks central or subcentral 2
   Beaks subterminal, shell inequilateral, anterior
        end of valves longer; usually about 7 mm,
        sometimes longer; two cardinal teeth in
        each valve ....*Pisidium*
2. Shoulders low, shell oval, thick, and
        with two cardinal teeth in the left
        valve, and one in the right; 7–15 mm long ....*Sphaerium* (Fig. 4–8w)
   Shoulders high; shell slightly smaller
        than that of *Sphaerium* ....*Musculium* (Fig. 4–8k)

Pisidium, Sphaerium, and *Musculium* are widely distributed in North America. The members of another genus, *Eupera*, for example, *E. singleyi*, occur in those states bordering the Gulf of Mexico. The shell is characteristically rhomboidal, often mottled, with one weak tooth in each valve.

TREMATODES THAT OCCUR IN BIVALVES

Generally, gorgoderid, allocreadiid, and gasterostome trematodes* utilize bivalves as first intermediate hosts. The following list includes a few representatives of the trematode families mentioned and their bivalve hosts.

Gorgoderidae (adults in amphibians): *Gorgodera amplicava* in *Musculium partumeium*; *Gorgoderina attenuata* in *Sphaerium occidentale*; *Phyllodistomum solidum* in *Pisidium abditum*; and *Phylodistomum staffordi* in *Musculium ryckholti*.

Allocreadiidae (adults in fish): *Crepidostomum cooperi, C. cornutum*, and *Megalogonia ictaluri* in *Musculium transversum*; *Crepidostomum metoecus* in *Pisidium* sp.; *Allocreadium isopora* in *Sphaerium* spp.; and *Bunoderella metteri* in *Pisidium idahoense*.

Bucephalidae (adults in fish): *Bucephalus elegans* in *Eurynia iris*; *Rhipidocotyle* (= *Bucephalus*) *papillosa* in *Elliptio dilatatus; Rhipidocotyle septpapillata* in *Lampsilis siliquoidea*; *Prosorhynchus uniporus* in *Crassostrea denselamellosa*; *Bucephaloides haimeana* in *Ostrea edulis* and *Cardium rusticum*; and *Bucephalopsis pusillum* in *Anodonta grandis*.

INFECTION OF MOLLUSKS WITH TREMATODES

The number of trematodes parasitic in man is small when compared with the very large number found in other vertebrates, both poikilotherms and homeotherms. It is the task of the malacologist working in places where human trematodes are endemic to be able to distinguish between those species infective to humans from those infective to other animals by examining the larval forms associated with mollusks. Although specific identification usually requires study by a helminthologist, the malacologist should be acquainted with the major groups of trematodes and their larval stages so as to be able to recognize those categories of trematodes that include human-infecting species. For this reason, the following laboratory exercises have been included to introduce the student of medical malacology to some basic aspects of trematode biology as related to mollusks.

Laboratory Exercise

Carefully wash the freshwater snails and bivalves that have either been provided or that you have collected in the field and sort them out by species. Isolate each species singly or in groups of five or six in bottles or fingerbowls about half filled with dechlorinated water. Expose the mollusks for a few

---

*For a general discussion of the various families of trematodes, see Dawes (1956) and Cheng (1973).

hours or overnight to a light source, for example, by placing the containers under a gooseneck lamp. After exposure to light, examine each bottle or fingerbowl with a dissection microscope. If you observe cercariae in any of the containers, isolate the mollusks, one in each bottle, to determine which mollusk or mollusks are infected. If the mollusks had been initially singly isolated this would not be necessary. Examine the emitted cercariae under the dissection microscope and note their swimming behavior, their reaction to light, and the flexure of the body and tail while swimming and when at rest.

In order to study cercarial morphology, remove a few cercariae from the water with a pipette, transfer them to a glass slide, and add a cover slip. The activity of the cercariae can be slowed down by either exerting a slight pressure when water is withdrawn from under the cover slip or by killing them by holding a lit match under the slide for a few seconds.

Weak aqueous dilutions (1:1000) of supravital stains introduced under the cover slip will reveal certain internal organs of the cercariae more clearly. Neutral red, methylene blue, or Nile blue sulfate are useful for this purpose.

Cercariae and sporocysts or rediae removed from infected mollusks can be fixed in warm Bouin's fluid (p. 367), preserved in 70% ethanol, and later stained. To obtain measurements, specimens are usually fixed in 10% formalin, although it is best to measure living specimens.

Not all infected mollusks will shed cercariae; therefore, in order to ascertain the percentage of infection, mollusks that do not shed cercariae should be gently crushed and the occurrence of sporocysts and/or rediae examined for under the dissection microscope. One disadvantage of this method as far as identification is concerned is that some of the cercariae obtained by this manner may be immature and are therefore unsuitable for identification.

For the examination of trematode infections in land snails, the shell is crushed, the broken shell fragments are removed, and pieces of tissues are examined microscopically. In the case of infection with *Leucochloridium* spp. in *Succinea* spp., the sausage-shaped branches of the sporocysts extend into the tentacles and are very obvious without microscopical examination (Fig. 14-17).

After having examined the various types of cercariae emitted from the mollusks, it may be a profitable experience to describe their movement and structure and to record whether they are produced within rediae or sporocysts. Furthermore, in order to appreciate the structure of rediae, sporocysts, and cercariae fully, make detailed drawings of these.

Types of Cercariae.   A variety of types of cercariae exist. A detailed description of the various types can be found in Cheng (1973). In order to give the student of medical malacology some idea of the types of cercariae

Fig. 14-17. *Leucochloridium macrostomum* in *Succinea*. (A) Anterior end of nonparasitized snail. (B) Parasitized and nonparasitized snail. Notice the swollen tentacles of the parasitized snail. (C) Sporocysts of *L. macrostomum* dissected from snail host. (D) Anterior end of parasitized snail showing tentacles distended by enclosed sporocysts. After Wickler (1968).

that may be encountered and some background relative to the biology of these cercariae, the following information is presented.

GYMNOCEPHALUS CERCARIAE (Fig. 14-18A). Cercariae belonging to this morphological group possess an oral and a ventral sucker. There is a tail, which is with or without a fin-fold. These cercariae are usually poor swimmers and are slightly positively phototactic. They develop in rediae, encyst in fishes, rarely in amphibians, or may encyst in the same snail in which the rediae occur, or on aquatic vegetation. Families of trematodes that possess gymnocephalus cercariae include the Heterophyidae, the adults of which are parasitic in the intestine of birds, mammals, and sometimes of man; the Opisthorchiidae, the adults of which occur in the gall bladder and bile ducts of reptiles, birds, mammals, and sometimes of man; and the Fasciolidae, the adults of which are parasitic in the livers and bile ducts of cattle, sheep, and sometimes man, for example, *Fasciola* spp.

MONOSTOME CERCARIAE (Fig. 14-18B). These cercariae are characterized by the possession of only one sucker, a small oral sucker, and the absence of a pharynx. There are two or three eyespots present. The cercarial tail is simple, very retractile, and is slightly longer than the body. Monostome cercariae

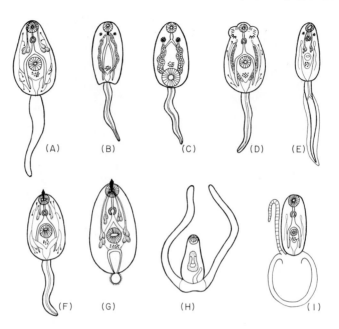

Fig. 14-18. Some types of cercariae. (A) Gymnophallid cercaria. (B) Monostome. (C) Amphistome. (D) Echinostome. (E) Pleurolophocercous cercaria. (F) Xiphidiocercaria. (G) Microcercous cercaria. (H) Gasterostome. (I) Cystophorous cercaria. After Malek (1962).

develop in rediae, encyst on snail shells, and on stones or vegetation. Examples of monostome cercariae include the cercaria of *Notocotylus seineti*, the adult of which occurs in the ceca of ducks. Other species of *Notocotylus* are parasitic in rodents and other mammals.

AMPHISTOME CERCARIAE (Fig. 14-18C).   This group of cercariae possess a large ventral sucker situated at the posterior margin of the body. The oral sucker is small, the body is large, and the tail is simple and globular, with refractile excretory concretions in the main excretory canals. They develop in rediae, encyst on aquatic vegetation, on the bottom of bodies of water, or on the skin of frogs. Examples of amphistome cercariae, which almost always possess eyespots, include the cercariae of *Paramphistomum* spp., parasites in the rumen of cattle; *Megalodiscus* spp., parasitic in the rectum of frogs; *Gastrodiscus aegyptiacus*, parasitic in the colon and cecum of equines in Africa and Asia (Malek, 1971); and *Allassostoma* spp., parasitic in the rectum of frogs and turtles.

ECHINOSTOME CERCARIAE (Fig. 14-18D).   This group of cercariae is characterized by the presence of a collar near the anterior end. This collar may or may not bear spines, although spines are usually present. These cercariae are usually good swimmers and possess long powerful tails. They develop in rediae with either a short or a long intestinal cecum and upon escaping, encyst as metacercariae in the same snail, or in another snail. They may also encyst in tadpoles or fishes. Adult echinostomes are usually intestinal parasites of birds and mammals, occasionally in man. Some species occur in their hosts' bile ducts. Representative species are *Echinostoma revolutum*, parasitic in the ceca and rectum of birds; *Echinoparyphium recurvatum* in the intestine of birds; *Echinochasmus* spp. in the intestine of mammals; and *Stephanoprora* spp. in birds (Beaver, 1937; Malek, 1952c).

XIPHIDIOCERCARIAE (Fig. 14-18F). These are the stylet-bearing cercariae. The various species share one characteristic in common, the occurrence of a stylet at the anterior margin of the oral sucker. These cercariae are poor swimmers, and are often found creeping or attached with their ventral suckers and lashing their tails in all directions.

Some species of xiphidiocercariae develop in rediae while others develop in sporocysts. Some examples of each of these two groups are presented below.

Cercariae developing in rediae:

1. Allocreadiidae. The cercariae of members of this family develop in rediae occurring in bivalve mollusks. The escaping cercariae encyst as metacercariae in insects and crayfish. The adult trematodes are intestinal parasites of fishes.

2. Troglotrematidae. The cercariae of members of this family develop in rediae occurring in operculate gastropods. The escaping cercariae encyst as metacercariae in fish, crabs, or crayfish. Adult troglotrematids are intestinal parasites of birds and mammals. The cercariae of troglotrematids are also known as microcercous cercariae because of their small, stumpy tail (Fig. 14-18G).

3. Microphallidae. The cercariae of members of this family develop in rediae in operculate gastropods but also occasionally in bivalves. The metacercariae generally are encysted in crustaceans, and the adults are intestinal parasites of birds and mammals.

Cercariae developing in sporocysts:

1. Microphallidae. The cercariae of some species of this family develop in sporocysts.

2. Lecithodendriidae. The cercariae of members of this family develop in sporocysts in pulmonate snails. The metacercariae are encysted in insects while the adult trematodes are intestinal parasites of birds and mammals, especially bats.

3. Plagiorchiidae. The cercariae of members of this family develop in

sporocysts in pulmonate snails while the metacercariae encyst in insects. Adult plagiorchiid trematodes are parasites of fishes, amphibians, reptiles, birds, and mammals.

4. Gorgoderidae. Gorgoderid cercariae develop in sporocysts in bivalves while the metacercariae encyst in insects, and the adults occur in amphibians. These cercariae are also known as cystocercous or gorgoderine cercariae because their tails form a cystlike chamber in which the body is enclosed (Fig. 14-18I).

5. Dicrocoeliidae. Dicrocoeliid cercariae, represented by that of *Dicrocoelium dendriticum*, develop in sporocysts in terrestrial gastropods. In the case of *D. dendriticum*, *Cionella lubrica* is the molluscan host in New

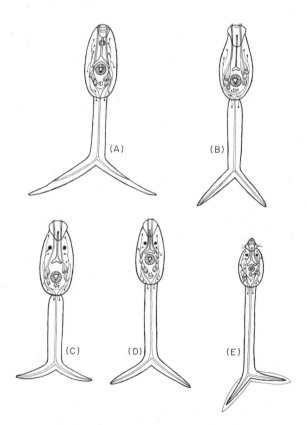

Fig. 14-19. Some furcocercous cercariae. (A) Strigeid. (B) Human-infecting schistosome cercaria. (C) Cercaria of *Schistosomatium douthitti*. (D) Cercaria of an avian schistosome. (E) Cercaria of a spirorchid trematode. After Malek (1962).

York State. The cercariae, escaping from sporocysts, are passed to the exterior in the mollusk's slime balls and are ingested by the second intermediate host, which is an ant. When ants harboring metacercariae are accidentally eaten by foraging sheep, the adult trematode eventually comes to lie within the bile duct and develops to maturity. In Europe the snail hosts are *Helicella ericetorum*, *H. candidula*, and *Zebrina detrita*.

FURCOCERCOUS CERCARIAE (Fig. 14-19). These are the forked-tail cercariae, that is, their long tails terminate as a bifurcation. These cercariae are generally distomate, that is, with two suckers, the anterior, oral sucker and the ventral acetabulum; however, the latter may be absent or only rudimentary. These cercariae usually develop in sparocysts. Several families of trematodes possess furcocercous cercariae, including the following.

1. Strigeidae. The strigeid cercariae (14-19A) are distomate, and a muscular pharynx is present. Their stout tails terminate as two elongate furcae. When these cercariae enter a suitable second intermediate host, they develop into encysted or nonencysted metacercariae. Encysted metacercariae, each known as a tetracotyle or a neascus, usually occur in the muscles of fish while unencysted metacercariae, each known as a diplostomulum, occur in the cranial cavity or eyes of fishes, amphibians, and reptiles.

Examples of strigeid trematodes are *Cotylurus communis*, a parasite of herring gulls; *Diplostomum flexicaudum*, a parasite of fish-eating birds; *Pharyngostomoides procyonis*, a parasite of raccoons; and *Prohemistomum vivax*, an intestinal parasite of dogs, cats, kites, and occasionally of humans.

2. Schistosomatidae. The cercariae of schistosomes can be distinguished from those of strigeids by the absence of a pharynx. The caudal furcae of schistosome cercariae are comparatively short, and their bodies are slender. Eyespots may be present or absent. Conspicuous pre- and postacetabular glands are present, and these are readily visible in stained specimens (Fig. 14–20).

All the adult schistosomes are blood flukes, and they occur primarily in birds and mammals. Those cercariae of avian schistosomes that bear eyespots belong to the genus *Trichobilharzia*; for example, the cercariae of *T. ocellata*, *T. stagnicolae*, and *T. physellae* (Fig. 14-19D). These species are among a fairly large group of avian schistosomes that can cause "swimmer's itch" or cercarial dermatitis in man. Other dermatitis-producing schistosome cercariae belong to the genera *Austrobilharzia* and *Gigantobilharzia*.

The cercariae of certain mammalian schistosomes also bear eyespots; for example, the cercariae of *Schistosomatium douthitti* (Fig. 14-19C) and *Heterobilharzia americana*. *Schistosomatium douthitti* is a blood parasite of muskrats, rabbits, and mice and utilizes *Lymnaea stagnalis*, *L. palustris*, *Stagnicola emarginata*, and *S. palustris* as the intermediate host. *Hetero-*

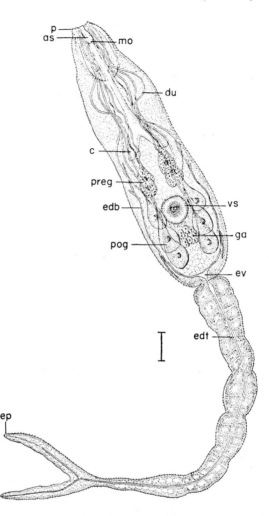

Fig. 14-20. Cercaria of *Schistosoma mansoni* showing internal structures including the pre-
and postacetabular glands. as, Anterior sucker; c, intestinal cecum; du, duct of postacetabular
gland; edb, excretory duct in body; edt, excretory duct in cercarial tail; ep, excretory pore;
ev, excretory vesicle; ga, genital anlagen; mo, mouth; p, papillae; pog, postacetabular gland;
preg, preacetabular gland; vs, ventral sucker. After Cheng and Bier (1972). Bar = 20 μm.

bilharzia americana is a blood parasite of the lynx and raccoon in North
America (Malek *et al.*, 1961; Malek, 1967, 1970).

The cercariae of the human-infecting schistosomes (Fig. 14-19B), for
example, *Schistosoma mansoni, S. japonicum*, and *S. haematobium*, do not
bear eyespots.

GASTEROSTOME CERCARIAE. (Fig. 14-18H). These are the cercariae of trematodes belonging to the family Bucephalidae. They develop in sporocysts parasitic in bivalves. The gasterostome cercariae are characterized by a midventrally situated mouth and a very short tail stem on which is attached two long furcae. The entire tail complex resembles the horns of an ox. Metacercariae developing from gasterostome cercariae are found encysted under the skin and in the nerves of certain fishes. Adult bucephalid trematodes are gastrointestinal parasites of carnivorous fishes.

CERCARIAEAE. These cercariae, the majority of which develop in sporocysts in terrestrial snails, lack a tail or only possess a rudimentary tail. An example is *Leucochloridium* spp., which in the snail *Succinea* spp., develops in sporocysts with sausage-shaped pulsating branches extending into distended tentacles of the snail (Fig. 14-17). Other members of Brachylaemidae have similar cercariae, for example, *Brachylaima virginianum*, the adult of which is an intestinal parasite of the opossum and armadillo and which utilizes *Mesodon thyroidus*, *Succinea* spp., and the slug *Deroceras laeve* as intermediate hosts.

OTHER TYPES OF CERCARIAE. In addition to the more common types of cercariae mentioned, there are additional ones. It is beyond the scope of this volume to present a comprehensive review of all the known cercarial types. Such information is more appropriate for a volume devoted to helminth parasitology. Interested individuals are referred to Cheng (1973).

HISTOPATHOLOGICAL CHANGES IN MOLLUSKS PARASITIZED BY TREMATODES

The known pathological alterations in mollusks due to parasitism by larval trematodes have been reviewed in Chapter 10. The following laboratory exercise is designed to acquaint the student with the more salient histopathological features of a gastropod infected with a larval trematode. More specifically, since most medical malacologists are interested in the relationship between the human-infecting schistosomes and their molluscan hosts, the histopathological change in *Biomphalaria glabrata* infected with *Schistosoma mansoni* is to be examined. For a detailed account of this topic see Pan (1965).

Laboratory Exercise

Examine histological sections of *Biomphalaria glabrata* (or *B. alexandrina*) infected with the larval stages of *Schistosoma mansoni*. If the snail had been infected by miracidia less than 12 days before it was fixed, then one would expect to find sections of mother sporocysts in the head–foot region (Fig. 14-21). Furthermore, if the strain of *S. mansoni* used to infect the snails was

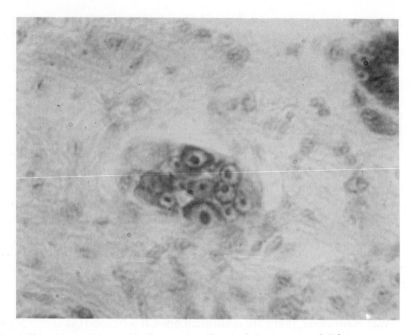

Fig. 14-21. Photomicrograph of a section of a mother sporocyst of *Schistosoma mansoni* in the head–foot region of *Biomphalaria glabrata*. The snail had been infected for 2 days (× 800).

a compatible one, one would not expect to find any host cellular reactions directed at the mother sporocysts. However, there is usually some displacement of the myofibers in the immediate proximity of these sporocysts.

If the snail had been infected for more than 12 days at the time it was fixed, one would expect to find daughter sporocysts of *S. mansoni* concentrated in the region of the digestive gland and to some extent in the region of the ovotestis, but they may be also present in the various anteriorly situated organs. They do not invade the tubules of the digestive gland and, unlike the redial stages of some other species of trematodes, they usually do not invade the acini of the ovotestis (Malek, 1955, 1958a). As a result of the infection, there is a heavy production and accumulation of excretory granules, calcium spherites, and lipid globules in the cells of the digestive gland and a concurrent proliferation of interlobular connective tissue.

Note that there are usually several cercariae in the region of the ovotestis and digestive gland, in the blood sinuses in the region of the esophagus, in the genital tracts, and especially in the perirectal sinuses. These cercariae are en route to the head–foot and mantle collar regions from which they make their way out of the snail into the water.

Examine sections of *B. glabrata* infected with sporocysts of *S. mansoni* that had been treated with the periodic acid-Schiff (PAS) reaction. Notice the lesser amount of PAS-positive (and diastase labile) granules in the cells of the digestive gland. This PAS-positive material is glycogen, and the presence of parasites causes a gradual depletion of this polysaccharide.

In addition to histopathological changes in *B. glabrata* caused by mother and daughter sporocysts of *S. mansoni*, there are also minor disruptions due to penetration by miracidia. If sections of penetrating miracidia are available, examine the sites of entry and attempt to identify alterations in the host's tissue. Figure 2-9 depicts the sites of miracidial penetration, the route of migration of daughter sporocysts to posterior portions of the snail, and that of the cercariae toward the sites of emergence from the snail.

ESTABLISHING TREMATODE LIFE CYCLES IN THE LABORATORY

Laboratory Rearing of Medically and Economically Important Snails

FRESHWATER SNAILS

Aquaria

The most convenient type of aquarium to use is a commercially available glass one. In setting up an aquarium, a mixture of washed sand and gravel with a little silt is placed at the bottom to occupy about one-half an inch on the bottom of the aquarium. This substrate, however, is not absolutely necessary. The aquarium is filled with dechlorinated water, covered with a glass plate, and left for a few days, after which the water is changed. Broad-leafed, rooted aquatic vegetation and floating aquatic vegetation can be placed in the aquarium. These aid in the oxygenation and removal of carbon dioxide in the water and provide a surface on which the snails can crawl and deposit their eggs. Again, however, such vegetation is not necessary if the water is changed once every two weeks. Compressed air may be piped into the water after being filtered by passing through glass wool and charcoal. Fluorescent lights are reflected over the aquaria, and algae are introduced. If substrate, vegetation, aeration, and lighting are provided, a balanced condition in the aquarium is usually attained after a few weeks, and the snails can then be placed into it.

Various other types of containers can also serve as aquaria. Enamel trays or dishes, 2 to 5 inches deep, or enamel or plastic refrigerator vegetable trays make good aquaria when aeration is supplied and adequate food is present.

Snail feces and waste food should be removed by aspiration whenever they accumulate in large quantities. In addition to enamel trays, glass jars or even large beakers are suitable for maintaining snails, including *Biomphalaria* spp. and *Bulinus* spp., and aeration from pumps is not absolutely necessary if the area of the water–air interface is sufficiently large. The only containers that are unsuitable are metal ones that give off heavy metal ions, which are lethal to most snails, and paper containers because of their temporary nature.

Temperature

It is important to remember that snails being maintained in the laboratory must be kept at temperatures essentially equal to those occurring in their natural habitats. Thus, *Biomphalaria* spp. are most satisfactorily maintained at 25°–27°C. Although specimens maintained at lower temperatures may survive, they usually do not lay eggs. On the other hand, the maintenance of even tropical and subtropical species at temperatures above 29°–30°C usually leads to premature death.

Water

If tap water is to be used in maintaining snails, it must be dechlorinated. This can be accomplished by either letting tap water "age" for a week or two in an uncovered large storage container or by passing the water from the tap directly through a column of sand and activated charcoal.

In areas where the quantity of inorganic salts is low in the municipal water, addition of the Nolan–Carriker salt mixture is necessary. This mixture includes:

Calcium carbonate	50 g
Magnesium carbonate	5 g
Sodium chloride	5 g
Potassium chloride	1 g

This mixture is added to 3 liters of water to make up the stock solution. When used, 120 ml of this stock solution is added to 20 gallons of aquarium water.

Snail Food

Snails feed on microflora, primarily algae that accumulate on the aquarium wall, and on other types of vegetation. A supplemental diet, however, is necessary if a large number of snails are reared. Tree-dried leaves (maple or mango leaves can be used) that have been soaked for about 2 weeks in water to get rid of the tannic acid can be used as a supplement. Fresh crisp lettuce or boiled lettuce is eaten readily by the snails and is the diet commonly used in research laboratories. Dried and powdered lettuce is ideal for young snails.

When large colonies of snails are maintained and large numbers of progeny are needed, another diet richer in its nutritional components has been recommended (Standen, 1951). The formula of this diet is as follows:

    Cerophyl (dehydrated cereal grass leaves.
        Cerophyl Laboratories, Inc., Kansas City,
        Missouri) .... 10 g
    Powdered whole milk .... 2.5 g
    Powdered wheat germ .... 5 g
    Sodium alginate .... 5 g

The diet as originally made contained powdered dry lettuce instead of the Cerophyl.

These ingredients are homogenized in a Waring blender in 500 ml of water at 50°C. When the homogenized viscous liquid is placed into a 2-liter suction flask and is forced by compressed air into a cold 2% calcium chloride solution in an enamel tray, a continuous strand of insoluble calcium alginate food is formed. The food is then washed in running tap water and can be frozen and stored until needed.

If the above ingredients are not available, a simpler diet consisting of cooked wheat cereal served on cork floats increased considerably the egg-laying capacity of *Biomphalaria alexandrina* when compared to lettuce (Malek, 1952a). However, the water in the container needs to be changed often.

Recently, Mecham and Holliman (1972) have recommended Purina Rat Chow® (Ralston Purina Co., St. Louis, Missouri) as a diet for *Biomphalaria glabrata*. The pellets are fed whole, and, reportedly, snails maintained on this diet grow faster. Snails maintained on this diet tend to deposit more eggs.

AMPHIBIOUS SNAILS

For maintaining amphibious snails such as *Oncomelania* spp., *Pomatiopsis* spp., and *Fossaria* (= *Lymnaea*) *truncatula*, the containers are designed so as to provide a terrestrial habitat at one end, or in the center, sloping down to an aquatic habitat. Such containers are of various types of which the two most popular are described below.

Clay Saucers

Saucers about 5 inches or larger in diameter and 1.5 inches deep can be used. The terrestrial portion is constructed of a mixture of soil, sand, and a few pebbles or crushed bricks. Glass lids are used as covers. The saucers are then placed inside a large glass dish or an enamel tray. About 1 inch of water is added into the glass dish or tray. Algae will grow on the rough, inner surface of the saucers, especially when light is reflected on the containers day and night.

Glass petri dishes are also used to maintain *Oncomelania* spp. (van der Schalie and Davis, 1968).

Glass Aquaria

Glass aquaria similar to those used for the freshwater snails can also be used. The soil used to provide the terrestrial habitat should be a sandy loam with decaying vegetation. Continuous aeration may be provided to the aqueous portion of the aquaterrarium. A glass plate is placed on top, leaving a small passage for the aerator tube. There is usually enough moisture in such an aquaterrarium.

Snail Food

One or more of the following supplementary diets can be given to the snails in clay saucers or aquaterraria: maple leaves, powdered rice, Standen's (1951) diet described earlier, alginate, and filter paper.

For maintaining *Fossaria truncatula* (=*Lymnaea truncatula*) and *L. tomentosa*, both intermediate hosts of *Fasciola hepatica*, the following diet is recommended as a supplement to lettuce and algae:

> Purina guinea pig chow (mortar ground) . . . .   1 g
> Wheat germ (mortar ground) . . . .   1 g
> Calcium sulfate   . . . . 0.6 g
> (Mix the ingredients and pass through a 40-mesh sieve. This supplement is added to the container at one-half a teaspoon full per week).

TERRESTRIAL SNAILS

Terrestrial snails and slugs can be reared effectively in aquaterraria with about an inch of moist mud covered with moss and moist dead leaves as the substrate. The snails and slugs can be fed on lettuce in addition to the leaves.

For rearing *Achatina fulica*, a common intermediate host for *Angiostrongylus cantonensis*, and other achatinids, a large plastic garbage can containing moist soil overlaid with dried leaves is recommended. This substrate is moistened periodically, and the snails will forge on practically any type of vegetable scraps.

MARINE SNAILS

Marine snails can be raised effectively in the laboratory. *Batillaria minima*, the intermediate host of the avian schistosome *Ornithobilharzia canaliculata*, has been reared successfully in enamel pans containing seawater changed at monthly intervals. Sticks of blackboard chalk are added, and the water is aerated with compressed air passed through air stones. The snails are fed bits of frozen shrimp, fresh yeast, baker's yeast, and Vita-Min bricks in 4-inch fingerbowls about twice weekly.

Another marine gastropod, *Nassarius obsoletus*, the molluscan host for *Austrobilharzia variglandis*, another cercarial dermatitis-causing avian schistosome, can be successfully maintained in Instant Ocean ® aquaria maintained at 22°C, with a salinity of 30–31‰. The snails are fed frozen turbot or fresh oysters ad libidum (Hoskin and Cheng, 1973). This method is suitable for most carnivorous mollusks.

For the maintenace of economically important marine mollusks such as clams and oysters, the procedures described in Chapter 12 should be consulted.

Procedure for Infecting Snails and Mammals

In experimental studies on schistosomiasis, fascioliasis, and certain other helminthic diseases, it is usually necessary not only to maintain the causative parasites in the laboratory by sustaining the various life cycle stages *in vivo* in compatible hosts but also to experimentally infect the hosts. In this section the procedures for infecting both molluscan and mammalian hosts of schistosomes, especially *Schistosoma mansoni*, are presented.

Laboratory Exercise (Obtaining Miracidia)

Eggs of *Schistosoma mansoni* are readily obtained from the livers and to some extent the intestines of white mice that had been exposed to cercariae. The prepatent period, that is, the time interval between entry of cercariae and the recovering of viable eggs, in the case of mice infected with *S. mansoni* is approximately 45 days.

Remove the livers from one to four infected mice and homogenize them for 20–30 seconds in 10 ml of a 0.85% NaCl solution in a Waring blender. Since salt inhibits the hatching of miracidia from the eggs, the liver homogenates should not be exposed to salt crystals or high concentrations of saline. Pour the homogenate into a flask (preferably a Pilsner glass) and allow to settle for 10–20 minutes, after which carefully pour off the supernatant. The eggs are in the sediment.

Repeat washing the sediment two or three times by adding 0.85% NaCl solution, mixing, allowing the material to settle for 10–20 minutes, and decanting the supernatant. By this time the supernatant should be fairly clear.

Rinse the sediment into a 1-liter side-arm flask (Fig. 14-22) with dechlorinated water. If a side-arm flask in unavailable, use an Erlenmeyer

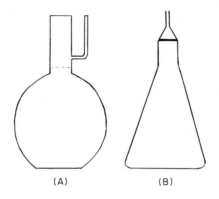

Fig. 14-22.   Flasks used to collect schistosome miracidia. (A) McMullen and Beaver side-arm flask. (B) Erlenmeyer flask.

flask. Fill the flask nearly to the top with dechlorinated water, and, after shaking vigorously, carefully fill it to the brim with water. Expose the flask to a gooseneck lamp for 5 minutes. This stimulus enhances the hatching of miracidia.

Cover the entire flask, except for the side arm, with a piece of black cloth. If an Erlenmeyer flask is used, cover the entire flask except for the top. Direct a bright light towards the uncovered portion. The negatively geotactic and positively phototactic behavior of the miracidia of *S. mansoni* will cause them to aggregate in the side arm about 15 minutes later. They can be removed from this site with a pipette and transferred to a small dish from which they can be used to infect snails.

After a few hours miracidia may cease to appear. When this happens, siphon off most of the water originally placed in the flask and replace it with freshwater as indicated before. Usually more eggs will hatch and miracidia will collect in the side arm.

In the case of the miracidia of *Schistosomatium douthitti* and *Hetero-bilharzia americana*, they can be effectively collected if the feces or liver homogenate of infected hosts are placed in an Erlenmeyer flask with an inverted small funnel placed on its mouth (Fig. 14-22B; unpublished studies by Malek).

Trematode eggs in the feces of laboratory vertebrate hosts can be concentrated by sedimentation. In endemic areas eggs can also be obtained from humans by sedimentation of urine in the case of *Schistosoma haematobium* or sedimentation of feces in the case of *S. mansoni* and *S. japonicum*. The sediment is then treated as presented above to obtain miracidia.

Laboratory Exercise (Infecting Snails with Miracidia)

Not all *Biomphalaria glabrata* are susceptible to *Schistosoma mansoni*. It has now been established that certain geographic strains of *B. glabrata* are refractory to certain strains of *S. mansoni*. Furthermore, there is at least one strain of *B. glabrata*, designated as the "juvenile susceptible" strain, which is only susceptible to *S. mansoni* during the juvenile period, becoming refractory when they become young adults. The physiological basis for this alteration in susceptibility remains undetermined.

Test the susceptibility of the strains of *B. glabrata* made available. In view of the above, also test their susceptibility at different ages by carrying out the following procedure.

Select ten snails of each of three size classes from the different strains. The first class should consist of snails measuring less than 5 mm in shell diameter (juveniles), the second class measuring from 7 to 10 mm in shell diameter (young adults), and the third class measuring approximately 15 mm in shell diameter. Place each snail with a little water in 2.5 cm (diameter) Stender dish or in a vial or glass cup about 10 mm in diameter and about 15 mm in depth. Place from four to five miracidia in the water with the snail. Snails can also be exposed to miracidia en masse by exposing from thirty to fifty to a large number of miracidia in a larger container. By observing under a dissection microscope, watch the reaction of the miracidia and the snail, and record your observations (Malek, 1950, 1958b, 1967).

Cover the containers to prevent the snails from crawling out and leave them for 4–5 hours. Place the exposed snails in a separate aquarium and mark the date and time of exposure to miracidia. Record the conditions under which the exposed snails are maintained, for example, temperature, pH of the water, and diet of the snails.

About 30 days postexposure to miracidia, start checking for the emergence of cercariae by isolating the snails in small bottles or Stendor dishes with water. Repeat the isolation every day, and when infected snails are identified, transfer them to a separate aquarium.

For establishing the life cycle of trematodes other than the schistosomes, it should be remembered that eggs of such trematodes as *Paragonimus*, *Fasciola*, *Fasciolopsis*, and certain amphistomes require an incubation period outside of a host during which the development of the miracidia occurs. The hatching of these eggs after the incubation period is influenced by a sudden change in the water temperature. Procedure for exposing the snail hosts to these miracidia is the same as described above for schistosomes. It is also possible in the case of amphibious snail hosts of *Paragonimus kellicotti* (and probably also those of *Schistosoma japonicum*) to allow the snails to feed on the fully developed eggs in feces on moist strips of filter paper as advocated by Beaver *et al.* (1964).

Laboratory Experiment (Infecting the Mammalian Host)

Various methods have been proposed for exposing laboratory animals to the schistosome cercariae depending on the intended experiment and the size of the host. The mammalian host is either bathed in water containing cercariae, or the animal may be restrained or anesthetized, and the cercariae, in a few drops of water, are placed on the shaved skin on gauze or in a glass or plastic ring. Another method is to expose the tail of a mouse by placing it in a narrow tube about 10 mm in diameter containing the cercariae in water.

For routine infections, the following is the most convenient and satisfactory method: Place from one to four mice or a hamster in a large fingerbowl of lukewarm tap water to stimulate defecation and urination. The animals should be covered to prevent escape, and the water level should just reach the animal's belly. After 10–15 minutes transfer the animals to a clean bowl and add 50–200 freshly emitted cercariae per animal in 100 ml of deionized or dechlorinated water. Allow the animals to be exposed to the cercariae for about 60 minutes.

Since schistosome cercariae are infective to humans, be sure to wear rubber gloves while infecting mice or hamsters and do not transfer cercariae by using a pipette by mouth. Use a bulb.

After the mice or hamsters have been infected, place them in a dry cage and feed as usual. Mature *Schistosoma mansoni* can be recovered from the mesenteric veins after 40 days, and eggs can be found in the feces.

LABORATORY TECHNIQUES

Shell Collection

To clean gastropod shells for a collection, extract the dead animal from the shell with a pair of forceps, preferably one with curved points. Place the shells in boiling water for half an hour. Carefully scrub the inside and outside of the shell with a soft brush, and permit them to air dry. In the case of operculate snails, retain the opercula as they are of importance in identification.

Keep the small, clean, dry shells in glass vials with cotton and the large ones in open cardboard boxes. Each specimen should be identified relative to species, collection locality, date, and collector's name.

In the case of large bivalves, such as oysters, a hard brush can be used to clean the exterior of the valves.

Fixation and Preservation

Infected and noninfected snails intended for histological studies can be directly fixed in either hot Bouin's fixative or Formalin–acetic acid–alcohol (FAA). The formulas for the preparation of these fixatives are as follows.

Bouin's Fixative (Fix for 24 Hours or Longer*)

Picric acid, saturated aqueous solution . . . . 75 ml
Formalin, concentrated . . . . 25 ml
Glacial acetic acid . . . . 5 ml

(After fixation in Bouin's, wash in 50% ethanol. The yellow color must be washed out before staining sections. Usually the color is removed in the alcohol series, but, if not, treat slides in 70% alcohol plus a few drops of saturated lithium carbonate until the color is extracted.)

Formalin-Acetic Acid-Alcohol Fixative (Fix for 3–24 Hours)

70% ethyl alcohol . . . . 100 ml
Formalin, concentrated . . . . 5 ml
Glacial acetic acid . . . . 5 ml

(After fixation in FAA, transfer to 85% ethanol.)

Since both Bouin's and the FAA fixatives include acetic acid, the mollusk's shell will be dissolved.

As an alternate method, the shell of the snail is gently cracked prior to fixation, and the fragments are removed with a pair of fine forceps after fixation under a dissection microscope.

In addition to the two fixatives presented above, a number of others may be used. Among these are Carnoy's, if cytological detail is desired, Newcomer's, and 10% neutral formalin. The formulas for Carnoy's and Newcomer's fixatives are as follows.

Carnoy's Fixative (Fix for 3–6 Hours)

Glacial acetic acid .... 10 ml
Chloroform .... 30 ml
Absolute ethyl alcohol .... 60 ml

(After fixation in Carnoy's, wash for 2–3 hours in absolute ethanol to remove the chloroform.)

---

*Several weeks of fixation will not cause damage.

Newcomber's Fixative (Fix for 6–18 Hours)

Isopropyl alcohol .... 60 ml
Proprionic acid .... 30 ml
Acetone .... 10 ml
Dioxane .... 10 ml

(After fixation in Newcomber's, the specimens must be washed in running tap water for approximately 6 hours.)

In the case of such large snails as *Achatina fulica*, *Viviparus malleatus*, and others that measure 2 cm or more in greatest diameter, special preparation prior to fixation is necessary. Specifically, such snails should be placed overnight in a refrigerator in aquarium water, and the next morning, after the shell is carefully pierced, they are fixed by injecting a previously cooled fixative into the heart. Alternatively, after the shell is quickly broken, the animal is immersed directly into the fixative. These methods are recommended to avoid the possible autolysis of tissues.

The presence of sand granules in the gizzard portion of the stomach causes a major problem in sectioning whole snails. To avoid this, before dehydrating and embedding in paraffin, a small incision (puncture) is made in the stomach wall, and the sand grains washed out.

Narcotization and Anesthetization

In several types of experiments on mollusks that involve implanting exogenous materials, tissue grafting, or injecting foreign materials, it is essential that the mollusk be anesthetized. Furthermore, it is necessary to relax mollusks, especially the larger species, prior to fixation for dissection. How a mollusk can be narcotized or anesthetized is, therefore, extremely important to malacologists. A comparison of the various procedures for doing this has been made by Runham *et al.* (1965). Narcotization is defined as the relaxation of the animal in as lifelike a position as possible and to such an extent that it does not contract when subjected to fixation. On the other hand, anesthetization is defined as the relaxation of the animal's muscles and extension of the animal so that various experimental procedures can be carried out and the animal can then be allowed to recover.

NARCOTIZATION

Although the use of freezing and Stovaine has been suggested for the narcotization of mollusks, these procedures are not recommended (Runham *et al.*, 1965).

Formalin is recommended for the narcotization of nudibranch gastropods. The exact technique involves placing the animal in 50 to 500 times its volume of seawater and allowing it to expand. When this has occurred, 3 drops of 1% formalin per 100 ml of seawater are added every 15 minutes for 1 hour and the amount of formalin is doubled every hour. When the animal becomes insensitive to probing, it can be fixed. This method does not work with freshwater gastropods.

Nembutal (sodium pentabarbitone) has been reported to be a very satisfactory narcotizing agent for pulmonates other than slugs. To use this compound, the snail is placed in a 0.08% solution of pure Nembutal and left to relax. Perfect relaxation is achieved between 12 and 55 hours, depending on the species. The only disadvantage is that there is a slight swelling of the animal; however, this swelling can be reduced by fixing the animal in hot formalin before complete relaxation occurs (van der Schalie, 1953).

Nembutal/propylene phenoxetol is an effective narcotizing agent for slugs. The animal is placed in a 0.08% Nembutal and 1% propylene phenoxetol aqueous solution for a few minutes, and this will cause it to relax. Although many specimens will have retracted tentacles when narcotized with this solution, this condition can be remedied by gently squeezing the head. After narcotizing with this solution, the specimen can be fixed with cold or hot formalin, although the latter is recommended.

A combination of Sevin (1-naphthyl N-methyl carbamate) and carbon dioxide is a useful general narcotizing agent for most gastropods but especially marine species. The procedure to be followed involves relaxing the mollusk for 1 hour in 10 ppm of Sevin in seawater (or freshwater in the case of freshwater species) followed by emersion for 3 hours in a fresh Sevin solution of the same concentration but saturated with carbon dioxide. Snails relaxed by this method will still contract to some extent when fixed; however, minimal retraction is attained if the specimens are placed on dry ice prior to fixation or by employing hot formalin as the fixative.

Propylene phenoxetol has been reported to be a satisfactory narcotizing agent for terrestrial and marine snails, slugs, and nudibranchs, although it is most effective for terrestrial pulmonates. This method involves the placing of a globule of propylene phenoxetol at the bottom of a container, and water (seawater or freshwater depending on the species) is added so that the narcotic constitutes less than 1% of the total volume. The mollusk is emersed in this solution and left overnight.

The use of menthol as a narcotizing agent for mollusks is an old practice. Snails to be relaxed are placed in a Stender or petri dish in water and powdered or crystalline menthol is sprinkled on the surface. The dish is then covered, and the animal is allowed to relax. The length of time required for total relaxation depends on the species. After the menthol treatment the snails can be fixed in formalin or 30% alcohol for dissection (Malek, 1951).

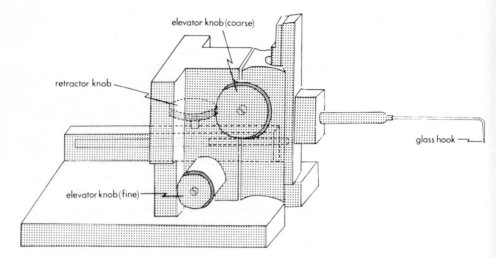

Fig. 14-23. Illustration of a microretractor used to extend anesthetized snails. After Cheng and Galloway (1970).

ANESTHETIZATION

Urethane is a suitable anesthetic for gastropods. We have used it successfully with *Biomphalaria glabrata* and *Helisoma duryi*, both pulmonates. Snails become relaxed when placed in a 0.5% or aqueous solution although a strong stimulus will cause contraction. Snails anesthetized with urethane can be subjected to retraction with a microretractor (Fig. 14-23) (after Cheng and Galloway, 1970).

In the case of *Helix pomatia* and possibly other species of large gastropods, the injection of 1 ml of a Ringer's solution saturated with either will cause the production of large quantities of mucus and retraction. However, in about 15 minutes the animal is sufficiently relaxed so that it can be pulled out of the aperture of the shell.

Nembutal is a recommended anesthetic for marine opisthobranchs. The animals are submerged in a solution containing 0.1 mg of Nembutal/ml of seawater. It takes about 20–30 minutes for the snails to relax.

Propylene phenoxetol can be used as an anesthetic for bivalves as well as slugs. The animal is placed in a 0.5–1% aqueous solution (seawater in the case of marine bivalves), and relaxation occurs in about 15 minutes.

Magnesium chloride is probably the most widely employed anesthetic for mollusks. The injection of a 10% aqueous solution will cause relaxation in 5–15 minutes. An alternative method suitable for marine operculates such as *Littorina* spp. and *Nucella* spp. is to place the animal in clean seawater, and slowly add a 20% magnesium chloride solution from a burette, the tip of which is submerged in the water. The amount of magnesium chloride solution added should not exceed a volume ratio of 1:10 of $MgCl_2$ solution to water. It usually takes 8 or more hours for total relaxation. To prevent the snails from crawling out of the water, the wall of the vessel is coated with the 20% $MgCl_2$ solution.

A rapid anesthetization method effective within 15 minutes with adult *Lymnaea stagnalis* was described by Lever *et al.* (1962). The substances used are: nitrogen gas to drive dissolved oxygen out of the water, Nembutal (0.1%), M.S. 222 (Sandoz), and carbon dioxide. For recovery the snails need only to be kept in tap water, preferably aerated. If maintained at 20° and 27°C, the snails regain normal behavior in 20 minutes to 2 hours.

Preparation of Permanent Mounts of Genitalia and Radulae
(after Dr. E. G. Berry, personal communication, 1949)

GENITALIA

The genitalia of gastropods can be measured and drawn with the specimen bathed in a 30% ethanol. If permanent preparations are desired, the following procedure should be followed.

1. Dissect out the genitalia.
2. Hydrate gradually via a graded series of ethyl alcohol.
3. Stain for at least 4 hours with Delafield's hematoxylin (see below for formula).
4. Wash in water and destain in a 2% aqueous solution of HCl until the color is light pink.
5. Dehydrate via a graded series of ethyl alcohol, clear in xylene, and mount in thick drop of mounting medium on a well-slide or an ordinary slide with a plastic or metal ring.

Delafield's Hematoxylin

Dissolve 4 g of hematoxylin in 25 ml of absolute ethyl alcohol. Mix gradually into 400 ml of a saturated aqueous solution of ammonia alum [$NH_4Al(SO_4)_2 \cdot 12H_2O$]. This solution is prepared by adding 1 part ammonia alum to 11 parts of distilled water. Expose the solution to light in a flask with a cotton plug for 3–5 days and then filter. Add 100 ml of glycerine and 100 ml of methyl alcohol to the filtrate and allow the stain to stand for at least 6 weeks before using. Delafield's hematoxylin will keep for years in a stoppered bottle.

RADULA

1. From the snail's head–foot region remove the buccal mass together with the jaws surrounding the mouth.
2. Transfer to a 10% solution of sodium or potassium hydroxide. It takes at least 1 day for all the tissues around the radular ribbon to be digested away. This procedure can be accelerated by placing the buccal mass in laundry bleach. If this is done, it takes only 15–30 minutes to recover the radular ribbon.
3. Wash the radula and jaws in water.
4. Stain with an aqueous solution of Orange G (see below for formula) for 1 hour (hematoxylin stains can also be used).
5. Wash in water and destain with a 2% aqueous solution of HCl.
6. Transfer the radula to a small drop of glycerine on a slide and with a fine brush clean the ribbon, especially the lower surface. The ribbon should then be flattened in the center of a glass slide with the teeth directed upwards.
7. Remove the glycerine with 95% ethyl alcohol.
8. Place the jaws on the same slide or on a separate slide.
9. Dehydrate with two successive changes of absolute alcohol on the slide, one drop each.
10. Clear the ribbon in a drop of xylene and mount in Canada balsam or some other medium.

Orange G Stain

Orange G	1 g
Distilled water	100 ml

Methods for Studying Molluscan Hemolymph

A review of what is known about molluscan hemolymph has been presented in Chapter 8. It should be apparent from that chapter that the understanding of several aspects of molluscan biology is dependent on information pertaining to the composition and function of the hemolymph. For this reason, the following laboratory exercises have been included to acquaint the reader with certain fundamental techniques.

HEMOLYMPH SMEARS

Smears of the hemolymph of mollusks are simple to prepare in the case of some species and extremely difficult in others.

In the case of the thin-shelled gastropods such as *Biomphalaria glabrata*, samples of hemolymph, including cells, can be obtained by inserting a 30 lambda capillary tube (Drummond Microcaps®) into the heart through the shell. This is especially simple if the NIH albino strain of *B. glabrata* is used. Alternatively, the capillary tube can be inserted into the cephalopedal sinus, but this may require prior anesthetizing, especially if the animal is to be kept alive.

In the case of the thick-shelled gastropods, a careful dissection of a few specimens will acquaint the investigator with the location of the heart. When this information is obtained, a minute hole can then be made over the heart with a dental drill, and a capillary can be inserted into the heart. Of course, hemolymph samples can also be obtained from the cephalopedal sinus.

If there is no need to keep the specimen alive, the easiest method of obtaining hemolymph is to crack the shell gently, making sure not to injure the underlying soft tissues, and to collect the hemolymph as it oozes from the sinuses in a tilted petri dish in which the snail had been placed.

If hemolymph samples are desired from bivalves, these can be obtained in several ways. One method is to remove the left valve by cutting the adductor muscles and then to use a syringe armed with a 26-gauge hypodermic needle inserted directly into the pulsating heart. A second method is to file a notch along the edge of both valves (Fig. 11-3), insert a hypodermic needle into the adductor muscle, and collect hemolymph from the sinus situated therein.

A third method, commonly used with oysters, is to file a hole over the heart and insert a hypodermic needle into it. Both the second and third methods are especially useful if the specimens are to be kept alive. In the case of the third method, the hole in the shell can be sealed with paraffin or a small piece of gauze saturated with nail polish after the hemolymph sample has been taken.

For fixing and staining hemolymph cells of mollusks, refer to Table 8-2.

AUTORADIOGRAPHIC TECHNIQUES

Autoradiographic techniques designed to determine the uptake and deposition of radioisotopes by mollusks are available for ^{65}Zn, ^{115M}Cd, ^{67}Cu, and ^{59}Fe. These are presented below.

^{65}Zn

According to Yager and Harry (1966) autoradiographs of *Biomphalaria glabrata* can be obtained by the following procedure. The snails are placed in distilled water for 24 hours prior to exposure. Subsequent to this, the snails are exposed individually in 100 ml of the dosing solution in polyethylene beakers. The dosing solution is prepared by mixing enough of the radioactive stock solution of ^{65}Zn as $ZnCl_2$ in HCl with distilled water to produce counts within a reasonable range. Specifically, suitable amounts are in the order of 0.25 $\mu c/ml$ of the dosing solution when a scintillation counter is used and of the order of 0.1 $\mu c/ml$ when a Geiger counter is used. The pH of the dosing solution is checked initially and, if necessary, adjusted to pH 4.5–6.0 (pH 5.5 is recommended) with NaOH. The ambient temperature should be 27°C.

After exposure for 24 hours, the shells of the snails are removed, the animals are fixed in 70% ethanol, embedded in paraffin, and sectioned at 10 μm. The sections are stretched by flotation on water and subsequently transferred to absolute ethanol. From the alcohol they are floated onto film (Eastman P426 fine-grain positive), pressed into it, and allowed to dry. They are then placed in a refrigerator at 5°C for the required exposure time, which is from 14 to 21 days. After exposure, the film is developed with Kodak D-19.

^{115M} Cd

The method for producing autoradiographs involving ^{115M}Cd is essentially the same as that for ^{65}Zn (Yager and Harry, 1966). The radioactive cadmium added to the dosing solution is in the form of $Cd(NO_3)_2$ in HND_3.

^{67}Cu

In unpublished studies by Cheng and Sullivan, satisfactory autoradiographs of *Biomphalaria glabrata* exposed to ^{67}Cu have been obtained. The method is as follows. A 6.5 ml sample of ^{67}Cu as $CuCl_2$ was diluted in 1000 ml of 1 ppm Cu as $CuSO_4$, and 0.5 ml of this dilution was further diluted in 1000 ml of a 1 ppm Cu as $CuSO_4$ solution. The snails are submerged into this final dilution (dosing solution), after having been maintained in deionized water for 24 hours at room temperature (22°C) during which they were fed lettuce. Exposure to ^{67}Cu was accomplished by placing the snails individually in small fingerbowls, each containing 10 ml of the dosing solution. It has been found that 8 and 10 hours of exposure gave the best results, although adequate autoradiographs can be obtained after 2, 4, and 6 hours of exposure.

The tissues of the exposed snails are routinely processed as histological sections, which are placed on glass slides, dipped in Kodak NTB-2 emulsion in the dark, and allowed to air dry for 1 hour. They are then placed in a black box and stored at 4°C for 21 hours, after which they are developed in Kodak D-19 developer and fixed in Kodak fixer.

[59]Fe

Lee and Cheng (1972) have reported satisfactory autoradiographs of *Biomphalaria glabrata* exposed to [59]Fe. By their method, snails that had been washed clean of extraneous material are exposed to ^{59}Fe in finger-bowls (11 cm diameter), five snails per bowl. This method ensures even uptake. Each bowl contains 100 ml of filtered dechlorinated tap water plus 0.4 $\mu c/ml$ of ^{59}Fe in the chloride form. After exposure for 12 hours during which the snails are permitted to feed ad libidum on lettuce, they are washed thoroughly and exsanguinated. The shells are gently crushed, and the specimens are fixed overnight in 10% neutral, buffered formalin. Subsequently, the shell fragments are removed, and the animals are washed, dehydrated in a graded alcohol series, and embedded in Paraplast. Sections cut at 4 μm are floated on scrupulously cleaned and "subbed" glass slides (Gude, 1968). The sections are then deparaffinized, hydrated, dipped in Kodak NTB-2 emulsion melted at 40°C, and air dried for 15 minutes. They are then stored in black boxes containing fused $CaCl_2$, sealed with black tape, and kept in a refrigerator at 4°C. Five days after exposure, the slides are developed with Kodak D-19 at 19°C for 2.5 minutes, rapidly rinsed in distilled water, and fixed in Kodak fixer for 15 minutes. After several changes of water, the slides are stained with Ehrlich's hematoxylin for 30 minutes at 4°C. Excess stain is removed with acid alcohol, and the sections are permitted to blue in alkaline alcohol. They are subsequently dehydrated in an ethyl alcohol series, cleared in xylene, and mounted in Damar.

References

Aboliņš-Krogis, A. (1960). The histochemistry of the hepatopancreas of *Helix pomatia* (L.) in relation to the regeneration of the shell. *Ark. Zool.* **13**, 159–201.

Aboliņš-Krogis, A. (1963a). Some features of the chemical composition of isolated cytoplasmic inclusions from the cells of the hepatopancreas of *Helix pomatia* (L.). *Ark. Zool.* **15**, 393–429.

Aboliņš-Krogis, A. (1963b). The histochemistry of the mantle of *Helix pomatia* (L.) in relation to the repair of the damaged shell. *Ark. Zool.* **15**, 461–474.

Baecher, R. (1932). Die Mikromorphologie von *Helix pomatia* und einigen anderen Stylommatophoren. *Z. Gesam. Anat. Ergeb. Anat. Entwick.* **29**, 449–585.

Basch, P. F. (1969). The arterial system of *Biomphalaria glabrata* (Say). *Malacologia* **7**, 169–181.

Beaver, P. C. (1937). Experimental studies on *Echinostoma revolutum* (Froelich), a fluke from birds and mammals. *Ill. Biol. Monog.* **15**, 1–96.

Beaver, P. C., Malek, E. A., and Little, M. D. (1964). Development of *Spirometra* and *Paragonimus* eggs in Harada-Mori cultures. *J. Parasitol.* **50**, 664–666.

Brown, D. S., and Burch, J. B. (1967). Distribution of cytologically different populations of the genus *Bulinus* (Basommatophora: Planorbidae) in Ethiopia. *Malacologia* **6**, 189–198.

Burch, J. B. (1960a). Chromosome studies of aquatic pulmonate snails. *Nucleus* **3**, 177–208.

Burch, J. B. (1960b). Chromosome numbers of schistosome vector snails. *Z. Tropenmed. Parasitol.* **11**, 449–452.

Burch, J. B. (1967). Chromosomes of intermediate hosts of human bilharziasis. *Malacologia* **5**, 127–135.

Burch, J. B., and Lindsay, G. K. (1970). An immunocytological study of *Bulinus* s.s. (Basommatophora, Planorbidae). *Malacol. Rev.* **3**, 1–18.

Cheng, T. C. (1971). Enhanced growth as a manifestation of parasitism and shell deposition in parasitized mollusks. *In* "Aspects of the Biology of Symbiosis" (T. C. Cheng, ed.), pp. 103–137. Univ. Park Press, Baltimore, Maryland.

Cheng, T. C. (1973). "General Parasitology." Academic Press, New York.

Cheng, T. C., and Galloway, P. C. (1970). Transplantation immunity in mollusks: The histoincompatibility of *Helisoma duryi normale* with allografts and xenografts. *J. Invertebr. Pathol.* **15**, 177–192.

Davis, G. M. (1968). A systematic study of *Oncomelania hupensis chiui* (Gastropoda: Hydrobiidae). *Malacologia* **7**, 17–70.

Dawes, B. (1956). "The Trematoda with special reference to British and other European forms." Univ. Press, Cambridge, England.

Gude, W. D. (1968). "Autoradiographic Techniques: Localization of Radioisotopes in Biological Material." Prentice-Hall, Englewood Cliffs, New Jersey.

Hoskin, G. P., and Cheng, T. C. (1974). *Himasthla quissetensis*: Uptake and utilization of glucose by rediae as determined by autoradiography and respirometry. *Exp. Parasitol.* (in press).

Lee, C. L., and Lewert, R. M. (1956). The maintenance of *Schistosoma mansoni* in the laboratory. *J. Infec. Dis.* **99**, 15–20.

Lee, F. O., and Cheng, T. C. (1972). Incorporation of ^{59}Fe in the snail *Biomphalaria glabrata* parasitized by *Schistosoma mansoni*. *J. Parasitol.* **58**, 481–488.

Lever, J., Jager, J. C., and Westerveld, A. (1962). A new anaesthetization technique for freshwater snails tested on *Lymnaea stagnalis*. *Malacologia* **1**, 331–337.

Malek, E. A. (1950). Susceptibility of the snail *Biomphalaria boissyi* to infection with certain strains of *Schistosoma mansoni*. *Amer. J. Trop. Med.* **30**, 887–894.

Malek, E. A. (1951). Menthol relaxation of helminths before fixation. *J. Parasitol.* **37**, 321.

Malek, E. A. (1952a). Morphology, bionomics and host-parasite relations of Planorbidae (Mollusca: Pulmonata). Ph.D. thesis, University of Michigan, Ann Arbor.

Malek, E. A. (1952b). The preputial organ of snails in the genus *Helisoma* (Gastropoda: Pulmonata). *Amer. Midl. Natur.* **48**, 94–102.

Malek, E. A. (1952c). *Cercaria chandleri*, a new echinostome species from the snail *Helisoma corpulentum* in Lake Itasca, Minnesota. *Trans. Amer. Micros. Soc.* **71**, 277–281.

Malek, E. A. (1954a). Morphological studies on the family Planorbidae (Mollusca: Pulmonata). I. Genital organs of *Helisoma trivolvis* (Say) (Subfamily Helisomatinae F. C. Baker, 1945). *Trans. Amer. Micros. Soc.* **73**, 103–124.

Malek, E. A. (1954b). Morphological studies on the family Planorbidae (Mollusca: Pulmonata). II. The genital organs of *Biomphalaria boissyi* (Subfamily Planorbinae H. A. Pilsbry, 1934). *Trans. Amer. Micros. Soc.* **73**, 285–296.

Malek, E. A. (1955). Anatomy of *Biomphalaria boissyi* as related to its infection with *Schistosoma mansoni. Amer. Midl. Natur.* **54**, 394–404.

Malek, E. A. (1958a). Factors conditioning the habitat of bilharziasis intermediate hosts of the family Planorbidae. *Bull. W.H.O.* **18**, 785–818.

Malek, E. A. (1958b). Natural and experimental infection of some bulinid snails in the Sudan with *Schistosoma haematobium. Proc. 6th Internl. Congress Trop. Med. Malaria, Lisbon* **2**, 5–13.

Malek, E. A. (1962). "Laboratory Guide and Notes for Medical Malacology." Burgess Co., Minneapolis, Minn.

Malek, E. A. (1967). Experimental infection of several lymnaeid snails with *Heterobilharzia americana. J. Parasitol.* **53**, 700–702.

Malek, E. A. (1969). Studies on "tropicorbid" snails (*Biomphalaria*: Planorbidae) from the Caribbean and Gulf of Mexico areas, including the southern United States. *Malacologia* **7**, 183–209.

Malek, E. A. (1970). Further studies on mammalian susceptibility to experimental infection with *Heterobilharzia americana. J. Parasitol.* **56**, 64–66.

Malek, E. A. (1971). The life cycle of *Gastrodiscus aegyptiacus* (Cobbold, 1876) Looss, 1896, (Trematoda: Paramphistomatidae: Gastrodiscinae). *J. Parasitol.* **57**, 975–979.

Malek, E. A., and File, S. K. (1971). Electrophoretic studies on the digestive gland esterases of some biomphalarid and lymnaeid snails. *Bull. W.H.O.* **45**, 819–825.

Malek, E. A., Ash, L. R., Lee, H. F., and Little, M. D. (1961). *Heterobilharzia* infection in the dog and other mammals in Louisiana. *J. Parasitol.* **47**, 619–623.

Mecham, J. A., and Holliman, R. B. (1972). An improved feeding procedure for *Biomphalaria glabrata. J. Parasitol.* **58**, 835.

Michelson, E. H. (1966). Specificity of hemolymph antigens in taxonomic discrimination of medically important snails. *J. Parasitol.* **52**, 466–472.

Pan, C. T. (1965). Studies on the host-parasite relationship between *Schistosoma mansoni* and the snail *Australorbis glabratus. Amer. J. Trop. Med. Hyg.* **14**, 931–976.

Pan, C. T. (1971). The arterial system of the planorbid snail *Biomphalaria glabrata. Trans. Amer. Microsc. Soc.* **90**, 434–440.

Runham, N. W., Isarankura, K., and Smith, B. J. (1965). Methods for narcotizing and anaesthetizing gastropods. *Malacologia* **2**, 231–238.

Standen, O. D. (1951). Some observations upon the maintenance of *Australorbis glabratus* in the laboratory. *Ann. Trop. Med. Parasitol.* **45**, 80–83.

van der Schalie, H. (1953). Nembutal as a relaxing agent for molluscs. *Amer. Midl. Natur.* **50**, 511.

van der Schalie, H., and Davis, G. W. (1968). Culturing *Oncomelania* snails (Prosobranchia: Hydrobiidae) for studies of oriental schistosomiasis. *Malacologia* **6**, 321–367.

Wright, C. A., and Klein, J. (1967). Serological studies on the taxonomy of planorbid snails. *J. Zool.* **151**, 489–495.

Wright, C. A., and Ross, G. C. (1965). Electrophoretic studies of some planorbid egg proteins. *Bull. W.H.O.* **32**, 709–712.

Wright, C. A., and Ross, G. C. (1966). Electrophoretic studies on planorbid egg-proteins. The *Bulinus africanus* and *B. forskalii* species groups. *Bull. W.H.O.* **35**, 727–731.

Wright, C. A., File, S. K., and Ross, G. C. (1966). Studies on the enzyme systems of planorbid snails. *Ann. Trop. Med. Parasitol.* **60**, 522–525.

Yager, C. M., and Harry, H. W. (1966). Uptake of heavy metal ions by *Taphius glabratus*, a snail host of *Schistosoma mansoni. Exp. Parasitol.* **19**, 174–182.

15 Field Work: Equipment and Methods

For medical malacologists intending to work in areas of the world where schistosomiasis and other snail-borne parasites are public health problems it is essential to become familiar with methods for collecting snails, in order to make quantitative and qualitative estimates of molluscan populations. Furthermore, it is also essential to recognize the fact that a number of ambient ecological factors directly or indirectly influence the biology of mollusks, including their role as intermediate hosts of helminth parasites (Malek, 1958, 1969, 1972). Thus, the intent of this brief chapter is to introduce the student to the necessary field equipment, survey methods, and how to keep a useful log.

Equipment

To conduct field studies relative to medical malacology, the investigator should have a scoop net, small cloth bags, a number of screw-top jars with wire fitted in their lids, specimen bottles, labels, a field notebook, a thermometer, hip-wading boots, forceps, and insect repellent.

An appropriate scoop net is one with 30 × 30 cm frame of steel bars and wire netting with a mesh of 16 to the linear inch (Fig. 15-1). The scoop is 10 cm deep and has an 8 cm blade soldered to the frame. A wooden handle is attached at the other end.

In schistosomiasis endemic areas, wading boots must be used, and great care must be taken in handling the snails. Bare hands must not be used while collecting snails. A pair of forceps, which exerts very light pressure on the

Fig. 15-1.   Metal scoop used to collect mollusks in the field.

snails, is recommended rather than wearing rubber gloves. It is a good practice that hands and arms are repeatedly rubbed with 70% alcohol, especially if they get wet accidentally.

Survey Methods

The area to be surveyed for snails, should be mapped. For surveying freshwater snails, all hydrographic details pertaining to the area, including man-made and natural bodies of water, should be indicated. The dry season, rainy season, and flood periods are to be recorded. Other data should also include the distance between the water courses and the houses, the use of the water by human inhabitants in the area, and any aquatic birds and mammals frequenting the area. The vegetation and topography must be indicated when terrestrial and amphibious snails are to be surveyed.

Other data should include the number of snails collected, sex in the case of operculate snails, the size of the snails, the presence or absence of egg masses, their number if present and number of eggs per egg mass.

Records of the air temperature and the temperature of the water, especially that of the microhabitat, that is, in the immediate vicinity of the snails, should be made. In addition, exposure of the habitat to the sun, the color of the water, and the presence or absence of silt should be recorded. The pH of the water should be determined either in the field or in the laboratory from water samples taken for analysis. The above data must be recorded periodically throughout the year and correlated with seasonal fluctuations in the life cycle of the snail and its infection with parasites (Malek, 1962; W.H.O., 1965).

Figure 15-2 is a facsimile of a snail-collection record sheet. Copies of this should be made and filled out in the field and later completed in the laboratory.

The snails are brought from the field in moist vegetation, not in water. They should be placed in separate, labeled jars or small cardboard boxes with perforated tops. Sometimes it is better not to attempt picking out the snails from weeds collected on the scoop net but to dump the contents into a pail. By thoroughly going through the weeds and debris in the laboratory, one avoids overlooking the smaller species of snails.

Determining Snail Densities in the Field

In certain studies a qualitative account of the snails occurring in the survey area is adequate while in others it is necessary to determine quantitatively the snail population density. There is no uniform method applicable to all areas that can be used for such quantitative determinations. The objective of the study, the nature of the habitat, and the equipment that is available determine the sampling method to be selected.

For terrestrial and amphibious snails and for aquatic snails in shallow waters the so-called tube method has been advocated. This method involves a sharpened brass pipe, about 14 cm in diameter, which is pushed into the mud with the help of handles. The plug of earth thus obtained is removed in the laboratory and washed thoroughly through a series of sieves. The snails present are collected from the finer-mesh sieves.

Other types of collecting instruments, such as the Dendy and Elsman bottom samplers, which are used in limnological studies, can also be used to sample the molluscan population at the bottom of bodies of water.

The quadrat method, which is commonly used in ecological surveys, has been adapted for work on snails. It is especially useful in the case of terrestrial and amphibious snails and in surveying aquatic snails in swampy habitats. This method involves dropping a metal ring or square into the habitat and collecting and counting all the snails inside the ring. This procedure is

Snail-Collection Record*

Date:
Parish (county):
Locality:
Waterbody: _____ Time: _____ Name _____
Type _____ Man-made: reservoir, irrigation canal, fish pond, etc.
Natural: river, lake, creek, bayou, etc.
permanent, stagnant, clear, seasonal, running, muddy
Nature of bottom: rocks, sand, clay, humus, decaying matter
Pollution:
Aquatic vegetation: dense, light   Type:

Density of snails: many, few
Egg masses: present, absent
Snails collected _____

                          Snail   Cercaria   Metacercaria

Trematode infection:
Nematode infection:
Other parasites: leeches, oligochaetes, etc.
Sun exposure of habitat:
Color of water:
Air temperature: Temperature of surface water:
Temperature of the microhabitat:
Hydrogen ion concentration:
Water analysis: Dissolved O$_2$:   Hardness:
Aquatic birds or mammals:
Contact with and use by population:
Other information:

*To be filled out in the field and completed in the laboratory.

Fig. 15-2. Facsimile of page from field notebook.

381

repeated a number of times at regular spatial intervals, and the results are subjected to statistical treatment for mean and standard deviation.

Standard sieves, scoops, and dredges have been used for both qualitative and quantitative studies. In the case of the scoop, it is passed through the water and vegetation at intervals along a canal or shore line, and the number of snails obtained with each scoop is counted. The total number of snails collected by this method will give a rough but usually sufficient reliable determination of the population density in the area. This is especially true if only a relative and not the absolute number of snails is required and if the same scoop, the same technique, and preferably the same person or persons carry out the sampling procedure.

The "counts per unit of time" method has been recommended by Olivier and Schneiderman (1956). This technique involves counting the number of snails that are collected systematically with sieves mounted on handles by one or more experienced collectors in a measured and marked area of the habitat for a given interval of time. This method measures the density of the snail population in the marked area only and not the total population, but it is statistically reliable.

Another method by which estimates of snail populations can be ascertained without tedious collecting involves placing palm-leaf traps in the water at regular intervals along both banks of canals or along shore lines of other types of bodies of water and, after exposing these traps for a period of time, counting the number of snails attached on the leaves. This method is effective in situations where the assessment information desired is the number of snails per linear meter of water. It has been widely employed in many Middle Eastern countries during surveys of *Biomphalaria* spp. and *Bulinus* spp., and it is of interest to note that in areas where no snails are detectable by using scoops and sieves, snails have been found attached to palm leaf traps.

References

Malek, E. A. (1958). Factors conditioning the habitat of bilharziasis intermediate hosts of the family Planorbidae. *Bull. W.H.O.* **18**, 785–818.

Malek, E. A. (1962). Bilharziasis control in pump schemes near Khartoum, Sudan and an evaluation of the efficacy of chemical and mechanical barriers. *Bull. W.H.O.* **27**, 41–58.

Malek, E. A. (1969). Studies on bovine schistosomiasis in the Sudan. *Ann. Trop. Med. Parasitol.* **63**, 501–513.

Malek, E. A. (1972). Environmental control: Snail ecology and man-made habitats. *In* "Proceedings of a Symposium on the Future of Schistosomiasis Control." (M. J. Miller, ed.). Pp. 57–60. Tulane University, New Orleans, Louisiana.

Olivier, L. J., and Schneiderman, M. (1956). A method for estimating the density of aquatic snail population. *Exp. Parasitol.* **5**, 109–117.

World Health Organization (1965). "Snail Control in the Prevention of Bilharziasis." *W.H.O. Monograph Series*, No. 50.

Subject Index

A

Acella, shell features, 54
Acella haldemani, 39
Achatina fulica, 122
  economic importance of, 285
  natural enemies of, 287
  nematode relations of, 120, 121, 126
  rearing of, 362
Aeleurostrongylus abstrusus, 120
Aequipecten gibbus, 125
Aequipecten irradians, 125
Aequipecten maximus, 125
Age of snail, effect on parasitism, 106, 199
Agriolimax, see Deroceras
Alaria marcianae, 51
Allassostoma parvum, 50
Allocreadium isopora, 349
Alloglosidium corti, 50, 51
Allogona profunda, 78, 81
Amnicola, 59, 61
Amnicola limosa, 39
  trematodes in, 61
Amnicola peracuta, trematodes in, 61
Amnicola pilsbryi, trematodes in, 61
Amoebae, in snails, 135, 136, 137
Amphibious snails, 5, 56, 59, 69
  control of, 289
  ecology of, 59
  molluscicide-testing, 299, 301
  rearing of, 361
Amphineura, 2
Ampullaridae, 6, 36, 69
Anafilaroides rostratus, 120

Ancylidae, 7, 36
  shell and anatomy, 56
Angiostrongylus cantonensis, 120, 122,
  195, 219
  larva in snail of, 126
  molluscan hosts of, 121
Angiostrongylus costaricensis, 120, 123
Angiostrongylus vasorum, 123
Anguispira alternata, 77, 80, 81
Anguispira solitaria, 78
Anodonta grandis, 349
Anodonta imbecillus, 33
Anomia simplex, 277
Apatemon gracilis, 63
Aplexa, 58
Aplexa hypnorum, 39
Apophallus brevis, 61
Apophallus venustus, 67
Aquaculture, 264
Aqualin, as molluscicide, 294
Aquaria, 359
Arca transversa, 276
Archaeogastropoda, 4
Arion ater, 120
Arion empiricorum, 119
Arion hortensis, 120
Arion rufus, 123
Arionidae, 8
Aroapyrgus colombiensis, trematodes in,
  62
Aroapyrgus costaricensis, 62
Ascocotyle pachycystis, 62
Assiminea latericea, 97
Assiminea japonica, 97

383

A 4
B 5
C 6
D 7
E 8
F 9
G 0
H 1
I 2
J 3